Complete Poems
and
Selected Letters of
John Keats

COMPLETE POEMS
AND
SELECTED LETTERS OF
JOHN KEATS

Introduction by Edward Hirsch

Notes by Jim Pollock,
University of Houston

THE MODERN LIBRARY

NEW YORK

Grateful acknowledgment is made to Alfred A. Knopf,
a division of Random House, Inc., for permission to reprint eleven lines
from "Belief" from *New Selected Poems* by Philip Levine. Copyright © 1991
by Philip Levine. Reprinted by permission of Alfred A. Knopf,
a division of Random House, Inc.

LIBRARY OF CONGRESS CATALOGING-IN-PUBLICATION DATA
Keats, John, 1795–1821.
[Selections. 2001]
Complete poems and selected letters of John Keats/John Keats;
introduction by Edward Hirsch—Modern Library pbk. ed.
p. cm.
Includes reading group guide.
Includes bibliographical references and indexes.
ISBN 0-375-75669-8
1. Keats, John, 1795–1821—Correspondence. 2. Poets, English—
19th century—Correspondence. I. Title.
PR4832 .H55 2001
821'.7—dc21 00-62460

Modern Library website address: www.modernlibrary.com

Printed in the United States of America

4 6 8 9 7 5 3

JOHN KEATS

John Keats was born in London in living quarters connected with his maternal grandfather's livery stable, the Swan and Hoop Inn, on October 31, 1795. He was the eldest of five children (one of whom died in infancy) begot by Thomas and Frances Jennings Keats. His father was the chief hostler at the Swan and Hoop, and the family prospered. The boy was eight years old when Thomas Keats was killed in a riding accident; the next year, in 1805, Keats's grandfather died. When the future poet was fourteen, his mother (after an unsuccessful remarriage) succumbed to tuberculosis. By then, however, Keats had received a liberal education at the progressive Clarke school, a private academy in the village of Enfield, twelve miles north of London, where for eight years he studied English literature, modern languages, and Latin. (He began translating Virgil's *Aeneid* while still at school.) Charles Cowden Clarke, the headmaster's son, remembered him as an outgoing youth who made friends easily and fought passionately in their defense. A fellow student recalled his pugnacious spirit: "Keats was not in childhood attached to books. His *penchant* was for fighting. He would fight any one." Yet George Keats spoke of his brother's "nervous, morbid temperament" (perhaps attributable to a complex about being short—"poor little Johnny Keats" was barely five feet tall) and of his having "many a bitter fit of hypochondriasm." Indeed Keats himself wrote: "My mind has been the most discontented and restless one that ever was put into a body too small for it."

In 1811 Keats left the Clarke school to become a surgeon's apprentice—first at Thomas Hammond's apothecary shop in a small town near Enfield and later in London at Guy's Hospital. (Surgery would have been a respectable and reasonable calling for someone of Keats's means: unlike the profession of medicine, it did not require a university degree. Moreover, Keats always maintained he was "ambitious of doing the world some good.") During his five years of study for a license, the young apprentice completed his translation of the *Aeneid* and "devoured rather than read" Ovid's *Metamorphoses,* Milton's *Paradise Lost,* and other books he borrowed from the Clarke school. But the work that decisively awakened his love of poetry—indeed shocked him suddenly into self-awareness of his own powers of imagination—was Edmund Spenser's *Faerie Queene.* At some point in 1814 Keats composed his first poem, "In Imitation of Spenser." Although he struck medical colleagues as an "idle loafing fellow, always writing poetry," on July 25, 1816, Keats passed the apothecaries' examination that allowed him to practice surgery.

In the meantime, his poetic genius was being recognized and encouraged by early friends like Charles Cowden Clarke and J. H. Reynolds, and in October 1816 Clarke introduced him to Leigh Hunt, whose *Examiner,* the leading liberal magazine of the day, had recently published Keats's sonnet "O Solitude." Five months later, on March 3, 1817, *Poems,* his first volume of verse, appeared. Despite the high hopes of the Hunt circle, it was a failure. During the fall of that year, Keats stayed with Oxford student Benjamin Bailey at Magdalen College. While Bailey crammed for exams, Keats worked on *Endymion,* his four-thousand-line romantic allegory; the two read and discussed Wordsworth, Hazlitt, Milton, Dante, and Shakespeare. Back in London, on November 22, 1817, Keats wrote to Bailey the first of his famous letters to friends (and siblings) on aesthetics, the social role of poetry, and his own sense of poetic mission. Rarely has a poet left such a remarkable record of his thoughts on his own career and its relation to the history of poetry. (The letters also reveal the astonishing speed with which Keats matured as an artist.) Yet by the time *Endymion* was published in April 1818, Keats's name had been identified with Hunt's "Cockney School," and the Tory *Blackwood's Magazine* delivered a violent attack on Keats as an "ignorant and unsettled pretender" to culture who had no right to aspire to poetry.

Although the critical reaction to *Endymion* was infamous for its ferocity, the youthful bard was hardly destroyed by it—despite Byron's famous quip that Keats was "snuffed out by an Article." The surprising truth is that he entered upon an interval of astonishing productivity, perhaps the most concentrated period of creativity any English poet has ever known. In the summer of 1818, Keats journeyed to Scotland with Charles Brown, the rugged, worldly businessman who was one of his most loyal friends. There he vowed: "I shall learn poetry here and shall henceforth write more than ever." That fall he began composing *Hyperion,* his imitation of and challenge to Milton's *Paradise Lost;* even critics saw the work as a major achievement. In December, following his brother Tom's death from tuberculosis, Keats went to live with Charles Brown in Wentworth Place, Hampstead. There, almost in spite of himself, the young poet fell helplessly in love with Fanny Brawne, the eighteen-year-old daughter of a widowed neighbor; a year later they were betrothed. In 1819 Keats produced "The Eve of St. Agnes," "La Belle Dame sans Merci," the major odes, *Lamia,* the Dantean dream-vision *The Fall of Hyperion,* and the five-act verse tragedy *Otho the Great* (written in collaboration with Brown).

On February 3, 1820, Keats suffered a pulmonary hemorrhage that signaled an advanced stage of tuberculosis. He quickly broke off his engagement and began what he called a "posthumous existence." His career as a poet was effectively ended, although the volume *Lamia, Isabella, The Eve of St. Agnes, and Other Poems,* containing the bulk of Keats's claim to immortality, was published that July. In a desperate attempt to recover his health in a milder climate, Keats sailed for Italy in September accompanied by the painter Joseph

Severn. Declining an invitation to stay with Shelley in Pisa, the two arrived in Rome on November 15 and took up residence in rooms overlooking the Piazza di Spagna. John Keats died in Rome on the night of February 23, 1821, and was buried there on February 26 in the Protestant Cemetery. On his deathbed Keats requested that his tombstone bear no name, only the words "Here lies one whose name was writ in water."

Contents

ENDYMION: A POETIC ROMANCE 59

LAMIA, ISABELLA, THE EVE OF ST. AGNES AND OTHER POEMS (1820)

POSTHUMOUS AND FUGITIVE POEMS

LONGER POSTHUMOUS POEMS: NARRATIVE AND DRAMATIC

SELECTED LETTERS

INTRODUCTION

Edward Hirsch

John Keats's poems and letters were for me—as they have been for so many others over the past two centuries—the portals of poetry itself, the highly decorated doors through which one passed into a magisterial kingdom, a realm of pure feeling, passionate thought. "I am certain of nothing but of the holiness of the Heart's affections and the truth of Imagination," Keats wrote to Benjamin Bailey in November 1817. "What the imagination seizes as Beauty must be truth." This is the sort of certainty that announces a vocation—it helped to seal mine—and opens the pathway to a life's work. "The Imagination may be compared to Adam's dream," Keats continued, "he awoke and found it truth." So many of Keats's formulations are like a bell, a trumpet call, leading us to our deepest, most imaginative selves.

Keats believed that "the excellence of every Art is its intensity." One discovers in the luxuriant lyric spaces of his art that the emotions are deemed sacred and the daydreaming capacities of the mind are given free rein to join with a feverishly active consciousness, with what he calls in "Ode to Psyche" "a working brain." He left ample room in his poems for reverie and trance, for waking into a "slumberous tenderness" ("The Eve of St. Agnes"), and he combined that associative drift with a startling openheartedness and a ferocious working intellect, the mind of a maker. He believed in the essential healthiness of the lyric—the healing powers of art—and early on borrowed a metaphor from medicine to declare that poetry itself "should be a friend/To soothe the cares, and lift the thoughts of man" ("Sleep and Poetry").

Keats was a keen, indelible phrase maker—"I look upon fine Phrases like a Lover," he wrote—and his work has great verbal sumptuousness. Many of his phrases and lines seem almost to have been formulated by the English language itself, as if he had become its vehicle, a transparent vessel, like Shakespeare, who was his supreme source.

> The poetry of earth is never dead.
>   ("On the Grasshopper and Cricket")

> When I have fears that I may cease to be
>   ("When I have fears . . .")

> A thing of beauty is a joy for ever.
>   (*Endymion*)

> Tender is the night,
>   ("Ode to a Nightingale")

> Where are the songs of Spring?
>   ("To Autumn")

When I was a boy my grandfather used to quote Keats's lines to me, like proverbs or psalms. I had no idea where these phrases, these formulas and equations (such as the urn's claim, "Beauty is truth, truth beauty") actually originated. I felt as if he had pulled them out of the summer air or summoned them from the collective pool of all the poetry he knew. Later, when I was in high school, I was surprised, and a little discomfited, to discover that so many of his lines had come from the teeming brain of a single nineteenth-century author. It was as if my grandfather had taken to heart

Keats's own formulation that "Poetry should ... strike the Reader as a wording of his own highest thoughts, and appear almost a Remembrance...." Sometimes, reading Keats's poems late at night, on my own, I still feel as if I am hearing not the beautifully formed cadences of a solitary writer, one of the major Romantic poets, but the Orphic voice of English poetry itself.

———

John Keats belongs to the second wave, second generation, of Romantic poets. He was the last born (1795), the most short-lived (twenty-five years old), the most easily endearing, obviously lovable, and the first to die (1821) of the key Romantic figures. Shelley, for example, was born three years before him and outlasted him by one year, long enough to write one of his best poems for him, the elegy "Adonais." ("And Love taught Grief to fall like music from his tongue.") Coleridge, who once shook hands with Keats on Hampstead Heath and declared "There is death in that hand," outlived him by thirteen years. Wordsworth, who was twenty-five years Keats's senior, survived him by nearly three decades.

Keats's background was obscure. He came from a lower-middle-class milieu in an extremely class-bound society, and thereby entered poetry without the advantages of birth, wealth, or university education. An aura of class still sometimes hovers around his achievement and reputation. This comes not only from his early detractors, the nasty politically motivated Tory critics from *Blackwood's Magazine* and the *Quarterly Review* who labeled him part of "the Cockney School of Poetry," but also from some of his later admirers, such as W. B. Yeats who in the poem "Ego Dominus Tuus" characterized Keats as "poor, ailing, and ignorant," and defined him as "the coarse-bred son of a livery-stable keeper" who made "luxuriant song" out of his frustrated disadvantages. Yeats's snobbery was gratuitous since he was primarily using Keats to demonstrate his own theory of how every poet seeks his or her own opposite. But from the first there seem always to have been readers who could not abide Keats's liberal sympathies and "Cockney" roots, his radical sensuality and democratic feeling for literary culture, his mask of— to use Yeats's fine phrase—"deliberate happiness."

Keats was the eldest of five children and learned to greet death early. By the time he was fifteen he had lost an infant brother, two uncles, his kindly maternal grandfather, and both his parents, whose death left him, as he said, with "a personal soreness which the world had exacerbated." To add to the misfortune, the orphaned children were then cheated out of their modest inheritance by an unscrupulous guardian. Keats nursed his mother through much of her final eighteen-month illness—she died, presumably from tuberculosis—just as he would later nurse his brother Tom, and the experience seems to have spilled over into the decision to apprentice himself to a surgeon-apothecary. He always was ambitious, as he said, "of doing the world some good." In one of his last poems, "*The Fall of Hyperion: a Vision*," written well after he had abandoned medicine for poetry, he describes the poet as "a sage;/A humanist, physician to all men."

Keats offers us the very model of a self-directed artistic development as a life well lived. He was entirely self-actualized, self-actualizing. There would be no Harrow or Eton, no Oxford or Cambridge in his experience, though he was fortunate to attend Clarke School in Enfield (1803–1811), a small progressive, enlightened academy on the outskirts of London. There he became particular friends with the headmaster's son, Charles Cowden Clarke, who was eight years his senior. Many years after Keats's death, Clarke recalled how as a schoolboy Keats had been "highly pugnacious" with an "ungovernable" temper and a "terrier courage." Clarke's portrait stands as a corrective to the myth of "poor Keats," the fatal victim of hostile reviews (Byron tartly claimed that Keats was "snuffed out by an article") and replaces it with a more accurate portrait of a person who plunged into things, who was scrappy, volatile, and impetuous, both physically vital and mentally robust.

At Clarke Keats became a voracious reader with an insatiable appetite for poetry, for Latin authors and mythological keys to classical culture, such as Lemprière's *Classical Dictionary*, Tooke's *Pantheon*, and Spence's *Polymetis*. "I know nothing, I have read nothing and I mean to follow Solomon's directions of 'get Wisdom—get understanding.'" He vowed with iron resolve: "There is but one

way for me—the road lies th[r]ough application study and thought.
I will pursue it...." The unappeasable hunger for books, for ancient
stories and myths, for beautiful works of art only increased after
Keats left school at sixteen—it was lifelong, needful to him as food.
Clarke recalled how ardently his young friend responded to
Spenser's "Epithalamion" and then went through the first volume
of the *Faerie Queene* "as a young horse would through a spring
meadow—ramping!" Spenser's highly descriptive passages opened
Keats up to his own wondrously florid isle, his own laurel groves, a
shady Bower of Bliss.

Keats wrote his first known poem in 1814 ("Imitation of
Spenser") under the excited spell of a writer who instigated his
own dreamy sensuousness, whose imagery fomented his enchant-
ments. Many of his early poems exhibit his dissenting political
spirit ("On Peace," "Written on the Day that Mr. Leigh Hunt left
Prison"), his sense of the grandeur of poetry ("Ode to Apollo"), and
his feeling for the way nature inspires and instructs poets ("To one
who has been long in city pent," "I stood tip-toe upon a little hill").
I have always been moved by Keats's tribute poem and verse epistle
"To Charles Cowden Clarke," which speaks to Clarke's mentorship
but also to their exalted experience of reading poetry together.
"That you first taught me all the sweets of song," Keats remembers
in a series of richly balanced couplets:

> The grand, the sweet, the terse, the free, the fine;
> What swell'd with pathos, and what right divine:
> Spenserian vowels that elope with ease,
> And float along like birds o'er summer seas;
> Miltonian storms, and more, Miltonian tenderness;
> Michael in arms, and more, meek Eve's fair slenderness.

Keats summarizes the wide range he hears in "the sweets of song,"
the particular mellifluous sounds ("Spenserian vowels") and en-
abling tones ("Miltonian storms and ... tenderness") he discovers in
two keys poets who spurred and made possible his own practice. He
also goes on to glory in the swelling capabilities—the immense

possibilities—of the poetic forms themselves: the sonnet, the ode, the epigram, and the epic. One feels that Keats's generous poem of acknowledgment, written in September 1816, signals the virtual completion of his poetic apprenticeship. A few weeks later he penned his first major poem, "On first looking into Chapman's Homer," which, as Leigh Hunt recognized, "completely announced the new poet taking possession."

Keats wrote his breakthrough poem at a fever pitch in a couple of enthralling early morning hours. He always did love the intoxication of creating in a fine frenzy. This is an emblematic or allegorical moment in Keats's writing life—in the life of any young poet—because his reading vitally seizes him and spurs him into his own extravagant making. It delivers him to himself. Keats and Clarke had spent the entire night excitedly poring over a borrowed 1616 folio edition of George Chapman's translation of Homer, which contained both the *Iliad* and the *Odyssey*. They searched out the great passages, the heart-stopping scenes, comparing Pope's well-tempered eighteenth-century couplets with Chapman's more propulsive, free-striding Elizabethan verse. Keats finally tore himself away at six A.M. He departed "at day-spring," as Clarke later recalled, "yet he contrived that I should receive the poem, from a distance of nearly two miles, before 10 A.M." A fair copy of the poem was sitting on Clarke's table when he came down to breakfast.

Keats's poem enacts a feeling of rapturous discovery. It breathes its own wonderment. It creates the sensation of tremendous vastness within the prescribed space of the Petrarchan form. The twenty-year-old poet builds his case so fully and convincingly that readers ever after have been powerfully affected by the swelling turn in the sonnet, the reverberations of the final sestet. It was only when he heard Chapman's bold rendition of "deep-browed Homer," the speaker argues:

> Then felt I like some watcher of the skies
> When a new planet swims into his ken;
> Or like stout Cortez when with eagle eyes
> He star'd at the Pacific—and all his men

> Look'd at each other with a wild surmise—
> Silent, upon a peak in Darien.

There's a touching way that Keats reveals himself to be a new-comer to high culture here. He implicitly acknowledges, for example, that he doesn't read Homer in the original Greek, that he is just now coming upon Chapman's translation ("On *first* looking . . ."). He mistakes Cortez for Balboa, as Tennyson first pointed out to Palgrave. But what seems to matter even more deeply is the rising excitement and sense of limitless possibility created in him by reading Homer, so that he feels poised on the brink of a great discovery, like Herschel finding the planet Uranus or Balboa suddenly sighting the Pacific. Reading Homer, even in translation, Keats feels the excitement of entering a fabulous New World; he, too, crescendos into a space of silent awe. And he instills that same feeling in us. Some contemporary readers, especially materialist critics, worry that Keats's aspirations to high culture are suspect, but I believe they have an almost Blakean political dignity. They speak to what we all might gain access to, what we would joyously create within ourselves. Chapman's Homer becomes Keats's marvelous method of transport, his way of joining with "the mighty dead" (*Endymion*), attaining the sublime. He had found a means for declaring, possessing, and authoring himself.

———

Keats published three books of poems in his lifetime: *Poems* (1817), *Endymion* (1818), and, when he was already mortally ill, *Lamia, Isabella, The Eve of St. Agnes, and Other Poems* (1820). His mature creative life was intensely full but shockingly brief. I still find it piercing that in "Sleep and Poetry," his first extended poem of substance, the twenty-one-year-old poet asked for ten years, one solid decade, to "overwhelm" himself in poetry, but was in fact given slightly less than three years more—from, say, December 1816, when he finished the poem, to September 1819, when he completed "To Autumn." He was only twenty-four, but he had registered his claim with astonishing rapidity, as he well knew. For as he notably put it to his brother George in the wake of the hostile reception to

Endymion, "I think I shall be among the English Poets after my death."

Keats was always deeply impressed by imaginative things. He loved to be overwhelmed, to wander in the fictive spaces, the secondary worlds, of classical stories and myths. He experienced poetry on his pulse. He felt that his success as a poet depended on acquiring material—it was not his by birthright—and he was attracted to poems of pre-existing figures (drawn from Ovid, from Shakespeare) and incited by mythological tales, stories of pagan gods, which stood for him as an alternative to a forbidding and restrictive Christianity. These gods were not abstractions to him but literal and metaphorical figures whose desires activated his mind and stimulated his senses. He tended to displace and embody his quest for a highly sensual love, for superhuman beauty, in the form of various supernatural enchantresses and Muse figures—some idealized, like the moon goddess in *Endymion,* some demonic, like the fairy mistress in "La Belle Dame sans Merci." He needed these enabling figures, which opened up for him a Shakespearean theater of the mind. Keats was psychically constituted so that his mythological predecessors induced and released the erotic animism in his poetic procedures. They unleashed his sensibility. They gave him access to his own deliriums—his sexual longings and desires, his pressing ambition to inscribe "the immortality of passion," (*Endymion*), his metaphorical turn of mind, his ardent, permeable, and empathic imagination. He could transpose the life force into a mythic mode, and the gift put him in touch with the oldest English poetry.

So, too, Keats was actively taken—almost physically seized—by art and often pulled into the visual realm of paintings, engravings, and sculptures. The grandeur of high art—what had previously been made great—could be both enabling and daunting to him. It could have forbidding power. One thinks, for example, of that day in the winter of 1817 when Keats's older friend, the historical painter Benjamin Haydon, took him to see the Parthenon sculptures exhibited for the first time at the British Museum. Keats's visceral response must have shocked Haydon, for instead of being intoxicated by the splendor, as the painter fully expected, he was dazed and even silenced by what he saw. Keats had received the first copy of his first book just a day or two earlier, and it seems to me that the excitement—and the shock—must have driven his museum experience, his overpowering encounter. There was still such an enormous gap—such a palpable abyss—between what he hoped to do and what he had actually accomplished. The magnificence of the Elgin Marbles brought it home to him in a devastating way—he took the greatness personally, almost competitively.

The sonnet "On Seeing the Elgin Marbles" enacts a sense of speechless astonishment. The mutable passage of time counterpoised against the immutable grandeur of Grecian art induced in him a debilitating vertigo, a dizzying panic. He could but dimly apprehend the magnitude he was seeking. Yet he had already begun to apprentice himself to what he called "the religion of Joy," the Greek spirit made flesh ("I never cease to wonder at all that incarnate delight," he told his friend, the painter Joseph Severn). I suspect he was steeling himself for a fresh start, for the "godlike hardship" of the Great Work. Keats could be overwhelmed by the threat of failure, as in his dirgelike Shakespearean sonnet "When I have fears that I may cease to be," but he ultimately responded by rededicating himself to the creative task with a deeper candor, a more furious resolve.

———

Keats is one of the great poets of sympathetic absorption. He disperses the self and inhabits alternative worlds. He had a gift for breeding fanciful figures, for thrusting himself into the natural world, for letting his spirit wander, soar, and descend. "[Byron] describes what he sees—I describe what I imagine—Mine is the hardest task," Keats said in 1819. I think of that key moment, for example, in "Sleep and Poetry" when a charioteer suddenly descends and starts talking directly to the natural world:

> The charioteer with wond'rous gesture talks
> To the trees and mountains; and there soon appear
> Shapes of delight, of mystery, and fear,

> Passing along before a dusky space
> Made by some mighty oaks . . .

The trees and mountains come alive almost as people—they are person-like—("Lo! how they murmur, laugh, and smile, and weep") rather than abstract emotions, under the "wond'rous gesture"—the Orphic enchantment—of the poet.

There is a startling quality of animism in much of Keats's best work (Hunt said amusingly that Keats never beheld an oak tree without seeing a dryad). He opened outward and showed an unabashed tenderness toward the Other. The first sentence of *Endymion* justifies beauty in terms of joy, radically enjambs and thereby rethinks—reenvisions—the "rocking horse" of the Augustan heroic couplet, and grants the pagan world its animistic wonder:

> A thing of beauty is a joy for ever:
> Its loveliness increases; it will never
> Pass into nothingness; but still will keep
> A bower quiet for us, and a sleep
> Full of sweet dreams, and health, and quiet breathing.

Keats wrote much of *Endymion* under the aspiring dream—the phantasm—of Shakespeare ("Is it too daring to Fancy Shakespeare this Presider?" he asked Hunt), and although there is something immature and oddly willed about the forced march of the long poem, which he himself viewed as "a feverish attempt, rather than a deed accomplished," it did provide him with the wide-open space to practice and employ the language of dramatic projection, a Shakespearean inheritance that flowered into the great odes. "In Endymion I leaped headlong into the Sea," he wrote, "and thereby have become better acquainted with the Soundings, the quicksands, & the rocks, than if I had stayed upon the green shore, and piped a silly pipe, and took tea & comfortable advice." The risky extended poetic romance also contains dazzling shorter passages, descriptive set pieces that prefigure the high lyrics and odal hymns to come, such as the defense of love as "the chiefest intensity" (Book II, lines

1–43), the "Ode to Sorrow" (Book V, lines 146–181), and the stanzaic hymn to Pan (Book I, lines 232–306), which Wordsworth condescended to as "a Very pretty piece of Paganism" but Shelley recognized for its "promise of ultimate excellence."

It was largely from reading and imitating Shakespeare that Keats came to understand and theorize ductility as an essential feature of artistic imagination, which is replete with what, in a letter to his brothers, he famously called "Negative Capability."

> *Negative Capability*, that is when man is capable of being in uncertainties, Mysteries, doubts, without any irritable reaching after fact & reason. . . . (December 21, 1817)

The displacement of the poet's protean self into another existence was for Keats a key feature of the highest poetic imagination. It was part of the native genius of English poetry. He attended William Hazlitt's brilliant Lectures on the English Poets, and he was spurred further to his own thinking by Hazlitt's groundbreaking idea that Shakespeare was "the least of an egotist that it was possible to be" and "nothing in himself," that he embodied "all that others were, or that they could become," that he "had in himself the germs of every faculty and feeling," and "he had only to think of anything in order to become that thing, with all the circumstances belonging to it." Keats also registered Hazlitt's reservations about the prominence of the self in modern poetry. He took to heart the ideal of "disinterestedness," of the wholly adaptable "characterless" poet, and he went on to contrast Wordsworth's capacity for self-projection, which he names "the egotistical sublime," with Shakespeare's essential selflessness, his capacity for anonymous shape-shifting. Everyone who cares about poetry should know his galvanizing letter to Richard Woodhouse:

> As to the poetical Character itself . . . it is not itself—it has no self—it is every thing and nothing—It has no character—it enjoys light and shade; it lives in gusto, be it foul or fair, high or low, rich or poor, mean or elevated—It has as much delight in conceiving an Iago as an Imogen. What shocks the virtuous philosop[h]er, delights the camelion Poet. . . .

> A Poet is the most unpoetical of any thing in existence; because he has
> no Identity—he is continually in for—and filling some other Body—
> The Sun, the Moon, The Sea and Men and Women who are creatures
> of impulse are poetical and have about them an unchangeable
> attribute—the poet has none; no identity.... (October 27, 1818)

Keats eagerly sought what he called the "ardent listlessness"
(*Endymion*) of the trance state. He exalted poetic thinking freed
from habitual trains of thought, from analytic, logical procedures.
"I am the more zealous in this affair," he wrote, "because I have
never yet been able to perceive how any thing can be known for
truth by consequitive reasoning...." He favored a drifting imagina-
tive logic, and in this, as in so much else, he anticipated romantic
American modernists such as Hart Crane and Wallace Stevens. His
fascination with associative drift put him in advance of the French
Surrealists.

Keats delighted in dramatically propelling himself into a wide
array of figures, of mythical stories. He combined a wholehearted
imaginative openness to the moment with a heightened receptivity
to the world in all its diverse particularity, its bodily concreteness.
"I scarcely remember counting upon any Happiness—I look not
for it if it be not in the present hour, ..." he told his friend Bailey:

> nothing startles me beyond the Moment. The setting sun will always
> set me to rights—or if a Sparrow come before my Window I take part
> in its existence and pick about the Gravel.

Keats hungered insatiably for concrete experiences ("O for a Life of
Sensations rather than of Thoughts!" he cried out in one letter) and
exhibited a tremendous capacity for grasping the inner life—the
innermost character—of things. He explicitly refused a didactic
poetry of moral doctrine or self-aggrandizement which, as he put
it, "has a palpable design upon us." Matthew Arnold rightly pointed
out that "he is with Shakespeare." He is also with Ovid who placed
metamorphic transformation, the interpenetrating of identities, at
the heart of his masterwork, Metamorphosis. And he is with the

archaic poets who greeted the world as alive in all its parts. To fill the body of the sun and moon, to speak not just to the other but also from its vantage point is to harness something of its numinous primitive power.

"Every mental pursuit takes its reality and worth from the ardour of the pursuer—being in itself a nothing," Keats said. There is an ethic of reciprocity in Keats's poetry in general and in the odes in particular—one feels in reading him that external reality has been touched by a human recognition. Despair comes when the mutable world goes dead on him, when it feels uninhabited, vacated, emptied of the magical presences he found necessary. Absence reigns, and he is tolled back in darkness to the mortal body, the imperiled psyche, the isolate self.

> Forlorn! The very word is like a bell
> To toll me back from thee to my sole self!
> ("ODE TO A NIGHTINGALE")

Keats was obsessed with fusion experiences, with moments when the membrane dissolves between being and non-being, life and death. Rapture comes when he achieves a moment of absolute cooperative harmony between mind and nature, a dawning into unity, when he crosses over and fully grasps, fully enters, the sensational world:

> Now more than ever seems it rich to die,
> To cease upon the midnight with no pain,
> While thou art pouring forth thy soul abroad
> In such an ecstasy!
> ("ODE TO A NIGHTINGALE")

It is a continual marvel that Keats wrote almost all of his greatest poetry in one exhilarating, headlong twelve-month stretch from, say, mid-September 1818 to mid-September 1819. The period has been variously called the living year, the fertile year, and Keats's annus mirabilis. But it is also something additional: I think of it as one of those inspired, superabundant, visionary moments that announces itself in poetry like a prophecy, that thunderously bursts out into Keats's odes and Rimbaud's Illuminations and Rilke's Duino Elegies. It overflows into the "Hyperion" fragments and A Season in Hell and The Sonnets to Orpheus. At these extended peak moments, in these atemporal storms, it seems as if the poet is taking dictation from a god—"Every angel is terrifying," Rilke cries out—and the experience is ruthless, trancelike, submissive, and annihilating. Keats's demonic song, like Rimbaud's derangement of the senses and Rilke's Orphic declarations, culminates in a poetry of the highest spiritual access, a human attainment nearly limitless in its apocalyptic splendor.

Keats's most vital year is framed by the two Miltonic "Hyperions"—the first a fragment written at the bedside of his dying brother Tom, the second a dream vision that takes up, among other things, the nature of poetry itself. Any account of that year must also include "The Eve of St. Agnes," a voluptuously pagan hymn to Eros that was probably impelled by his falling in love with Fanny Brawne (Hazlitt said that reading it made him regret that he wasn't young any longer) and its unfinished companion piece, "The Eve of Saint Mark," a lyric whose atmosphere grows out of Keats's fondness for Chatterton and wholly anticipates Pre-Raphaelite poetry (Rossetti said that it "shows astonishingly real medievalism"). The year also fertilized two startlingly erotic poems, "La Belle Dame sans Merci" (a ballad Robert Graves took to be the ultimate celebration of the White Goddess, a figure for the poet's destruction by his Muse) and *Lamia* (the spooky tale of a serpent-woman that Robert Bridges called "the most perfect of the narratives"). Both pay homage to the figure Keats called "my demon Poesy" ("Ode on Indolence"), the lustrous, immortal, predatory Muse.

It is worth pausing to consider that Keats was depicting in these poems mythic personifications, not literal lives. He created and found—he was visited by—soulful figures of staunchless allure who initiated him into his own death, deaths, afterlives. Deathless yet death encompassing, these nonliteral female-like presences abnegate no one, no group's literal human rights. Rather, Keats's poems of the goddess (the figure with "a wan face,/Not pin'd by human sorrows, but bright-blanch'd/By an immortal sickness which kills not;" as she is described in *The Fall of Hyperion*) deliver us up to an immanent, bone-rattling mystery. They are a means for us to register or reckon the sacred in a world in which every human being is born to a woman and every human being born must die.

I've always been haunted by Keats's sonnet "Why did I laugh tonight?" It vividly shows how illness preyed on his consciousness, how the thought of rapidly progressing death could paralyze even his three deepest impulses and longings:

> Verse, Fame, and Beauty are intense indeed,
> But Death intenser—Death is Life's high meed.

In a short period Keats also writes four sonnets that remarkably test and experiment with the sonnet structure: "To Sleep," "On Fame" (I and II), and "If by dull rhymes our English must be chain'd," which is a formal directive, an *ars poetica*.

Keats was compelled by technical problems of assonance, of vowel music, and his working ideas came to full fruition during the living year. "One of his favorite topics of discourse was the principle of melody in Verse," Benjamin Bailey remembered:

> Keats's theory was, that the vowels should be so managed as not to clash one with another so as to mar the melody,—& yet that they should be interchanged, like differing notes of music. . . .

Keats's verbal tactics of repetition and variation, his subtle way of mixing and matching long and short vowels, enabled him to fashion a music of enduring sonorousness. His vowels dilate the line into a numinous presence, creating a feeling both of intensity and spiritual easefulness. One thinks, for example, of how he grasps and modulates the pitch of a nightingale across several lines, how suggestively he invokes "a light-winged Dryad of the trees" who

> In some melodious plot
> Of beechen green, and shadows numberless,
> Singest of summer in full-throated ease.

Or of how he captures the sound of the wind (listen for the light *i* sounds as well as the *f* and *w* consonants) in a famous line from "To Autumn":

> Thy hair soft-lifted by the winnowing wind;

Readers have also enjoyed Keats's mastery of the consonants. One thinks, for example, of the Anglo-Saxon firmness of the consonants used for declaration, as in the last line of his program poem, "If by dull rhymes . . ."

> She will be bound with garlands of her own.

Keats's particular way with words—his strategic deployments—serve as the very means by which the transcendent becomes immanent, becomes ours. His shimmering word art was the only method by which he could achieve the status—the carved solidity—of the Elgin Marbles. He had schooled his fluencies (his work is filled with metrical hauntings, melodic departures), and a relentless poetic dedication and craftsmanship stood behind his axiom of Romantic spontaneity: "That which is creative must create itself."

——

The English language reached one of its pinnacles—it attained itself—in one three-and-a-half week period in April and May 1819, when a twenty-three-year-old poet living in Hampstead composed "Ode to Psyche," "Ode on a Grecian Urn," "Ode to a Nightingale," "Ode on Melancholy," and "Ode on Indolence." He then completed the sequence on September 19 with one of the most perfect poems in English, "To Autumn."

"Who found for me the grandeur of the ode,/Growing, like Atlas, stronger from its load?" Keats had asked in his dedicatory poem "To Charles Cowden Clarke." When the right time came, he responded to the ancient heft and grandeur of the form, challenging himself to fulfill a certain loftiness of tone, a certain noble aspiration built into the concept of a celebratory poem written in an elevated language on a theme of acknowledged importance. Keats's praise poems—partly rhapsodic, partly forlorn—are driven by an aching sense of mortality. They are suffused with an excruciating sense of beauty born of death. Indeed, the awareness of death seems to me everywhere present in these joyful addresses: to the goddess Psyche (the word signifies "soul"), to a composite Greek vase—"Thou still unravish'd bride of quietness"—that might defy the flow of time (an urn for holding the ashes of the dead), to the most glorious and poetical of European songbirds ("Thou wast not born for death, immortal Bird!"), to a savory sad emotion, melancholy ("Ay, in the very temple of delight/Veil'd Melancholy has her sovran shrine"), to a drowsy state of mind necessary for the making of genuine art (indolence), and, finally, to a season of exquisite fugitive beauty (autumn). These poems are Keats's mutability odes. They represent the claiming of an obligation, an inner feeling rising up to meet an outer occasion, something owed.

The odes return often to the nature and necessity of human suffering. In one of his most profound letters, written to his brother and sister-in-law, Keats called the world "The vale of Soul-making." He was thinking through an alternative to the concept of the world as a "vale of tears," a springboard to Christian redemption. He writes:

> I will call the *world* a School instituted for the purpose of teaching little children to read—I will call the *human heart* the *horn Book* used in that School—and I will call the *Child able to read, the Soul* made from that *school* and its *hornbook*. Do you not see how necessary a World of Pains and troubles is to school an Intelligence and make it a soul? A place where the heart must feel and suffer in a thousand diverse ways!

This is an allegory of hard-won earthly meaning. Keats's notion is that heart and mind cooperate in soul-making, soul knowledge. He speaks to the idea of the soul as something created and forged through experience. It is not inborn but something nurtured and made, like art, something that gives validity and meaning to suffering during our time on earth and thereby deepens our humanity. He calls it "a system of Spirit-creation."

The odes represent a poetry of human recourse. They speak to suffering and death, to human impermanence. Keats's capacity for sympathetic absorption also made him especially vulnerable to the anguish of others. Considering his life, he once said, "the death or sickness of some one has always spoilt my hours." He was no doubt thinking about his brother Tom when he penned the line—

Where youth grows pale, and spectre-thin, and dies;

and he recognized a world repeatedly disfigured by disease:

> Where but to think is to be full of sorrow
> And leaden-eyed despairs,
> Where Beauty cannot keep her lustrous eyes,
> Or new Love pine at them beyond to-morrow.
> ("ODE TO A NIGHTINGALE")

In the grip of loss, in the deathlike clutch of the transitory, the poet craves permanence. In the midst of sorrow, he is suddenly stunned by the invisible splendor of a nightingale's song, an immortal natural music, and he is overcome by the silent visual perfection—"Cold Pastoral!"—of an Attic shape. He finds refuge from human woe in the high artifice of a Grecian urn, which he calls "a friend to man." Keats is overwhelmed by an evanescence—a "wild ecstasy"—that can scarcely be captured in words. And he vocalizes the wisdom of a work of art that surpasses time and embodies imperishable joy, that speaks to our flawed and mortal selves with the equation of beauty and truth.

Keats concludes his sequence in "To Autumn" by embracing a season of abundance whose splendor depends upon its transience. As Wallace Stevens put it, in a wholly Keatsian formulation, "Death is the mother of beauty" ("Sunday Morning"). Keats finds the mournful majesty of the cresting moment—the autumnal peak—fatefully poignant because it cannot last, because it perishes, like us.

The three stanzas of Keats's poem progress through the season it-self—from the "ripeness to the core" to the harvest reaping to the rich depletion after the gathering but before the onslaught of bar-ren winter. The final stanza is one of the culminating moments in the poetry of earth:

> Where are the songs of Spring? Ay, where are they?
>   Think not of them, thou hast thy music too,—
> While barred clouds bloom the soft-dying day,
>   And touch the stubble-plains with rosy hue;
> Then in a wailful choir the small gnats mourn
>   Among the river sallows, borne aloft
>   Or sinking as the light wind lives or dies;
> And full-grown lambs loud bleat from hilly bourn;
>   Hedge-crickets sing; and now with treble soft
> The red-breast whistles from a garden-croft;
>   And gathering swallows twitter in the skies.

Human and nonhuman life welcome and recognize each other in these harmonious lines, which have so much warmth and breadth, so much calm poise. "To Autumn" is a poem of mournful amplitudes—of singing completions and earthly regeneration—and it comes to such a serene, conclusive affirmation of the natural processes of the world that it seems to me it could only come at the end of a life's work. It crosses a final threshold.

———

There are four invaluable biographies of Keats—by Walter Jackson Bate, Aileen Ward, Robert Gittings, and Andrew Motion—and all tell his story movingly well. It's as if something of his spirit rubbed off on each of his biographers. But no one can assuage his ending. Keats had a special kind of goodness, a vivid nobility, both as a man and as a poet, that makes the last year and a half of his life particu-larly heartbreaking. He was cut off tragically soon. "Life must be undergone," he said, and so must death, but it is impossible to con-sider the end of his life with equanimity.

I think often, for example, of the eight-line fragment, "This living hand, now warm and capable," which he penned in the margin of his unfinished satire, "The Cap and Bells." These are probably the last serious lines of poetry Keats ever wrote:

> This living hand, now warm and capable
> Of earnest grasping, would, if it were cold
> And in the icy silence of the tomb,
> So haunt thy days and chill thy dreaming nights
> That thou would wish thine own heart dry of blood
> So in my veins red life might stream again,
> And thou be conscience-calmed—see here it is—
> I hold it towards you.

These lines were written by someone who knew, at the moment of writing, that the "warm" hand with which he could touch another person would soon be "cold" and unable to grasp anyone, anything. He reaches out for contact because he can't stand it. He is distraught, enraged, terrified. He would prove to you, whoever "you" are, that he still exists: "see here it is," he declares, interrupting himself, urgently holding out his hand: "I hold it towards you." The fury behind this gesture is immense—the fury of the desire to live, the fury of the consciousness of death, the fury that some love might have assuaged all this suffering. Keats keeps the desperation going in this lyric: he embodies it in a Shakespearean rhetoric. The desperation gives voltage to the well-wrought lines, almost lifting them off the page, almost scorching them. I hear it in the beseeching, agonized, infuriated voice. I feel it incarnated in the physical image of his once-living hand. He holds his hand toward you—toward each of us—in a fierce and plaintive gesture of poetry that tries to go beyond poetry. One imagines his hand moving furiously across the page and then suddenly stopping. The truth was intolerable. The reality that his actual hand would be replaced by these living lines of poetry seems to have given him no comfort. Still, these lines must carry as much of him as possible now; they are all that is left. The poet perceived this in advance. He gave his word for it.

I suppose that all of us who care about Keats have been haunted by various details connected to the end of his life—how, for example, he staggered into the house at eleven P.M. after his first severe hemorrhage and announced to Charles Brown, "I know the colour of that blood;—it is arterial blood;—I cannot be deceived in that colour;—that drop of blood is my death-warrant;—I must die." Or of how he set off for Italy, as he put it to Shelley, "as a soldier marches up to a battery." He told him, "I am pick'd up and sorted to a pip. My Imagination is a Monastry and I am its Monk. . . ." Or of how he was torn away from Fanny Brawne with such intolerable agony ("I can bear to die—I cannot bear to leave her." He wrote from Naples: "Oh, God! God! God! Every thing I have in my trunks that reminds me of her goes through me like a spear"). He wrote home to Charles Brown, on his way to Italy, "Land and Sea, weakness and decline are great seperators, but death is the great divorcer for ever." In a letter to Fanny's mother he burst out, "O what a misery it is to have an intellect in splints!" Keats's final desperation hit a fever pitch—he was coughing out his lungs. "This noble fellow lying on the bed—is dying in horror," Severn wrote to William Haslam in England. It is unbearable to think about the physical torture and mental wretchedness Keats suffered night and day during his last few months in Rome.

There have been many of us eager to pay Keats tribute over the decades. You, too, could voyage to Rome, climb the Spanish Steps humming with rude red life, enter the Memorial House at 26 Piazza di Spagna, and stand with numb grief in the tiny corner bedroom—airless container!—where he died. You could stare at the painted flowers on the ceiling and gaze into the fireplace where Severn sometimes heated up their meals. You could marvel at the famous death-bed drawing Severn sketched at three A.M. on January 28, 1821 ("Drawn to keep me awake—a deadly sweat was on him all this night") and recall Rilke's poem "On the Drawing Depicting John Keats's Death." You could wander above the Spanish Steps on the Pincio, where Keats also briefly walked and rode horseback, and look down at the brilliant, buzzing, carelessly gleaming city and summon up what Keats called his "posthumous existence" ("I have an habitual feeling of my real life having past," he wrote to Brown in his last letter, "and that I am leading a posthumous existence"). You could walk slowly under the green umbrella pines, gaze at the incongruous pyramid of the Consul Cestius, and pause for a long time at the place where Keats is buried next to Severn in the Protestant Cemetery. Has anyone ever looked down without trembling at the inscription—"Here lies one whose name was writ in water." It was close by, for example, that Henry James brooded over what he called "that trouble within trouble, misfortune in a foreign land." And it was here at what he called "the holiest place in Rome" that Oscar Wilde prostrated himself on the grass. "As I stood beside the mean grave of this divine boy," he wrote later, "I thought of him as of a Priest of Beauty slain before his time. . . ."

There are dozens of memorial poems in Keats's honor—from Shelley's earthshaking "Adonais" to contemporary sequences by Amy Clampitt ("Voyages: A Homage to John Keats," 1986) and Tom Clark (*Junkets on a Sad Planet: Scenes from the Life of John Keats,* 1994). Keats wrote some sixty-seven sonnets throughout his writing life—he experimented with the form constantly, from one of his first poems, "On Peace," to one of his last, "Bright star—would I were steadfast as thou art," which he copied out on a blank page in Severn's copy of Shakespeare on their voyage to Italy. It is therefore fitting that there is a tradition of testimonial sonnets in his honor—from John Clare (1821) to Karl Shapiro (1944), which includes fourteeners by Thomas Hood, Christina Rossetti, James Russell Lowell, Henry Wadsworth Longfellow, Oscar Wilde, Dante Gabriel Rossetti, Algernon Charles Swinburne, and Christopher Morley. I have a special affection for Alice Meynell's ardent 1869 tribute "On Keats's Grave," Thomas Hardy's 1887 poem "Rome: At the Pyramid of Cestius Near the Graves of Keats and Shelley," Countee Cullen's Harlem Renaissance lyrics, "For John Keats, Apostle of Beauty" and "To John Keats, Poet. At Spring Time" (1925), and Larry Levis's 1985 poem "Those Graves in Rome" ("And here is the Protestant Cemetery/Where Keats & Joseph Severn join hands/Forever under a little shawl of grass"). There are lively allegorizing lyrics by Stanley Plumly ("Posthumous Keats"),

Jorie Graham ("Scirocco"), and George Bradley ("Keats's Handkerchief"). I think of how Tony Harrison offers the poet a fruit in "A Kumquat for John Keats" ("You'll find that one part is sweet and one part's tart") and of how Galway Kinnell imagines sitting down to breakfast with him in the poem "Oatmeal" (hadn't Robert Browning concluded his poem "Popularity" with the question "What porridge had John Keats?") and of how Philip Levine dreams of taking up—taking in—Keats's own breath in the poem "Belief":

> No one believes
> that the lost breath of a man
> who died in 1821 is my breath
> and that I will live until
> I no longer want to, and then
> I will write my name
> in water, as he did, and pass
> this breath to anyone who can
> believe that life comes back
> again and again without end
> and always with the same face—

These poems remind us how deeply and persistently Keats circulates in the bloodstream of other poets. He is a spirit to breathe in, to live up to.

One never gets tired of thinking about Keats. His life, like his work, is inexhaustible, even Shakespearean. His poems and letters are a continual joy, an enduring consolation in our mortality. "I have lov'd the principle of beauty in all things," he said, and he continues to bring that principle intimately home to us. His work delivers us up to ourselves, more fully and more wholly, through the sensuous, rhythmic, musical language of attainment. He is an adept of inhabitable awe. He takes us to the heights. He propels us into a fusion—an ecstatic consummation—with the Other, but the moment cannot stay—it is reneged upon—and we are delivered back to ourselves with an overpowering self-awareness. Keats is expert at these vacillations. He carries the burden of their mysteries. He brings us an abiding reverence for the human heart; he testifies to— and emanates—the eternal eloquence of the imagination. We are befriended by art, Keats teaches us, in our struggle with ourselves, in our urgent soul-making. We are made more human—and more noble—by reading him, for he is a hero of our jubilant, flawed, tragic humanity. I would call him, as Marina Tsvetaeva called Rainer Maria Rilke, "the fifth element incarnate: poetry itself."

———————

EDWARD HIRSCH has published five books of poems—among them, *Wild Gratitude* (1986), *Earthly Measures* (1994), and *On Love* (1998) as well as *How to Read a Poem and Fall in Love with Poetry* (1999). A 1998 MacArthur Fellow, he teaches in the Creative Writing Program at the University of Houston.

POEMS

1817

'What more felicity can fall to creature,
Than to enjoy delight with liberty.'
—SPENSER, *Fate of the Butterfly*

DEDICATION

To Leigh Hunt, Esq.

GLORY and loveliness have pass'd away;
    For if we wander out in early morn,
    No wreathed incense do we see upborne
Into the east, to meet the smiling day:
No crowd of nymphs soft-voiced and young and gay,
    In woven baskets bringing ears of corn,
    Roses, and pinks, and violets, to adorn
The shrine of Flora in her early May.
But there are left delights as high as these.
    And I shall ever bless my destiny,
That in a time when under pleasant trees
    Pan is no longer sought, I feel a free,
A leafy luxury, seeing I could please,
    With these poor offerings, a man like thee.

'I stood tip-toe upon a little hill'

'Places of nestling green for poets made.'
—*Story of Rimini*

I STOOD tip-toe upon a little hill,
The air was cooling, and so very still,
That the sweet buds which with a modest pride
Pull droopingly, in slanting curve aside,
Their scantly leaved, and finely tapering stems,
Had not yet lost their starry diadems
Caught from the early sobbing of the morn.
The clouds were pure and white as flocks new shorn,

And fresh from the clear brook; sweetly they slept
On the blue fields of heaven, and then there crept   10
A little noiseless noise among the leaves,
Born of the very sigh that silence heaves:
For not the faintest motion could be seen
Of all the shades that slanted o'er the green.
There was wide wand'ring for the greediest eye,
To peer about upon variety;
Far round the horizon's crystal air to skim,
And trace the dwindled edgings of its brim;
To picture out the quaint, and curious bending
Of the fresh woodland alley never ending;   20
Or by the bowery clefts, and leafy shelves,
Guess where the jaunty streams refresh themselves.
I gazed awhile, and felt as light and free
As though the fanning wings of Mercury
Had play'd upon my heels: I was light-hearted,
And many pleasures to my vision started;
So I straightway began to pluck a posey
Of luxuries bright, milky, soft, and rosy.

A bush of May-flowers with the bees about them;
Ah, sure no tasteful nook would be without them;   30
And let a lush laburnum oversweep them,
And let long grass grow round the roots to keep them
Moist, cool, and green; and shade the violets,
That they may bind the moss in leafy nets.
A filbert hedge with wild briar overtwined,
And clumps of woodbine taking the soft wind
Upon their summer thrones; there too should be
The frequent chequer of a youngling tree,
That with a score of light green brethren shoots
From the quaint mossiness of aged roots: 40
Round which is heard a spring-head of clear waters,
Babbling so wildly of its lovely daughters,
The spreading blue-bells: it may haply mourn

That such fair clusters should be rudely torn
From their fresh beds, and scatter'd thoughtlessly
By infant hands, left on the path to die.

Open afresh your round of starry folds,
Ye ardent marigolds!
Dry up the moisture from your golden lids,
For great Apollo bids   50
That in these days your praises should be sung
On many harps, which he has lately strung;
And when again your dewiness he kisses,
Tell him, I have you in my world of blisses:
So haply when I rove in some far vale,
His mighty voice may come upon the gale.

Here are sweet peas, on tip-toe for a flight
With wings of gentle flush o'er delicate white,
And taper fingers catching at all things,
To bind them all about with tiny rings.   60

Linger awhile upon some bending planks
That lean against a streamlet's rushy banks,
And watch intently Nature's gentle doings:
They will be found softer than ring-dove's cooings.
How silent comes the water round that bend!
Not the minutest whisper does it send
To the o'erhanging sallows: blades of grass
Slowly across the chequer'd shadows pass.
Why, you might read two sonnets, ere they reach
To where the hurrying freshnesses aye preach   70
A natural sermon o'er their pebbly beds;
Where swarms of minnows show their little heads,
Staying their wavy bodies 'gainst the streams,
To taste the luxury of sunny beams
Temper'd with coolness. How they ever wrestle
With their own sweet delight, and ever nestle

Their silver bellies on the pebbly sand!
If you but scantily hold out the hand,
That very instant not one will remain;
But turn your eye, and they are there again.   80
The ripples seem right glad to reach those cresses,
And cool themselves among the em'rald tresses;
The while they cool themselves, they freshness give,
And moisture, that the bowery green may live:
So keeping up an interchange of favours,
Like good men in the truth of their behaviours.
Sometimes goldfinches one by one will drop
From low-hung branches: little space they stop.
But sip, and twitter, and their feathers sleek;
Then off at once, as in a wanton freak: 90
Or perhaps, to show their black and golden wings,
Pausing upon their yellow flutterings.
Were I in such a place, I sure should pray
That nought less sweet might call my thoughts away,
Than the soft rustle of a maiden's gown
Fanning away the dandelion's down;
Than the light music of her nimble toes
Patting against the sorrel as she goes.
How she would start, and blush, thus to be caught
Playing in all her innocence of thought!   100
O let me lead her gently o'er the brook,
Watch her half-smiling lips and downward look;
O let me for one moment touch her wrist;
Let me one moment to her breathing list;
And as she leaves me, may she often turn
Her fair eyes looking through her locks auburne.
What next? A tuft of evening primroses,
O'er which the mind may hover till it dozes;
O'er which it well might take a pleasant sleep,
But that 'tis ever startled by the leap   110
Of buds into ripe flowers; or by the flitting
Of divers moths, that aye their rest are quitting;

Or by the moon lifting her silver rim
Above a cloud, and with a gradual swim
Coming into the blue with all her light.
O Maker of sweet poets! dear delight
Of this fair world and all its gentle livers;
Spangler of clouds, halo of crystal rivers,
Mingler with leaves, and dew and tumbling streams,
Closer of lovely eyes to lovely dreams,   120
Lover of loneliness, and wandering,
Of upcast eye, and tender pondering!
Thee must I praise above all other glories
That smile us on to tell delightful stories.
For what has made the sage or poet write
But the fair paradise of Nature's light?
In the calm grandeur of a sober line,
We see the waving of the mountain pine;
And when a tale is beautifully staid,
We feel the safety of a hawthorn glade: 130
When it is moving on luxurious wings,
The soul is lost in pleasant smotherings:
Fair dewy roses brush against our faces,
And flowering laurels spring from diamond vases;
O'erhead we see the jasmine and sweet briar,
And bloomy grapes laughing from green attire,
While at our feet, the voice of crystal bubbles
Charms us at once away from all our troubles:
So that we feel uplifted from the world,
Walking upon the white clouds wreath'd and curl'd.   140
So felt he, who first told how Psyche went
On the smooth wind to realms of wonderment;
What Psyche felt, and Love, when their full lips
First touch'd; what amorous and fondling nips
They gave each other's cheeks; with all their sighs,
And how they kist each other's tremulous eyes:
The silver lamp, – the ravishment – the wonder –
The darkness – loneliness – the fearful thunder;

Their woes gone by, and both to heaven upflown,
To bow for gratitude before Jove's throne.   150
So did he feel, who pull'd the boughs aside,
That we might look into a forest wide,
To catch a glimpse of Fauns, and Dryades
Coming with softest rustle through the trees;
And garlands woven of flowers wild, and sweet,
Upheld on ivory wrists, or sporting feet:
Telling us how fair, trembling Syrinx fled
Arcadian Pan, with such a fearful dread.
Poor nymph, – poor Pan, – how he did weep to find
Nought but a lovely sighing of the wind   160
Along the reedy stream; a half-heard strain,
Full of sweet desolation – balmy pain.

What first inspir'd a bard of old to sing
Narcissus pining o'er the untainted spring
In some delicious ramble, he had found
A little space, with boughs all woven round;
And in the midst of all, a clearer pool
Than e'er reflected in its pleasant cool
The blue sky, here and there serenely peeping,
Through tendril wreaths fantastically creeping.   170
And on the bank a lonely flower he spied,
A meek and forlorn flower, with nought of pride,
Drooping its beauty o'er the watery clearness,
To woo its own sad image into nearness:
Deaf to light Zephyrus, it would not move;
But still would seem to droop, to pine, to love.
So while the Poet stood in this sweet spot,
Some fainter gleamings o'er his fancy shot;
Nor was it long ere he had told the tale
Of young Narcissus, and sad Echo's bale.   180

Where had he been, from whose warm head outflew
That sweetest of all songs, that ever new,

That aye refreshing, pure deliciousness,
Coming ever to bless
The wanderer by moonlight? to him bringing
Shapes from the invisible world, unearthly singing
From out the middle air, from flowery nests,
And from the pillowy silkiness that rests
Full in the speculation of the stars.
Ah! surely he had burst our mortal bars: 190
Into some wond'rous region he had gone,
To search for thee, divine Endymion!

He was a Poet, sure a lover too,
Who stood on Latmus' top, what time there blew
Soft breezes from the myrtle vale below:
And brought, in faintness solemn, sweet and slow,
A hymn from Dian's temple; while upswelling,
The incense went to her own starry dwelling.
But though her face was clear as infant's eyes,
Though she stood smiling o'er the sacrifice,   200
The Poet wept at her so piteous fate,
Wept that such beauty should be desolate:
So in fine wrath some golden sounds he won,
And gave meek Cynthia her Endymion.

Queen of the wide air; thou most lovely queen
Of all the brightness that mine eyes have seen!
As thou exceedest all things in thy shine,
So every tale does this sweet tale of thine.
O for three words of honey, that I might
Tell but one wonder of thy bridal night!   210

Where distant ships do seem to show their keels,
Phœbus awhile delay'd his mighty wheels,
And turn'd to smile upon thy bashful eyes,
Ere he his unseen pomp would solemnise.
The evening weather was so bright, and clear,

That men of health were of unusual cheer;
Stepping like Homer at the trumpet's call,
Or young Apollo on the pedestal:
And lovely women were as fair and warm
As Venus looking sideways in alarm.   220
The breezes were ethereal, and pure,
And crept through half-closed lattices to cure
The languid sick; it cool'd their fever'd sleep,
And soothed them into slumbers full and deep.
Soon they awoke clear eyed: nor burnt with thirsting,
Nor with hot fingers, nor with temples bursting:
And springing up, they met the wond'ring sight
Of their dear friends, nigh foolish with delight;
Who feel their arms, and breasts, and kiss, and stare,
And on their placid foreheads part the hair.   230
Young men and maidens at each other gazed,
With hands held back, and motionless, amazed
To see the brightness in each other's eyes;
And so they stood, fill'd with a sweet surprise,
Until their tongues were loosed in poesy.
Therefore no lover did of anguish die:
But the soft numbers, in that moment spoken,
Made silken ties, that never may be broken.
Cynthia! I cannot tell the greater blisses
That follow'd thine, and thy dear shepherd's kisses: 240
Was there a Poet born? – but now no more –
My wand'ring spirit must no farther soar.

Specimen of an Induction to a Poem

Lo! I must tell a tale of chivalry;
For large white plumes are dancing in mine eye.
Not like the formal crest of latter days,
But bending in a thousand graceful ways;
So graceful, that it seems no mortal hand,
Or e'en the touch of Archimago's wand,

Could charm them into such an attitude.
We must think rather, that in playful mood
Some mountain breeze had turn'd its chief delight
To show this wonder of its gentle might.   10
Lo! I must tell a tell of chivalry;
For while I muse, the lance points slantingly
Athwart the morning air: some lady sweet,
Who cannot feel for cold her tender feet,
From the worn top of some old battlement
Hails it with tears, her stout defender sent;
And from her own pure self no joy dissembling,
Wraps round her ample robe with happy trembling.
Sometimes, when the good knight his rest would take,
It is reflected, clearly, in a lake,   20
With the young ashen boughs, 'gainst which it rests,
And th' half-seen mossiness of linnets' nests.
Ah! shall I ever tell its cruelty,
When the fire flashes from a warrior's eye,
And his tremendous hand is grasping it,
And his dark brow for very wrath is knit?
Or when his spirit, with more calm intent,
Leaps to the honours of a tournament,
And makes the gazers round about the ring
Stare at the grandeur of the balancing!   30
No, no! this is far off: – then how shall I
Revive the dying tones of minstrelsy,
Which linger yet about lone gothic arches,
In dark green ivy, and among wild larches?
How sing the splendour of the revelries,
When butts of wine are drunk off to the lees?
And that bright lance, against the fretted wall,
Beneath the shade of stately banneral,
Is slung with shining cuirass, sword, and shield?
Where ye may see a spur in bloody field.   40
Light-footed damsels move with gentle paces
Round the wide hall, and show their happy faces;

Or stand in courtly talk by fives and sevens:
Like those fair stars that twinkle in the heavens.
Yet must I tell a tale of chivalry:
Or wherefore comes that steed so proudly by?
Wherefore more proudly does the gentle knight
Rein in the swelling of his ample might?

Spenser! thy brows are archèd, open, kind,
And come like a clear sunrise to my mind;   50
And always does my heart with pleasure dance,
When I think on thy noble countenance:
Where never yet was aught more earthly seen
Than the pure freshness of thy laurels green.
Therefore, great bard, I not so fearfully
Call on thy gentle spirit to hover nigh
My daring steps: or if thy tender care,
Thus startled unaware,
Be jealous that the foot of other wight
Should madly follow that bright path of light   60
Traced by thy lov'd Libertas; he will speak,
And tell thee that my prayer is very meek;
That I will follow with due reverence,
And start with awe at mine own strange pretence.
Him thou wilt hear; so I will rest in hope
To see wide plains, fair trees, and lawny slope;
The morn, the eve, the light, the shade, the flowers;
Clear streams, smooth lakes, and overlooking towers.

Calidore

A Fragment

YOUNG Calidore is paddling o'er the lake;
His healthful spirit eager and awake
To feel the beauty of a silent eve,
Which seem'd full loth this happy world to leave,

The light dwelt o'er the scene so lingeringly.
He bares his forehead to the cool blue sky,
And smiles at the far clearness all around,
Until his heart is well-nigh overwound,
And turns for calmness to the pleasant green
Of easy slopes, and shadowy trees that lean   10
So elegantly o'er the waters' brim
And show their blossoms trim.
Scarce can his clear and nimble eyesight follow
The freaks and dartings of the black-wing'd swallow,
Delighting much to see it, half at rest,
Dip so refreshingly its wings and breast
'Gainst the smooth surface, and to mark anon
The widening circles into nothing gone.

And now the sharp keel of his little boat
Comes up with ripple, and with easy float,   20
And glides into a bed of water-lilies:
Broad-leaved are they, and their white canopies
Are upward turn'd to catch the heavens' dew
Near to a little island's point they grew;
Whence Calidore might have the goodliest view
Of this sweet spot of earth. The bowery shore
Went off in gentle windings to the hoar
And light blue mountains: but no breathing man,
With a warm heart, and eye prepared to scan
Nature's clear beauty, could pass lightly by   30
Objects that look'd out so invitingly
On either side. These gentle Calidore
Greeted, as he had known them long before.

The sidelong view of swelling leafiness,
Which the glad setting sun in gold doth dress,
Whence, ever and anon, the jay outsprings,
And scales upon the beauty of its wings.

The lonely turret, shatter'd and outworn,
Stands venerably proud; too proud to mourn
Its long-lost grandeur: fir-trees grow around,   40
Aye dropping their hard fruit upon the ground.

The little chapel, with the cross above,
Upholding wreaths of ivy; the white dove,
That on the windows spreads his feathers light,
And seems from purple clouds to wing its flight.
Green tufted islands casting their soft shades
Across the lake; sequester'd leafy glades,
That through the dimness of their twilight show
Large dock-leaves, spiral foxgloves, or the glow
Of the wild cat's eyes, or the silvery stems   50
Of delicate birch-trees, or long grass which hems
A little brook. The youth had long been viewing
These pleasant things, and heaven was bedewing
The mountain flowers, when his glad senses caught
A trumpet's silver voice. Ah! it was fraught
With many joys for him: the warder's ken
Had found white coursers prancing in the glen:
Friends very dear to him he soon will see;
So pushes off his boat most eagerly.
And soon upon the lake he skims along,   60
Deaf to the nightingale's first under-song;
Nor minds he the white swans that dream so sweetly,
His spirit flies before him so completely.

And now he turns a jutting point of land,
Whence may be seen the castle gloomy and grand:
Nor will a bee buzz round two swelling peaches,
Before the point of his light shallop reaches
Those marble steps that through the water dip:
Now over them he goes with hasty trip,
And scarcely stays to ope the folding doors;   70

Anon he leaps along the oaken floors
Of halls and corridors.
Delicious sounds! those little bright-eyed things
That float about the air on azure wings,
Had been less heartfelt by him than the clang
Of clattering hoofs: into the court he sprang,
Just as two noble steeds, and palfreys twain,
Were slanting out their necks with loosen'd rein;
While from beneath the threat'ning portcullis
They brought their happy burthens. What a kiss,   80
What gentle squeeze he gave each lady's hand!
How tremblingly their delicate ankles spann'd!
Into how sweet a trance his soul was gone,
While whisperings of affection
Made him delay to let their tender feet
Come to the earth; with an incline so sweet
From their low palfreys o'er his neck they bent:
And whether there were tears of languishment,
Or that the evening dew had pearl'd their tresses,
He feels a moisture on his cheek, and blesses,   90
With lips that tremble, and with glistening eye,
All the soft luxury
That nestled in his arms. A dimpled hand,
Fair as some wonder out of fairyland,
Hung from his shoulder like the drooping flowers
Of whitest cassia, fresh from summer showers:
And this he fondled with his happy cheek,
As if for joy he would no further seek:
When the kind voice of good Sir Clerimond
Came to his ear, like something from beyond   100
His present being: so he gently drew
His warm arms, thrilling now with pulses new,
From their sweet thrall, and forward gently bending,
Thank'd heaven that his joy was never-ending;
While 'gainst his forehead he devoutly press'd

A hand heaven made to succour the distress'd;
A hand that from the world's bleak promontory
Had lifted Calidore for deeds of glory.

Amid the pages, and the torches' glare,
There stood a knight, patting the flowing hair   110
Of his proud horse's mane: he was withal
A man of elegance, and stature tall:
So that the waving of his plumes would be
High as the berries of a wild ash tree,
Or as the wingèd cap of Mercury.
His armour was so dexterously wrought
In shape, that sure no living man had thought
It hard, and heavy steel: but that indeed
It was some glorious form, some splendid weed,
In which a spirit new come from the skies   120
Might live, and show itself to human eyes.
'Tis the far-famed, the brave Sir Gondibert,
Said the good man to Calidore alert;
While the young warrior with a step of grace
Came up, – a courtly smile upon his face,
And mailèd hand held out, ready to greet
The large-eyed wonder and ambitious heat
Of the aspiring boy; who as he led
Those smiling ladies, often turn'd his head
To admire the visor arch'd so gracefully   130
Over a knightly brow; while they went by,
The lamps that from the high roof'd hall were pendent,
And gave the steel a shining quite transcendent.

Soon in a pleasant chamber they are seated;
The sweet-lipp'd ladies have already greeted
All the green leaves that round the window clamber,
To show their purple stars, and bells of amber.
Sir Gondibert has doff'd his shining steel,
Gladdening in the free and airy feel

Of a light mantle; and while Clerimond   140
Is looking round about him with a fond
And placid eye, young Calidore is burning
To hear of knightly deeds, and gallant spurning
Of all unworthiness; and how the strong of arm
Kept off dismay, and terror, and alarm
From lovely woman: while brimful of this,
He gave each damsel's hand so warm a kiss,
And had such manly ardour in his eye,
That each at other look'd half-staringly:
And then their features started into smiles,   150
Sweet as blue heavens o'er enchanted isles.

Softly the breezes from the forest came,
Softly they blew aside the taper's flame;
Clear was the song from Philomel's far bower;
Grateful the incense from the lime-tree flower;
Mysterious, wild, the far-heard trumpet's tone;
Lovely the moon in ether, all alone:
Sweet too, the converse of these happy mortals,
As that of busy spirits when the portals
Are closing in the west; or that soft humming   160
We hear around when Hesperus is coming.
Sweet be their sleep. * * * *

To Some Ladies

WHAT though, while the wonders of nature exploring,
    I cannot your light, mazy footsteps attend;
Nor listen to accents, that almost adoring,
    Bless Cynthia's face, the enthusiast's friend?

Yet over the steep, whence the mountain stream rushes,
    With you, kindest friends, in idea I muse;
Mark the clear tumbling crystal, its passionate gushes,
    Its spray, that the wild flower kindly bedews.

Why linger ye so, the wild labyrinth strolling?
   Why breathless, unable your bliss to declare?   10
Ah! you list to the nightingale's tender condoling,
   Responsive to sylphs, in the moonbeamy air.

'Tis morn, and the flowers with dew are yet drooping,
   I see you are treading the verge of the sea:
And now! ah, I see it – you just now are stooping
   To pick up the keepsake intended for me.

If a cherub, on pinions of silver descending,
   Had brought me a gem from the fretwork of heaven;
And, smiles with his star-cheering voice sweetly blending,
   The blessings of Tighe had melodiously given;   20

It had not created a warmer emotion
   Than the present, fair nymphs, I was blest with from you;
Than the shell, from the bright golden sands of the ocean,
   Which the emerald waves at your feet gladly threw.

For, indeed, 'tis a sweet and peculiar pleasure
   (And blissful is he who such happiness finds),
To possess but a span of the hour of leisure
   In elegant, pure, and aerial minds.

On receiving a Curious Shell
and a Copy of Verses from the Same Ladies

HAST thou from the caves of Golconda, a gem
   Pure as the ice-drop that froze on the mountain?
Bright as the humming-bird's green diadem,
   When it flutters in sunbeams that shine through a fountain?

Hast thou a goblet for dark sparkling wine;
   That goblet right heavy, and massy, and gold?

And splendidly marked with the story divine
  Of Armida the fair, and Rinaldo the bold?

Hast thou a steed with a mane richly flowing?
  Hast thou a sword that thine enemy's smart is?   10
Hast thou a trumpet rich melodies blowing?
  And wear'st thou the shield of the famed Britomartis?

What is it that hangs from thy shoulder so brave,
  Embroider'd with many a spring-peering flower?
Is it a scarf that thy fair lady gave?
  And hastest thou now to that fair lady's bower?

Ah! courteous Sir Knight, with large joy thou art crown'd;
  Full many the glories that brighten thy youth!
I will tell thee my blisses, which richly abound
  In magical powers to bless and to soothe.   20

On this scroll thou seest written in characters fair
  A sunbeamy tale of a wreath, and a chain:
And, warrior, it nurtures the property rare
  Of charming my mind from the trammels of pain.

This canopy mark: 'tis the work of a fay;
  Beneath its rich shade did King Oberon languish,
When lovely Titania was far, far away,
  And cruelly left him to sorrow and anguish.

There, oft would he bring from his soft-sighing lute
  Wild strains to which, spell-bound, the nightingales listen'd!   30
The wondering spirits of heaven were mute,
  And tears 'mong the dewdrops of morning oft glisten'd.

In this little dome, all those melodies strange,
  Soft, plaintive, and melting, for ever will sigh;

Nor e'er will the notes from their tenderness change,
    Nor e'er will the music of Oberon die.

So when I am in a voluptuous vein,
    I pillow my head on the sweets of the rose,
And list to the tale of the wreath, and the chain,
    Till its echoes depart; then I sink to repose.   40

Adieu! valiant Eric! with joy thou art crown'd,
    Full many the glories that brighten thy youth,
I too have my blisses, which richly abound
    In magical powers to bless and to soothe.

To * * * *

HADST thou lived in days of old,
O what wonders had been told
Of thy lively countenance,
And thy humid eyes, that dance
In the midst of their own brightness,
In the very fane of lightness;
Over which thine eyebrows, leaning,
Picture out each lovely meaning:
In a dainty bend they lie,
Like the streaks across the sky,   10
Or the feathers from a crow
Fallen on a bed of snow:
Of thy dark hair, that extends
Into many graceful bends;
As the leaves of hellebore
Turn to whence they sprung before;
And behind each ample curl
Peeps the richness of a pearl.
Downward too flows many a tress
With a glossy waviness,   20
Full, and round like globes that rise

From the censer to the skies
Through sunny air. Add too the sweetness
Of thy honey'd voice; the neatness
Of thine ankle lightly turn'd:
With those beauties, scarce discern'd,
Kept with such sweet privacy,
That they seldom meet the eye
Of the little loves that fly
Round about with eager pry. 30
Saving when, with freshening lave,
Thou dipp'st them in the taintless wave;
Like twin water-lilies, born
In the coolness of the morn.
O, if thou hadst breathèd then,
Now the Muses had been ten.
Couldst thou wish for lineage higher
Than twin-sister of Thalia?
At least for ever, evermore,
Will I call the Graces four. 40

Hadst thou lived when chivalry
Lifted up her lance on high,
Tell me what thou wouldst have been?
Ah! I see the silver sheen
Of thy broider'd floating vest
Cov'ring half thine ivory breast:
Which, O heavens! I should see,
But that cruel destiny
Has placed a golden cuirass there,
Keeping secret what is fair. 50
Like sunbeams in a cloudlet nested,
Thy locks in knightly casque are rested;
O'er which bend four milky plumes
Like the gentle lily's blooms
Springing from a costly vase.
See with what a stately pace

Comes thine alabaster steed;
Servant of heroic deed!
O'er his loins, his trappings glow
Like the northern lights on snow.   60
Mount his back! thy sword unsheath!
Sign of the enchanter's death;
Bane of every wicked spell;
Silencer of dragon's yell.
Alas! thou this wilt never do,
Thou art an enchantress too,
And wilt never surely spill
Blood of those whose eyes can kill.

To Hope

WHEN by my solitary hearth I sit,
    And hateful thoughts enwrap my soul in gloom;
When no fair dreams before my 'mind's eye' flit,
    And the bare heath of life presents no bloom;
Sweet Hope! ethereal balm upon me shed,
And wave thy silver pinions o'er my head.

Whene'er I wander, at the fall of night,
    Where woven boughs shut out the moon's bright ray,
Should sad Despondency my musings fright,
    And frown, to drive fair Cheerfulness away,   10
Peep with the moonbeams through the leafy roof,
And keep that fiend Despondence far aloof.

Should Disappointment, parent of Despair,
    Strive for her son to seize my careless heart
When, like a cloud, he sits upon the air,
    Preparing on his spell-bound prey to dart:
Chase him away, sweet Hope, with visage bright,
And fright him, as the morning frightens night.

Whene'er the fate of those I hold most dear
    Tells to my fearful breast a tale of sorrow,   20
O bright-eyed Hope, my morbid fancy cheer;
    Let me awhile thy sweetest comforts borrow:
Thy heaven-born radiance around me shed,
And wave thy silver pinions o'er my head!

Should e'er unhappy love my bosom pain,
    From cruel parents, or relentless fair,
O let me think it is not quite in vain
    To sigh out sonnets to the midnight air!
Sweet Hope! ethereal balm upon me shed,
And wave thy silver pinions o'er my head.   30

In the long vista of the years to roll,
    Let me not see our country's honour fade,
O let me see our land retain her soul,
    Her pride, her freedom; and not freedom's shade.
From thy bright eyes unusual brightness shed –
Beneath thy pinions canopy my head!

Let me not see the patriot's high bequest,
    Great liberty! how great in plain attire!
With the base purple of a court oppress'd,
    Bowing her head, and ready to expire: 40
But let me see thee stoop from heaven on wings
That fill the skies with silver glitterings!

And as, in sparkling majesty, a star
    Gilds the bright summit of some gloomy cloud:
Brightening the half-veil'd face of heaven afar:
    So, when dark thoughts my boding spirit shroud,
Sweet Hope! celestial influence round me shed,
Waving thy silver pinions o'er my head.

Imitation of Spenser

• • •

Now Morning from her orient chamber came,
And her first footsteps touch'd a verdant hill:
Crowning its lawny crest with amber flame,
Silv'ring the untainted gushes of its rill;
Which, pure from mossy beds, did down distil,
And after parting beds of simple flowers,
By many streams a little lake did fill,
Which round its marge reflected woven bowers,
And, in its middle space, a sky that never lowers.

There the kingfisher saw his plumage bright,   10
Vying with fish of brilliant dye below;
Whose silken fins, and golden scales' light
Cast upward, through the waves, a ruby glow:
There saw the swan his neck of archèd snow,
And oar'd himself along with majesty:
Sparkled his jetty eyes; his feet did show
Beneath the waves like Afric's ebony,
And on his back a fay reclined voluptuously.

Ah! could I tell the wonders of an isle
That in that fairest lake had placèd been,   20
I could e'en Dido of her grief beguile;
Or rob from aged Lear his bitter teen:
For sure so fair a place was never seen
Of all that ever charm'd romantic eye:
It seem'd an emerald in the silver sheen
Of the bright waters; or as when on high,
Through clouds of fleecy white, laughs the cærulean sky.

And all around it dipp'd luxuriously
Slopings of verdure through the glossy tide,
Which, as it were in gentle amity,   30

Rippled delighted up the flowery side;
As if to glean the ruddy tears it tried,
Which fell profusely from the rose-tree stem!
Haply it was the workings of its pride,
In strife to throw upon the shore a gem
Outvying all the buds in Flora's diadem.

'Woman! when I behold thee flippant, vain'

WOMAN! when I behold thee flippant, vain,
   Inconstant, childish, proud, and full of fancies;
   Without that modest softening that enhances
The downcast eye, repentant of the pain
That its mild light creates to heal again;
   E'en then, elate, my spirit leaps and prances,
   E'en then my soul with exultation dances,
For that to love, so long, I've dormant lain:
But when I see thee meek, and kind, and tender,
   Heavens! how desperately do I adore   10
Thy winning graces; – to be thy defender
   I hotly burn – to be a Calidore –
A very Red Cross Knight – a stout Leander –
   Might I be loved by thee like these of yore.

Light feet, dark violet eyes, and parted hair;
   Soft dimpled hands, white neck and creamy breast;
   Are things on which the dazzled senses rest
Till the fond, fixed eyes forget they stare.
From such fine pictures, heavens! I cannot dare
   To turn my admiration, though unpossess'd   20
   They be of what is worthy, – though not drest
In lovely modesty, and virtues rare.
Yet these I leave as thoughtless as a lark:
   These lures I straight forget, – e'en ere I dine,
Or thrice my palate moisten: but when I mark
   Such charms with mild intelligences shine,

My ear is open like a greedy shark,
   To catch the tunings of a voice divine.
Ah! who can e'er forget so fair a being?
   Who can forget her half-retiring sweets?   30
   God! she is like a milk-white lamb that bleats
For man's protection. Surely the All-seeing,
Who joys to see us with his gifts agreeing,
   Will never give him pinions, who entreats
   Such innocence to ruin, – who vilely cheats
A dove-like bosom. In truth there is no freeing
One's thoughts from such a beauty; when I hear
   A lay that once I saw her hand awake,
Her form seems floating palpable, and near:
   Had I e'er seen her from an arbour take   40
A dewy flower, oft would that hand appear,
   And o'er my eyes the trembling moisture shake.

EPISTLES

To George Felton Mathew

SWEET are the pleasures that to verse belong,
And doubly sweet a brotherhood in song;
Nor can remembrance, Mathew! bring to view
A fate more pleasing, a delight more true
Than that in which the brother Poets joy'd,
Who, with combinèd powers, their wit employ'd
To raise a trophy to the drama's muses.
The thought of this great partnership diffuses
Over the genius-loving heart, a feeling
Of all that's high, and great, and good, and healing.   10

Too partial friend! fain would I follow thee
Past each horizon of fine poesy;
Fain would I echo back each pleasant note,
As o'er Sicilian seas clear anthems float
'Mong the light skimming gondolas far parted,
Just when the sun his farewell beam has darted:
But 'tis impossible; far different cares
Beckon me sternly from soft 'Lydian airs,'
And hold my faculties so long in thrall,
That I am oft in doubt whether at all   20
I shall again see Phœbus in the morning:
Or flush'd Aurora in the roseate dawning!
Or a white Naiad in a rippling stream;

Or a rapt seraph in a moonlight beam;
Or again witness what with thee I've seen,
The dew by fairy feet swept from the green,
After a night of some quaint jubilee
Which every elf and fay had come to see:
When bright processions took their airy march
Beneath the curvèd moon's triumphal arch.   30

But might I now each passing moment give
To the coy muse, with me she would not live
In this dark city, nor would condescend
'Mid contradictions her delights to lend.
Should e'er the fine-eyed maid to me be kind,
Ah! surely it must be whene'er I find
Some flowery spot, sequester'd, wild, romantic,
That often must have seen a poet frantic;
Where oaks, that erst the Druid knew, are growing,
And flowers, the glory of one day, are blowing;   40
Where the dark-leaved laburnum's drooping clusters
Reflect athwart the stream their yellow lustres,
And intertwined the cassia's arms unite,
With its own drooping buds, but very white.
Where on one side are covert branches hung,
'Mong which the nightingales have always sung
In leafy quiet; where to pry, aloof
Atween the pillars of the sylvan roof,
Would be to find where violet beds were nestling,
And where the bee with cowslip bells was wrestling.   50
There must be too a ruin dark and gloomy,
To say, 'Joy not too much in all that's bloomy.'

Yet that is vain – O Mathew! lend thy aid
To find a place where I may greet the maid –
Where we may soft humanity put on,
And sit, and rhyme, and think on Chatterton;

And that warm-hearted Shakespeare sent to meet him
Four laurell'd spirits, heavenward to entreat him.
With reverence would we speak of all the sages
Who have left streaks of light athwart their ages: 60
And thou shouldst moralize on Milton's blindness,
And mourn the fearful dearth of human kindness
To those who strove with the bright golden wing
Of genius, to flap away each sting
Thrown by the pitiless world. We next could tell
Of those who in the cause of freedom fell;
Of our own Alfred, of Helvetian Tell;
Of him whose name to ev'ry heart's a solace,
High-minded and unbending William Wallace.
While to the rugged north our musing turns,   70
We well might drop a tear for him and Burns.

Felton! without incitements such as these,
How vain for me the niggard Muse to tease!
For thee, she will thy every dwelling grace,
And make 'a sunshine in a shady place':
For thou wast once a flow'ret blooming wild,
Close to the source, bright, pure, and undefiled,
Whence gush the streams of song: in happy hour
Came chaste Diana from her shady bower,
Just as the sun was from the east uprising;   80
And, as for him some gift she was devising,
Beheld thee, pluck'd thee, cast thee in the stream
To meet her glorious brother's greeting beam.
I marvel much that thou hast never told
How, from a flower, into a fish of gold
Apollo changed thee: how thou next didst seem
A black-eyed swan upon the widening stream;
And when thou first didst in that mirror trace
The placid features of a human face;
That thou hast never told thy travels strange,   90

And all the wonders of the mazy range
  O'er pebbly crystal, and o'er golden sands;
  Kissing thy daily food from Naiads' pearly hands.

To my Brother George

FULL many a dreary hour have I past,
My brain bewilder'd, and my mind o'ercast
With heaviness; in seasons when I've thought
No sphery strains by me could e'er be caught
From the blue dome, though I to dimness gaze
On the far depth where sheeted lightning plays;
Or, on the wavy grass outstretch'd supinely,
Pry 'mong the stars, to strive to think divinely:
That I should never hear Apollo's song,
Though feathery clouds were floating all along   10
The purple west, and, two bright streaks between,
The golden lyre itself were dimly seen:
That the still murmur of the honey-bee
Would never teach a rural song to me:
That the bright glance from beauty's eyelids slanting
Would never make a lay of mine enchanting,
Or warm my breast with ardour to unfold
Some tale of love and arms in time of old.

But there are times, when those that love the bay,
Fly from all sorrowing far, far away;   20
A sudden glow comes on them, nought they see
In water, earth, or air, but poesy.
It has been said, dear George, and true I hold it,
(For knightly Spenser to Libertas told it)
That when a Poet is in such a trance,
In air he sees white coursers paw and prance,
Bestridden of gay knights, in gay apparel,
Who at each other tilt in playful quarrel;
And what we, ignorantly, sheet-lightning call,

Is the swift opening of their wide portal,   30
When the bright warder blows his trumpet clear,
Whose tones reach nought on earth but Poet's ear,
When these enchanted portals open wide,
And through the light the horsemen swiftly glide,
The Poet's eye can reach those golden halls,
And view the glory of their festivals:
Their ladies fair, that in the distance seem
Fit for the silvering of a seraph's dream;
Their rich brimmed goblets, that incessant run,
Like the bright spots that move about the sun;   40
And when upheld, the wine from each bright jar
Pours with the lustre of a falling star.
Yet further off are dimly seen their bowers,
Of which no mortal eye can reach the flowers;
And 'tis right just, for well Apollo knows
'Twould make the Poet quarrel with the rose.
All that's reveal'd from that far seat of blisses,
Is, the clear fountains' interchanging kisses,
As gracefully descending, light and thin,
Like silver streaks across a dolphin's fin,   50
When he upswimmeth from the coral caves,
And sports with half his tail above the waves.

These wonders strange he sees, and many more,
Whose head is pregnant with poetic lore:
Should he upon an evening ramble fare
With forehead to the soothing breezes bare,
Would he nought see but the dark, silent blue,
With all its diamonds trembling through and through?
Or the coy moon, when in the waviness
Of whitest clouds she does her beauty dress,   60
And staidly paces higher up, and higher,
Like a sweet nun in holiday attire?
Ah, yes! much more would start into his sight –
The revelries and mysteries of night:

And should I ever see them, I will tell you
Such tales as needs must with amazement spell you.

These are the living pleasures of the bard:
But richer far posterity's award.
What does he murmur with his latest breath,
While his proud eye looks through the film of death? 70
'What though I leave this dull and earthly mould,
Yet shall my spirit lofty converse hold
With after times. – The patriot shall feel
My stern alarum, and unsheath his steel;
Or in the senate thunder out my numbers,
To startle princes from their easy slumbers.
The sage will mingle with each moral theme
My happy thoughts sententious: he will teem
With lofty periods when my verses fire him,
And then I'll stoop from heaven to inspire him. 80
Lays have I left of such a dear delight
That maids will sing them on their bridal night;
Gay villagers, upon a morn of May,
When they have tired their gentle limbs with play
And form'd a snowy circle on the grass,
And placed in midst of all that lovely lass
Who chosen is their queen, – with her fine head
Crowned with flowers purple, white, and red:
For there the lily and the musk-rose sighing,
Are emblems true of hapless lovers dying: 90
Between her breasts, that never yet felt trouble,
A bunch of violets full blown, and double,
Serenely sleep: – she from a casket takes
A little book, – and then a joy awakes
About each youthful heart, – with stifled cries,
And rubbing of white hands, and sparkling eyes:
For she's to read a tale of hopes and fears:
One that I foster'd in my youthful years:
The pearls, that on each glistening circlet sleep,

Gush ever and anon with silent creep,   100
Lured by the innocent dimples. To sweet rest
Shall the dear babe, upon its mother's breast,
Be lull'd with songs of mine. Fair world, adieu!
Thy dales and hills are fading from my view:
Swiftly I mount, upon wide-spreading pinions,
Far from the narrow bounds of thy dominions.
Full joy I feel, while thus I cleave the air,
That my soft verse will charm thy daughters fair,
And warm thy sons!' Ah, my dear friend and brother,
Could I, at once, my mad ambition smother,   110
For tasting joys like these, sure I should be
Happier, and dearer to society.
At times, 'tis true, I've felt relief from pain
When some bright thought has darted through my brain:
Through all that day I've felt a greater pleasure
Than if I'd brought to light a hidden treasure.
As to my sonnets, though none else should heed them,
I feel delighted, still, that you should read them.
Of late, too, I have had much calm enjoyment,
Stretch'd on the grass at my best-loved employment   120
Of scribbling lines for you. These things I thought
While, in my face, the freshest breeze I caught.
E'en now I'm pillow'd on a bed of flowers
That crowns a lofty clift, which proudly towers
Above the ocean waves. The stalks and blades
Chequer my tablet with their quivering shades.
On one side is a field of drooping oats,
Through which the poppies show their scarlet coats;
So pert and useless, that they bring to mind
The scarlet coats that pester humankind.   130
And on the other side, outspread, is seen
Ocean's blue mantle, streak'd with purple and green!
Now, 'tis I see a canvas'd ship, and now
Mark the bright silver curling round her prow;
I see the lark down-dropping to his nest,

And the broad-wing'd sea-gull never at rest;
For when no more he spreads his feathers free,
His breast is dancing on the restless sea.
Now I direct my eyes into the west,
Which at this moment is in sunbeams drest: 140
Why westward turn? 'Twas but to say adieu!
'Twas but to kiss my hand, dear George, to you!

To Charles Cowden Clarke

OFT have you seen a swan superbly frowning,
And with proud breast his own white shadow crowning;
He slants his neck beneath the waters bright
So silently, it seems a beam of light
Come from the galaxy: anon he sports, –
With outspread wings the Naiad Zephyr courts,
Or ruffles all the surface of the lake
In striving from its crystal face to take
Some diamond water-drops, and them to treasure
In milky nest, and sip them off at leisure.   10
But not a moment can he there insure them,
Nor to such downy rest can he allure them;
For down they rush as though they would be free,
And drop like hours into eternity.
Just like that bird am I in loss of time,
Whene'er I venture on the stream of rhyme;
With shatter'd boat, oar snapt, and canvas rent,
I slowly sail, scarce knowing my intent;
Still scooping up the water with my fingers,
In which a trembling diamond never lingers.   20

By this, friend Charles, you may full plainly see
Why I have never penn'd a line to thee:
Because my thoughts were never free and clear,
And little fit to please a classic ear;
Because my wine was of too poor a savour

For one whose palate gladdens in the flavour
Of sparkling Helicon: – small good it were
To take him to a desert rude and bare,
Who had on Baiæ's shore reclined at ease,
While Tasso's page was floating in a breeze   30
That gave soft music from Armida's bowers,
Mingled with fragrance from her rarest flowers:
Small good to one who had by Mulla's stream
Fondled the maidens with the breasts of cream;
Who had beheld Belphœbe in a brook,
And lovely Una in a leafy nook,
And Archimago leaning o'er his book:
Who had of all that's sweet tasted, and seen,
From silvery ripple, up to beauty's queen;
From the sequester'd haunts of gay Titania,   40
To the blue dwelling of divine Urania:
One who of late had ta'en sweet forest walks
With him who elegantly chats and talks –
The wrong'd Libertas – who has told you stories
Of laurel chaplets, and Apollo's glories;
Of troops chivalrous prancing through a city,
And tearful ladies, made for love and pity:
With many else which I have never known.
Thus have I thought; and days on days have flown
Slowly, or rapidly – unwilling still   50
For you to try my dull, unlearned quill.
Nor should I now, but that I've known you long;
That you first taught me all the sweets of song:
The grand, the sweet, the terse, the free, the fine:
What swell'd with pathos, and what right divine:
Spenserian vowels that elope with ease,
And float along like birds o'er summer seas:
Miltonian storms, and more, Miltonian tenderness,
Michael in arms, and more, meek Eve's fair slenderness.
Who read for me the sonnet swelling loudly   60
Up to its climax, and then dying proudly?

Who found for me the grandeur of the ode,
Growing, like Atlas, stronger from its load?
Who let me taste that more than cordial dram,
The sharp, the rapier-pointed epigram?
Show'd me that epic was of all the king,
Round, vast, and spanning all, like Saturn's ring?
You too upheld the veil from Clio's beauty,
And pointed out the patriot's stern duty;
The might of Alfred, and the shaft of Tell;   70
The hand of Brutus, that so grandly fell
Upon a tyrant's head. Ah! had I never seen
Or known your kindness, what might I have been?
What my enjoyments in my youthful years,
Bereft of all that now my life endears?
And can I e'er these benefits forget?
And can I e'er repay the friendly debt?
No, doubly no; – yet should these rhymings please,
I shall roll on the grass with twofold ease;
For I have long time been my fancy feeding   80
With hopes that you would one day think the reading
Of my rough verses not an hour misspent;
Should it e'er be so, what a rich content!
Some weeks have pass'd since last I saw the spires
In lucent Thames reflected: – warm desires
To see the sun o'erpeep the eastern dimness,
And morning shadows streaking into slimness
Across the lawny fields, and pebbly water;
To mark the time as they grow broad, and shorter;
To feel the air that plays about the hills,   90
And sips its freshness from the little rills;
To see high, golden corn wave in the light
When Cynthia smiles upon a summer's night,
And peers among the cloudlets, jet and white,
As though she were reclining in a bed
Of bean-blossoms, in heaven freshly shed.
No sooner had I stepp'd into these pleasures,

Than I began to think of rhymes and measures:
The air that floated by me seem'd to say,
'Write! thou wilt never have a better day.'   100
And so I did. When many lines I'd written,
Though with their grace I was not oversmitten,
Yet, as my hand was warm, I thought I'd better
Trust to my feelings, and write you a letter.
Such an attempt required an inspiration
Of a peculiar sort, – a consummation; –
Which, had I felt, these scribblings might have been
Verses from which the soul would never wean;
But many days have passed since last my heart
Was warm'd luxuriously by divine Mozart;   110
By Arne delighted, or by Handel madden'd;
Or by the song of Erin pierced and sadden'd:
What time you were before the music sitting,
And the rich notes to each sensation fitting.
Since I have walk'd with you through shady lanes
That freshly terminate in open plains,
And revell'd in a chat that ceased not,
When, at night-fall, among your books we got:
No, nor when supper came, nor after that, –
Nor when reluctantly I took my hat;   120
No, nor till cordially you shook my hand
Mid-way between our homes: – your accents bland
Still sounded in my ears, when I no more
Could hear your footsteps touch the gravelly floor.
Sometimes I lost them, and then found again;
You changed the footpath for the grassy plain.
In those still moments I have wish'd you joys
That well you know to honour: – 'Life's very toys,
With him,' said I, 'will take a pleasant charm;
It cannot be that aught will work him harm.'   130
These thoughts now come o'er me with all their might: –
Again I shake your hand, – friend Charles, good-night.

SONNETS

1

To my Brother George

MANY the wonders I this day have seen:
    The sun, when first he kist away the tears
    That fill'd the eyes of morn; – the laurell'd peers
Who from the feathery gold of evening lean; –
The ocean with its vastness, its blue green,
    Its ships, its rocks, its caves, its hopes, its fears,
    Its voice mysterious, which whoso hears
Must think on what will be, and what has been.
E'en now, dear George, while this for you I write,
    Cynthia is from her silken curtains peeping
So scantly, that it seems her bridal night,
    And she her half-discover'd revels keeping.
But what, without the social thought of thee,
Would be the wonders of the sky and sea?

2

To * * * * *

HAD I a man's fair form, then might my sighs
    Be echoed swiftly through that ivory shell,
    Thine ear, and find thy gentle heart; so well
Would passion arm me for the enterprise:
But ah! I am no knight whose foeman dies;
    No cuirass glistens on my bosom's swell;
    I am no happy shepherd of the dell
Whose lips have trembled with a maiden's eyes.
Yet must I dote upon thee, – call thee sweet,
    Sweeter by far than Hybla's honey'd roses

When steep'd in dew rich to intoxication.
Ah! I will taste that dew, for me 'tis meet,
    And when the moon her pallid face discloses,
I'll gather some by spells, and incantation.

3

Written on the Day that Mr. Leigh Hunt left Prison

WHAT though, for showing truth to flatter'd state,
    Kind Hunt was shut in prison, yet has he,
    In his immortal spirit, been as free
As the sky-searching lark, and as elate.
Minion of grandeur! think you he did wait?
    Think you he nought but prison walls did see,
    Till, so unwilling, thou unturn'dst the key?
Ah, no! far happier, nobler was his fate!
In Spenser's halls he stray'd, and bowers fair,
    Culling enchanted flowers; and he flew
With daring Milton through the fields of air:
    To regions of his own his genius true
Took happy flights. Who shall his fame impair
    When thou art dead, and all thy wretched crew?

4

'How many bards gild the lapses of time!'

How many bards gild the lapses of time!
    A few of them have ever been the food
    Of my delighted fancy, – I could brood
Over their beauties, earthly, or sublime:
And often, when I sit me down to rhyme,
    These will in throngs before my mind intrude:
    But no confusion, no disturbance rude
Do they occasion; 'tis a pleasing chime.
So the unnumber'd sounds that evening store;
    The songs of birds – the whispering of the leaves –

The voice of waters – the great bell that heaves
With solemn sound, – and thousand others more,
    That distance of recognizance bereaves,
Make pleasing music, and not wild uproar.

5

To a Friend who sent me some Roses

As late I rambled in the happy fields,
    What time the skylark shakes the tremulous dew
    From his lush clover covert; – when anew
Adventurous knights take up their dinted shields;
I saw the sweet flower wild nature yields,
    A fresh-blown musk-rose: 'twas the first that threw
    Its sweets upon the summer: graceful it grew
As is the wand that queen Titania wields.
And, as I feasted on its fragrancy,
    I thought the garden-rose it far excell'd;
But when, O Wells! thy roses came to me,
    My sense with their deliciousness was spell'd:
Soft voices had they, that with tender plea
    Whisper'd of peace, and truth, and friendliness
            unquell'd.

6

To G. A. W.

NYMPH of the downward smile and sidelong glance,
    In what diviner moments of the day
    Art thou most lovely? when gone far astray
Into the labyrinths of sweet utterance?
Or when serenely wandering in a trance
    Of sober thought? Or when starting away,
    With careless robe to meet the morning ray,
Thou spar'st the flowers in thy mazy dance?
Haply 'tis when thy ruby lips part sweetly,

And so remain, because thou listenest:
But thou to please were nurtured so completely
   That I can never tell what mood is best,
I shall as soon pronounce which Grace more neatly
   Trips it before Apollo than the rest.

7

'O solitude! if I must with thee dwell'

O SOLITUDE! if I must with thee dwell,
   Let it not be among the jumbled heap
   Of murky buildings: climb with me the steep, –
Nature's observatory – whence the dell,
Its flowery slopes, its river's crystal swell,
   May seem a span; let me thy vigils keep
   'Mongst boughs pavilion'd, where the deer's swift leap
Startles the wild bee from the foxglove bell.
But though I'll gladly trace these scenes with thee,
   Yet the sweet converse of an innocent mind,
   Whose words are images of thoughts refined,
Is my soul's pleasure; and it sure must be
   Almost the highest bliss of human-kind,
When to thy haunts two kindred spirits flee.

8

To my Brothers

SMALL, busy flames play through the fresh-laid coals,
   And their faint cracklings o'er our silence creep
   Like whispers of the household gods that keep
A gentle empire o'er fraternal souls,
And while, for rhymes, I search around the poles,
   Your eyes are fix'd, as in poetic sleep,
   Upon the lore so voluble and deep,
That aye at fall of night our care condoles.
This is your birth-day, Tom, and I rejoice

That thus it passes smoothly, quietly.
Many such eves of gently whispering noise
    May we together pass, and calmly try
What are this world's true joys, – ere the great voice
    From its fair face shall bid our spirits fly.

9

'Keen fitful gusts are whispering here and there'

KEEN fitful gusts are whispering here and there
    Among the bushes, half leafless and dry;
    The stars look very cold about the sky,
And I have many miles on foot to fare;
Yet feel I little of the cool bleak air,
    Or of the dead leaves rustling drearily,
    Or of those silver lamps that burn on high,
Or of the distance from home's pleasant lair:
For I am brimful of the friendliness
    That in a little cottage I have found;
Of fair-haired Milton's eloquent distress,
    And all his love for gentle Lycid' drown'd,
Of lovely Laura in her light green dress,
    And faithful Petrarch gloriously crown'd.

1 0

'To one who has been long in city pent,'

To one who has been long in city pent,
    'Tis very sweet to look into the fair
    And open face of heaven, – to breathe a prayer
Full in the smile of the blue firmament.
Who is more happy, when, with heart's content,
    Fatigued he sinks into some pleasant lair
    Of wavy grass, and reads a debonair
And gentle tale of love and languishment?
Returning home at evening, with an ear

Catching the notes of Philomel, – an eye
Watching the sailing cloudlet's bright career,
    He mourns that day so soon has glided by,
E'en like the passage of an angel's tear
    That falls through the clear ether silently.

1 1

On first looking into Chapman's Homer

MUCH have I travell'd in the realms of gold,
    And many goodly states and kingdoms seen;
    Round many western islands have I been
Which bards in fealty to Apollo hold.
Oft of one wide expanse had I been told,
    That deep-brow'd Homer ruled as his demesne:
    Yet did I never breathe its pure serene
Till I heard Chapman speak out loud and bold:
Then felt I like some watcher of the skies
    When a new planet swims into his ken;
Or like stout Cortez when with eagle eyes
    He stared at the Pacific – and all his men
Look'd at each other with a wild surmise –
    Silent, upon a peak in Darien.

1 2

On leaving some Friends at an Early Hour

GIVE me a golden pen, and let me lean
    On heap'd-up flowers, in regions clear, and far;
    Bring me a tablet whiter than a star,
Or hand of hymning angel, when 'tis seen
The silver strings of heavenly harp atween:
    And let there glide by many a pearly car,
    Pink robes, and wavy hair, and diamond jar,
And half-discover'd wings, and glances keen.
The while let music wander round my ears,

And as it reaches each delicious ending,
　　Let me write down a line of glorious tone,
　　And full of many wonders of the spheres:
　　For what a height my spirit is contending!
　　'Tis not content so soon to be alone.

1 3

Addressed to Haydon

HIGH-MINDEDNESS, a jealousy for good,
　　A loving-kindness for the great man's fame,
　　Dwells here and there with people of no name,
In noisome alley, and in pathless wood:
And where we think the truth least understood,
　　Oft may be found a 'singleness of aim,'
　　That ought to frighten into hooded shame
A money-mongering, pitiable brood.
How glorious this affection for the cause
　　Of stedfast genius, toiling gallantly!
What when a stout unbending champion awes
　　Envy and Malice to their native sty!
Unnumber'd souls breathe out a still applause,
　　Proud to behold him in his country's eye.

1 4

Addressed to the Same

GREAT spirits now on earth are sojourning:
　　He of the cloud, the cataract, the lake,
　　Who on Helvellyn's summit, wide awake,
Catches his freshness from Archangel's wing:
He of the rose, the violet, the spring,
　　The social smile, the chain for Freedom's sake:
　　And lo! whose stedfastness would never take
A meaner sound than Raphael's whispering.
And other spirits there are standing apart

Upon the forehead of the age to come;
These, these will give the world another heart,
    And other pulses. Hear ye not the hum
Of mighty workings? –
    Listen awhile, ye nations, and be dumb.

1 5

On the Grasshopper and Cricket

THE poetry of earth is never dead:
    When all the birds are faint with the hot sun,
    And hide in cooling trees, a voice will run
From hedge to hedge about the new-mown mead.
That is the Grasshopper's – he takes the lead
    In summer luxury, – he has never done
    With his delights; for when tired out with fun,
He rests at ease beneath some pleasant weed.
The poetry of earth is ceasing never:
    On a lone winter evening, when the frost
        Has wrought a silence, from the stove there shrills
The Cricket's song, in warmth increasing ever,
    And seems to one in drowsiness half lost,
        The Grasshopper's among some grassy hills.

1 6

To Kosciusko

GOOD Kosciusko! thy great name alone
    Is a full harvest whence to reap high feeling;
    It comes upon us like the glorious pealing
Of the wide spheres – an everlasting tone.
And now it tells me, that in worlds unknown,
    The names of heroes burst from clouds concealing,
    And change to harmonies, for ever stealing
Through cloudless blue, and round each silver throne.
It tells me too, that on a happy day,

When some good spirit walks upon the earth,
Thy name with Alfred's, and the great of yore,
   Gently commingling, gives tremendous birth
To a loud hymn, that sounds far, far away
To where the great God lives for evermore.

1 7

Happy is England

HAPPY is England! I could be content
   To see no other verdure than its own;
   To feel no other breezes than are blown
Through its tall woods with high romances blent;
Yet do I sometimes feel a languishment
   For skies Italian, and an inward groan
   To sit upon an Alp as on a throne,
And half forget what world or worldling meant.
Happy is England, sweet her artless daughters:
   Enough their simple loveliness for me,
      Enough their whitest arms in silence clinging:
   Yet do I often warmly burn to see
      Beauties of deeper glance, and hear their singing,
And float with them about the summer waters.

Sleep and Poetry

'As I lay in my bed slepe full unmete
Was unto me, but why that I ne might
Rest I ne wist, for there n'as erthly wight
(As I suppose) had more of hertis ese
Than I, for I n'ad sicknesse nor disese.'

—CHAUCER

What is more gentle than a wind in summer?
What is more soothing than the pretty hummer
That stays one moment in an open flower,
And buzzes cheerily from bower to bower?
What is more tranquil than a musk-rose blowing
In a green island, far from all men's knowing?
More healthful than the leafiness of dales?
More secret than a nest of nightingales?
More serene than Cordelia's countenance?
More full of visions than a high romance?
What, but thee, Sleep? Soft closer of our eyes!
Low murmurer of tender lullabies!
Light hoverer around our happy pillows!
Wreather of poppy buds, and weeping willows!
Silent entangler of a beauty's tresses!
Most happy listener! when the morning blesses
Thee for enlivening all the cheerful eyes
That glance so brightly at the new sun-rise.

But what is higher beyond thought than thee?
Fresher than berries of a mountain tree?
More strange, more beautiful, more smooth, more regal,
Than wings of swans, than doves, than dim-seen eagle?
What is it? And to what shall I compare it?
It has a glory, and nought else can share it:
The thought thereof is awful, sweet, and holy,
Chasing away all worldliness and folly:
Coming sometimes like fearful claps of thunder;
Or the low rumblings earth's regions under;

And sometimes like a gentle whispering
Of all the secrets of some wondrous thing   30
That breathes about us in the vacant air;
So that we look around with prying stare,
Perhaps to see shapes of light, aerial limning;
And catch soft floatings from a faint-heard hymning;
To see the laurel wreath, on high suspended,
That is to crown our name when life is ended.
Sometimes it gives a glory to the voice,
And from the heart up-springs, rejoice! rejoice!
Sounds which will reach the Framer of all things,
And die away in ardent mutterings.   40

No one who once the glorious sun has seen,
And all the clouds, and felt his bosom clean
For his great Maker's presence, but must know
What 'tis I mean, and feel his being glow:
Therefore no insult will I give his spirit,
By telling what he sees from native merit.

O Poesy! for thee I hold my pen,
That am not yet a glorious denizen
Of thy wide heaven – Should I rather kneel
Upon some mountain-top until I feel   50
A glowing splendour round about me hung,
And echo back the voice of thine own tongue?
O Poesy! for thee I grasp my pen,
That am not yet a glorious denizen
Of thy wide heaven; yet, to my ardent prayer,
Yield from thy sanctuary some clear air,
Smoothed for intoxication by the breath
Of flowering bays, that I may die a death
Of luxury, and my young spirit follow
The morning sunbeams to the great Apollo,   60
Like a fresh sacrifice; or, if I can bear

The o'erwhelming sweets, 'twill bring me to the fair
Visions of all places: a bowery nook
Will be elysium – an eternal book
Whence I may copy many a lovely saying
About the leaves, and flowers – about the playing
Of nymphs in woods and fountains; and the shade
Keeping a silence round a sleeping maid;
And many a verse from so strange influence
That we must ever wonder how, and whence   70
It came. Also imaginings will hover
Round my fire-side, and haply there discover
Vistas of solemn beauty, where I'd wander
In happy silence, like the clear Meander
Through its lone vales; and where I found a spot
Of awfuller shade, or an enchanted grot,
Or a green hill o'erspread with chequer'd dress
Of flowers, and fearful from its loveliness,
Write on my tablets all that was permitted,
All that was for our human senses fitted.   80
Then the events of this wide world I'd seize
Like a strong giant, and my spirit tease,
Till at its shoulders it should proudly see
Wings to find out an immortality.

Stop and consider! life is but a day;
A fragile dewdrop on its perilous way
From a tree's summit; a poor Indian's sleep
While his boat hastens to the monstrous steep
Of Montmorenci. Why so sad a moan?
Life is the rose's hope while yet unblown;   90
The reading of an ever-changing tale;
The light uplifting of a maiden's veil;
A pigeon tumbling in clear summer air;
A laughing schoolboy, without grief or care,
Riding the springy branches of an elm.

O for ten years, that I may overwhelm
Myself in poesy! so I may do the deed
That my own soul has to itself decreed.
Then I will pass the countries that I see
In long perspective, and continually   100
Taste their pure fountains. First the realm I'll pass
Of Flora, and old Pan: sleep in the grass,
Feed upon apples red, and strawberries,
And choose each pleasure that my fancy sees;
Catch the white-handed nymphs in shady places,
To woo sweet kisses from averted faces, –
Play with their fingers, touch their shoulders white
Into a pretty shrinking with a bite
As hard as lips can make it: till agreed,
A lovely tale of human life we'll read.   110
And one will teach a tame dove how it best
May fan the cool air gently o'er my rest;
Another, bending o'er her nimble tread,
Will set a green robe floating round her head,
And still will dance with ever varied ease,
Smiling upon the flowers and the trees;
Another will entice me on, and on,
Through almond blossoms and rich cinnamon;
Till in the bosom of a leafy world
We rest in silence, like two gems upcurl'd   120
In the recesses of a pearly shell.
And can I ever bid these joys farewell?
Yes, I must pass them for a nobler life,
Where I may find the agonies, the strife
Of human hearts: for lo! I see afar,
O'er-sailing the blue cragginess, a car
And steeds with streamy manes – the charioteer
Looks out upon the winds with glorious fear;
And now the numerous tramplings quiver lightly
Along a huge cloud's ridge; and now with sprightly   130
Wheel downward come they into fresher skies,

Tipt round with silver from the sun's bright eyes.
Still downward with capacious whirl they glide;
And now I see them on a green hill's side
In breezy rest among the nodding stalks.
The charioteer with wondrous gesture talks
To the trees and mountains; and there soon appear
Shapes of delight, of mystery, and fear,
Passing along before a dusky space
Made by some mighty oaks: as they would chase   140
Some ever-fleeting music, on they sweep.
Lo! how they murmur, laugh, and smile, and weep:
Some with upholden hand and mouth severe;
Some with their faces muffled to the ear
Between their arms; some, clear in youthful bloom,
Go glad and smilingly athwart the gloom;
Some looking back, and some with upward gaze;
Yes, thousands in a thousand different ways
Flit onward – now a lovely wreath of girls
Dancing their sleek hair into tangled curls;   150
And now broad wings. Most awfully intent
The driver of those steeds is forward bent,
And seems to listen: O that I might know
All that he writes with such a hurrying glow!

The visions all are fled – the car is fled
Into the light of heaven, and in their stead
A sense of real things comes doubly strong,
And, like a muddy stream, would bear along
My soul to nothingness: but I will strive
Against all doubtings, and will keep alive   160
The thought of that same chariot, and the strange
Journey it went.
                    Is there so small a range
In the present strength of manhood, that the high
Imagination cannot freely fly
As she was wont of old? prepare her steeds,

Paw up against the light, and do strange deeds
Upon the clouds? Has she not shown us all?
From the clear space of ether, to the small
Breath of new buds unfolding? From the meaning
Of Jove's large eyebrow, to the tender greening   170
Of April meadows? Here her altar shone,
E'en in this isle; and who could paragon
The fervid choir that lifted up a noise
Of harmony, to where it aye will poise
Its mighty self of convoluting sound,
Huge as a planet, and like that roll round,
Eternally around a dizzy void?
Ay, in those days the Muses were nigh cloy'd
With honours: nor had any other care
Than to sing out and soothe their wavy hair.   180

Could all this be forgotten? Yes, a schism
Nurtured by foppery and barbarism
Made great Apollo blush for this his land.
Men were thought wise who could not understand
His glories; with a puling infant's force
They sway'd about upon a rocking-horse,
And thought it Pegasus. Ah, dismal-soul'd!
The winds of heaven blew, the ocean roll'd
Its gathering waves – ye felt it not. The blue
Bared its eternal bosom, and the dew   190
Of summer nights collected still to make
The morning precious: beauty was awake!
Why were ye not awake? But ye were dead
To things ye knew not of; – were closely wed
To musty laws lined out with wretched rule
And compass vile; so that ye taught a school
Of dolts to smooth, inlay, and clip, and fit,
Till, like the certain wands of Jacob's wit,
Their verses tallied. Easy was the task:
A thousand handicraftsmen wore the mask   200

Of Poesy. Ill-fated, impious race!
That blasphemed the bright Lyrist to his face,
And did not know it, – no, they went about,
Holding a poor, decrepit standard out,
Mark'd with most flimsy mottoes, and in large
The name of one Boileau!

                 O ye whose charge
It is to hover round our pleasant hills!
Whose congregated majesty so fills
My boundly reverence, that I cannot trace
Your hallow'd names, in this unholy place,   210
So near those common folk; did not their shames
Affright you? Did our old lamenting Thames
Delight you? Did ye never cluster round
Delicious Avon, with a mournful sound,
And weep? Or did ye wholly bid adieu
To regions where no more the laurel grew?
Or did ye stay to give a welcoming
To some lone spirits who could proudly sing
Their youth away, and die? 'Twas even so.
But let me think away those times of woe: 220
Now 'tis a fairer season; ye have breathed
Rich benedictions o'er us; ye have wreathed
Fresh garlands: for sweet music has been heard
In many places; some has been upstirr'd
From out its crystal dwelling in a lake,
By a swan's ebon bill; from a thick brake,
Nested and quiet in a valley mild,
Bubbles a pipe; fine sounds are floating wild
About the earth: happy are ye and glad.

These things are doubtless; yet in truth we've had   230
Strange thunders from the potency of song;
Mingled indeed with what is sweet and strong,
From majesty: but in clear truth the themes
Are ugly clubs, the poets Polyphemes

Disturbing the grand sea. A drainless shower
Of light is poesy; 'tis the supreme of power;
'Tis might half slumb'ring on its own right arm:
The very archings of her eyelids charm
A thousand willing agents to obey,
And still she governs with the mildest sway: 240
But strength alone, though of the Muses born,
Is like a fallen angel: trees uptorn,
Darkness, and worms, and shrouds, and sepulchres
Delight it; for it feeds upon the burrs
And thorns of life; forgetting the great end
Of poesy, that it should be a friend
To soothe the cares, and lift the thoughts of man.

Yet I rejoice: a myrtle fairer than
E'er grew in Paphos, from the bitter weeds
Lifts its sweet head into the air, and feeds 250
A silent space with ever-sprouting green.
All tenderest birds there find a pleasant screen,
Creep through the shade with jaunty fluttering,
Nibble the little cuppèd flowers and sing.
Then let us clear away the choking thorns
From round its gentle stem; let the young fawns,
Yeanèd in after-times, when we are flown,
Find a fresh sward beneath it, overgrown
With simple flowers: let there nothing be
More boisterous than a lover's bended knee; 260
Nought more ungentle than the placid look
Of one who leans upon a closed book;
Nought more untranquil than the grassy slopes
Between two hills. All hail, delightful hopes!
As she was wont, th' imagination
Into most lovely labyrinths will be gone,
And they shall be accounted poet kings
Who simply tell the most heart-easing things.
Oh may these joys be ripe before I die!

Will not some say that I presumptuously   270
Have spoken? that from hastening disgrace
'Twere better far to hide my foolish face?
That whining boyhood should with reverence bow
Ere the dread thunderbolt could reach me? How!
If I do hide myself, it sure shall be
In the very fane, the light of Poesy:
If I do fall, at least I will be laid
Beneath the silence of a poplar shade;
And over me the grass shall be smooth shaven;
And there shall be a kind memorial graven.   280
But off, Despondence! miserable bane!
They should not know thee, who athirst to gain
A noble end, are thirsty every hour.
What though I am not wealthy in the dower
Of spanning wisdom; though I do not know
The shiftings of the mighty winds that blow
Hither and thither all the changing thoughts
Of man: though no great minist'ring reason sorts
Out the dark mysteries of human souls
To clear conceiving: yet there ever rolls   290
A vast idea before me, and I glean
Therefrom my liberty; thence too I've seen
The end and aim of Poesy. 'Tis clear
As anything most true; as that the year
Is made of the four seasons – manifest
As a large cross, some old cathedral's crest,
Lifted to the white clouds. Therefore should I
Be but the essence of deformity,
A coward, did my very eyelids wink
At speaking out what I have dared to think.   300
Ah! rather let me like a madman run
Over some precipice; let the hot sun
Melt my Dedalian wings, and drive me down
Convulsed and headlong! Stay! an inward frown
Of conscience bids me be more calm awhile.

An ocean dim, sprinkled with many an isle,
Spreads awfully before me. How much toil!
How many days! what desperate turmoil!
Ere I can have explored its widenesses.
Ah, what a task! upon my bended knees,   310
I could unsay those – no, impossible!
Impossible!
        For sweet relief I'll dwell
On humbler thoughts, and let this strange assay
Begun in gentleness die so away.
E'en now all tumult from my bosom fades:
I turn full-hearted to the friendly aids
That smooth the path of honour; brotherhood,
And friendliness, the nurse of mutual good.
The hearty grasp that sends a pleasant sonnet
Into the brain ere one can think upon it;   320
The silence when some rhymes are coming out;
And when they're come, the very pleasant rout:
The message certain to be done to-morrow.
'Tis perhaps as well that it should be to borrow
Some precious book from out its snug retreat,
To cluster round it when we next shall meet.
Scarce can I scribble on: for lovely airs
Are fluttering round the room like doves in pairs;
Many delights of that glad day recalling,
When first my senses caught their tender falling.   330
And with these airs come forms of elegance
Stooping their shoulders o'er a horse's prance,
Careless, and grand – fingers soft and round
Parting luxuriant curls; and the swift bound
Of Bacchus from his chariot, when his eye
Made Ariadne's cheek look blushingly.
Thus I remember all the pleasant flow
Of words at opening a portfolio.
Things such as these are ever harbingers
To trains of peaceful images: the stirs   340

Of a swan's neck unseen among the rushes;
A linnet starting all about the bushes:
A butterfly, with golden wings broad parted,
Nestling a rose, convulsed as though it smarted
With over-pleasure – many, many more,
Might I indulge at large in all my store
Of luxuries: yet I must not forget
Sleep, quiet with his poppy coronet:
For what there may be worthy in these rhymes
I partly owe to him: and thus, the chimes   350
Of friendly voices had just given place
To as sweet a silence, when I 'gan retrace
The pleasant day, upon a couch at ease.
It was a poet's house who keeps the keys
Of pleasure's temple. Round about were hung
The glorious features of the bards who sung
In other ages – cold and sacred busts
Smiled at each other. Happy he who trusts
To clear Futurity his darling fame!
Then there were fauns and satyrs taking aim   360
At swelling apples with a frisky leap
And reaching fingers, 'mid a luscious heap
Of vine-leaves. Then there rose to view a fane
Of liny marble, and thereto a train
Of nymphs approaching fairly o'er the sward:
One, loveliest, holding her white hand toward
The dazzling sun-rise; two sisters sweet
Bending their graceful figures till they meet
Over the trippings of a little child:
And some are hearing, eagerly, the wild   370
Thrilling liquidity of dewy piping.
See, in another picture, nymphs are wiping
Cherishingly Diana's timorous limbs;
A fold of lawny mantle dabbling swims
At the bath's edge, and keeps a gentle motion
With the subsiding crystal: as when ocean

Heaves calmly its broad swelling smoothness o'er
Its rocky marge, and balances once more
The patient weeds, that now unshent by foam
Feel all about their undulating home. 380
Sappho's meek head was there half smiling down
At nothing; just as though the earnest frown
Of over-thinking had that moment gone
From off her brow, and left her all alone.

Great Alfred's too, with anxious, pitying eyes,
As if he always listen'd to the sighs
Of the goaded world; and Kosciusko's, worn
By horrid suffrance – mightily forlorn.

Petrarch, outstepping from the shady green,
Starts at the sight of Laura; nor can wean 390
His eyes from her sweet face. Most happy they!
For over them was seen a free display
Of outspread wings, and from between them shone
The face of Poesy: from off her throne
She overlook'd things that I scarce could tell.
The very sense of where I was might well
Keep Sleep aloof: but more than that there came
Thought after thought to nourish up the flame
Within my breast; so that the morning light
Surprised me even from a sleepless night; 400
And up I rose refresh'd, and glad, and gay,
Resolving to begin that very day
These lines; and howsoever they be done,
I leave them as a father does his son.

ENDYMION

A POETIC ROMANCE

'The stretchèd metre of an antique song.'

INSCRIBED

TO THE MEMORY

OF

THOMAS CHATTERTON

1818

PREFACE

Knowing within myself the manner in which this Poem has been produced, it is not without a feeling of regret that I make it public.

What manner I mean, will be quite clear to the reader, who must soon perceive great inexperience, immaturity, and every error denoting a feverish attempt, rather than a deed accomplished. The two first books, and indeed the two last, I feel sensible are not of such completion as to warrant their passing the press; nor should they if I thought a year's castigation would do them any good; – it will not: the foundations are too sandy. It is just that this youngster should die away: a sad thought for me, if I had not some hope that while it is dwindling I may be plotting, and fitting myself for verses fit to live.

This may be speaking too presumptuously, and may deserve a punishment: but no feeling man will be forward to inflict it: he will leave me alone, with the conviction that there is not a fiercer hell than the failure in a great object. This is not written with the least atom of purpose to forestall criticisms of course, but from the desire I have to conciliate men who are competent to look, and who do look with a zealous eye, to the honour of English literature.

The imagination of a boy is healthy, and the mature imagination of a man is healthy; but there is a space of life between, in which the soul is in a ferment, the character undecided, the way of life uncertain, the ambition thick-sighted: thence proceeds mawkishness, and all the thousand bitters which those men I speak of must necessarily taste in going over the following pages.

I hope I have not in too late a day touched the beautiful mythology of Greece, and dulled its brightness: for I wish to try once more, before I bid it farewell.

TEIGNMOUTH, 10 APRIL 1818

BOOK I

A THING of beauty is a joy for ever:
Its loveliness increases; it will never
Pass into nothingness; but still will keep
A bower quiet for us, and a sleep
Full of sweet dreams, and health, and quiet breathing.
Therefore, on every morrow, are we wreathing
A flowery band to bind us to the earth,
Spite of despondence, of the inhuman dearth
Of noble natures, of the gloomy days,
Of all the unhealthy and o'er-darken'd ways   10
Made for our searching: yes, in spite of all,
Some shape of beauty moves away the pall
From our dark spirits. Such the sun, the moon,
Trees old and young, sprouting a shady boon
For simple sheep; and such are daffodils
With the green world they live in; and clear rills
That for themselves a cooling covert make
'Gainst the hot season; the mid-forest brake,
Rich with a sprinkling of fair musk-rose blooms:
And such too is the grandeur of the dooms   20
We have imagined for the mighty dead;
All lovely tales that we have heard or read:
An endless fountain of immortal drink,
Pouring unto us from the heaven's brink.

   Nor do we merely feel these essences
For one short hour; no, even as the trees
That whisper round a temple become soon
Dear as the temple's self, so does the moon,
The passion poesy, glories infinite,

Haunt us till they become a cheering light   30
Unto our souls, and bound to us so fast,
That, whether there be shine, or gloom o'ercast,
They always must be with us, or we die.
    Therefore, 'tis with full happiness that I
Will trace the story of Endymion.
The very music of the name has gone
Into my being, and each pleasant scene
Is growing fresh before me as the green
Of our own valleys: so I will begin
Now while I cannot hear the city's din;   40
Now while the early budders are just new
And run in mazes of the youngest hue
About old forests; while the willow trails
Its delicate amber; and the dairy pails
Bring home increase of milk. And, as the year
Grows lush in juicy stalks, I'll smoothly steer
My little boat, for many quiet hours,
With streams that deepen freshly into bowers.
Many and many a verse I hope to write,
Before the daisies, vermeil rimm'd and white,   50
Hide in deep herbage; and ere yet the bees
Hum about globes of clover and sweet peas,
I must be near the middle of my story.
O may no wintry season, bare and hoary,
See it half-finish'd: but let Autumn bold,
With universal tinge of sober gold,
Be all about me when I make an end.
And now at once, adventuresome, I send
My herald thought into a wilderness:
There let its trumpet blow, and quickly dress   60
My uncertain path with green, that I may speed
Easily onward, thorough flowers and weed.

    Upon the sides of Latmos was outspread
A mighty forest; for the moist earth fed

So plenteously all weed-hidden roots
Into o'erhanging boughs, and precious fruits.
And it had gloomy shades, sequester'd deep,
Where no man went; and if from shepherd's keep
A lamb stray'd far a-down those inmost glens,
Never again saw he the happy pens   70
Whither his brethren, bleating with content,
Over the hills at every nightfall went.
Among the shepherds 'twas believèd ever,
That not one fleecy lamb which thus did sever
From the white flock, but pass'd unworried
By any wolf, or pard with prying head,
Until it came to some unfooted plains
Where fed the herds of Pan: aye, great his gains
Who thus one lamb did lose. Paths there were many,
Winding through palmy fern, and rushes fenny,   80
And ivy banks; all leading pleasantly
To a wide lawn, whence one could only see
Stems thronging all around between the swell
Of turf and slanting branches; who could tell
The freshness of the space of heaven above,
Edged round with dark tree-tops? through which a dove
Would often beat its wings, and often too
A little cloud would move across the blue.

    Full in the middle of this pleasantness
There stood a marble altar, with a tress   90
Of flowers budded newly; and the dew
Had taken fairy phantasies to strew
Daisies upon the sacred sward last eve,
And so the dawnèd light in pomp receive.
For 'twas the morn: Apollo's upward fire
Made every eastern cloud a silvery pyre
Of brightness so unsullied, that therein
A melancholy spirit well might win
Oblivion, and melt out his essence fine

Into the winds: rain-scented eglantine   100
Gave temperate sweets to that well-wooing sun:
The lark was lost in him; cold springs had run
To warm their chilliest bubbles in the grass;
Man's voice was on the mountains; and the mass
Of nature's lives and wonders pulsed tenfold,
To feel this sun-rise and its glories old.

　　Now while the silent workings of the dawn
Were busiest, into that self-same lawn
All suddenly, with joyful cries, there sped
A troop of little children garlanded;   110
Who gathering round the altar, seem'd to pry
Earnestly round as wishing to espy
Some folk of holiday; nor had they waited
For many moments, ere their ears were sated
With a faint breath of music, which even then
Fill'd out its voice, and died away again.
Within a little space again it gave
Its airy swellings, with a gentle wave,
To light-hung leaves, in smoothest echoes breaking
Through copse-clad valleys, – ere their death, o'ertaking   120
The surgy murmurs of the lonely sea.

　　And now, as deep into the wood as we
Might mark a lynx's eye, there glimmer'd light
Fair faces and a rush of garments white,
Plainer and plainer showing, till at last
Into the widest alley they all past,
Making directly for the woodland altar.
O kindly muse! let not my weak tongue falter
In telling of this goodly company,
Of their old piety, and of their glee: 130
But let a portion of ethereal dew
Fall on my head, and presently unmew

My soul; that I may dare, in wayfaring,
To stammer where old Chaucer used to sing.

Leading the way, young damsels danced along,
Bearing the burden of a shepherd song;
Each having a white wicker, overbrimm'd
With April's tender younglings: next, well trimm'd,
A crowd of shepherds with as sunburnt looks
As may be read of in Arcadian books;   140
Such as sat listening round Apollo's pipe,
When the great deity, for earth too ripe,
Let his divinity o'erflowing die
In music, through the vales of Thessaly:
Some idly trail'd their sheep-hooks on the ground,
And some kept up a shrilly mellow sound
With ebon-tippèd flutes: close after these,
Now coming from beneath the forest trees,
A venerable priest full soberly
Begirt, with minist'ring looks: always his eye   150
Stedfast upon the matted turf he kept,
And after him his sacred vestments swept.
From his right hand there swung a vase, milk-white,
Of mingled wine, out-sparkling generous light;
And in his left he held a basket full
Of all sweet herbs that searching eye could cull:
Wild thyme, and valley-lilies whiter still
Than Leda's love, and cresses from the rill.
His aged head, crownèd with beechen wreath,
Seem'd like a poll of ivy in the teeth   160
Of winter hoar. Then came another crowd
Of shepherds, lifting in due time aloud
Their share of the ditty. After them appear'd,
Up-follow'd by a multitude that rear'd
Their voices to the clouds, a fair-wrought car,
Easily rolling, so as scarce to mar
The freedom of three steeds of dapple brown:

Who stood therein did seem of great renown
Among the throng. His youth was fully blown,
Showing like Ganymede to manhood grown;   170
And, for those simple times, his garments were
A chieftain king's: beneath his breast, half bare,
Was hung a silver bugle, and between
His nervy knees there lay a boar-spear keen.
A smile was on his countenance; he seem'd
To common lookers-on, like one who dream'd
Of idleness in groves Elysian:
But there were some who feelingly could scan
A lurking trouble in his nether lip,
And see that oftentimes the reins would slip   180
Through his forgotten hands: then would they sigh
And think of yellow leaves, of owlets' cry,
Of logs piled solemnly. – Ah, well-a-day,
Why should our young Endymion pine away?

      Soon the assembly, in a circle ranged,
Stood silent round the shrine: each look was changed
To sudden veneration: women meek
Beckon'd their sons to silence; while each cheek
Of virgin bloom paled gently for slight fear.
Endymion too, without a forest peer,   190
Stood, wan, and pale, and with an awèd face,
Among his brothers of the mountain chase.
In midst of all, the venerable priest
Eyed them with joy from greatest to the least,
And, after lifting up his aged hands,
Thus spake he: 'Men of Latmos! shepherd bands!
Whose care it is to guard a thousand flocks:
Whether descended from beneath the rocks
That overtop your mountains; whether come
From valleys where the pipe is never dumb;   200
Or from your swelling downs, where sweet air stirs
Blue hare-bells lightly, and where prickly furze

Buds lavish gold; or ye, whose precious charge
Nibble their fill at ocean's very marge,
Whose mellow reeds are touch'd with sounds forlorn
By the dim echoes of old Triton's horn:
Mothers and wives! who day by day prepare
The scrip, with needments, for the mountain air;
And all ye gentle girls who foster up
Udderless lambs, and in a little cup   210
Will put choice honey for a favour'd youth:
Yea, every one attend! for in good truth
Our vows are wanting to our great god Pan.
Are not our lowing heifers sleeker than
Night-swollen mushrooms? Are not our wide plains
Speckled with countless fleeces? Have not rains
Green'd over April's lap? No howling sad
Sickens our fearful ewes; and we have had
Great bounty from Endymion our lord.
The earth is glad: the merry lark has pour'd   220
His early song against yon breezy sky,
That spreads so clear o'er our solemnity.'

      Thus ending, on the shrine he heap'd a spire
Of teeming sweets, enkindling sacred fire;
Anon he stain'd the thick and spongy sod
With wine, in honour of the shepherd-god.
Now while the earth was drinking it, and while
Bay leaves were crackling in the fragrant pile,
And gummy frankincense was sparkling bright
'Neath smothering parsley, and a hazy light   230
Spread greyly eastward, thus a chorus sang:

      'O thou, whose mighty palace roof doth hang
From jagged trunks, and overshadoweth
Eternal whispers, glooms, the birth, life, death
Of unseen flowers in heavy peacefulness;
Who lov'st to see the hamadryads dress

Their ruffled locks where meeting hazels darken;
And through whole solemn hours dost sit, and hearken
The dreary melody of bedded reeds –
In desolate places, where dank moisture breeds   240
The pipy hemlock to strange overgrowth,
Bethinking thee, how melancholy loth
Thou wast to lose fair Syrinx – do thou now,
By thy love's milky brow!
By all the trembling mazes that she ran,
Hear us, great Pan!

   'O thou, for whose soul-soothing quiet, turtles
Passion their voices cooingly 'mong myrtles,
What time thou wanderest at eventide
Through sunny meadows, that outskirt the side   250
Of thine enmossèd realms: O thou, to whom
Broad-leavèd fig-trees even now foredoom
Their ripen'd fruitage; yellow-girted bees
Their golden honeycombs; our village leas
Their fairest-blossom'd beans and poppied corn;
The chuckling linnet its five young unborn,
To sing for thee; low-creeping strawberries
Their summer coolness; pent-up butterflies
Their freckled wings; yea, the fresh-budding year
All its completions – be quickly near,   260
By every wind that nods the mountain pine,
O forester divine!

   'Thou, to whom every faun and satyr flies
For willing service; whether to surprise
The squatted hare while in half-sleeping fit;
Or upward ragged precipices flit
To save poor lambkins from the eagle's maw;
Or by mysterious enticement draw
Bewilder'd shepherds to their path again;
Or to tread breathless round the frothy main,   270

And gather up all fancifullest shells
For thee to tumble into Naiads' cells,
And, being hidden, laugh at their out-peeping;
Or to delight thee with fantastic leaping,
The while they pelt each other on the crown
With silvery oak-apples, and fir-cones brown –
By all the echoes that about thee ring,
Hear us, O satyr king!

'O Hearkener to the loud-clapping shears,
While ever and anon to his shorn peers   280
A ram goes bleating: Winder of the horn,
When snouted wild-boars routing tender corn
Anger our huntsman: Breather round our farms,
To keep off mildews, and all weather harms:
Strange ministrant of undescribèd sounds,
That come a-swooning over hollow grounds,
And wither drearily on barren moors:
Dread opener of the mysterious doors
Leading to universal knowledge – see,
Great son of Dryope,   290
The many that are come to pay their vows
With leaves about their brows!

'Be still the unimaginable lodge
For solitary thinkings; such as dodge
Conception to the very bourne of heaven,
Then leave the naked brain: be still the leaven
That spreading in this dull and clodded earth,
Gives it a touch ethereal – a new birth:
Be still a symbol of immensity;
A firmament reflected in a sea;   300
An element filling the space between;
An unknown – but no more: we humbly screen
With uplift hands our foreheads, lowly bending,
And giving out a shout most heaven-rending,

Conjure thee to receive our humble Pæan,
Upon thy Mount Lycean!'

    Even while they brought the burden to a close
A shout from the whole multitude arose,
That linger'd in the air like dying rolls
Of abrupt thunder, when Ionian shoals   310
Of dolphins bob their noses through the brine.
Meantime, on shady levels, mossy fine,
Young companies nimbly began dancing
To the swift treble pipe, and humming string.
Ay, those fair living forms swam heavenly
To tunes forgotten – out of memory:
Fair creatures! whose young children's children bred
Thermopylæ its heroes – not yet dead,
But in old marbles ever beautiful.
High genitors, unconscious did they cull   320
Time's sweet firstfruits – they danced to weariness,
And then in quiet circles did they press
The hillock turf, and caught the latter end
Of some strange history, potent to send
A young mind from its bodily tenement.
Or they might watch the quoit-pitchers, intent
On either side; pitying the sad death
Of Hyacinthus, when the cruel breath
Of Zephyr slew him, – Zephyr penitent,
Who now, ere Phœbus mounts the firmament,   330
Fondles the flower amid the sobbing rain.
The archers too, upon a wider plain,
Beside the feathery whizzing of the shaft,
And the dull twanging bowstring, and the raft
Branch down sweeping from a tall ash top,
Call'd up a thousand thoughts to envelope
Those who would watch. Perhaps, the trembling knee
And frantic gape of lonely Niobe,
Poor, lonely Niobe! when her lovely young

Were dead and gone, and her caressing tongue   340
Lay a lost thing upon her paly lip,
And very, very deadliness did nip
Her motherly cheeks. Aroused from this sad mood
By one, who at a distance loud halloo'd,
Uplifting his strong bow into the air,
Many might after brighter visions stare:
After the Argonauts, in blind amaze
Tossing about on Neptune's restless ways,
Until, from the horizon's vaulted side,
There shot a golden splendour far and wide,   350
Spangling those million poutings of the brine
With quivering ore: 'twas even an awful shine
From the exaltation of Apollo's bow;
A heavenly beacon in their dreary woe.
Who thus were ripe for high contemplating,
Might turn their steps towards the sober ring
Where sat Endymion and the aged priest
'Mong shepherds gone in eld, whose looks increased
The silvery setting of their mortal star.
There they discoursed upon the fragile bar   360
That keeps us from our homes ethereal;
And what our duties there: to nightly call
Vesper, the beauty-crest of summer weather;
To summon all the downiest clouds together
For the sun's purple couch; to emulate
In minist'ring the potent rule of fate
With speed of fire-tail'd exhalations;
To tint her pallid cheek with bloom, who cons
Sweet poesy by moonlight: besides these,
A world of other unguess'd offices.   370
Anon they wander'd, by divine converse,
Into Elysium; vying to rehearse
Each one his own anticipated bliss.
One felt heart-certain that he could not miss
His quick-gone love, among fair blossom'd boughs,

Where every zephyr-sigh pouts, and endows
Her lips with music for the welcoming.
Another wish'd, 'mid that eternal spring,
To meet his rosy child, with feathery sails,
Sweeping, eye-earnestly, through almond vales: 380
Who, suddenly, should stoop through the smooth wind
And with the balmiest leaves his temples bind;
And, ever after, through those regions be
His messenger, his little Mercury.
Some were athirst in soul to see again
Their fellow huntsmen o'er the wide champaign
In times long past; to sit with them, and talk
Of all the chances in their earthly walk;
Comparing, joyfully, their plenteous stores
Of happiness, to when upon the moors,   390
Benighted, close they huddled from the cold,
And shared their famish'd scrips. Thus all out-told
Their fond imaginations, – saving him
Whose eyelids curtain'd up their jewels dim,
Endymion: yet hourly had he striven
To hide the cankering venom, that had riven
His fainting recollections. Now indeed
His senses had swoon'd off: he did not heed
The sudden silence, or the whispers low,
Or the old eyes dissolving at his woe,   400
Or anxious calls, or close of trembling palms,
Or maiden's sigh, that grief itself embalms;
But in the self-same fixèd trance he kept,
Like one who on the earth had never stept,
Ay, even as dead-still as a marble man,
Frozen in that old tale Arabian.

Who whispers him so pantingly and close?
Peona, his sweet sister: of all those,
His friends, the dearest. Hushing signs she made,
And breathed a sister's sorrow to persuade   410

A yielding up, a cradling on her care.
Her eloquence did breathe away the curse:
She led him, like some midnight spirit nurse
Of happy changes in emphatic dreams,
Along a path between two little streams, –
Guarding his forehead, with her round elbow,
From low-grown branches, and his footsteps slow
From stumbling over stumps and hillocks small;
Until they came to where these streamlets fall,
With mingled bubblings and a gentle rush,   420
Into a river, clear, brimful, and flush
With crystal mocking of the trees and sky.
A little shallop, floating there hard by,
Pointed its beak over the fringèd bank;
And soon it lightly dipt, and rose, and sank,
And dipt again, with the young couple's weight, –
Peona guiding, through the water straight,
Towards a bowery island opposite;
Which gaining presently, she steerèd light
Into a shady, fresh, and ripply cove,   430
Where nested was an arbour, overwove
By many a summer's silent fingering;
To whose cool bosom she was used to bring
Her playmates, with their needle broidery,
And minstrel memories of times gone by.

So she was gently glad to see him laid
Under her favourite bower's quiet shade,
On her own couch, new made of flower leaves,
Dried carefully on the cooler side of sheaves
When last the sun his autumn tresses shook,   440
And the tann'd harvesters rich armfuls took.
Soon was he quieted to slumbrous rest:
But, ere it crept upon him, he had prest
Peona's busy hand against his lips,
And still, a-sleeping, held her finger-tips

In tender pressure. And as a willow keeps
A patient watch over the stream that creeps
Windingly by it, so the quiet maid
Held her in peace: so that a whispering blade
Of grass, a wailful gnat, a bee bustling   450
Down in the blue-bells, or a wren light rustling
Among sere leaves and twigs, might all be heard.

    O magic sleep! O comfortable bird,
That broodest o'er the troubled sea of the mind
Till it is hush'd and smooth! O unconfined
Restraint! imprison'd liberty! great key
To golden palaces, strange minstrelsy,
Fountains grotesque, new trees, bespangled caves,
Echoing grottoes, full of tumbling waves
And moonlight; ay, to all the mazy world   460
Of silvery enchantment! – who, upfurl'd
Beneath thy drowsy wing a triple hour,
But renovates and lives? – Thus, in the bower,
Endymion was calm'd to life again.
Opening his eyelids with a healthier brain,
He said: 'I feel this thine endearing love
All through my bosom: thou art as a dove
Trembling its closèd eyes and sleekèd wings
About me; and the pearliest dew not brings
Such morning incense from the fields of May,   470
As do those brighter drops that twinkling stray
From those kind eyes, – the very home and haunt
Of sisterly affection. Can I want
Aught else, aught nearer heaven, than such tears?
Yet dry them up, in bidding hence all fears
That, any longer, I will pass my days
Alone and sad. No, I will once more raise
My voice upon the mountain-heights; once more
Make my horn parley from their foreheads hoar;
Again my trooping hounds their tongues shall loll 480

Around the breathèd boar: again I'll poll
The fair-grown yew-tree, for a chosen bow:
And, when the pleasant sun is getting low,
Again I'll linger in a sloping mead
To hear the speckled thrushes, and see feed
Our idle sheep. So be thou cheerèd, sweet!
And, if thy lute is here, softly entreat
My soul to keep in its resolvèd course.'

Hereat Peona, in their silver source,
Shut her pure sorrow-drops with glad exclaim,   490
And took a lute, from which there pulsing came
A lively prelude, fashioning the way
In which her voice should wander. 'Twas a lay
More subtle-cadencèd, more forest wild
Than Dryope's lone lulling of her child;
And nothing since has floated in the air
So mournful strange. Surely some influence rare
Went, spiritual, through the damsel's hand;
For still, with Delphic emphasis, she spann'd
The quick invisible strings, even though she saw   500
Endymion's spirit melt away and thaw
Before the deep intoxication.
But soon she came, with sudden burst, upon
Her self-possession – swung the lute aside,
And earnestly said: 'Brother, 'tis vain to hide
That thou dost know of things mysterious,
Immortal, starry; such alone could thus
Weigh down thy nature. Hast thou sinn'd in aught
Offensive to the heavenly powers? Caught
A Paphian dove upon a message sent?   510
Thy deathful bow against some deer-herd bent,
Sacred to Dian? Haply, thou hast seen
Her naked limbs among the alders green;
And that, alas! is death. No, I can trace
Something more high perplexing in thy face!'

Endymion look'd at her, and press'd her hand,
And said, 'Art thou so pale, who was so bland
And merry in our meadows? How is this?
Tell me thine ailment: tell me all amiss!
Ah! thou hast been unhappy at the change   520
Wrought suddenly in me. What indeed more strange?
Or more complete to overwhelm surmise?
Ambition is no sluggard: 'tis no prize,
That toiling years would put within my grasp,
That I have sigh'd for: with so deadly gasp
No man e'er panted for a mortal love.
So all have set my heavier grief above
These things which happen. Rightly have they done:
I, who still saw the horizontal sun
Heave his broad shoulder o'er the edge of the world,   530
Out-facing Lucifer, and then had hurl'd
My spear aloft, as signal for the chase –
I, who, for very sport of heart, would race
With my own steed from Araby; pluck down
A vulture from his towery perching; frown
A lion into growling, loth retire –
To lose, at once, all my toil-breeding fire,
And sink thus low! but I will ease my breast
Of secret grief, here in this bowery nest.

'This river does not see the naked sky,   540
Till it begins to progress silverly
Around the western border of the wood,
Whence, from a certain spot, its winding flood
Seems at the distance like a crescent moon:
And in that nook, the very pride of June,
Had I been used to pass my weary eves;
The rather for the sun unwilling leaves
So dear a picture of his sovereign power,
And I could witness his most kingly hour,
When he doth tighten up the golden reins,   550

And paces leisurely down amber plains
His snorting four. Now when his chariot last
Its beams against the zodiac-lion cast,
There blossom'd suddenly a magic bed
Of sacred ditamy, and poppies red:
At which I wonder'd greatly, knowing well
That but one night had wrought this flowery spell;
And, sitting down close by, began to muse
What it might mean. Perhaps, thought I, Morpheus,
In passing here, his owlet pinions shook;   560
Or, it may be, ere matron Night uptook
Her ebon urn, young Mercury, by stealth,
Had dipt his rod in it: such garland wealth
Came not by common growth. Thus on I thought,
Until my head was dizzy and distraught.
Moreover, through the dancing poppies stole
A breeze, most softly lulling to my soul;
And shaping visions all about my sight
Of colours, wings, and bursts of spangly light:
The which became more strange, and strange,
   and dim,   570
And then were gulph'd in a tumultuous swim:
And then I fell asleep. Ah, can I tell
The enchantment that afterwards befell?
Yet it was but a dream: yet such a dream
That never tongue, although it overteem
With mellow utterance, like a cavern spring,
Could figure out and to conception bring
All I beheld and felt. Methought I lay
Watching the zenith, where the milky way
Among the stars in virgin splendour pours;   580
And travelling my eye, until the doors
Of heaven appeared to open for my flight,
I became loth and fearful to alight
From such high soaring by a downward glance;
So kept me stedfast in that airy trance,

Spreading imaginary pinions wide.
When, presently, the stars began to glide,
And faint away, before my eager view:
At which I sigh'd that I could not pursue,
And dropt my vision to the horizon's verge;   590
And lo! from opening clouds, I saw emerge
The loveliest moon, that ever silver'd o'er
A shell for Neptune's goblet; she did soar
So passionately bright, my dazzled soul
Commingling with her argent spheres did roll
Through clear and cloudy, even when she went
At last into a dark and vapoury tent –
Whereat, methought, the lidless-eyèd train
Of planets all were in the blue again.
To commune with those orbs, once more I raised   600
My sight right upward: but it was quite dazed
By a bright something, sailing down apace,
Making me quickly veil my eyes and face:
Again I look'd, and, O ye deities,
Who from Olympus watch our destinies!
Whence that completed form of all completeness?
Whence came that high perfection of all sweetness?
Speak, stubborn earth, and tell me where, O where
Hast thou a symbol of her golden hair?
Not oat-sheaves drooping in the western sun;   610
Not – thy soft hand, fair sister! let me shun
Such follying before thee – yet she had,
Indeed, locks bright enough to make me mad;
And they were simply gordian'd up and braided,
Leaving, in naked comeliness, unshaded,
Her pearl round ears, white neck, and orbèd brow;
The which were blended in, I know not how,
With such a paradise of lips and eyes,
Blush-tinted cheeks, half smiles, and faintest sighs,
That, when I think thereon, my spirit clings   620
And plays about its fancy, till the stings

Of human neighbourhood envenom all.
Unto what awful power shall I call?
To what high fane? – Ah! see her hovering feet,
More bluely vein'd, more soft, more whitely sweet
Than those of sea-born Venus, when she rose
From out her cradle shell. The wind outblows
Her scarf into a fluttering pavilion;
'Tis blue, and over-spangled with a million
Of little eyes, as though thou wert to shed,   630
Over the darkest, lushest blue-bell bed,
Handfuls of daisies.' – 'Endymion, how strange!
Dream within dream!' – 'She took an airy range,
And then, towards me, like a very maid,
Came blushing, waning, willing, and afraid,
And press'd me by the hand: Ah! 'twas too much;
Methought I fainted at the charmèd touch,
Yet held my recollection, even as one
Who dives three fathoms where the waters run
Gurgling in beds of coral: for anon,   640
I felt upmounted in that region
Where falling stars dart their artillery forth,
And eagles struggle with the buffeting north
That balances the heavy meteor-stone; –
Felt too, I was not fearful, nor alone,
But lapp'd and lull'd along the dangerous sky.
Soon, as it seem'd, we left our journeying high,
And straightway into frightful eddies swoop'd;
Such as aye muster where grey time has scoop'd
Huge dens and caverns in a mountain's side: 650
There hollow sounds aroused me, and I sigh'd
To faint once more by looking on my bliss –
I was distracted; madly did I kiss
The wooing arms which held me, and did give
My eyes at once to death: but 'twas to live,
To take in draughts of life from the gold fount
Of kind and passionate looks; to count, and count

The moments, by some greedy help that seem'd
A second self, that each might be redeem'd
And plunder'd of its load of blessedness.   660
Ah, desperate mortal! I even dared to press
Her very cheek against my crownèd lip,
And, at that moment, felt my body dip
Into a warmer air: a moment more,
Our feet were soft in flowers. There was store
Of newest joys upon that alp. Sometimes
A scent of violets, and blossoming limes,
Loiter'd around us; then of honey cells,
Made delicate from all white-flower bells, –
And once, above the edges of our nest,   670
An arch face peep'd, – an Oread as I guess'd.

     'Why did I dream that sleep o'erpower'd me
In midst of all this heaven? Why not see,
Far off, the shadows of his pinions dark,
And stare them from me? But no, like a spark
That needs must die, although its little beam
Reflects upon a diamond, my sweet dream
Fell into nothing – into stupid sleep.
And so it was, until a gentle creep,
A careful moving caught my waking ears,   680
And up I started: Ah! my sighs, my tears,
My clenchèd hands; – for lo! the poppies hung
Dew-dabbled on their stalks, the ouzel sung
A heavy ditty, and the sullen day
Had chidden herald Hesperus away,
With leaden looks: the solitary breeze
Bluster'd, and slept, and its wild self did tease
With wayward melancholy; and I thought,
Mark me, Peona! that sometimes it brought
Faint fare-thee-wells, and sigh-shrilled adieus! –   690
Away I wander'd – all the pleasant hues
Of heaven and earth had faded: deepest shades

Were deepest dungeons; heaths and sunny glades
Were full of pestilent light; our taintless rills
Seem'd sooty, and o'erspread with upturn'd gills
Of dying fish; the vermeil rose had blown
In frightful scarlet, and its thorns outgrown
Like spikèd aloe. If an innocent bird
Before my heedless footsteps stirr'd, and stirr'd
In little journeys, I beheld in it   700
A disguised demon, missionèd to knit
My soul with under darkness; to entice
My stumblings down some monstrous precipice:
Therefore I eager follow'd, and did curse
The disappointment. Time, that aged nurse,
Rock'd me to patience. Now, thank gentle heaven,
These things, with all their comfortings, are given
To my down-sunken hours, and with thee,
Sweet sister, help to stem the ebbing sea
Of weary life.'

        Thus ended he, and both   710
Sat silent: for the maid was very loth
To answer; feeling well that breathèd words
Would all be lost, unheard, and vain as swords
Against the enchased crocodile, or leaps
Of grasshoppers against the sun. She weeps,
And wonders; struggles to devise some blame
To put on such a look as would say, *Shame
On this poor weakness!* but, for all her strife,
She could as soon have crush'd away the life
From a sick dove. At length, to break the pause,   720
She said with trembling chance: 'Is this the cause?
This all? Yet it is strange, and sad, alas!
That one who through this middle earth should pass
Most like a sojourning demi-god, and leave
His name upon the harp-string, should achieve
No higher bard than simple maidenhood,

Singing alone, and fearfully, – how the blood
Left his young cheek; and how he used to stray
He knew not where: and how he would say, *nay,*
If any said 'twas love: and yet 'twas love;   730
What could it be but love? How a ring-dove
Let fall a sprig of yew-tree in his path
And how he died: and then, that love doth scathe
The gentle heart, as northern blasts do roses;
And then the ballad of his sad life closes
With sighs, and an alas! – Endymion!
Be rather in the trumpet's mouth, – anon
Among the winds at large – that all may hearken!
Although, before the crystal heavens darken,
I watch and dote upon the silver lakes   740
Pictured in western cloudiness, that takes
The semblance of gold rocks and bright gold sands,
Islands, and creeks, and amber-fretted strands
With horses prancing o'er them, palaces
And towers of amethyst, – would I so tease
My pleasant days, because I could not mount
Into those regions? The Morphean fount
Of that fine element that visions, dreams,
And fitful whims of sleep are made of, streams
Into its airy channels with so subtle,   750
So thin a breathing, not the spider's shuttle,
Circled a million times within the space
Of a swallow's nest-door, could delay a trace,
A tinting of its quality: how light
Must dreams themselves be; seeing they're more slight
Than the mere nothing that engenders them!
Then wherefore sully the entrusted gem
Of high and noble life with thoughts so sick?
Why pierce high-fronted honour to the quick
For nothing but a dream?' Hereat the youth   760
Look'd up: a conflicting of shame and ruth
Was in his plaited brow: yet his eyelids

Widen'd a little, as when Zephyr bids
A little breeze to creep between the fans
Of careless butterflies; amid his pains
He seem'd to taste a drop of manna-dew,
Full palatable; and a colour grew
Upon his cheek, while thus he lifeful spake.

   'Peona! ever have I long'd to slake
My thirst for the world's praises: nothing base,   770
No merely slumberous phantasm, could unlace
The stubborn canvas for my voyage prepared –
Though now 'tis tatter'd; leaving my bark bared
And sullenly drifting: yet my higher hope
Is of too wide, too rainbow-large a scope,
To fret at myriads of earthly wrecks.
Wherein lies happiness? In that which becks
Our ready minds to fellowship divine,
A fellowship with essence; till we shine,
Full alchemized, and free of space. Behold   780
The clear religion of heaven! Fold
A rose-leaf round thy finger's taperness,
And soothe thy lips: hist! when the airy stress
Of music's kiss impregnates the free winds,
And with a sympathetic touch unbinds
Æolian magic from their lucid wombs:
Then old songs waken from enclouded tombs;
Old ditties sigh above their father's grave;
Ghosts of melodious prophesyings rave
Round every spot where trod Apollo's foot;   790
Bronze clarions awake, and faintly bruit,
Where long ago a giant battle was;
And, from the turf, a lullaby doth pass
In every place where infant Orpheus slept.
Feel we these things? – that moment have we stept
Into a sort of oneness, and our state
Is like a floating spirit's. But there are

Richer entanglements, enthralments far
More self-destroying, leading, by degrees,
To the chief intensity: the crown of these   800
Is made of love and friendship, and sits high
Upon the forehead of humanity.
All its more ponderous and bulky worth
Is friendship, whence there ever issues forth
A steady splendour; but at the tip-top,
There hangs by unseen film, an orbèd drop
Of light, and that is love: its influence,
Thrown in our eyes, genders a novel sense,
At which we start and fret; till in the end,
Melting into its radiance, we blend,   810
Mingle, and so become a part of it, –
Nor with aught else can our souls interknit
So wingedly: when we combine therewith,
Life's self is nourish'd by its proper pith,
And we are nurtured like a pelican brood.
Ay, so delicious is the unsating food,
That men, who might have tower'd in the van
Of all the congregated world, to fan
And winnow from the coming step of time
All chaff of custom, wipe away all slime   820
Left by men-slugs and human serpentry,
Have been content to let occasion die,
Whilst they did sleep in love's Elysium.
And, truly, I would rather be struck dumb
Than speak against this ardent listlessness:
For I have ever thought that it might bless
The world with benefits unknowingly;
As does the nightingale, up-perchèd high,
And cloister'd among cool and bunchèd leaves –
She sings but to her love, nor e'er conceives   830
How tiptoe Night holds back her dark-grey hood.
Just so may love, although 'tis understood
The mere commingling of passionate breath,

Produce more than our searching witnesseth:
What I know not: but who, of men, can tell
That flowers would bloom, or that green fruit
      would swell
To melting pulp, that fish would have bright mail,
The earth its dower of river, wood, and vale,
The meadows runnels, runnels pebble-stones,
The seed its harvest, or the lute its tones,   840
Tones ravishment, or ravishment its sweet,
If human souls did never kiss and greet?

   'Now, if this earthly love has power to make
Men's being mortal, immortal; to shake
Ambition from their memories, and brim
Their measure of content; what merest whim,
Seems all this poor endeavour after fame,
To one, who keeps within his stedfast aim
A love immortal, an immortal too.
Look not so wilder'd; for these things are true,   850
And never can be born of atomies
That buzz about our slumbers, like brain-flies,
Leaving us fancy-sick. No, no, I'm sure,
My restless spirit never could endure
To brood so long upon one luxury,
Unless it did, though fearfully, espy
A hope beyond the shadow of a dream.
My sayings will the less obscurèd seem
When I have told thee how my waking sight
Has made me scruple whether that same night   860
Was pass'd in dreaming. Hearken, sweet Peona!
Beyond the matron-temple of Latona,
Which we should see but for these darkening boughs,
Lies a deep hollow, from whose ragged brows
Bushes and trees do lean all round athwart,
And meet so nearly, that with wings outraught,
And spreaded tail, a vulture could not glide

Past them, but he must brush on every side.
Some moulder'd steps lead into this cool cell,
Far as the slabbèd margin of a well,   870
Whose patient level peeps its crystal eye
Right upward, through the bushes, to the sky.
Oft have I brought thee flowers, on their stalks set
Like vestal primroses, but dark velvet
Edges them round, and they have golden pits:
'Twas there I got them, from the gaps and slits
In a mossy stone, that sometimes was my seat,
When all above was faint with mid-day heat.
And there in strife no burning thoughts to heed,
I'd bubble up the water through a reed;   880
So reaching back to boyhood: make me ships
Of moulted feathers, touchwood, alder chips,
With leaves stuck in them; and the Neptune be
Of their petty ocean. Oftener, heavily,
When lovelorn hours had left me less a child,
I sat contemplating the figures wild
Of o'erhead clouds melting the mirror through,
Upon a day, while thus I watch'd, by flew
A cloudy Cupid, with his bow and quiver;
So plainly character'd, no breeze would shiver   890
The happy chance: so happy, I was fain
To follow it upon the open plain,
And, therefore, was just going; when, behold!
A wonder, fair as any I have told –
The same bright face I tasted in my sleep,
Smiling in the clear well. My heart did leap
Through the cool depth. – It moved as if to flee –
I started up, when lo! refreshfully,
There came upon my face, in plenteous showers,
Dew-drops, and dewy buds, and leaves, and flowers,   900
Wrapping all objects from my smother'd sight,
Bathing my spirit in a new delight.
Ay, such a breathless honey-feel of bliss

Alone preserved me from the drear abyss
Of death, for the fair form had gone again.
Pleasure is oft a visitant; but pain
Clings cruelly to us, like the gnawing sloth
On the deer's tender haunches: late, and loth,
'Tis scared away by slow-returning pleasure.
How sickening, how dark the dreadful leisure   910
Of weary days, made deeper exquisite,
By a foreknowledge of unslumbrous night!
Like sorrow came upon me, heavier still,
Than when I wander'd from the poppy hill:
And a whole age of lingering moments crept
Sluggishly by, ere more contentment swept
Away at once the deadly yellow spleen.
Yes, thrice have I this fair enchantment seen;
Once more been tortured with renewèd life.
When last the wintry gusts gave over strife   920
With the conquering sun of spring, and left the skies
Warm and serene, but yet with moisten'd eyes
In pity of the shatter'd infant buds, –
That time thou didst adorn, with amber studs,
My hunting-cap, because I laugh'd and smiled,
Chatted with thee, and many days exiled
All torment from my breast; – 'twas even then,
Straying about, yet, coop'd up in the den
Of helpless discontent, – hurling my lance
From place to place, and following at chance,   930
At last, by hap, through some young trees it struck,
And, plashing among bedded pebbles, stuck
In the middle of a brook, – whose silver ramble
Down twenty little falls, through reeds and bramble,
Tracing along, it brought me to a cave,
Whence it ran brightly forth, and white did lave
The nether sides of mossy stones and rock, –
'Mong which it gurgled blithe adieus, to mock
Its own sweet grief at parting. Overhead

Hung a lush screen of drooping weeds, and spread   940
Thick, as to curtain up some wood-nymph's home.
"Ah! impious mortal, whither do I roam?"
Said I, low-voiced: "Ah, whither! 'Tis the grot
Of Proserpine, when Hell, obscure and hot,
Doth her resign: and where her tender hands
She dabbles, on the cool and sluicy sands;
Or 'tis the cell of Echo, where she sits,
And babbles thorough silence, till her wits
Are gone in tender madness, and anon,
Faints into sleep, with many a dying tone   950
Of sadness. O that she would take my vows,
And breathe them sighingly among the boughs,
To sue her gentle ears for whose fair head,
Daily, I pluck sweet flowerets from their bed,
And weave them dyingly – send honey-whispers
Round every leaf, that all those gentle lispers
May sigh my love unto her pitying!
O charitable Echo! hear, and sing
This ditty to her! – tell her" – So I stay'd
My foolish tongue, and listening, half afraid,   960
Stood stupefied with my own empty folly,
And blushing for the freaks of melancholy.
Salt tears were coming, when I heard my name
Most fondly lipp'd, and then these accents came:
"Endymion! the cave is secreter
Than the isle of Delos. Echo hence shall stir
No sighs but sigh-warm kisses, or light noise
Of thy combing hand, the while it travelling cloys
And trembles through my labyrinthine hair."
At that oppress'd, I hurried in. – Ah! where   970
Are those swift moments? Whither are they fled?
I'll smile no more, Peona; nor will wed
Sorrow, the way to death; but patiently
Bear up against it: so farewell, sad sigh;
And come instead demurest meditation,

To occupy me wholly, and to fashion
My pilgrimage for the world's dusky brink.
No more will I count over, link by link,
My chain of grief: no longer strive to find
A half-forgetfulness in mountain wind   980
Blustering about my ears: ay, thou shalt see,
Dearest of sisters, what my life shall be;
What a calm round of hours shall make my days.
There is a paly flame of hope that plays
Where'er I look: but yet, I'll say 'tis nought –
And here I bid it die. Have not I caught,
Already, a more healthy countenance?
By this the sun is setting; we may chance
Meet some of our near-dwellers with my car.'

    This said, he rose, faint-smiling like a star   990
Through autumn mists, and took Peona's hand:
They stept into the boat, and launch'd from land.

BOOK II

O SOVEREIGN power of love! O grief! O balm!
All records, saving thine, come cool, and calm,
And shadowy, through the mist of passèd years:
For others, good or bad, hatred and tears
Have become indolent; but touching thine,
One sigh doth echo, one poor sob doth pine,
One kiss brings honey-dew from buried days.
The woes of Troy, towers smothering o'er their blaze,
Stiff-holden shields, far-piercing spears, keen blades,
Struggling, and blood, and shrieks – all dimly fades   10
Into some backward corner of the brain;
Yet, in our very souls, we feel amain
The close of Troilus and Cressid sweet.
Hence, pageant history! hence, gilded cheat!
Swart planet in the universe of deeds!
Wide sea, that one continuous murmur breeds
Along the pebbled shore of memory!
Many old rotten-timber'd boats there be
Upon thy vaporous bosom, magnified
To goodly vessels; many a sail of pride,   20
And golden-keel'd, is left unlaunch'd and dry.
But wherefore this? What care, though owl did fly
About the great Athenian admiral's mast?
What care, though striding Alexander past
The Indus with his Macedonian numbers?
Though old Ulysses tortured from his slumbers
The glutted Cyclops, what care? – Juliet leaning
Amid her window-flowers, – sighing, – weaning
Tenderly her fancy from its maiden snow,
Doth more avail than these: the silver flow   30

Of Hero's tears, the swoon of Imogen,
Fair Pastorella in the bandit's den,
Are things to brood on with more ardency
Than the death-day of empires. Fearfully
Must such conviction come upon his head,
Who, thus far, discontent, has dared to tread,
Without one muse's smile, or kind behest,
The path of love and poesy. But rest,
In chafing restlessness, is yet more drear
Than to be crush'd, in striving to uprear   40
Love's standard on the battlements of song.
So once more days and nights aid me along,
Like legion'd soldiers.

                Brain-sick shepherd prince,
What promise hast thou faithful guarded since
The day of sacrifice? Or, have new sorrows
Come with the constant dawn upon thy morrows?
Alas! 'tis his old grief. For many days,
Has he been wandering in uncertain ways:
Through wilderness, and woods of mossèd oaks;
Counting his woe-worn minutes, by the strokes   50
Of the lone wood-cutter; and listening still,
Hour after hour, to each lush-leav'd rill.
Now he is sitting by a shady spring,
And elbow-deep with feverous fingering
Stems the upbursting cold: a wild rose-tree
Pavilions him in bloom, and he doth see
A bud which snares his fancy: lo! but now
He plucks it, dips its stalk in the water: how!
It swells, it buds, it flowers beneath his sight;
And, in the middle, there is softly pight   60
A golden butterfly; upon whose wings
There must be surely character'd strange things,
For with wide eye he wonders, and smiles oft.

Lightly this little herald flew aloft,
Follow'd by glad Endymion's claspèd hands:
Onward it flies. From languor's sullen bands
His limbs are loosed, and eager, on he hies
Dazzled to trace it in the sunny skies.
It seem'd he flew, the way so easy was;
And like a new-born spirit did he pass   70
Through the green evening quiet in the sun,
O'er many a heath, through many a woodland dun,
Through buried paths, where sleepy twilight dreams
The summer time away. One track unseams
A wooded cleft, and, far away, the blue
Of ocean fades upon him; then, anew,
He sinks adown a solitary glen,
Where there was never sound of mortal men,
Saving, perhaps, some snow-light cadences
Melting to silence, when upon the breeze   80
Some holy bark let forth an anthem sweet,
To cheer itself to Delphi. Still his feet
Went swift beneath the merry-wingèd guide,
Until it reach'd a splashing fountain's side
That, near a cavern's mouth, for ever pour'd
Unto the temperate air; then high it soar'd,
And, downward, suddenly began to dip,
As if, athirst with so much toil, 'twould sip
The crystal spout-head; so it did, with touch
Most delicate, as though afraid to smutch   90
Even with mealy gold the waters clear.
But, at that very touch, to disappear
So fairy-quick, was strange! Bewilderèd,
Endymion sought around, and shook each bed
Of covert flowers in vain; and then he flung
Himself along the grass. What gentle tongue,
What whisperer disturb'd his gloomy rest?
It was a nymph uprisen to the breast
In the fountain's pebbly margin, and she stood

'Mong lilies, like the youngest of the brood.   100
To him her dripping hand she softly kist,
And anxiously began to plait and twist
Her ringlets round her fingers, saying: 'Youth!
Too long, alas, hast thou starved on the ruth,
The bitterness of love: too long indeed,
Seeing thou art so gentle. Could I weed
Thy soul of care, by heavens, I would offer
All the bright riches of my crystal coffer
To Amphitrite; all my clear-eyed fish,
Golden, or rainbow-sided, or purplish,   110
Vermilion-tail'd, or finn'd with silvery gauze;
Yea, or my veinèd pebble-floor, that draws
A virgin light to the deep; my grotto-sands,
Tawny and gold, oozed slowly from far lands
By my diligent springs: my level lilies, shells,
My charming-rod, my potent river spells;
Yes, everything, even to the pearly cup
Meander gave me, – for I bubbled up
To fainting creatures in a desert wild.
But woe is me, I am but as a child   120
To gladden thee; and all I dare to say,
Is, that I pity thee; that on this day
I've been thy guide; that thou must wander far
In other regions, past the scanty bar
To mortal steps, before thou canst be ta'en
From every wasting sigh, from every pain,
Into the gentle bosom of thy love.
Why it is thus, one knows in heaven above:
But, a poor Naiad, I guess not. Farewell!
I have a ditty for my hollow cell.'   130

    Hereat she vanish'd from Endymion's gaze,
Who brooded o'er the water in amaze:
The dashing fount pour'd on, and where its pool
Lay, half asleep, in grass and rushes cool,

Quick waterflies and gnats were sporting still,
And fish were dimpling, as if good nor ill
Had fallen out that hour. The wanderer,
Holding his forehead, to keep off the burr
Of smothering fancies, patiently sat down;
And, while beneath the evening's sleepy frown   140
Glow-worms began to trim their starry lamps,
Thus breathed he to himself: 'Whoso encamps
To take a fancied city of delight,
O what a wretch is he! and when 'tis his,
After long toil and travelling, to miss
The kernel of his hopes, how more than vile!
Yet, for him there's refreshment even in toil;
Another city doth he set about,
Free from the smallest pebble-bead of doubt
That he will seize on trickling honey-combs: 150
Alas! he finds them dry; and then he foams,
And onward to another city speeds.
But this is human life: the war, the deeds,
The disappointment, the anxiety,
Imagination's struggles, far and nigh,
All human; bearing in themselves this good,
That they are still the air, the subtle food,
To make us feel existence, and to show
How quiet death is. Where soil is men grow,
Whether to weeds or flowers; but for me,   160
There is no depth to strike in: I can see
Nought earthly worth my compassing; so stand
Upon a misty, jutting head of land –
Alone? No, no; and by the Orphean lute,
When mad Eurydice is listening to 't,
I'd rather stand upon this misty peak,
With not a thing to sigh for, or to seek,
But the soft shadow of my thrice-seen love,
Than be – I care not what. O meekest dove
Of heaven! O Cynthia, ten-times bright and fair!   170

From thy blue throne, now filling all the air,
Glance but one little beam of temper'd light
Into my bosom, that the dreadful might
And tyranny of love be somewhat scared!
Yet do not so, sweet queen; one torment spared
Would give a pang to jealous misery,
Worse than the torment's self: but rather tie
Large wings upon my shoulders, and point out
My love's far dwelling. Though the playful rout
Of Cupids shun thee, too divine art thou,   180
Too keen in beauty, for thy silver prow
Not to have dipp'd in love's most gentle stream.
O be propitious, nor severely deem
My madness impious; for, by all the stars
That tend thy bidding, I do think the bars
That kept my spirit in are burst – that I
Am sailing with thee through the dizzy sky!
How beautiful thou art! The world how deep!
How tremulous-dazzlingly the wheels sweep
Around their axle! Then these gleaming reins,   190
How lithe! When this thy chariot attains
Its airy goal, haply some bower veils
Those twilight eyes? Those eyes! – my spirit fails;
Dear goddess, help! or the wide-gaping air
Will gulph me – help!' – At this, with madden'd stare,
And lifted hands, and trembling lips, he stood;
Like old Deucalion mountain'd o'er the flood,
Or blind Orion hungry for the morn.
And, but from the deep cavern there was borne
A voice, he had been froze to senseless stone;   200
Nor sigh of his, nor plaint, nor passion'd moan
Had more been heard. Thus swell'd it forth: 'Descend,
Young mountaineer! descend where alleys bend
Into the sparry hollows of the world!
Oft hast thou seen bolts of the thunder hurl'd
As from thy threshold; day by day hast been

A little lower than the chilly sheen
Of icy pinnacles, and dipp'dst thine arms
Into the deadening ether that still charms
Their marble being; now, as deep profound   210
As those are high, descend! He ne'er is crown'd
With immortality, who fears to follow
Where airy voices lead: so through the hollow,
The silent mysteries of earth, descend!'

    He heard but the last words, nor could contend
One moment in reflection: for he fled
Into the fearful deep, to hide his head
From the clear moon, the trees, and coming madness.

    'Twas far too strange and wonderful for sadness;
Sharpening, by degrees, his appetite   220
To dive into the deepest. Dark, nor light,
The region; nor bright, nor sombre wholly,
But mingled up; a gleaming melancholy;
A dusky empire and its diadems;
One faint eternal eventide of gems.
Ay, millions sparkled on a vein of gold,
Along whose track the prince quick footsteps told,
With all its lines abrupt and angular:
Out-shooting sometimes, like a meteor-star,
Through a vast antre; then the metal woof,   230
Like Vulcan's rainbow, with some monstrous roof
Curves hugely: now, far in the deep abyss,
It seems an angry lightning, and doth hiss
Fancy into belief: anon it leads
Through winding passages, where sameness breeds
Vexing conceptions of some sudden change;
Whether to silver grots, or giant range
Of sapphire columns, or fantastic bridge
Athwart a flood of crystal. On a ridge
Now fareth he, that o'er the vast beneath   240

Towers like an ocean-cliff, and whence he seeth
A hundred waterfalls, whose voices come
But as the murmuring surge. Chilly and numb
His bosom grew, when first he, far away,
Descried an orbèd diamond, set to fray
Old Darkness from his throne: 'twas like the sun
Uprisen o'er chaos: and with such a stun
Came the amazement, that, absorb'd in it,
He saw not fiercer wonders – past the wit
Of any spirit to tell, but one of those   250
Who, when this planet's sphering time doth close,
Will be its high remembrancers: who they?
The mighty ones who have made eternal day
For Greece and England. While astonishment
With deep-drawn sighs was quieting, he went
Into a marble gallery, passing through
A mimic temple, so complete and true
In sacred custom, that he well-nigh fear'd
To search it inwards; whence far off appear'd,
Through a long pillar'd vista, a fair shrine,   260
And, just beyond, on light tiptoe divine,
A quiver'd Dian. Stepping awfully,
The youth approach'd; oft turning his veil'd eye
Down sidelong aisles, and into niches old:
And, when more near against the marble cold
He had touch'd his forehead, he began to thread
All courts and passages, where silence dead,
Roused by his whispering footsteps, murmur'd faint:
And long he traversed to and fro, to acquaint
Himself with every mystery, and awe;   270
Till, weary, he sat down before the maw
Of a wide outlet, fathomless and dim,
To wild uncertainty and shadows grim.
There, when new wonders ceased to float before,
And thoughts of self came on, how crude and sore
The journey homeward to habitual self!

A mad-pursuing of the fog-born elf,
Whose flitting lantern, through rude nettle-brier,
Cheats us into a swamp, into a fire,
Into the bosom of a hated thing.   280

What misery most drowningly doth sing
In lone Endymion's ear, now he has raught
The goal of consciousness? Ah, 'tis the thought,
The deadly feel of solitude: for lo!
He cannot see the heavens, nor the flow
Of rivers, nor hill-flowers running wild
In pink and purple chequer, nor, up-piled,
The cloudy rack slow journeying in the west,
Like herded elephants; nor felt, nor prest
Cool grass, nor tasted the fresh slumberous air;   290
But far from such companionship to wear
An unknown time, surcharged with grief, away,
Was now his lot. And must he patient stay,
Tracing fantastic figures with his spear?
'No!' exclaimed he, 'why should I tarry here?'
No! loudly echoed times innumerable.
At which he straightway started, and 'gan tell
His paces back into the temple's chief;
Warming and glowing strong in the belief
Of help from Dian: so that when again   300
He caught her airy form, thus did he plain,
Moving more near the while: 'O Haunter chaste
Of river sides, and woods, and heathy waste,
Where with thy silver bow and arrows keen
Art thou now forested? O woodland Queen,
What smoothest air thy smoother forehead woos?
Where dost thou listen to the wide halloos
Of thy disparted nymphs? Through what dark tree
Glimmers thy crescent? Wheresoe'er it be,
'Tis in the breath of heaven: thou dost taste   310
Freedom as none can taste it, nor dost waste

Thy loveliness in dismal elements;
But, finding in our green earth sweet contents,
There livest blissfully. Ah, if to thee
It feels Elysian, how rich to me,
An exiled mortal, sounds its pleasant name!
Within my breast there lives a choking flame –
O let me cool 't the zephyr-boughs among!
A homeward fever parches up my tongue –
O let me slake it at the running springs!   320
Upon my ear a noisy nothing rings –
O let me once more hear the linnet's note!
Before mine eyes thick films and shadows float –
O let me 'noint them with the heaven's light:
Dost thou now lave thy feet and ankles white?
O think how sweet to me the freshening sluice!
Dost thou now please thy thirst with berry-juice?
O think how this dry palate would rejoice!
If in soft slumber thou dost hear my voice,
O think how I should love a bed of flowers! –   330
Young goddess! let me see my native bowers!
Deliver me from this rapacious deep!'

    Thus ending loudly, as he would o'erleap
His destiny, alert he stood: but when
Obstinate silence came heavily again,
Feeling about for its old couch of space
And airy cradle, lowly bow'd his face,
Desponding, o'er the marble floor's cold thrill.
But 'twas not long; for, sweeter than the rill
To its old channel, or a swollen tide   340
To margin sallows, were the leaves he spied,
And flowers, and wreaths, and ready myrtle crowns
Up heaping through the slab: refreshment drowns
Itself, and strives its own delights to hide –
Nor in one spot alone; the floral pride
In a long whispering birth enchanted grew

Before his footsteps; as when heaved anew
Old ocean rolls a lengthen'd wave to the shore,
Down whose green back the short-lived foam, all hoar,
Bursts gradual, with a wayward indolence.   350

    Increasing still in heart, and pleasant sense,
Upon his fairy journey on he hastes;
So anxious for the end, he scarcely wastes
One moment with his hand among the sweets:
Onward he goes – he stops – his bosom beats
As plainly in his ear, as the faint charm
Of which the throbs were born. This still alarm,
This sleepy music, forced him walk tiptoe;
For it came more softly than the east could blow
Arion's magic to the Atlantic isles;   360
Or than the west, made jealous by the smiles
Of throned Apollo, could breathe back the lyre
To seas Ionian and Tyrian.

    O did he ever live, that lonely man,
Who loved – and music slew not? 'Tis the pest
Of love, that fairest joys give most unrest;
That things of delicate and tenderest worth
Are swallow'd all, and make a searèd dearth,
By one consuming flame: it doth immerse
And suffocate true blessings in a curse.   370
Half-happy, by comparison of bliss,
Is miserable. 'Twas even so with this
Dew-dropping melody, in the Carian's ear;
First heaven, then hell, and then forgotten clear,
Vanish'd in elemental passion.

    And down some swart abysm he had gone,
Had not a heavenly guide benignant led
To where thick myrtle branches, 'gainst his head
Brushing, awaken'd: then the sounds again

Went noiseless as a passing noontide rain   380
Over a bower, where little space he stood;
For as the sunset peeps into a wood,
So saw he panting light, and towards it went
Through winding alleys; and lo, wonderment!
Upon soft verdure saw, one here, one there,
Cupids a-slumbering on their pinions fair.

    After a thousand mazes overgone,
At last, with sudden step, he came upon
A chamber, myrtle-wall'd, embower'd high,
Full of light, incense, tender minstrelsy,   390
And more of beautiful and strange beside:
For on a silken couch of rosy pride,
In midst of all, there lay a sleeping youth
Of fondest beauty; fonder, in fair sooth,
Than sighs could fathom, or contentment reach:
And coverlids gold-tinted like the peach,
Or ripe October's faded marigolds,
Fell sleek about him in a thousand folds –
Not hiding up an Apollonian curve
Of neck and shoulder, nor the tenting swerve   400
Of knee from knee, nor ankles pointing light;
But rather, giving them to the fill'd sight
Officiously. Sideway his face reposed
On one white arm, and tenderly unclosed,
By tenderest pressure, a faint damask mouth
To slumbery pout: just as the morning south
Disparts a dew-lipp'd rose. Above his head,
Four lily stalks did their white honours wed
To make a coronal; and round him grew
All tendrils green, of every bloom and hue,   410
Together intertwined and trammell'd fresh:
The vine of glossy sprout; the ivy mesh,
Shading its Ethiop berries; and woodbine,
Of velvet leaves and bugle-blooms divine;

Convolvulus in streakèd vases flush;
The creeper, mellowing for an autumn blush;
And virgin's bower, trailing airily;
With others of the sisterhood. Hard by,
Stood serene Cupids watching silently.
One, kneeling to a lyre, touch'd the strings,   420
Muffling to death the pathos with his wings;
And, ever and anon, uprose to look
At the youth's slumber; while another took
A willow bough, distilling odorous dew,
And shook it on his hair; another flew
In through the woven roof, and fluttering-wise
Rain'd violets upon his sleeping eyes.

At these enchantments, and yet many more,
The breathless Latmian wonder'd o'er and o'er;
Until, impatient in embarrassment,   430
He forthright pass'd, and lightly treading went
To that same feather'd lyrist, who straightway,
Smiling, thus whisper'd: 'Though from upper day
Thou art a wanderer, and thy presence here
Might seem unholy, be of happy cheer!
For 'tis the nicest touch of human honour,
When some ethereal and high-favouring donor
Presents immortal bowers to mortal sense;
As now 'tis done to thee, Endymion. Hence
Was I in no wise startled. So recline   440
Upon these living flowers. Here is wine,
Alive with sparkles – never, I aver,
Since Ariadne was a vintager,
So cool a purple: taste these juicy pears,
Sent me by sad Vertumnus, when his fears
Were high about Pomona; here is cream,
Deepening to richness from a snowy gleam;
Sweeter than that nurse Amalthea skimm'd
For the boy Jupiter: and here, undimm'd

By any touch, a bunch of blooming plums   450
Ready to melt between an infant's gums:
And here is manna pick'd from Syrian trees,
In starlight, by the three Hesperides.
Feast on, and meanwhile I will let thee know
Of all these things around us.' He did so,
Still brooding o'er the cadence of his lyre;
And thus: 'I need not any hearing tire
By telling how the sea-born goddess pined
For a mortal youth, and how she strove to bind
Him all in all unto her doting self.   460
Who would not be so prison'd? but, fond elf
He was content to let her amorous plea
Faint through his careless arms; content to see
An unseized heaven dying at his feet;
Content, O fool! to make a cold retreat,
When on the pleasant grass such love, lovelorn,
Lay sorrowing; when every tear was born
Of diverse passion; when her lips and eyes
Were closed in sullen moisture, and quick sighs
Came vex'd and pettish through her nostrils small.   470
Hush! no exclaim – yet, justly might'st thou call
Curses upon his head. – I was half glad,
But my poor mistress went distract and mad,
When the boar tusk'd him: so away she flew
To Jove's high throne, and by her plainings drew
Immortal tear-drops down the Thunderer's beard;
Whereon, it was decreed he should be rear'd
Each summer-time to life. Lo! this is he,
That same Adonis, safe in the privacy
Of this still region all his winter-sleep.   480
Ay, sleep; for when our love-sick queen did weep
Over his wanèd corse, the tremulous shower
Heal'd up the wound, and, with a balmy power,
Medicined death to a lengthen'd drowsiness:
The which she fills with visions, and doth dress

In all this quiet luxury; and hath set
Us young immortals, without any let,
To watch his slumber through. 'Tis well-nigh pass'd,
Even to a moment's filling up, and fast
She scuds with summer breezes, to pant through   490
The first long kiss, warm firstling, to renew
Embower'd sports in Cytherea's isle.
Look, how those wingèd listeners all this while
Stand anxious: see! behold!' – This clamant word
Broke through the careful silence; for they heard
A rustling noise of leaves, and out there flutter'd
Pigeons and doves: Adonis something mutter'd,
The while one hand, that erst upon his thigh
Lay dormant, moved convulsed and gradually
Up to his forehead. Then there was a hum   500
Of sudden voices, echoing, 'Come! come!
Arise! awake! Clear summer has forth walk'd
Unto the clover-sward, and she has talk'd
Full soothingly to every nested finch:
Rise, Cupids! or we'll give the blue-bell pinch
To your dimpled arms. Once more sweet life begin!'
At this, from every side they hurried in,
Rubbing their sleepy eyes with lazy wrists,
And doubling overhead their little fists
In backward yawns. But all were soon alive: 510
For as delicious wine doth, sparkling, dive
In nectar'd clouds and curls through water fair,
So from the arbour roof down swell'd an air
Odorous and enlivening; making all
To laugh, and play, and sing, and loudly call
For their sweet queen: when lo! the wreathèd green
Disparted, and far upward could be seen
Blue heaven, and a silver car, air-borne,
Whose silent wheels, fresh wet from clouds of morn,
Spun off a drizzling dew, – which falling chill   520
On soft Adonis' shoulders, made him still

Nestle and turn uneasily about.
Soon were the white doves plain, with necks stretched
        out,
And silken traces lighten'd in descent;
And soon, returning from love's banishment,
Queen Venus leaning downward open-arm'd:
Her shadow fell upon his breast, and charm'd
A tumult to his heart, and a new life
Into his eyes. Ah, miserable strife,
But for her comforting! unhappy sight,   530
But meeting her blue orbs! Who, who can write
Of these first minutes? The unchariest muse
To embracements warm as theirs makes coy excuse.

   O it has ruffled every spirit there,
Saving Love's self, who stands superb to share
The general gladness: awfully he stands;
A sovereign quell is in his waving hands;
No sight can bear the lightning of his bow;
His quiver is mysterious, none can know
What themselves think of it; from forth his eyes   540
There darts strange light of varied hues and dyes:
A scowl is sometimes on his brow, but who
Look full upon it feel anon the blue
Of his fair eyes run liquid through their souls.
Endymion feels it, and no more controls
The burning prayer within him; so, bent low,
He had begun a plaining of his woe.
But Venus, bending forward, said: 'My child,
Favour this gentle youth; his days are wild
With love – he – but alas! too well I see   550
Thou know'st the deepness of his misery.
Ah, smile not so, my son: I tell thee true,
That when through heavy hours I used to rue
The endless sleep of this new-born Adon',
This stranger aye I pitied. For upon

A dreary morning once I fled away
Into the breezy clouds, to weep and pray
For this my love: for vexing Mars had teased
Me even to tears: thence, when a little eased,
Down-looking, vacant, through a hazy wood,   560
I saw this youth as he despairing stood:
Those same dark curls blown vagrant in the wind:
Those same full fringèd lids a constant blind
Over his sullen eyes: I saw him throw
Himself on wither'd leaves, even as though
Death had come sudden; for no jot he moved,
Yet mutter'd wildly. I could hear he loved
Some fair immortal, and that his embrace
Had zoned her through the night. There is no trace
Of this in heaven: I have mark'd each cheek,   570
And find it is the vainest thing to seek;
And that of all things 'tis kept secretest.
Endymion! one day thou wilt be blest:
So still obey the guiding hand that fends
Thee safely through these wonders for sweet ends.
'Tis a concealment needful in extreme;
And if I guess'd not so, the sunny beam
Thou shouldst mount up to with me. Now adieu!
Here must we leave thee.' – At these words up flew
The impatient doves, up rose the floating car,   580
Up went the hum celestial. High afar
The Latmian saw them minish into nought;
And, when all were clear vanish'd, still he caught
A vivid lightning from that dreadful bow.
When all was darken'd, with Ætnean throe
The earth closed – gave a solitary moan –
And left him once again in twilight lone.

    He did not rave, he did not stare aghast,
For all those visions were o'ergone, and past,
And he in loneliness: he felt assured   590

Of happy times, when all he had endured
Would seem a feather to the mighty prize.
So, with unusual gladness, on he hies
Through caves, and palaces of mottled ore,
Gold dome, and crystal wall, and turquois floor,
Black polish'd porticoes of awful shade,
And, at the last, a diamond balustrade,
Leading afar past wild magnificence,
Spiral through ruggedest loop-holes, and thence
Stretching across a void, then guiding o'er   600
Enormous chasms, where, all foam and roar,
Streams subterranean tease their granite beds;
Then heighten'd just above the silvery heads
Of a thousand fountains, so that he could dash
The waters with his spear; but at the splash,
Done heedlessly, those spouting columns rose
Sudden a poplar's height, and 'gan to enclose
His diamond path with fretwork, streaming round
Alive, and dazzling cool, and with a sound,
Haply, like dolphin tumults, when sweet shells   610
Welcome the float of Thetis. Long he dwells
On this delight; for, every minute's space,
The streams with changèd magic interlace:
Sometimes like delicatest lattices,
Cover'd with crystal vines; then weeping trees,
Moving about as in a gentle wind,
Which, in a wink, to watery gauze refined,
Pour'd into shapes of curtain'd canopies,
Spangled, and rich with liquid broideries
Of flowers, peacocks, swans, and naiads fair.   620
Swifter than lightning went these wonders rare;
And then the water, into stubborn streams
Collecting, mimick'd the wrought oaken beams,
Pillars, and frieze, and high fantastic roof,
Of those dusk places in times far aloof
Cathedrals call'd. He bade a loth farewell

To these founts Protean, passing gulph, and dell,
And torrent, and ten thousand jutting shapes,
Half seen through deepest gloom, and griesly gapes,
Blackening on every side, and overhead   630
A vaulted dome like heaven's, far bespread
With starlight gems: ay, all so huge and strange,
The solitary felt a hurried change
Working within him into something dreary, –
Vex'd like a morning eagle, lost, and weary,
And purblind amid foggy midnight wolds,
But he revives at once: for who beholds
New sudden things, nor casts his mental slough?
Forth from a rugged arch, in the dusk below,
Came mother Cybele! alone – alone –   640
In sombre chariot; dark foldings thrown
About her majesty, and front death-pale,
With turrets crown'd. Four manèd lions hale
The sluggish wheels; solemn their toothèd maws,
Their surly eyes brow-hidden, heavy paws
Uplifted drowsily, and nervy tails
Cowering their tawny brushes. Silent sails
This shadowy queen athwart, and faints away
In another gloomy arch.

                          Wherefore delay,
Young traveller, in such a mournful place?   650
Art thou wayworn, or canst not further trace
The diamond path? And does it indeed end
Abrupt in middle air? Yet earthward bend
Thy forehead, and to Jupiter cloud-borne
Call ardently! He was indeed wayworn;
Abrupt, in middle air, his way was lost;
To cloud-borne Jove he bowed, and there crost
Towards him a large eagle, 'twixt whose wings,
Without one impious word, himself he flings,
Committed to the darkness and the gloom: 660

Down, down, uncertain to what pleasant doom,
Swift as a fathoming plummet down he fell
Through unknown things; till exhaled asphodel,
And rose, with spicy fannings interbreathed,
Came swelling forth where little caves were wreathed
So thick with leaves and mosses, that they seem'd
Large honeycombs of green, and freshly teem'd
With airs delicious. In the greenest nook
The eagle landed him, and farewell took.

It was a jasmine bower, all bestrown   670
With golden moss. His every sense had grown
Ethereal for pleasure; 'bove his head
Flew a delight half graspable; his tread
Was Hesperean; to his capable ears
Silence was music from the holy spheres;
A dewy luxury was in his eyes;
The little flowers felt his pleasant sighs
And stirr'd them faintly. Verdant cave and cell
He wander'd through, oft wondering at such swell
Of sudden exaltation: but, 'Alas!'   680
Said he, 'will all this gush of feeling pass
Away in solitude? And must they wane,
Like melodies upon a sandy plain,
Without an echo? Then shall I be left
So sad, so melancholy, so bereft!
Yet still I feel immortal! O my love,
My breath of life, where art thou? High above,
Dancing before the morning gates of heaven?
Or keeping watch among those starry seven,
Old Atlas' children? Art a maid of the waters   690
One of shell-winding Triton's bright-hair'd daughters?
Or art, impossible! a nymph of Dian's,
Weaving a coronal of tender scions
For very idleness? Where'er thou art,
Methinks it now is at my will to start

Into thine arms; to scare Aurora's train,
And snatch thee from the morning; o'er the main
To scud like a wild bird, and take thee off
From thy sea-foamy cradle; or to doff
Thy shepherd vest, and woo thee 'mid fresh leaves.   700
No, no, too eagerly my soul deceives
Its powerless self: I know this cannot be.
O let me then by some sweet dreaming flee
To her entrancements: hither sleep awhile!
Hither, most gentle sleep! and soothing foil
For some few hours the coming solitude.'

　　Thus spake he, and that moment felt endued
With power to dream deliciously; so wound
Through a dim passage, searching till he found
The smoothest mossy bed and deepest, where   710
He threw himself, and just into the air
Stretching his indolent arms, he took, O bliss!
A naked waist: 'Fair Cupid, whence is this?'
A well-known voice sigh'd, 'Sweetest, here am I!'
At which soft ravishment, with doting cry
They trembled to each other. – Helicon!
O fountain'd hill! Old Homer's Helicon!
That thou wouldst spout a little streamlet o'er
These sorry pages; then the verse would soar
And sing above this gentle pair, like lark   720
Over his nested young: but all is dark
Around thine aged top, and thy clear fount
Exhales in mists to heaven. Ay, the count
Of mighty Poets is made up; the scroll
Is folded by the Muses; the bright roll
Is in Apollo's hand: our dazèd eyes
Have seen a new tinge in the western skies:
The world has done its duty. Yet, oh yet,
Although the sun of poesy is set,
These lovers did embrace, and we must weep   730

That there is no old power left to steep
A quill immortal in their joyous tears.
Long time in silence did their anxious fears
Question that thus it was; long time they lay
Fondling and kissing every doubt away;
Long time ere soft caressing sobs began
To mellow into words, and then there ran
Two bubbling springs of talk from their sweet lips.
'O known Unknown! from whom my being sips
Such darling essence, wherefore may I not   740
Be ever in these arms? in this sweet spot
Pillow my chin for ever? ever press
These toying hands and kiss their smooth excess?
Why not for ever and for ever feel
That breath about my eyes? Ah, thou wilt steal
Away from me again, indeed, indeed –
Thou wilt be gone away, and wilt not heed
My lonely madness. Speak, my kindest fair!
Is – is it to be so? No! Who will dare
To pluck thee from me? And, of thine own will   750
Full well I feel thou wouldst not leave me. Still
Let me entwine thee surer, surer – now
How can we part? Elysium! who art thou?
Who, that thou canst not be for ever here,
Or lift me with thee to some starry sphere?
Enchantress! tell me by this soft embrace,
By the most soft completion of thy face,
Those lips, O slippery blisses! twinkling eyes,
And by these tenderest, milky sovereignties –
These tenderest, and by the nectar-wine,   760
The passion' – 'O loved Ida the divine!
Endymion! dearest! Ah, unhappy me!
His soul will 'scape us – O felicity!
How he does love me! His poor temples beat
To the very tune of love – how sweet, sweet, sweet!
Revive, dear youth, or I shall faint and die;

Revive, or these soft hours will hurry by
In trancèd dullness; speak, and let that spell
Affright this lethargy! I cannot quell
Its heavy pressure, and will press at least   770
My lips to thine, that they may richly feast
Until we taste the life of love again.
What! dost thou move? dost kiss? O bliss! O pain!
I love thee, youth, more than I can conceive;
And so long absence from thee doth bereave
My soul of any rest: yet must I hence:
Yet, can I not to starry eminence
Uplift thee; nor for very shame can own
Myself to thee. Ah, dearest! do not groan,
Or thou wilt force me from this secrecy,   780
And I must blush in heaven. O that I
Had done it already! that the dreadful smiles
At my lost brightness, my impassion'd wiles,
Had waned from Olympus' solemn height,
And from all serious Gods; that our delight
Was quite forgotten, save of us alone!
And wherefore so ashamed? 'Tis but to atone
For endless pleasure, by some coward blushes:
Yet must I be a coward! Horror rushes
Too palpable before me – the sad look   790
Of Jove – Minerva's start – no bosom shook
With awe of purity – no Cupid pinion
In reverence vail'd – my crystalline dominion
Half lost, and all old hymns made nullity!
But what is this to love? O I could fly
With thee into the ken of heavenly powers,
So thou wouldst thus, for many sequent hours,
Press me so sweetly. Now I swear at once
That I am wise, that Pallas is a dunce –
Perhaps her love like mine is but unknown –   800
O I do think that I have been alone
In chastity! yes, Pallas has been sighing,

While every eve saw me my hair uptying
With fingers cool as aspen leaves. Sweet love,
I was as vague as solitary dove,
Nor knew that nests were built. Now a soft kiss –
Ay, by that kiss, I vow an endless bliss,
An immortality of passion's thine:
Ere long I will exalt thee to the shine
Of heaven ambrosial; and we will shade   810
Ourselves whole summers by a river glade;
And I will tell thee stories of the sky,
And breathe thee whispers of its minstrelsy,
My happy love will overwing all bounds!
O let me melt into thee! let the sounds
Of our close voices marry at their birth;
Let us entwine hoveringly! O dearth
Of human words! roughness of mortal speech!
Lispings empyrean will I sometimes teach
Thine honey'd tongue – lute-breathings which I gasp   820
To have thee understand, now while I clasp
Thee thus, and weep for fondness – I am pain'd,
Endymion: woe! woe! is grief contain'd
In the very deeps of pleasure, my sole life?' –
Hereat, with many sobs, her gentle strife
Melted into a languor. He return'd
Entrancèd vows and tears.

                   Ye who have yearn'd
With too much passion, will here stay and pity,
For the mere sake of truth; as 'tis a ditty
Not of these days, but long ago 'twas told   830
By a cavern wind unto a forest old;
And then the forest told it in a dream
To a sleeping lake, whose cool and level gleam
A poet caught as he was journeying
To Phœbus' shrine; and in it he did fling
His weary limbs, bathing an hour's space,

And after, straight in that inspired place
He sang the story up into the air,
Giving it universal freedom. There
Has it been ever sounding for those ears   840
Whose tips are glowing hot. The legend cheers
Yon sentinel stars; and he who listens to it
Must surely be self-doom'd or he will rue it:
For quenchless burnings come upon the heart,
Made fiercer by a fear lest any part
Should be engulphed in the eddying wind.
As much as here is penn'd doth always find
A resting-place, thus much comes clear and plain;
Anon the strange voice is upon the wane –
And 'tis but echoed from departing sound,   850
That the fair visitant at last unwound
Her gentle limbs, and left the youth asleep. –
Thus the tradition of the gusty deep.

Now turn we to our former chroniclers. –
Endymion awoke, that grief of hers
Sweet paining on his ear: he sickly guess'd
How lone he was once more, and sadly press'd
His empty arms together, hung his head,
And most forlorn upon that widow'd bed
Sat silently. Love's madness he had known: 860
Often with more than tortured lion's groan
Moanings had burst from him; but now that rage
Had pass'd away: no longer did he wage
A rough-voiced war against the dooming stars.
No, he had felt too much for such harsh jars:
The lyre of his soul Æolian tuned
Forgot all violence, and but communed
With melancholy thought: O he had swoon'd
Drunken from pleasure's nipple! and his love
Henceforth was dove-like. – Loth was he to move   870
From the imprinted couch, and when he did,

'Twas with slow, languid paces, and face hid
In muffling hands. So temper'd, out he stray'd,
Half seeing visions that might have dismay'd
Alecto's serpents; ravishments more keen
Than Hermes' pipe, when anxious he did lean
Over eclipsing eyes: and at the last
It was a sounding grotto, vaulted, vast,
O'erstudded with a thousand, thousand pearls,
And crimson-mouthèd shells with stubborn curls   880
Of every shape and size, even to the bulk
In which whales harbour close, to brood and sulk
Against an endless storm. Moreover too,
Fish-semblances of green and azure hue,
Ready to snort their streams. In this cool wonder
Endymion sat down, and 'gan to ponder
On all his life: his youth, up to the day
When 'mid acclaim, and feasts, and garlands gay,
He stept upon his shepherd throne: the look
Of his white palace in wild forest nook,   890
And all the revels he had lorded there:
Each tender maiden whom he once thought fair,
With every friend and fellow-woodlander –
Pass'd like a dream before him. Then the spur
Of the old bards to mighty deeds: his plans
To nurse the golden age 'mong shepherd clans:
That wondrous night: the great Pan-festival:
His sister's sorrow; and his wanderings all,
Until into the earth's deep maw he rush'd:
Then all its buried magic, till it flush'd   900
High with excessive love. 'And now,' thought he,
'How long must I remain in jeopardy
Of blank amazements that amaze no more?
Now I have tasted her sweet soul to the core,
All other depths are shallow: essences,
Once spiritual, are like muddy lees,
Meant but to fertilize my earthly root,

And make my branches lift a golden fruit
Into the bloom of heaven: other light,
Though it be quick and sharp enough to blight   910
The Olympian eagle's vision, is dark,
Dark as the parentage of chaos. Hark!
My silent thoughts are echoing from these shells;
Or they are but the ghosts, the dying swells
Of noises far away? – list!' – Hereupon
He kept an anxious ear. The humming tone
Came louder, and behold, there as he lay,
On either side outgush'd, with misty spray,
A copious spring; and both together dash'd
Swift, mad, fantastic round the rocks, and lash'd   920
Among the conchs and shells of the lofty grot,
Leaving a trickling dew. At last they shot
Down from the ceiling's height, pouring a noise
As of some breathless racers whose hopes poise
Upon the last few steps, and with spent force
Along the ground they took a winding course.
Endymion follow'd – for it seem'd that one
Ever pursued, the other strove to shun –
Follow'd their languid mazes, till well-nigh
He had left thinking of the mystery, –   930
And was now rapt in tender hoverings
Over the vanish'd bliss. Ah! what is it sings
His dream away? What melodies are these?
They sound as through the whispering of trees,
Not native in such barren vaults. Give ear!

      'O Arethusa, peerless nymph! why fear
Such tenderness as mine? Great Dian, why,
Why didst thou hear her prayer? O that I
Were rippling round her dainty fairness now,
Circling about her waist, and striving how   940
To entice her to a dive! then stealing in
Between her luscious lips and eyelids thin.

O that her shining hair was in the sun,
And I distilling from it thence to run
In amorous rillets down her shrinking form!
To linger on her lily shoulders, warm
Between her kissing breasts, and every charm
Touch raptured! – See how painfully I flow:
Fair maid, be pitiful to my great woe.
Stay, stay thy weary course, and let me lead,   950
A happy wooer, to the flowery mead
Where all that beauty snared me.' – 'Cruel god,
Desist! or my offended mistress' nod
Will stagnate all thy fountains: – tease me not
With syren words – Ah, have I really got
Such power to madden thee? And is it true –
Away, away, or I shall dearly rue
My very thoughts: in mercy then away,
Kindest Alpheus, for should I obey
My own dear will, 'twould be a deadly bane.   960
O, Oread-Queen! would that thou hadst a pain
Like this of mine, then would I fearless turn
And be a criminal. Alas, I burn,
I shudder – gentle river, get thee hence.
Alpheus! thou enchanter! every sense
Of mine was once made perfect in these woods.
Fresh breezes, bowery lawns, and innocent floods,
Ripe fruits, and lonely couch, contentment gave;
But ever since I heedlessly did lave
In thy deceitful stream, a panting glow   970
Grew strong within me; wherefore serve me so,
And call it love? Alas! 'twas cruelty.
Not once more did I close my happy eye
Amid the thrushes' song. Away! Avaunt!
O 'twas a cruel thing.' – 'Now thou dost taunt
So softly, Arethusa, that I think
If thou wast playing on my shady brink,
Thou wouldst bathe once again. Innocent maid!

Stifle thine heart no more; nor be afraid
Of angry powers: there are deities   980
Will shade us with their wings. Those fitful sighs
'Tis almost death to hear: O let me pour
A dewy balm upon them! – fear no more,
Sweet Arethusa! Dian's self must feel
Sometime these very pangs. Dear maiden, steal
Blushing into my soul, and let us fly
These dreary caverns for the open sky.
I will delight thee all my winding course,
From the green sea up to my hidden source
About Arcadian forests; and will show   990
The channels where my coolest waters flow
Through mossy rocks; where, 'mid exuberant green,
I roam in pleasant darkness, more unseen
Than Saturn in his exile; where I brim
Round flowery islands, and take thence a skim
Of mealy sweets, which myriads of bees
Buzz from their honey'd wings: and thou shouldst please
Thyself to choose the richest, where we might
Be incense-pillow'd every summer night.
Doff all sad fears, thou white deliciousness,   1000
And let us be thus comforted; unless
Thou couldst rejoice to see my hopeless stream
Hurry distracted from Sol's temperate beam,
And pour to death along some hungry sands.' –
'What can I do, Alpheus? Dian stands
Severe before me: persecuting fate!
Unhappy Arethusa! thou wast late
A huntress free in –' At this, sudden fell
Those two sad streams adown a fearful dell.
The Latmian listen'd, but he heard no more,   1010
Save echo, faint repeating o'er and o'er
The name of Arethusa. On the verge
Of that dark gulph he wept, and said: 'I urge
Thee, gentle Goddess of my pilgrimage,

By our eternal hopes, to soothe, to assuage,
If thou art powerful, these lovers' pains;
And make them happy in some happy plains.'

    He turn'd – there was a whelming sound – he stept –
There was a cooler light; and so he kept
Towards it by a sandy path, and lo!   1020
More suddenly than doth a moment go,
The visions of the earth were gone and fled –
He saw the giant sea above his head.

BOOK III

THERE are who lord it o'er their fellow-men
With most prevailing tinsel: who unpen
Their baaing vanities, to browse away
The comfortable green and juicy hay
From human pastures; or, O torturing fact!
Who, through an idiot blink, will see unpack'd
Fire-branded foxes to sear up and singe
Our gold and ripe-ear'd hopes. With not one tinge
Of sanctuary splendour, not a sight
Able to face an owl's, they still are dight   10
By the blear-eyed nations in empurpled vests,
And crowns, and turbans. With unladen breasts,
Save of blown self-applause, they proudly mount
To their spirit's perch, their being's high account,
Their tip-top nothings, their dull skies, their thrones –
Amid the fierce intoxicating tones
Of trumpets, shoutings, and belabour'd drums,
And sudden cannon. Ah! how all this hums,
In wakeful ears, like uproar past and gone –
Like thunder-clouds that spake to Babylon,   20
And set those old Chaldeans to their tasks. –
Are then regalities all gilded masks?
No, there are thronèd seats unscalable
But by a patient wing, a constant spell,
Or by ethereal things that, unconfined,
Can make a ladder of the eternal wind,
And poise about in cloudy thunder-tents
To watch the abysm-birth of elements.
Ay, 'bove the withering of old-lipp'd Fate
A thousand Powers keep religious state,   30

In water, fiery realm, and airy bourne;
And, silent, as a consecrated urn,
Hold sphery sessions for a season due.
Yet few of these far majesties, ah, few!
Have bared their operations to this globe –
Few, who with gorgeous pageantry enrobe
Our piece of heaven – whose benevolence
Shakes hand with our own Ceres; every sense
Filling with spiritual sweets to plenitude,
As bees gorge full their cells. And by the feud   40
'Twixt Nothing and Creation, I here swear,
Eterne Apollo! that thy Sister fair
Is of all these the gentlier-mightiest.
When thy gold breath is misting in the west,
She unobservèd steals unto her throne,
And there she sits most meek and most alone;
As if she had not pomp subservient;
As if thine eye, high Poet! was not bent
Towards her with the Muses in thine heart;
As if the minist'ring stars kept not apart,   50
Waiting for silver-footed messages.
O Moon! the oldest shades 'mong oldest trees
Feel palpitations when thou lookest in.
O Moon! old boughs lisp forth a holier din
The while they feel thine airy fellowship.
Thou dost bless everywhere, with silver lip
Kissing dead things to life. The sleeping kine,
Couch'd in thy brightness, dream of fields divine:
Innumerable mountains rise, and rise,
Ambitious for the hallowing of thine eyes,   60
And yet thy benediction passeth not
One obscure hiding-place, one little spot
Where pleasure may be sent: the nested wren
Has thy fair face within its tranquil ken,
And from beneath a sheltering ivy leaf
Takes glimpses of thee; thou art a relief

To the poor patient oyster, where it sleeps,
Within its pearly house; – The mighty deeps,
The monstrous sea is thine – the myriad sea!
O Moon! far spooming Ocean bows to thee,   70
And Tellus feels his forehead's cumbrous load.

　　Cynthia! where art thou now? What far abode
Of green or silvery bower doth enshrine
Such utmost beauty? Alas, thou dost pine
For one as sorrowful: thy cheek is pale
For one whose cheek is pale: thou dost bewail
His tears who weep for thee. Where dost thou sigh?
Ah! surely that light peeps from Vesper's eye,
Or, what a thing is love! 'Tis She, but lo!
How changed, how full of ache, how gone in woe!   80
She dies at the thinnest cloud; her loveliness
Is wan on Neptune's blue: yet there's a stress
Of love-spangles, just off yon cape of trees,
Dancing upon the waves, as if to please
The curly foam with amorous influence.
O, not so idle! for down-glancing thence,
She fathoms eddies, and runs wild about
O'erwhelming water-courses; scaring out
The thorny sharks from hiding-holes, and fright'ning
Their savage eyes with unaccustom'd lightning.   90
Where will the splendour be content to reach?
O love! how potent hast thou been to teach
Strange journeyings! Wherever beauty dwells,
In gulph or aerie, mountains or deep dells,
In light, in gloom, in star or blazing sun,
Thou pointest out the way, and straight 'tis won.
Amid his toil thou gav'st Leander breath;
Thou leddest Orpheus through the gleams of death;
Thou madest Pluto bear thin element:
And now, O wingèd Chieftain! thou hast sent   100

A moon-beam to the deep, deep water-world,
To find Endymion.

       On gold sand impearl'd
With lily shells, and pebbles milky white,
Poor Cynthia greeted him, and soothed her light
Against his pallid face: he felt the charm
To breathlessness, and suddenly a warm
Of his heart's blood: 'twas very sweet; he stay'd
His wandering steps, and half-entrancèd laid
His head upon a tuft of straggling weeds,
To taste the gentle moon, and freshening beads,   110
Lash'd from the crystal roof by fishes' tails.
And so he kept, until the rosy veils
Mantling the east, by Aurora's peering hand
Were lifted from the water's breast, and fann'd
Into sweet air; and sober'd morning came
Meekly through billows: – when like taper-flame
Left sudden by a dallying breath of air,
He rose in silence, and once more 'gan fare
Along his fated way.

       Far had he roam'd,
With nothing save the hollow vast, that foam'd   120
Above, around, and at his feet; save things
More dead than Morpheus' imaginings:
Old rusted anchors, helmets, breastplates large
Of gone sea-warriors; brazen beaks and targe;
Rudders that for a hundred years had lost
The sway of human hand; gold vase emboss'd
With long-forgotten story, and wherein
No reveller had ever dipp'd a chin
But those of Saturn's vintage; mouldering scrolls,
Writ in the tongue of heaven, by those souls   130
Who first were on the earth; and sculptures rude

In ponderous stone, developing the mood
Of ancient Nox; – then skeletons of man,
Of beast, behemoth, and leviathan,
And elephant, and eagle, and huge jaw
Of nameless monster. A cold leaden awe
These secrets struck into him; and unless
Dian had chased away that heaviness,
He might have died: but now, with cheerèd feel,
He onward kept; wooing these thoughts to steal   140
About the labyrinth in his soul of love.

   'What is there in thee, Moon! that thou shouldst move
My heart so potently? When yet a child
I oft have dried my tears when thou hast smiled.
Thou seem'dst my sister: hand in hand we went
From eve to morn across the firmament.
No apples would I gather from the tree,
Till thou hadst cool'd their cheeks deliciously:
No tumbling water ever spake romance,
But when my eyes with thine thereon could dance: 150
No woods were green enough, no bower divine,
Until thou liftedst up thine eyelids fine:
In sowing-time ne'er would I dibble take,
Or drop a seed, till thou wast wide awake;
And, in the summer-tide of blossoming,
No one but thee hath heard me blithely sing
And mesh my dewy flowers all the night.
No melody was like a passing spright
If it went not to solemnize thy reign.
Yes, in my boyhood, every joy and pain   160
By thee were fashion'd to the self-same end;
And as I grew in years, still didst thou blend
With all my ardours: thou wast the deep glen –
Thou wast the mountain-top – the sage's pen –
The poet's harp – the voice of friends – the sun;
Thou wast the river – thou wast glory won;

Thou wast my clarion's blast – thou wast my steed –
My goblet full of wine – my topmost deed: –
Thou wast the charm of women, lovely Moon!
O what a wild and harmonizèd tune   170
My spirit struck from all the beautiful!
On some bright essence could I lean, and lull
Myself to immortality: I prest
Nature's soft pillow in a wakeful rest.
But, gentle Orb! there came a nearer bliss –
My strange love came – Felicity's abyss!
She came, and thou didst fade, and fade away –
Yet not entirely; no, thy starry sway
Has been an under-passion to this hour.
Now I begin to feel thine orby power   180
Is coming fresh upon me: O be kind!
Keep back thine influence, and do not blind
My sovereign vision. – Dearest love, forgive
That I can think away from thee and live! –
Pardon me, airy planet, that I prize
One thought beyond thine argent luxuries!
How far beyond!' At this a surprised start
Frosted the springing verdure of his heart;
For as he lifted up his eyes to swear
How his own goddess was past all things fair,   190
He saw far in the concave green of the sea
An old man sitting calm and peacefully.
Upon a weeded rock this old man sat,
And his white hair was awful, and a mat
Of weeds were cold beneath his cold thin feet;
And, ample as the largest winding-sheet,
A cloak of blue wrapp'd up his aged bones,
O'erwrought with symbols by the deepest groans
Of ambitious magic: every ocean-form
Was woven in with black distinctness; storm,   200
And calm, and whispering, and hideous roar,
Quicksand, and whirlpool, and deserted shore,

Were emblem'd in the woof; with every shape
That skims, or dives, or sleeps, 'twixt cape and cape.
The gulphing whale was like a dot in the spell,
Yet look upon it, and 'twould size and swell
To its huge self; and the minutest fish
Would pass the very hardest gazer's wish,
And show his little eye's anatomy.
Then there was pictured the regality   210
Of Neptune; and the sea-nymphs round his state,
In beauteous vassalage, look up and wait.
Beside this old man lay a pearly wand,
And in his lap a book, the which he conn'd
So stedfastly, that the new denizen
Had time to keep him in amazèd ken,
To mark these shadowings, and stand in awe.

   The old man raised his hoary head and saw
The wilder'd stranger – seeming not to see,
His features were so lifeless. Suddenly   220
He woke as from a trance; his snow-white brows
Went arching up, and like two magic ploughs
Furrow'd deep wrinkles in his forehead large,
Which kept as fixedly as rocky marge,
Till round his wither'd lips had gone a smile.
Then up he rose, like one whose tedious toil
Had watch'd for years in forlorn hermitage,
Who had not from mid-life to utmost age
Eased in one accent his o'erburden'd soul,
Even to the trees. He rose: he grasp'd his stole,   230
With convulsed clenches waving it abroad,
And in a voice of solemn joy, that awed
Echo into oblivion, he said: –

   'Thou art the man! Now shall I lay my head
In peace upon my watery pillow: now
Sleep will come smoothly to my weary brow.

O Jove! I shall be young again, be young!
O shell-borne Neptune, I am pierced and stung
With new-born life! What shall I do? Where go,
When I have cast this serpent-skin of woe? –   240
I'll swim to the syrens, and one moment listen
Their melodies, and see their long hair glisten;
Anon upon that giant's arm I'll be,
That writhes about the roots of Sicily;
To northern seas I'll in a twinkling sail,
And mount upon the snortings of a whale
To some black cloud; thence down I'll madly sweep
On forked lightning to the deepest deep,
Where through some sucking pool I will be hurl'd
With rapture to the other side of the world!   250
O, I am full of gladness! Sisters three,
I bow full-hearted to your old decree!
Yes, every god be thank'd, and power benign,
For I no more shall wither, droop, and pine.
Thou art the man!' Endymion started back
Dismay'd; and like a wretch from whom the rack
Tortures hot breath, and speech of agony,
Mutter'd: 'What lonely death am I to die
In this cold region? Will he let me freeze,
And float my brittle limbs o'er polar seas?   260
Or will he touch me with his searing hand,
And leave a black memorial on the sand?
Or tear me piecemeal with a bony saw,
And keep me as a chosen food to draw
His magian fish through hated fire and flame?
O misery of hell! resistless, tame,
Am I to be burnt up? No, I will shout,
Until the gods through heaven's blue look out! –
O Tartarus! but some few days agone
Her soft arms were entwining me, and on   270
Her voice I hung like fruit among green leaves:
Her lips were all my own, and – ah, ripe sheaves

Of happiness! ye on the stubble droop,
But never may be garner'd. I must stoop
My head, and kiss death's foot. Love! love, farewell!
Is there no hope from thee? This horrid spell
Would melt at thy sweet breath. – By Dian's hind
Feeding from her white fingers, on the wind
I see thy streaming hair! and now, by Pan,
I care not for this old mysterious man!'   280

He spake, and walking to that aged form,
Look'd high defiance. Lo! his heart 'gan warm
With pity, for the grey-hair'd creature wept.
Had he then wrong'd a heart where sorrow kept?
Had he, though blindly contumelious, brought
Rheum to kind eyes, a sting to human thought,
Convulsion to a mouth of many years?
He had in truth; and he was ripe for tears.
The penitent shower fell, as down he knelt
Before that care-worn sage, who trembling felt   290
About his large dark locks, and faltering spake:

'Arise, good youth, for sacred Phœbus' sake!
I know thine inmost bosom, and I feel
A very brother's yearning for thee steal
Into mine own: for why? thou openest
The prison-gates that have so long oppress'd
My weary watching. Though thou know'st it not,
Thou art commission'd to this fated spot
For great enfranchisement. O weep no more!
I am a friend to love, to loves of yore: 300
Ay, hadst thou never loved an unknown power,
I had been grieving at this joyous hour.
But even now, most miserable old,
I saw thee, and my blood no longer cold
Gave mighty pulses: in this tottering case

Grew a new heart, which at this moment plays
As dancingly as thine. Be not afraid,
For thou shalt hear this secret all display'd,
Now as we speed towards our joyous task.'

    So saying, this young soul in age's mask   310
Went forward with the Carian side by side:
Resuming quickly thus; while ocean's tide
Hung swollen at their backs, and jewell'd sands
Took silently their foot-prints.

                    'My soul stands
Now past the midway from mortality,
And so I can prepare without a sigh
To tell thee briefly all my joy and pain.
I was a fisher once, upon this main,
And my boat danced in every creek and bay;
Rough billows were my home by night and day, —   320
The sea-gulls not more constant; for I had
No housing from the storm and tempests mad,
But hollow rocks, — and they were palaces
Of silent happiness, of slumberous ease:
Long years of misery have told me so.
Ay, thus it was one thousand years ago.
One thousand years! — Is it then possible
To look so plainly through them? to dispel
A thousand years with backward glance sublime?
To breathe away as 'twere all scummy slime   330
From off a crystal pool, to see its deep,
And one's own image from the bottom peep?
Yes: now I am no longer wretched thrall,
My long captivity and moanings all
Are but a slime, a thin-pervading scum,
The which I breathe away, and thronging come
Like things of yesterday my youthful pleasures.

'I touch'd no lute, I sang not, trod no measures:
I was a lonely youth on desert shores.
My sports were lonely, 'mid continuous roars,   340
And craggy isles, and sea-mew's plaintive cry
Plaining discrepant between sea and sky.
Dolphins were still my playmates; shapes unseen
Would let me feel their scales of gold and green
Nor be my desolation; and, full oft,
When a dread waterspout had rear'd aloft
Its hungry hugeness, seeming ready ripe
To burst with hoarsest thunderings, and wipe
My life away like a vast sponge of fate,
Some friendly monster, pitying my sad state,   350
Has dived to its foundations, gulph'd it down,
And left me tossing safely. But the crown
Of all my life was utmost quietude:
More did I love to lie in cavern rude,
Keeping in wait whole days for Neptune's voice,
And if it came at last, hark, and rejoice!
There blush'd no summer eve but I would steer
My skiff along green shelving coasts, to hear
The shepherd's pipe come clear from aery steep,
Mingled with ceaseless bleatings of his sheep: 360
And never was a day of summer shine,
But I beheld its birth upon the brine:
For I would watch all night to see unfold
Heaven's gates, and Æthon snort his morning gold
Wide o'er the swelling streams: and constantly
At brim of day-tide, on some grassy lea,
My nets would be spread out, and I at rest.
The poor folk of the sea-country I blest
With daily boon of fish most delicate:
They knew not whence this bounty, and elate   370
Would strew sweet flowers on a sterile beach.

'Why was I not contented? Wherefore reach
At things which, but for thee, O Latmian!
Had been my dreary death! Fool! I began
To feel distemper'd longings: to desire
The utmost privilege that ocean's sire
Could grant in benediction: to be free
Of all his kingdom. Long in misery
I wasted, ere in one extremest fit
I plunged for life or death. To interknit   380
One's senses with so dense a breathing stuff
Might seem a work of pain; so not enough
Can I admire how crystal-smooth it felt,
And buoyant round my limbs. At first I dwelt
Whole days and days in sheer astonishment;
Forgetful utterly of self-intent;
Moving but with the mighty ebb and flow.
Then, like a new-fledged bird that first doth show
His spreaded feathers to the morrow chill,
I tried in fear the pinions of my will.   390
'Twas freedom! and at once I visited
The ceaseless wonders of this ocean-bed.
No need to tell thee of them, for I see
That thou hast been a witness – it must be –
For these I know thou canst not feel a drouth,
By the melancholy corners of that mouth.
So I will in my story straightway pass
To more immediate matter. Woe, alas!
That love should be my bane! Ah, Scylla, fair!
Why did poor Glaucus ever – ever dare   400
To sue thee to his heart? Kind stranger-youth!
I loved her to the very white of truth,
And she would not conceive it. Timid thing!
She fled me swift as sea-bird on the wing,
Round every isle, and point, and promontory,
From where large Hercules wound up his story

Far as Egyptian Nile. My passion grew
The more, the more I saw her dainty hue
Gleam delicately through the azure clear:
Until 'twas too fierce agony to bear;   410
And in that agony, across my grief
It flash'd, that Circe might find some relief –
Cruel enchantress! So above the water
I rear'd my head, and look'd for Phœbus' daughter.
Æææ's isle was wondering at the moon: –
It seem'd to whirl around me, and a swoon
Left me dead-drifting to that fatal power.

'When I awoke, 'twas in a twilight bower;
Just when the light of morn, with hum of bees,
Stole through its verdurous matting of fresh trees.   420
How sweet, and sweeter! for I heard a lyre,
And over it a sighing voice expire.
It ceased – I caught light footsteps; and anon
The fairest face that morn e'er looked upon
Push'd through a screen of roses. Starry Jove!
With tears, and smiles, and honey-words she wove
A net whose thraldom was more bliss than all
The range of flower'd Elysium. Thus did fall
The dew of her rich speech: "Ah! art awake?
O let me hear thee speak, for Cupid's sake!   430
I am so oppress'd with joy! Why, I have shed
An urn of tears, as though thou wert cold dead;
And now I find thee living, I will pour
From these devoted eyes their silver store,
Until exhausted of the latest drop,
So it will pleasure thee, and force thee stop
Here, that I too may live; but if beyond
Such cool and sorrowful offerings, thou art fond
Of soothing warmth, of dalliance supreme;
If thou art ripe to taste a long love-dream;   440
If smiles, if dimples, tongues for ardour mute,

Hang in thy vision like a tempting fruit,
O let me pluck it for thee!" Thus she link'd
Her charming syllables, till indistinct
Their music came to my o'er-sweeten'd soul;
And then she hover'd over me, and stole
So near, that if no nearer it had been
This furrow'd visage thou hadst never seen.

'Young man of Latmos! thus particular
Am I, that thou may'st plainly see how far   450
This fierce temptation went: and thou may'st not
Exclaim, How then? was Scylla quite forgot?

'Who could resist? Who in this universe?
She did so breathe ambrosia; so immerse
My fine existence in a golden clime.
She took me like a child of suckling time,
And cradled me in roses. Thus condemn'd,
The current of my former life was stemm'd,
And to this arbitrary queen of sense
I bow'd a trancèd vassal: nor would thence   460
Have moved, even though Amphion's harp had woo'd
Me back to Scylla o'er the billows rude.
For as Apollo each eve doth devise
A new apparelling for western skies;
So every eve, nay, every spendthrift hour
Shed balmy consciousness within that bower.
And I was free of haunts umbrageous;
Could wander in the mazy forest-house
Of squirrels, foxes shy, and antler'd deer,
And birds from coverts innermost and drear   470
Warbling for very joy mellifluous sorrow –
To me new-born delights!

                              'Now let me borrow
For moments few, a temperament as stern

As Pluto's sceptre, that my words not burn
These uttering lips, while I in calm speech tell
How specious heaven was changed to real hell.

'One morn she left me sleeping: half awake
I sought for her smooth arms and lips, to slake
My greedy thirst with nectarous camel-draughts;
But she was gone. Whereat the barbèd shafts   480
Of disappointment stuck in me so sore,
That out I ran and search'd the forest o'er.
Wandering about in pine and cedar gloom
Damp awe assail'd me, for there 'gan to boom
A sound of moan, an agony of sound,
Sepulchral from the distance all around.
Then came a conquering earth-thunder, and rumbled
That fierce complain to silence; while I stumbled
Down a precipitous path, as if impell'd.
I came to a dark valley. Groanings swell'd   490
Poisonous about my ears, and louder grew,
The nearer I approach'd a flame's gaunt blue,
That glared before me through a thorny brake.
This fire, like the eye of gordian snake,
Bewitch'd me towards; and I soon was near
A sight too fearful for the feel of fear:
In thicket hid I cursed the haggard scene –
The banquet of my arms, my arbour queen,
Seated upon an uptorn forest root;
And all around her shapes, wizard and brute,   500
Laughing, and wailing, grovelling, serpenting,
Showing tooth, tusk, and venom-bag, and sting.
O such deformities! Old Charon's self,
Should he give up awhile his penny pelf,
And take a dream 'mong rushes Stygian,
It could not be so phantasied. Fierce, wan,
And tyrannizing was the lady's look,

As over them a gnarlèd staff she shook.
Oft-times upon the sudden she laugh'd out,
And from a basket emptied to the rout   510
Clusters of grapes, the which they raven'd quick
And roar'd for more; with many a hungry lick
About their shaggy jaws. Avenging, slow,
Anon she took a branch of mistletoe,
And emptied on't a black dull-gurgling phial:
Groan'd one and all, as if some piercing trial
Was sharpening for their pitiable bones.
She lifted up the charm: appealing groans
From their poor breasts went suing to her ear
In vain; remorseless as an infant's bier   520
She whisk'd against their eyes the sooty oil,
Whereat was heard a noise of painful toil,
Increasing gradual to a tempest rage,
Shrieks, yells, and groans of torture-pilgrimage;
Until their grievèd bodies 'gan to bloat
And puff from the tail's end to stifled throat:
Then was appalling silence: then a sight
More wildering than all that hoarse affright;
For the whole herd, as by a whirlwind writhen,
Went through the dismal air like one huge Python   530
Antagonizing Boreas, – and so vanish'd.
Yet there was not a breath of wind: she banish'd
These phantoms with a nod. Lo! from the dark
Came waggish fauns, and nymphs, and satyrs stark,
With dancing and loud revelry, – and went
Swifter than centaurs after rapine bent. –
Sighing an elephant appear'd and bow'd
Before the fierce witch, speaking thus aloud
In human accent: "Potent goddess! chief
Of pains resistless! make my being brief,   540
Or let me from this heavy prison fly:
Or give me to the air, or let me die!

I sue not for my happy crown again;
I sue not for my phalanx on the plain;
I sue not for my lone, my widow'd wife;
I sue not for my ruddy drops of life,
My children fair, my lovely girls and boys!
I will forget them; I will pass these joys;
Ask nought so heavenward, so too – too high;
Only I pray, as fairest boon, to die,   550
Or be deliver'd from this cumbrous flesh,
From this gross, detestable, filthy mesh,
And merely given to the cold bleak air.
Have mercy, Goddess! Circe, feel my prayer!"

    'That curst magician's name fell icy numb
Upon my wild conjecturing: truth had come
Naked and sabre-like against my heart.
I saw a fury whetting a death-dart;
And my slain spirit, overwrought with fright,
Fainted away in that dark lair of night.   560
Think, my deliverer, how desolate
My waking must have been! disgust and hate
And terrors manifold divided me
A spoil amongst them. I prepared to flee
Into the dungeon core of that wild wood:
I fled three days – when lo! before me stood
Glaring the angry witch. O Dis, even now,
A clammy dew is beading on my brow,
At mere remembering her pale laugh, and curse.
"Ha! ha! Sir Dainty! there must be a nurse   570
Made of rose-leaves and thistle-down, express,
To cradle thee, my sweet, and lull thee: yes,
I am too flinty-hard for thy nice touch:
My tenderest squeeze is but a giant's clutch.
So, fairy-thing, it shall have lullabies
Unheard of yet; and it shall still its cries

Upon some breast more lily-feminine.
Oh, no – it shall not pine, and pine, and pine
More than one pretty, trifling thousand years;
And then 'twere pity, but fate's gentle shears   580
Cut short its immortality. Sea-flirt!
Young dove of the waters! truly I'll not hurt
One hair of thine: see how I weep and sigh,
That our heart-broken parting is so nigh.
And must we part? Ah, yes, it must be so.
Yet ere thou leavest me in utter woe,
Let me sob over thee my last adieus,
And speak a blessing: Mark me! thou hast thews
Immortal, for thou art of heavenly race:
But such a love is mine, that here I chase   590
Eternally away from thee all bloom
Of youth, and destine thee towards a tomb.
Hence shalt thou quickly to the watery vast;
And there, ere many days be overpast,
Disabled age shall seize thee; and even then
Thou shalt not go the way of aged men;
But live and wither, cripple and still breathe
Ten hundred years: which gone, I then bequeath
Thy fragile bones to unknown burial.
Adieu, sweet love, adieu!" – As shot stars fall,   600
She fled ere I could groan for mercy. Stung
And poison'd was my spirit: despair sung
A war-song of defiance 'gainst all hell.
A hand was at my shoulder to compel
My sullen steps; another 'fore my eyes
Moved on with pointed finger. In this guise
Enforcèd, at the last by ocean's foam
I found me; by my fresh, my native home.
Its tempering coolness, to my life akin,
Came salutary as I waded in;   610
And, with a blind voluptuous rage, I gave

Battle to the swollen billow-ridge, and drave
Large froth before me, while there yet remain'd
Hale strength, nor from my bones all marrow drain'd.

'Young lover, I must weep – such hellish spite
With dry cheek who can tell? Why thus my might
Proving upon this element, dismay'd,
Upon a dead thing's face my hand I laid;
I look'd – 'twas Scylla! Cursed, cursed Circe!
O vulture-witch, hast never heard of mercy!   620
Could not thy harshest vengeance be content,
But thou must nip this tender innocent
Because I loved her? – Cold, O cold indeed
Were her fair limbs, and like a common weed
The sea-swell took her hair. Dead as she was
I clung about her waist, nor ceased to pass
Fleet as an arrow through unfathom'd brine,
Until there shone a fabric crystalline,
Ribb'd and inlaid with coral, pebble, and pearl.
Headlong I darted; at one eager swirl   630
Gain'd its bright portal, enter'd, and behold!
'Twas vast, and desolate, and icy-cold;
And all around – But wherefore this to thee
Who in few minutes more thyself shalt see? –
I left poor Scylla in a niche and fled.
My fever'd parchings up, my scathing dread
Met palsy half way: soon these limbs became
Gaunt, wither'd, sapless, feeble, cramp'd, and lame.

'Now let me pass a cruel, cruel space,
Without one hope, without one faintest trace   640
Of mitigation, or redeeming bubble
Of colour'd phantasy; for I fear 'twould trouble
Thy brain to loss of reason: and next tell
How a restoring chance came down to quell
One half of the witch in me.

'On a day,
Sitting upon a rock above the spray,
I saw grow up from the horizon's brink
A gallant vessel: soon she seem'd to sink
Away from me again, as though her course
Had been resumed in spite of hindering force –   650
So vanish'd: and not long, before arose
Dark clouds, and muttering of winds morose.
Old Æolus would stifle his mad spleen,
But could not: therefore all the billows green
Toss'd up the silver spume against the clouds.
The tempest came: I saw that vessel's shrouds
In perilous bustle; while upon the deck
Stood trembling creatures. I beheld the wreck;
The final gulphing; the poor struggling souls:
I heard their cries amid loud thunder-rolls.   660
O they had all been saved but crazèd eld
Annull'd my vigorous cravings: and thus quell'd
And curb'd, think on 't, O Latmian! did I sit
Writhing with pity, and a cursing fit
Against that hell-born Circe. The crew had gone,
By one and one, to pale oblivion;
And I was gazing on the surges prone,
With many a scalding tear and many a groan,
When at my feet emerged an old man's hand,
Grasping this scroll, and this same slender wand.   670
I knelt with pain – reach'd out my hand – had grasp'd
These treasures – touch'd the knuckles – they unclasp'd –
I caught a finger; but the downward weight
O'erpower'd me – it sank. Then 'gan abate
The storm, and through chill aguish gloom outburst
The comfortable sun. I was athirst
To search the book, and in the warming air
Parted its dripping leaves with eager care.
Strange matters did it treat of, and drew on
My soul page after page, till well-nigh won   680

Into forgetfulness; when, stupefied,
I read these words, and read again, and tried
My eyes against the heavens, and read again.
O what a load of misery and pain
Each Atlas-line bore off! – a shine of hope
Came gold around me, cheering me to cope
Strenuous with hellish tyranny. Attend!
For thou hast brought their promise to an end.

    ' "In the wide sea there lives a forlorn wretch,
Doom'd with enfeebled carcase to outstretch   690
His loathed existence through ten centuries,
And then to die alone. Who can devise
A total opposition? No one. So
One million times ocean must ebb and flow,
And he oppressed. Yet he shall not die,
These things accomplish'd: – If he utterly
Scans all the depths of magic, and expounds
The meanings of all motions, shapes, and sounds;
If he explores all forms and substances
Straight homeward to their symbol-essences;   700
He shall not die. Moreover, and in chief,
He must pursue this task of joy and grief
Most piously; – all lovers tempest-tost,
And in the savage overwhelming lost,
He shall deposit side by side, until
Time's creeping shall the dreary space fulfil:
Which done, and all these labours ripened,
A youth, by heavenly power loved and led,
Shall stand before him; whom he shall direct
How to consummate all. The youth elect   710
Must do the thing, or both will be destroy'd." '

    'Then,' cried the young Endymion, overjoy'd,
'We are twin brothers in this destiny!
Say, I entreat thee, what achievement high

Is, in this restless world, for me reserved.
What! if from thee my wandering feet had swerved,
Had we both perish'd?' – 'Look!' the sage replied,
'Dost thou not mark a gleaming through the tide,
Of divers brilliances? 'tis the edifice
I told thee of, where lovely Scylla lies;   720
And where I have enshrinèd piously
All lovers, whom fell storms have doom'd to die
Throughout my bondage.' Thus discoursing, on
They went till unobscured the porches shone;
Which hurryingly they gain'd, and enter'd straight.
Sure never since king Neptune held his state
Was seen such wonder underneath the stars.
Turn to some level plain where haughty Mars
Has legion'd all his battle; and behold
How every soldier, with firm foot, doth hold   730
His even breast: see, many steelèd squares,
And rigid ranks of iron – whence who dares
One step? Imagine further, line by line,
These warrior thousands on the field supine: –
So in that crystal place, in silent rows,
Poor lovers lay at rest from joys and woes. –
The stranger from the mountains, breathless, traced
Such thousands of shut eyes in order placed;
Such ranges of white feet, and patient lips
All ruddy, – for here death no blossom nips.   740
He mark'd their brows and foreheads; saw their hair
Put sleekly on one side with nicest care;
And each one's gentle wrists, with reverence,
Put cross-wise to its heart.

                    'Let us commence,'
Whisper'd the guide, stuttering with joy, 'even now.'
He spake, and, trembling like an aspen-bough,
Began to tear his scroll in pieces small,
Uttering the while some mumblings funeral.

He tore it into pieces small as snow
That drifts unfeather'd when bleak northerns blow;   750
And having done it, took his dark blue cloak
And bound it round Endymion: then struck
His wand against the empty air times nine.
'What more there is to do, young man, is thine:
But first a little patience; first undo
This tangled thread, and wind it to a clue.
Ah, gentle! 'tis as weak as spider's skein;
And shouldst thou break it – What, is it done so clean?
A power overshadows thee! O, brave!
The spite of hell is tumbling to its grave.   760
Here is a shell; 'tis pearly blank to me,
Nor mark'd with any sign or charactery –
Canst thou read aught? O read for pity's sake!
Olympus! we are safe! Now, Carian, break
This wand against yon lyre on the pedestal.'

   'Twas done: and straight with sudden swell and fall
Sweet music breathed her soul away, and sigh'd
A lullaby to silence. – 'Youth! now strew
These mincèd leaves on me, and passing through
Those files of dead, scatter the same around,   770
And thou wilt see the issue.' – 'Mid the sound
Of flutes and viols, ravishing his heart,
Endymion from Glaucus stood apart,
And scatter'd in his face some fragments light.
How lightning-swift the change! a youthful wight
Smiling beneath a coral diadem,
Out-sparkling sudden like an upturn'd gem,
Appear'd, and, stepping to a beauteous corse,
Kneel'd down beside it, and with tenderest force
Press'd its cold hand, and wept – and Scylla sigh'd!   780
Endymion, with quick hand, the charm applied –
The nymph arose: he left them to their joy,

And onward went upon his high employ,
Showering those powerful fragments on the dead,
And, as he pass'd, each lifted up his head,
As doth a flower at Apollo's touch.
Death felt it to his inwards; 'twas too much:
Death fell a-weeping in his charnel-house.
The Latmian persevered along, and thus
All were reanimated. There arose   790
A noise of harmony, pulses and throes
Of gladness in the air – while many, who
Had died in mutual arms devout and true,
Sprang to each other madly; and the rest
Felt a high certainty of being blest.
They gazed upon Endymion. Enchantment
Grew drunken, and would have its head and bent.
Delicious symphonies, like airy flowers,
Budded, and swell'd, and, full-blown, shed full showers
Of light, soft, unseen leaves of sounds divine.   800
The two deliverers tasted a pure wine
Of happiness, from fairy press oozed out.
Speechless they eyed each other, and about
The fair assembly wander'd to and fro,
Distracted with the richest overflow
Of joy that ever pour'd from heaven.

                      – 'Away!'
Shouted the new-born god; 'Follow, and pay
Our piety to Neptunus supreme!'
Then Scylla, blushing sweetly from her dream,
They led on first, bent to her meek surprise,   810
Through portal columns of a giant size
Into the vaulted, boundless emerald.
Joyous all follow'd, as the leader call'd,
Down marble steps; pouring as easily
As hour-glass sand – and fast, as you might see

Swallows obeying the south summer's call,
Or swans upon a gentle waterfall.

Thus went that beautiful multitude, nor far,
Ere from among some rocks of glittering spar,
Just within ken, they saw descending thick   820
Another multitude. Whereat more quick
Moved either host. On a wide sand they met,
And of those numbers every eye was wet;
For each their old love found. A murmuring rose,
Like what was never heard in all the throes
Of wind and waters: 'tis past human wit
To tell; 'tis dizziness to think of it.

This mighty consummation made, the host
Moved on for many a league; and gain'd and lost
Huge sea-marks; vanward swelling in array,   830
And from the rear diminishing away,
Till a faint dawn surprised them. Glaucus cried,
'Behold! behold, the palace of his pride!
God Neptune's palaces!' With noise increased,
They shoulder'd on towards that brightening east,
At every onward step proud domes arose
In prospect; diamond gleams and golden glows
Of amber 'gainst their faces levelling.
Joyous, and many as the leaves in spring,
Still onward; still the splendour gradual swell'd.   840
Rich opal domes were seen, on high upheld
By jasper pillars, letting through their shafts
A blush of coral. Copious wonder-draughts
Each gazer drank; and deeper drank more near:
For what poor mortals fragment up, as mere
As marble was there lavish, to the vast
Of one fair palace, that far, far surpass'd,
Even for common bulk, those olden three,
Memphis, and Babylon, and Nineveh.

As large, as bright, as colour'd as the bow   850
Of Iris, when unfading it doth show
Beyond a silvery shower, was the arch
Through which this Paphian army took its march
Into the outer courts of Neptune's state:
Whence could be seen, direct, a golden gate,
To which the leaders sped; but not half raught
Ere it burst open swift as fairy thought,
And made those dazzled thousands veil their eyes
Like callow eagles at the first sunrise.
Soon with an eagle nativeness their gaze   860
Ripe from hue-golden swoons took all the blaze,
And then, behold! large Neptune on his throne
Of emerald deep: yet not exalt alone;
At his right hand stood wingèd Love, and on
His left sat smiling Beauty's paragon.

   Far as the mariner on highest mast
Can see all round upon the calmèd vast,
So wide was Neptune's hall: and as the blue
Doth vault the waters, so the waters drew
Their doming curtains, high, magnificent,   870
Awed from the throne aloof; – and when storm-rent
Disclosed the thunder-gloomings in Jove's air;
But soothed as now, flash'd sudden everywhere,
Noiseless, sub-marine cloudlets, glittering
Death to a human eye: for there did spring
From natural west, and east, and south, and north,
A light as of four sunsets, blazing forth
A gold-green zenith 'bove the Sea-God's head.
Of lucid depth the floor, and far outspread
As breezeless lake, on which the slim canoe   880
Of feather'd Indian darts about, as through
The delicatest air: air verily,
But for the portraiture of clouds and sky:
This palace floor breath-air, – but for the amaze

Of deep-seen wonders motionless, – and blaze
Of the dome pomp, reflected in extremes,
Globing a golden sphere.

                They stood in dreams
Till Triton blew his horn. The palace rang;
The Nereids danced; the Syrens faintly sang;
And the great Sea-King bow'd his dripping head.   890
Then Love took wing, and from his pinions shed
On all the multitude a nectarous dew.
The ooze-born Goddess beckoned and drew
Fair Scylla and her guides to conference;
And when they reach'd the throned eminence
She kist the sea-nymph's cheek, who sat her down
A toying with the doves. Then, 'Mighty crown
And sceptre of this kingdom!' Venus said,
'Thy vows were on a time to Nais paid:
Behold!' – Two copious tear-drops instant fell   900
From the God's large eyes; he smiled delectable,
And over Glaucus held his blessing hands. –
'Endymion! Ah! still wandering in the bands
Of love? Now this is cruel. Since the hour
I met thee in earth's bosom, all my power
Have I put forth to serve thee. What, not yet
Escaped from dull mortality's harsh net?
A little patience, youth! 'twill not be long,
Or I am skilless quite: an idle tongue,
A humid eye, and steps luxurious,   910
Where these are new and strange, are ominous.
Ay, I have seen these signs in one of heaven,
When others were all blind; and were I given
To utter secrets, haply I might say
Some pleasant words; but Love will have his day.
So wait awhile expectant. Pr'ythee soon,
Even in the passing of thine honey-moon,
Visit thou my Cythera: thou wilt find

Cupid well-natured, my Adonis kind;
And pray persuade with thee – Ah, I have done,   920
All blisses be upon thee, my sweet son!' –
Thus the fair Goddess: while Endymion
Knelt to receive those accents halcyon.

Meantime a glorious revelry began
Before the Water-Monarch. Nectar ran
In courteous fountains to all cups outreach'd;
And plunder'd vines, teeming exhaustless, pleach'd
New growth about each shell and pendent lyre;
The which, in disentangling for their fire,
Pull'd down fresh foliage and coverture   930
For dainty toy. Cupid, empire-sure,
Flutter'd and laugh'd, and oft-times through the throng
Made a delighted way. Then dance, and song,
And garlanding, grew wild; and pleasure reign'd.
In harmless tendril they each other chain'd,
And strove who should be smother'd deepest in
Fresh crush of leaves.

O 'tis a very sin
For one so weak to venture his poor verse
In such a place as this. O do not curse,
High Muses! let him hurry to the ending.   940

All suddenly were silent. A soft blending
Of dulcet instruments came charmingly;
And then a hymn.

'King of the stormy sea!
Brother of Jove, and co-inheritor
Of elements! Eternally before
Thee the waves awful bow. Fast, stubborn rock,
At thy fear'd trident shrinking, doth unlock
Its deep foundations, hissing into foam.

All mountain-rivers, lost in the wide home
Of thy capacious bosom, ever flow.   950
Thou frownest, and old Æolus thy foe
Skulks to his cavern, 'mid the gruff complaint
Of all his rebel tempests. Dark clouds faint
When, from thy diadem, a silver gleam
Slants over blue dominion. Thy bright team
Gulphs in the morning light, and scuds along
To bring thee nearer to that golden song
Apollo singeth, while his chariot
Waits at the doors of heaven. Thou art not
For scenes like this: an empire stern hast thou;   960
And it hath furrow'd that large front: yet now,
As newly come of heaven, dost thou sit
To blend and interknit
Subduèd majesty with this glad time.
O shell-borne King sublime!
We lay our hearts before thee evermore –
We sing, and we adore!

     'Breathe softly, flutes,
Be tender of your strings, ye soothing lutes;
Nor be the trumpet heard! O vain, O vain!   970
Not flowers budding in an April rain,
Nor breath of sleeping dove, nor river's flow, –
No, nor the Æolian twang of Love's own bow,
Can mingle music fit for the soft ear
Of goddess Cytherea!
Yet deign, white Queen of Beauty, thy fair eyes
On our souls' sacrifice.

     'Bright-wingèd Child!
Who has another care when thou hast smiled?
Unfortunates on earth, we see at last   980
All death-shadows, and glooms that overcast
Our spirits, fann'd away by thy light pinions.

O sweetest essence! sweetest of all minions!
God of warm pulses, and dishevell'd hair,
And panting bosoms bare!
Dear unseen light in darkness! eclipser
Of light in light! delicious poisoner!
Thy venom'd goblet will we quaff until
We fill – we fill!
And by thy Mother's lips – ' 990

                Was heard no more
For clamour, when the golden palace-door
Open'd again, and from without, in shone
A new magnificence. On oozy throne
Smooth-moving came Oceanus the old,
To take a latest glimpse at his sheep-fold,
Before he went into his quiet cave
To muse for ever – Then, a lucid wave,
Scoop'd from its trembling sisters of mid-sea,
Afloat, and pillowing up the majesty
Of Doris, and the Ægean seer, her spouse – 1000
Next, on a dolphin, clad in laurel boughs,
Theban Amphion leaning on his lute:
His fingers went across it – All were mute
To gaze on Amphitrite, queen of pearls,
And Thetis pearly too. –

                The palace whirls
Around giddy Endymion; seeing he
Was there far strayed from mortality.
He could not bear it – shut his eyes in vain;
Imagination gave a dizzier pain.
'O I shall die! sweet Venus, be my stay! 1010
Where is my lovely mistress? Well-away!
I die – I hear her voice – I feel my wing – '
At Neptune's feet he sank. A sudden ring
Of Nereids were about him, in kind strife

To usher back his spirit into life:
But still he slept. At last they interwove
Their cradling arms, and purposed to convey
Towards a crystal bower far away.

Lo! while slow carried through the pitying crowd,
To his inward senses these words spake aloud;   1020
Written in star-light on the dark above:
'Dearest Endymion! my entire love!
How have I dwelt in fear of fate: 'tis done –
Immortal bliss for me too hast thou won.
Arise then! for the hen-dove shall not hatch
Her ready eggs, before I'll kissing snatch
Thee into endless heaven. Awake! awake!'

The youth at once arose: a placid lake
Came quiet to his eyes; and forest green,
Cooler than all the wonder he had seen,   1030
Lull'd with its simple song his fluttering breast.
How happy once again in grassy nest!

BOOK IV

MUSE of my native land! loftiest Muse!
O first-born on the mountains! by the hues
Of heaven on the spiritual air begot:
Long didst thou sit alone in northern grot,
While yet our England was a wolfish den;
Before our forests heard the talk of men;
Before the first of Druids was a child; –
Long didst thou sit amid our regions wild,
Rapt in a deep prophetic solitude.
There came an eastern voice of solemn mood: –   10
Yet wast thou patient. Then sang forth the Nine,
Apollo's garland: – yet didst thou divine
Such home-bred glory, that they cried in vain,
'Come hither, Sister of the Island!' Plain
Spake fair Ausonia; and once more she spake
A higher summons: – still didst thou betake
Thee to thy native hopes. O thou hast won
A full accomplishment! The thing is done,
Which undone, these our latter days had risen
On barren souls. Great Muse, thou know'st what prison   20
Of flesh and bone, curbs, and confines, and frets
Our spirit's wings: despondency besets
Our pillows; and the fresh to-morrow morn
Seems to give forth its light in very scorn
Of our dull, uninspired, snail-paced lives.
Long have I said, how happy he who shrives
To thee! But then I thought on poets gone,
And could not pray: – nor can I now – so on
I move to the end in lowliness of heart. –

'Ah, woe is me! that I should fondly part   30
From my dear native land! Ah, foolish maid!
Glad was the hour, when, with thee, myriads bade
Adieu to Ganges and their pleasant fields!
To one so friendless the clear freshet yields
A bitter coolness; the ripe grape is sour:
Yet I would have, great gods! but one short hour
Of native air – let me but die at home.'

   Endymion to heaven's airy dome
Was offering up a hecatomb of vows,
When these words reach'd him. Whereupon he bows   40
His head through thorny-green entanglement
Of underwood, and to the sound is bent,
Anxious as hind towards her hidden fawn.

   'Is no one near to help me? No fair dawn
Of life from charitable voice? No sweet saying
To set my dull and sadden'd spirit playing?
No hand to toy with mine? No lips so sweet
That I may worship them? No eyelids meet
To twinkle on my bosom? No one dies
Before me, till from these enslaving eyes   50
Redemption sparkles! – I am sad and lost.'

   Thou, Carian lord, hadst better have been tost
Into a whirlpool. Vanish into air,
Warm mountaineer! for canst thou only bear
A woman's sigh alone and in distress?
See not her charms! Is Phœbe passionless?
Phœbe is fairer far – O gaze no more: –
Yet if thou wilt behold all beauty's store,
Behold her panting in the forest grass!
Do not those curls of glossy jet surpass   60
For tenderness the arms so idly lain
Amongst them? Feelest not a kindred pain,

To see such lovely eyes in swimming search
After some warm delight, that seems to perch
Dovelike in the dim cell lying beyond
Their upper lids? – Hist!

                'O for Hermes' wand,
To touch this flower into human shape!
That woodland Hyacinthus could escape
From his green prison, and here kneeling down
Call me his queen, his second life's fair crown!   70
Ah me, how I could love! – My soul doth melt
For the unhappy youth – Love! I have felt
So faint a kindness, such a meek surrender
To what my own full thoughts had made too tender,
That but for tears my life had fled away! –
Ye deaf and senseless minutes of the day,
And thou, old forest, hold ye this for true,
There is no lightning, no authentic dew
But in the eye of love: there's not a sound,
Melodious howsoever, can confound   80
The heavens and earth in one to such a death
As doth the voice of love: there's not a breath
Will mingle kindly with the meadow air,
Till it has panted round, and stolen a share
Of passion from the heart!' –

                 Upon a bough
He leant, wretched. He surely cannot now
Thirst for another love: O impious,
That he can even dream upon it thus!
Thought he, 'Why am I not as are the dead,
Since to a woe like this I have been led   90
Through the dark earth, and through the wondrous sea?
Goddess! I love thee not the less: from thee,
By Juno's smile, I turn not – no, no, no –
While the great waters are at ebb and flow.

I have a triple soul! O fond pretence –
For both, for both my love is so immense,
I feel my heart is cut for them in twain.'

   And so he groan'd, as one by beauty slain.
The lady's heart beat quick, and he could see
Her gentle bosom heave tumultuously.   100
He sprang from his green covert: there she lay,
Sweet as a musk-rose upon new-made hay;
With all her limbs on tremble, and her eyes
Shut softly up alive. To speak he tries:
'Fair damsel, pity me! forgive that I
Thus violate thy bower's sanctity!
O pardon me, for I am full of grief –
Grief born of thee, young angel! fairest thief!
Who stolen hast away the wings wherewith
I was to top the heavens. Dear maid, sith   110
Thou art my executioner, and I feel
Loving and hatred, misery and weal,
Will in a few short hours be nothing to me,
And all my story that much passion slew me;
Do smile upon the evening of my days;
And, for my tortured brain begins to craze,
Be thou my nurse; and let me understand
How dying I shall kiss that lily hand. –
Dost weep for me? Then should I be content.
Scowl on, ye fates! until the firmament   120
Outblackens Erebus, and the full-cavern'd earth
Crumbles into itself. By the cloud-girth
Of Jove, those tears have given me a thirst
To meet oblivion.' – As her heart would burst
The maiden sobb'd awhile, and then replied:
'Why must such desolation betide
As that thou speakest of? Are not these green nooks
Empty of all misfortune? Do the brooks

Utter a gorgon voice? Does yonder thrush,
Schooling its half-fledged little ones to brush   130
About the dewy forest, whisper tales? –
Speak not of grief, young stranger, or cold snails
Will slime the rose to-night. Though if thou wilt,
Methinks 'twould be a guilt – a very guilt –
Not to companion thee, and sigh away
The light – the dusk – the dark – till break of day!'
'Dear lady,' said Endymion, ' 'tis past:
I love thee! and my days can never last.
That I may pass in patience still speak:
Let me have music dying, and I seek   140
No more delight – I bid adieu to all.
Didst thou not after other climates call,
And murmur about Indian streams?' – Then she,
Sitting beneath the midmost forest tree,
For pity sang this roundelay –

    'O Sorrow!
    Why dost borrow
The natural hue of health, from vermeil lips? –
    To give maiden blushes
    To the white rose bushes?   150
Or is it thy dewy hand the daisy tips?

    'O Sorrow!
    Why dost borrow
The lustrous passion from a falcon-eye? –
    To give the glow-worm light?
    Or, on a moonless night,
To tinge, on syren shores, the salt sea-spry?

    'O Sorrow!
    Why dost borrow
The mellow ditties from a mourning tongue? –   160

To give at evening pale
Unto the nightingale,
That thou mayst listen the cold dews among?

'O Sorrow!
Why dost borrow
Heart's lightness from the merriment of May?
A lover would not tread
A cowslip on the head,
Though he should dance from eve till peep of day –
Nor any drooping flower
Held sacred for thy bower,
Wherever he may sport himself and play.

'To Sorrow
I bade good morrow,
And thought to leave her far away behind;
But cheerly, cheerly,
She loves me dearly;
She is so constant to me, and so kind:
I would deceive her,
And so leave her,
But ah! she is so constant and so kind.

'Beneath my palm-trees, by the river side,
I sat a-weeping: in the whole world wide
There was no one to ask me why I wept –
And so I kept
Brimming the water-lily cups with tears
Cold as my fears.

'Beneath my palm-trees, by the river side,
I sat a-weeping: what enamour'd bride,
Cheated by shadowy wooer from the clouds,
But hides and shrouds
Beneath dark palm-trees by a river side?

170

180

190

'And as I sat, over the light blue hills
There came a noise of revellers: the rills
Into the wide stream came of purple hue –
      'Twas Bacchus and his crew!
The earnest trumpet spake, and silver thrills
From kissing cymbals made a merry din –
      'Twas Bacchus and his kin!
Like to a moving vintage down they came,   200
Crown'd with green leaves, and faces all on flame;
All madly dancing through the pleasant valley,
      To scare thee, Melancholy!
O then, O then, thou wast a simple name!
And I forgot thee, as the berried holly
By shepherds is forgotten, when, in June,
Tall chestnuts keep away the sun and moon: –
      I rush'd into the folly!

'Within his car, aloft, young Bacchus stood,
Trifling his ivy-dart, in dancing mood,   210
      With sidelong laughing;
And little rills of crimson wine imbrued
His plump white arms, and shoulders, enough white,
      For Venus' pearly bite;
And near him rode Silenus on his ass,
Pelted with flowers as he on did pass
      Tipsily quaffing.

'Whence came ye, merry Damsels! whence came ye,
So many, and so many, and such glee?
Why have ye left your bowers desolate,   220
      Your lutes, and gentler fate?
"We follow Bacchus! Bacchus on the wing,
      A-conquering!
Bacchus, young Bacchus! good or ill betide,
We dance before him thorough kingdoms wide: –

Come hither, lady fair, and joinèd be
      To our wild minstrelsy!"

'Whence came ye, jolly Satyrs! whence came ye,
So many, and so many, and such glee?
Why have ye left your forest haunts, why left   230
      Your nuts in oak-tree cleft? –
"For wine, for wine we left our kernel tree;
For wine we left our heath, and yellow brooms,
      And cold mushrooms;
For wine we follow Bacchus through the earth;
Great god of breathless cups and chirping mirth! –
Come hither, lady fair, and joinèd be
      To our mad minstrelsy!"

'Over wide streams and mountains great we went,
And, save when Bacchus kept his ivy tent,   240
Onward the tiger and the leopard pants,
      With Asian elephants:
Onward these myriads – with song and dance,
With zebras striped, and sleek Arabians' prance,
Web-footed alligators, crocodiles,
Bearing upon their scaly backs, in files,
Plump infant laughers mimicking the coil
Of seamen, and stout galley-rowers' toil:
With toying oars and silken sails they glide,
      Nor care for wind and tide.   250

'Mounted on panthers' furs and lions' manes,
From rear to van they scour about the plains;
A three days' journey in a moment done;
And always, at the rising of the sun,
About the wilds they hunt with spear and horn,
      On spleenful unicorn.

'I saw Osirian Egypt kneel adown
      Before the vine-wreath crown!
I saw parch'd Abyssinia rouse and sing
      To the silver cymbals' ring!   260
I saw the whelming vintage hotly pierce
      Old Tartary the fierce!
The kings of Ind their jewel-sceptres vail,
And from their treasures scatter pearlèd hail;
Great Brahma from his mystic heaven groans,
      And all his priesthood moans;
Before young Bacchus' eye-wink turning pale.
Into these regions came I, following him,
Sick-hearted, weary – so I took a whim
To stray away into these forests drear,   270
      Alone, without a peer:
And I have told thee all thou mayest hear.

      'Young stranger!
      I've been a ranger
In search of pleasure throughout every clime:
      Alas, 'tis not for me!
      Bewitch'd I sure must be,
To lose in grieving all my maiden prime.

      'Come then, Sorrow,
      Sweetest Sorrow!   280
Like an own babe I nurse thee on my breast:
      I thought to leave thee,
      And deceive thee,
But now of all the world I love thee best.

      'There is not one,
      No, no, not one
But thee to comfort a poor lonely maid;
      Thou art her mother,

And her brother,
Her playmate, and her wooer in the shade.'   290

  O what a sigh she gave in finishing,
And look, quite dead to every worldly thing!
Endymion could not speak, but gazed on her:
And listen'd to the wind that now did stir
About the crispèd oaks full drearily,
Yet with as sweet a softness as might be
Remember'd from its velvet summer song.
At last he said: 'Poor lady! how thus long
Have I been able to endure that voice?
Fair Melody! kind Syren! I've no choice;   300
I must be thy sad servant evermore:
I cannot choose but kneel here and adore.
Alas, I must not think – by Phœbe, no!
Let me not think, soft Angel! shall it be so?
Say, beautifullest, shall I never think?
O thou couldst foster me beyond the brink
Of recollection! make my watchful care
Close up its bloodshot eyes, nor see despair!
Do gently murder half my soul, and I
Shall feel the other half so utterly! –   310
I'm giddy at that cheek so fair and smooth;
O let it blush so ever: let it soothe
My madness; let it mantle rosy-warm
With the tinge of love, panting in safe alarm.
This cannot be thy hand, and yet it is!
And this is sure thine other softling – this
Thine own fair bosom, and I am so near!
Wilt fall asleep? O let me sip that tear!
And whisper one sweet word that I may know
This is this world – sweet dewy blossom!' – *Woe!*   320
Woe! Woe to that Endymion! Where is he? –
Even these words went echoing dismally
Through the wide forest – a most fearful tone,

Like one repenting in his latest moan;
And while it died away a shade pass'd by,
As of a thunder-cloud. When arrows fly
Through the thick branches, poor ring-doves sleek forth
Their timid necks and tremble; so these both
Leant to each other trembling, and sat so
Waiting for some destruction – when lo!   330
Foot-feather'd Mercury appeared sublime
Beyond the tall tree tops; and in less time
Than shoots the slanted hail-storm, down he dropt
Towards the ground; but rested not, nor stopt
One moment from his home: only the sward
He with his wand light touch'd, and heavenward
Swifter than sight was gone – even before
The teeming earth a sudden witness bore
Of his swift magic. Diving swans appear
Above the crystal circlings white and clear;   340
And catch the cheated eye in wild surprise,
How they can dive in sight and unseen rise –
So from the turf outsprang two steeds jet-black,
Each with large dark blue wings upon his back.
The youth of Caria placed the lovely dame
On one, and felt himself in spleen to tame
The other's fierceness. Through the air they flew,
High as the eagles. Like two drops of dew
Exhaled to Phœbus' lips, away they are gone,
Far from the earth away – unseen, alone,   350
Among cool clouds and winds, but that the free,
The buoyant life of song can floating be
Above their heads, and follow them untired.
Muse of my native land! am I inspired?
This is the giddy air, and I must spread
Wide pinions to keep here; nor do I dread
Or height, or depth, or width, or any chance
Precipitous: I have beneath my glance
Those towering horses and their mournful freight.

Could I thus sail, and see, and thus await   360
Fearless for power of thought, without thine aid?
There is a sleepy dusk, an odorous shade
From some approaching wonder, and behold
Those winged steeds, with snorting nostrils bold
Snuff at its faint extreme, and seem to tire,
Dying to embers from their native fire!

    There curl'd a purple mist around them; soon,
It seem'd as when around the pale new moon
Sad Zephyr droops the clouds like weeping willow:
'Twas Sleep slow journeying with head on pillow,   370
For the first time, since he came nigh dead-born
From the old womb of night, his cave forlorn
Had he left more forlorn; for the first time,
He felt aloof the day and morning's prime –
Because into his depth Cimmerian
There came a dream, showing how a young man,
Ere a lean bat could plump its wintry skin,
Would at high Jove's empyreal footstool win
An immortality, and how espouse
Jove's daughter, and be reckon'd of his house.   380
Now was he slumbering towards heaven's gate,
That he might at the threshold one hour wait
To hear the marriage melodies, and then
Sink downward to his dusky cave again.
His litter of smooth semilucent mist,
Diversely tinged with rose and amethyst,
Puzzled those eyes that for the centre sought;
And scarcely for one moment could be caught
His sluggish form reposing motionless.
Those two on wingèd steeds, with all the stress   390
Of vision search'd for him, as one would look
Athwart the sallows of a river nook
To catch a glance at silver-throated eels, –
Or from old Skiddaw's top, when fog conceals

His rugged forehead in a mantle pale,
With an eye-guess towards some pleasant vale,
Descry a favourite hamlet faint and far.

    These raven horses, though they foster'd are
Of earth's splenetic fire, dully drop
Their full-vein'd ears, nostrils blood wide, and stop;   400
Upon the spiritless mist have they outspread
Their ample feathers, are in slumber dead, –
And on those pinions, level in mid-air
Endymion sleepeth and the lady fair.
Slowly they sail, slowly as icy isle
Upon a calm sea drifting; and meanwhile
The mournful wanderer dreams. Behold! he walks
On heaven's pavement, brotherly he talks
To divine powers; from his hand full fain
Juno's proud birds are pecking pearly grain: 410
He tries the nerve of Phœbus' golden bow,
And asketh where the golden apples grow:
Upon his arm he braces Pallas' shield,
And strives in vain to unsettle and wield
A Jovian thunderbolt: arch Hebe brings
A full-brimm'd goblet, dances lightly, sings
And tantalizes long; at last he drinks,
And lost in pleasure, at her feet he sinks,
Touching with dazzled lips her star-light hand;
He blows a bugle, – an ethereal band   420
Are visible above: the Seasons four, –
Green-kirtled Spring, flush Summer, golden store
In Autumn's sickle, Winter frosty hoar,
Join dance with shadowy Hours; while still the blast,
In swells unmitigated, still doth last
To sway their floating morris. 'Whose is this?
Whose bugle?' he inquires: they smile – 'O Dis!
Why is this mortal here? Dost thou not know
Its mistress' lips? Not thou? – 'Tis Dian's: lo!

She rises crescented!' He looks, 'tis she, 430
His very goddess: good-bye earth, and sea,
And air, and pains, and care, and suffering;
Good-bye to all but love! Then doth he spring
Towards her, and awakes – and, strange, o'erhead,
Of those same fragrant exhalations bred,
Beheld awake his very dream: the gods
Stood smiling; merry Hebe laughs and nods;
And Phœbe bends towards him crescented.
O state perplexing! On the pinion bed,
Too well awake, he feels the panting side 440
Of his delicious lady. He who died
For soaring too audacious in the sun,
Where that same treacherous wax began to run,
Felt not more tongue-tied than Endymion.
His heart leapt up as to its rightful throne,
To that fair-shadow'd passion pulsed its way –
Ah, what perplexity! Ah, well-a-day!
So fond, so beauteous was his bed-fellow,
He could not help but kiss her: then he grew
Awhile forgetful of all beauty save 450
Young Phœbe's, golden-hair'd; and so 'gan crave
Forgiveness: yet he turn'd once more to look
At the sweet sleeper, – all his soul was shook, –
She press'd his hand in slumber; so once more
He could not help but kiss her and adore.
At this the shadow wept, melting away.
The Latmian started up: 'Bright goddess, stay!
Search my most hidden breast! By truth's own tongue,
I have no dædale heart; why is it wrung
To desperation? Is there nought for me 460
Upon the bourne of bliss, but misery?'

These words awoke the stranger of dark tresses:
Her dawning love-look rapt Endymion blesses
With 'haviour soft. Sleep yawn'd from underneath.

'Thou swan of Ganges, let us no more breathe
This murky phantasm! thou contented seem'st,
Pillow'd in lovely idleness, nor dream'st
What horrors may discomfort thee and me.
Ah, shouldst thou die from my heart-treachery! –
Yet did she merely weep – her gentle soul   470
Hath no revenge in it; as it is whole
In tenderness, would I were whole in love!
Can I prize thee, fair maid, all price above,
Even when I feel as true as innocence!
I do, I do. – What is this soul then? Whence
Came it? It does not seem my own, and I
Have no self-passion or identity.
Some fearful end must be; where, where is it?
By Nemesis! I see my spirit flit
Alone about the dark – Forgive me, sweet!   480
Shall we away?' He roused the steeds; they beat
Their wings chivalrous into the clear air,
Leaving old Sleep within his vapoury lair.

    The good-night blush of eve was waning slow,
And Vesper, risen star, began to throe
In the dusk heavens silverly, when they
Thus sprang direct towards the Galaxy.
Nor did speed hinder converse soft and strange –
Eternal oaths and vows they interchange,
In such wise, in such temper, so aloof   490
Up in the winds, beneath a starry roof,
So witless of their doom, that verily
'Tis well nigh past man's search their hearts to see;
Whether they wept, or laugh'd or grieved, or toy'd –
Most like with joy gone mad, with sorrow cloy'd.

    Full facing their swift flight, from ebon streak,
The moon put forth a little diamond peak,
No bigger than an unobserved star,

Or tiny point of fairy scymitar;
Bright signal that she only stoop'd to tie   500
Her silver sandals, ere deliciously
She bow'd into the heavens her timid head.
Slowly she rose, as though she would have fled,
While to his lady meek the Carian turn'd,
To mark if her dark eyes had yet discern'd
This beauty in its birth – Despair! despair!
He saw her body fading gaunt and spare
In the cold moonshine. Straight he seized her wrist;
It melted from his grasp; her hand he kiss'd,
And, horror! kiss'd his own – he was alone.   510
Her steed a little higher soar'd, and then
Dropt hawk-wise to the earth.

                 There lies a den,
Beyond the seeming confines of the space
Made for the soul to wander in and trace
Its own existence, of remotest glooms.
Dark regions are around it, where the tombs
Of buried griefs the spirit sees, but scarce
One hour doth linger weeping, for the pierce
Of new-born woe it feels more inly smart;
And in these regions many a venom'd dart   520
At random flies; they are the proper home
Of every ill: the man is yet to come
Who hath not journey'd in this native hell.
But few have ever felt how calm and well
Sleep may be had in that deep den of all.
There anguish does not sting, nor pleasure pall;
Woe-hurricanes beat ever at the gate.
Yet all is still within and desolate.
Beset with plainful gusts, within ye hear
No sound so loud as when on curtain'd bier   530
The death-watch tick is stifled. Enter none
Who strive therefore; on the sudden it is won.

Just when the sufferer begins to burn,
Then it is free to him; and from an urn,
Still fed by melting ice, he takes a draught –
Young Semele such richness never quaft
In her maternal longing. Happy gloom!
Dark Paradise! where pale becomes the bloom
Of health by due; where silence dreariest
Is most articulate; where hopes infest;   540
Where those eyes are the brightest far that keep
Their lids shut longest in a dreamless sleep.
O happy spirit-home! O wondrous soul!
Pregnant with such a den to save the whole
In thine own depth. Hail, gentle Carian!
For, never since thy griefs and woes began,
Hast thou felt so content: a grievous feud
Hath led thee to this Cave of Quietude.
Ay, his lull'd soul was there, although upborne
With dangerous speed: and so he did not mourn   550
Because he knew not whither he was going.
So happy was he, not the aerial blowing
Of trumpets at clear parley from the east
Could rouse from that fine relish, that high feast.
They stung the feather'd horse; with fierce alarm
He flapped towards the sound. Alas! no charm
Could lift Endymion's head, or he had view'd
A skyey mask, a pinion'd multitude, –
And silvery was its passing: voices sweet
Warbling the while as if to lull and greet   560
The wanderer in his path. Thus warbled they,
While past the vision went in bright array.

'Who, who from Dian's feast would be away?
For all the golden bowers of the day
Are empty left? Who, who away would be
From Cynthia's wedding and festivity?
Not Hesperus: lo! upon his silver wings

He leans away for highest heaven and sings,
Snapping his lucid fingers merrily! –
Ah, Zephyrus! art here, and Flora too?   570
Ye tender bibbers of the rain and dew,
Young playmates of the rose and daffodil,
Be careful, ere ye enter in, to fill
            Your baskets high
With fennel green, and balm, and golden pines,
Savory, latter-mint, and columbines,
Cool parsley, basil sweet, and sunny thyme;
Yea, every flower and leaf of every clime,
All gather'd in the dewy morning: hie
            Away! fly, fly! –   580
Crystalline brother of the belt of heaven,
Aquarius! to whom king Jove has given
Two liquid pulse streams 'stead of feather'd wings,
Two fanlike fountains, – thine illuminings
            For Dian play:
Dissolve the frozen purity of air;
Let thy white shoulders silvery and bare
Show cold through watery pinions; make more bright
The Star-Queen's crescent on her marriage night:
            Haste, haste away! –   590
Castor has tamed the planet Lion, see!
And of the Bear has Pollux mastery:
A third is in the race! who is the third,
Speeding away swift as the eagle bird?
            The ramping Centaur!
The Lion's mane's on end: the Bear how fierce!
The Centaur's arrow ready seems to pierce
Some enemy: far forth his bow is bent
Into the blue of heaven. He'll be shent,
            Pale unrelentor,   600
When he shall hear the wedding lutes a-playing. –
Andromeda! sweet woman! why delaying
So timidly among the stars: come hither!

Join this bright throng, and nimbly follow whither
        They all are going.
Danae's Son, before Jove newly bow'd,
Has wept for thee, calling to Jove aloud.
Thee, gentle lady, did he disenthral:
Ye shall for ever live and love, for all
        Thy tears are flowing. –   610
By Daphne's fright, behold Apollo!' –

                More
Endymion heard not: down his steed him bore
Prone to the green head of a misty hill.

  His first touch of the earth went nigh to kill.
'Alas!' said he, 'were I but always borne
Through dangerous winds, but had my footsteps
      worn
A path in hell, for ever would I bless
Horrors which nourish an uneasiness
For my own sullen conquering: to him
Who lives beyond earth's boundary, grief is dim,   620
Sorrow is but a shadow: now I see
The grass; I feel the solid ground – Ah, me!
It is thy voice – divinest! Where? – who? who
Left thee so quiet on this bed of dew?
Behold upon this happy earth we are;
Let us aye love each other; let us fare
On forest-fruits, and never, never go
Among the abodes of mortals here below,
Or be by phantoms duped. O destiny!
Into a labyrinth now my soul would fly,   630
But with thy beauty will I deaden it.
Where didst thou melt to? By thee will I sit
For ever: let our fate stop here – a kid
I on this spot will offer: Pan will bid
Us live in peace, in love and peace among

His forest wildernesses. I have clung
To nothing, loved a nothing, nothing seen
Or felt but a great dream! O I have been
Presumptuous against love, against the sky,
Against all elements, against the tie   640
Of mortals each to each, against the blooms
Of flowers, rush of rivers, and the tombs
Of heroes gone! Against his proper glory
Has my own soul conspired: so my story
Will I to children utter, and repent.
There never lived a mortal man, who bent
His appetite beyond his natural sphere,
But starved and died. My sweetest Indian, here,
Here will I kneel, for thou redeemèd hast
My life from too thin breathing: gone and past   650
Are cloudy phantasms. Caverns lone, farewell!
And air of visions, and the monstrous swell
Of visionary seas! No, never more
Shall airy voices cheat me to the shore
Of tangled wonder, breathless and aghast.
Adieu, my daintiest Dream! although so vast
My love is still for thee. The hour may come
When we shall meet in pure elysium.
On earth I may not love thee, and therefore
Doves will I offer up, and sweetest store   660
All through the teeming year: so thou wilt shine
On me, and on this damsel fair of mine,
And bless our simple lives. My Indian bliss!
My river-lily bud! one human kiss!
One sigh of real breath — one gentle squeeze,
Warm as a dove's nest among summer trees,
And warm with dew at ooze from living blood!
Whither didst melt? Ah, what of that! — all good
We'll talk about — no more of dreaming. — Now,
Where shall our dwelling be? Under the brow   670
Of some steep mossy hill, where ivy dun

Would hide us up, although spring leaves were none;
And where dark yew-trees, as we rustle through,
Will drop their scarlet-berry cups of dew?
O thou wouldst joy to live in such a place!
Dusk for our loves, yet light enough to grace
Those gentle limbs on mossy bed reclined:
For by one step the blue sky shouldst thou find,
And by another, in deep dell below,
See, through the trees, a little river go   680
All in its mid-day gold and glimmering.
Honey from out the gnarled hive I'll bring,
And apples, wan with sweetness, gather thee, –
Cresses that grow where no man may them see,
And sorrel untorn by the dew-claw'd stag:
Pipes will I fashion of the syrinx flag,
That thou mayst always know whither I roam,
When it shall please thee in our quiet home
To listen and think of love. Still let me speak;
Still let me dive into the joy I seek, –   690
For yet the past doth prison me. The rill,
Thou haply mayst delight in, will I fill
With fairy fishes from the mountain tarn,
And thou shalt feed them from the squirrel's barn.
Its bottom will I strew with amber shells,
And pebbles blue from deep enchanted wells.
Its sides I'll plant with dew-sweet eglantine,
And honeysuckles full of clear bee-wine.
I will entice this crystal rill to trace
Love's silver name upon the meadow's face.   700
I'll kneel to Vesta, for a flame of fire;
And to God Phœbus, for a golden lyre;
To Empress Dian, for a hunting-spear,
To Vesper, for a taper silver-clear,
That I may see thy beauty through the night;
To Flora, and a nightingale shall light
Tame on thy finger; to the River-gods,

And they shall bring thee taper fishing-rods
Of gold, and lines of Naiads' long bright tress,
Heaven shield thee for thine utter loveliness!   710
Thy mossy footstool shall the altar be
'Fore which I'll bend, bending, dear love, to thee:
Those lips shall be my Delphos, and shall speak
Laws to my footsteps, colour to my cheek,
Trembling or stedfastness to this same voice,
And of three sweetest pleasurings the choice:
And that affectionate light, those diamond things,
Those eyes, those passions, those supreme pearl springs,
Shall be my grief, or twinkle me to pleasure.
Say, is not bliss within our perfect seizure?   720
O that I could not doubt!'

            The mountaineer
Thus strove by fancies vain and crude to clear
His brier'd path to some tranquillity.
It gave bright gladness to his lady's eye,
And yet the tears she wept were tears of sorrow;
Answering thus, just as the golden morrow
Beam'd upward from the valleys of the east:
'O that the flutter of this heart had ceased,
Or the sweet name of love had pass'd away!
Young feather'd tyrant! by a swift decay   730
Wilt thou devote this body to the earth:
And I do think that at my very birth
I lisp'd thy blooming titles inwardly;
For at the first, first dawn and thought of thee,
With uplift hands I bless'd the stars of heaven.
Art thou not cruel? Ever have I striven
To think thee kind, but ah, it will not do!
When yet a child, I heard that kisses drew
Favour from thee, and so I kisses gave
To the void air, bidding them find out love: 740

But when I came to feel how far above
All fancy, pride, and fickle maidenhood,
All earthly pleasure, all imagined good,
Was the warm tremble of a devout kiss, –
Even then, that moment, at the thought of this,
Fainting I fell into a bed of flowers,
And languish'd there three days. Ye milder powers,
Am I not cruelly wrong'd? Believe, believe
Me, dear Endymion, were I to weave
With my own fancies garlands of sweet life,   750
Thou shouldst be one of all. Ah, bitter strife!
I may not be thy love: I am forbidden –
Indeed I am – thwarted, affrighted, chidden,
By things I trembled at, and gorgon wrath.
Twice hast thou ask'd whither I went: henceforth
Ask me no more! I may not utter it,
Nor may I be thy love. We might commit
Ourselves at once to vengeance; we might die;
We might embrace and die: voluptuous thought!
Enlarge not to my hunger, or I'm caught   760
In trammels of perverse deliciousness.
No, no, that shall not be: thee will I bless,
And bid a long adieu.'

The Carian
No word return'd: both lovelorn, silent, wan,
Into the valleys green together went.
Far wandering, they were perforce content
To sit beneath a fair lone beechen tree;
Nor at each other gazed, but heavily
Pored on its hazel cirque of shedded leaves.

    Endymion! unhappy! it nigh grieves   770
Me to behold thee thus in last extreme:
Ensky'd ere this, but truly that I deem

Truth the best music in a first-born song.
Thy lute-voiced brother will I sing ere long,
And thou shalt aid – hast thou not aided me?
Yes, moonlight Emperor! felicity
Has been thy meed for many thousand years;
Yet often have I, on the brink of tears,
Mourn'd as if yet thou wert a forester; –
Forgetting the old tale.

          He did not stir   780
His eyes from the dead leaves, or one small pulse
Of joy he might have felt. The spirit culls
Unfaded amaranth, when wild it strays
Through the old garden-ground of boyish days.
A little onward ran the very stream
By which he took his first soft poppy dream;
And on the very bark 'gainst which he leant
A crescent he had carved, and round it spent
His skill in little stars. The teeming tree
Had swoll'n and green'd the pious charactery,   790
But not ta'en out. Why, there was not a slope
Up which he had not fear'd the antelope;
And not a tree, beneath whose rooty shade
He had not with his tamed leopards play'd;
Nor could an arrow light, or javelin,
Fly in the air where his had never been –
And yet he knew it not.

          O treachery!
Why does his lady smile, pleasing her eye
With all his sorrowing? He sees her not.
But who so stares on him? His sister sure!   800
Peona of the woods! – Can she endure? –
Impossible – how dearly they embrace!
His lady smiles; delight is in her face;
It is no treachery.

'Dear brother mine!
Endymion, weep not so! Why shouldst thou pine
When all great Latmos so exalt will be?
Thank the great gods, and look not bitterly;
And speak not one pale word, and sigh no more.
Sure I will not believe thou hast such store
Of grief, to last thee to my kiss again.   810
Thou surely canst not bear a mind in pain,
Come hand in hand with one so beautiful.
Be happy both of you! for I will pull
The flowers of autumn for your coronals.
Pan's holy priest for young Endymion calls;
And when he is restored, thou, fairest dame,
Shalt be our queen. Now, is it not a shame
To see ye thus, – not very, very sad?
Perhaps ye are too happy to be glad:
O feel as if it were a common day;   820
Free-voiced as one who never was away.
No tongue shall ask, whence come ye? but ye shall
Be gods of your own rest imperial.
Not even I, for one whole month, will pry
Into the hours that have pass'd us by,
Since in my arbour I did sing to thee.
O Hermes! on this very night will be
A hymning up to Cynthia, queen of light;
For the soothsayers old saw yesternight
Good visions in the air, – whence will befall,   830
As say these sages, health perpetual
To shepherds and their flocks; and furthermore
In Dian's face they read the gentle lore:
Therefore for her these vesper-carols are.
Our friends will all be there from nigh and far.
Many upon thy death have ditties made;
And many, even now, their foreheads shade
With cypress, on a day of sacrifice.
New singing for our maids shalt thou devise,

And pluck the sorrow from our huntsmen's brows,   840
Tell me, my lady-queen, how to espouse
This wayward brother to his rightful joys!
His eyes are on thee bent, as thou didst poise
His fate most goddess-like. Help me, I pray,
To lure – Endymion, dear brother, say
What ails thee?' He could bear no more, and so
Bent his soul fiercely like a spiritual bow,
And twang'd it inwardly, and calmly said:
'I would have thee my only friend, sweet maid!
My only visitor! not ignorant though,   850
That those deceptions which for pleasure go
'Mong men, are pleasures real as real may be:
But there are higher ones I may not see,
If impiously an earthly realm I take.
Since I saw thee, I have been wide awake
Night after night, and day by day, until
Of the empyrean I have drunk my fill.
Let it content thee, Sister, seeing me
More happy than betides mortality.
A hermit young, I'll live in mossy cave,   860
Where thou alone shalt come to me, and lave
Thy spirit in the wonders I shall tell.
Through me the shepherd realm shall prosper well;
For to thy tongue will I all health confide.
And for my sake, let this young maid abide
With thee as a dear sister. Thou alone,
Peona, mayst return to me. I own
This may sound strangely: but when, dearest girl,
Thou seest it for my happiness, no pearl
Will trespass down those cheeks. Companion fair!   870
Wilt be content to dwell with her, to share
This sister's love with me?' Like one resign'd
And bent by circumstance, and thereby blind
In self-commitment, thus, that meek unknown:
'Ay, but a buzzing by my ears has flown,

Of jubilee to Dian: – truth I heard!
Well then, I see there is no little bird,
Tender soever, but is Jove's own care.
Long have I sought for rest, and unaware,
Behold I find it! so exalted too!   880
So after my own heart! I knew, I knew
There was a place untenanted in it:
In that same void white Chastity shall sit,
And monitor me nightly to lone slumber.
With sanest lips I vow me to the number
Of Dian's sisterhood; and, kind lady,
With thy good help, this very night shall see
My future days to her fane consecrate.'

    As feels a dreamer what doth most create
His own particular fright, so these three felt.   890
Or like one who, in after ages, knelt
To Lucifer or Baal, when he'd pine
After a little sleep: or when in mine
Far under-ground, a sleeper meets his friends
Who know him not. Each diligently bends
Towards common thoughts and things for very fear;
Striving their ghastly malady to cheer,
By thinking it a thing of yes and no,
That housewives talk of. But the spirit-blow
Was struck, and all were dreamers. At the last   900
Endymion said: 'Are not our fates all cast?
Why stand we here? Adieu, ye tender pair!
Adieu!' Whereat those maidens, with wild stare,
Walk'd dizzily away. Pained and hot
His eyes went after them, until they got
Near to a cypress grove, whose deadly maw,
In one swift moment, would what then he saw
Engulph for ever. 'Stay!' he cried, 'ah, stay!
Turn, damsels! hist! one word I have to say:
Sweet Indian, I would see thee once again.   910

It is a thing I dote on: so I'd fain,
Peona, ye should hand in hand repair
Into those holy groves, that silent are
Behind great Dian's temple. I'll be yon,
At vesper's earliest twinkle – they are gone –
But once, once, once again – ' At this he prest
His hands against his face, and then did rest
His head upon a mossy hillock green,
And so remain'd as he a corpse had been
All the long day; save when he scantly lifted   920
His eyes abroad, to see how shadows shifted
With the slow move of time, – sluggish and weary
Until the poplar tops, in journey dreary,
Had reach'd the river's brim. Then up he rose,
And, slowly as that very river flows,
Walk'd towards the temple-grove with this lament:
'Why such a golden eve? The breeze is sent
Careful and soft, that not a leaf may fall
Before the serene father of them all
Bows down his summer head below the west.   930
Now am I of breath, speech, and speed possest,
But at the setting I must bid adieu
To her for the last time. Night will strew
On the damp grass myriads of lingering leaves,
And with them shall I die; nor much it grieves
To die, when summer dies on the cold sward.
Why, I have been a butterfly, a lord
Of flowers, garlands, love-knots, silly posies,
Groves, meadows, melodies, and arbour-roses;
My kingdom's at its death, and just it is   940
That I should die with it: so in all this
We miscall grief, bale, sorrow, heart-break, woe,
What is there to plain of? By Titan's foe
I am but rightly served.' So saying, he
Tripp'd lightly on, in sort of deathful glee;
Laughing at the clear stream and setting sun,

As though they jests had been: nor had he done
His laugh at nature's holy countenance,
Until that grove appear'd, as if perchance,
And then his tongue with sober seemlihed   950
Gave utterance as he enter'd: 'Ha! I said,
"King of the butterflies"; but by this gloom,
And by old Rhadamanthus' tongue of doom,
This dusk religion, pomp of solitude,
And the Promethean clay by thief endued,
By old Saturnus' forelock, by his head
Shook with eternal palsy, I did wed
Myself to things of light from infancy;
And thus to be cast out, thus lorn to die,
Is sure enough to make a mortal man   960
Grow impious.' So he inwardly began
On things for which no wording can be found
Deeper and deeper sinking, until drown'd
Beyond the reach of music: for the choir
Of Cynthia he heard not, though rough brier
Nor muffling thicket interposed to dull
The vesper hymn, far swollen, soft and full,
Through the dark pillars of those sylvan aisles.
He saw not the two maidens, nor their smiles,
Wan as primroses gather'd at midnight   970
By chilly-finger'd spring. Unhappy wight!
'Endymion!' said Peona, 'we are here!
What wouldst thou ere we all are laid on bier?'
Then he embraced her, and his lady's hand
Press'd, saying: 'Sister, I would have command,
If it were heaven's will, on our sad fate.'
At which that dark-eyed stranger stood elate
And said, in a new voice, but sweet as love,
To Endymion's amaze: 'By Cupid's dove,
And so thou shalt? and by the lily truth   980
Of my own breast thou shalt, belovèd youth!'
And as she spake, into her face there came,

Light, as reflected from a silver flame:
Her long black hair swell'd ampler, in display
Full golden: in her eyes a brighter day
Dawn'd blue, and full of love. Ay, he beheld
Phœbe, his passion! joyous she upheld
Her lucid bow, continuing thus: 'Drear, drear
Has our delaying been; but foolish fear
Withheld me first; and then decrees of fate: 990
And then 'twas fit that from this mortal state
Thou shouldst, my love, by some unlook'd-for change
Be spiritualized. Peona, we shall range
These forests, and to thee they safe shall be
As was thy cradle; hither shalt thou flee
To meet us many a time.' Next Cynthia bright
Peona kiss'd, and bless'd with fair good night:
Her brother kiss'd her too, and knelt adown
Before his goddess, in a blissful swoon.
She gave her fair hands to him, and behold,   1000
Before three swiftest kisses he had told,
They vanish'd far away! – Peona went
Home through the gloomy wood in wonderment.

LAMIA, ISABELLA, THE EVE OF ST. AGNES,

AND OTHER POEMS

1820

ADVERTISEMENT[*]

If any apology be thought necessary for the appearance of the un-
finished poem of HYPERION, the publishers beg to state that they
alone are responsible, as it was printed at their particular request,
and contrary to the wish of the author. The poem was intended to
have been of equal length with ENDYMION, but the reception given
to that work discouraged the author from proceeding.

Fleet-Street, 26 June, 1820

---

[*] *The publishers' advertisement for 1820*
This was probably written by John Taylor (see *The Keats Circle*, ed. Hyder Edward
Rollins, 1965, I., 115 n.). K remarked on it 'This is none of my doing–I was ill at the time.'
He added with respect to the final sentence: 'This is a lie.' See Amy Lowell, *John Keats* (2
vols, 1925), II. 424–5.

Lamia

PART I

UPON a time, before the faery broods
Drove Nymph and Satyr from the prosperous woods,
Before King Oberon's bright diadem,
Sceptre, and mantle, clasp'd with dewy gem,
Frighted away the Dryads and the Fauns
From rushes green, and brakes, and cowslipp'd lawns,
The ever-smitten Hermes empty left
His golden throne, bent warm on amorous theft:
From high Olympus had he stolen light,
On this side of Jove's clouds, to escape the sight   10
Of his great summoner, and made retreat
Into a forest on the shores of Crete.
For somewhere in that sacred island dwelt
A nymph to whom all hoofèd Satyrs knelt;
At whose white feet the languid Tritons pour'd
Pearls, while on land they wither'd and adored.
Fast by the springs where she to bathe was wont,
And in those meads where sometime she might haunt,
Were strewn rich gifts, unknown to any Muse,
Though Fancy's casket were unlock'd to choose.   20
Ah, what a world of love was at her feet!
So Hermes thought, and a celestial heat
Burn'd from his winged heels to either ear,
That from a whiteness as the lily clear,
Blush'd into roses 'mid his golden hair,
Fallen in jealous curls about his shoulders bare.
From vale to vale, from wood to wood, he flew,
Breathing upon the flowers his passion new,
And wound with many a river to its head,

To find where this sweet nymph prepared her secret bed   30
In vain; the sweet nymph might nowhere be found,
And so he rested on the lonely ground,
Pensive, and full of painful jealousies
Of the Wood-Gods, and even the very trees.
There as he stood he heard a mournful voice,
Such as once heard, in gentle heart, destroys
All pain but pity: thus the lone voice spake:
'When from this wreathèd tomb shall I awake?
When move in a sweet body fit for life,
And love, and pleasure, and the ruddy strife   40
Of hearts and lips? Ah, miserable me!'
The God, dove-footed, glided silently
Round bush and tree, soft-brushing in his speed
The taller grasses and full-flowering weed,
Until he found a palpitating snake,
Bright, and cirque-couchant in a dusky brake.

      She was a gordian shape of dazzling hue,
Vermilion-spotted, golden, green, and blue;
Striped like a zebra, freckled like a pard,
Eyed like a peacock, and all crimson-barr'd;   50
And full of silver moons, that, as she breathed,
Dissolved, or brighter shone, or interwreathed
Their lustres with the gloomier tapestries –
So rainbow-sided, touch'd with miseries,
She seem'd at once, some penanced lady elf,
Some demon's mistress, or the demon's self.
Upon her crest she wore a wannish fire
Sprinkled with stars, like Ariadne's tiar:
Her head was serpent, but ah, bitter-sweet!
She had a woman's mouth with all its pearls complete;   60
And for her eyes: what could such eyes do there
But weep, and weep, that they were born so fair?
As Proserpine still weeps for her Sicilian air.
Her throat was serpent, but the words she spake

Came, as through bubbling honey, for Love's sake,
And thus; while Hermes on his pinions lay,
Like a stoop'd falcon ere he takes his prey:

  'Fair Hermes, crown'd with feathers, fluttering light,
I had a splendid dream of thee last night:
I saw thee sitting, on a throne of gold,   70
Among the Gods, upon Olympus old,
The only sad one; for thou didst not hear
The soft lute-finger'd Muses chaunting clear,
Nor even Apollo when he sang alone,
Deaf to his throbbing throat's long, long melodious moan.
I dreamt I saw thee, robed in purple flakes,
Break amorous through the clouds, as morning breaks,
And swiftly as a bright Phœbean dart
Strike for the Cretan isle; and here thou art!
Too gentle Hermes, hast thou found the maid?'   80
Whereat the star of Lethe not delay'd
His rosy eloquence, and thus inquired:
'Thou smooth-lipp'd serpent, surely high inspired!
Thou beauteous wreath, with melancholy eyes,
Possess whatever bliss thou canst devise,
Telling me only where my nymph is fled –
Where she doth breathe!' 'Bright planet, thou hast said,'
Return'd the snake, 'but seal with oaths, fair God!'
'I swear,' said Hermes, 'by my serpent rod,
And by thine eyes, and by thy starry crown!'   90
Light flew his earnest words, among the blossoms blown.
Then thus again the brilliance feminine:
'Too frail of heart! for this lost nymph of thine,
Free as the air, invisibly, she strays
About these thornless wilds; her pleasant days
She tastes unseen; unseen her nimble feet
Leave traces in the grass and flowers sweet:
From weary tendrils and bow'd branches green
She plucks the fruit unseen, she bathes unseen:

And by my power is her beauty veil'd   100
To keep it unaffronted, unassail'd
By the love-glances of unlovely eyes,
Of Satyrs, Fauns, and blear'd Silenus' sighs.
Pale grew her immortality, for woe
Of all these lovers, and she grievèd so
I took compassion on her, bade her steep
Her hair in weïrd syrops, that would keep
Her loveliness invisible, yet free
To wander as she loves, in liberty.
Thou shalt behold her, Hermes, thou alone   110
If thou wilt, as thou swearest, grant my boon.'
Then, once again, the charmèd God began
An oath, and through the serpent's ears it ran
Warm, tremulous, devout, psalterian.
Ravish'd, she lifted her Circean head,
Blush'd a live damask, and swift-lisping said,
'I was a woman, let me have once more
A woman's shape, and charming as before.
I love a youth of Corinth – O the bliss!
Give me my woman's form, and place me where he is.   120
Stoop, Hermes, let me breathe upon thy brow,
And thou shalt see thy sweet nymph even now.'
The God on half-shut feathers sank serene,
She breathed upon his eyes, and swift was seen
Of both the guarded nymph near-smiling on the green.
It was no dream; or say a dream it was,
Real are the dreams of Gods, and smoothly pass
Their pleasures in a long immortal dream.
One warm, flush'd moment, hovering, it might seem,
Dash'd by the wood-nymph's beauty, so he burn'd;   130
Then, lighting on the printless verdure, turn'd
To the swoon'd serpent, and with languid arm,
Delicate, put to proof the lithe Caducean charm.
So done, upon the nymph his eyes he bent
Full of adoring tears and blandishment,

And towards her stept: she, like a moon in wane,
Faded before him, cower'd, nor could restrain
Her fearful sobs, self-folding like a flower
That faints into itself at evening hour:
But the God fostering her chillèd hand,   140
She felt the warmth, her eyelids open'd bland,
And, like new flowers at morning song of bees,
Bloom'd, and gave up her honey to the lees.
Into the green-recessèd woods they flew;
Nor grew they pale, as mortal lovers do.

    Left to herself, the serpent now began
To change; her elfin blood in madness ran;
Her mouth foam'd, and the grass, therewith besprent,
Wither'd at dew so sweet and virulent;
Her eyes in torture fix'd and anguish drear,   150
Hot, glazed, and wide, with lid-lashes all sear,
Flash'd phosphor and sharp sparks, without one cooling tear.
The colours all inflamed throughout her train,
She writhed about, convulsed with scarlet pain:
A deep volcanian yellow took the place,
Of all her milder-moonèd body's grace;
And, as the lava ravishes the mead,
Spoilt all her silver mail, and golden brede:
Made gloom of all her frecklings, streaks and bars,
Eclipsed her crescents, and lick'd up her stars: 160
So that, in moments few, she was undrest
Of all her sapphires, greens, and amethyst,
And rubious-argent: of all these bereft,
Nothing but pain and ugliness were left.
Still shone her crown; that vanish'd, also she
Melted and disappear'd as suddenly;
And in the air, her new voice luting soft,
Cried, 'Lycius! gentle Lycius!' – Borne aloft
With the bright mists about the mountains hoar
These words dissolved: Crete's forests heard no more.   170

Whither fled Lamia, now a lady bright,
A full-born beauty new and exquisite?
She fled into that valley they pass o'er
Who go to Corinth from Cenchreas' shore;
And rested at the foot of those wild hills,
The rugged founts of the Peræan rills,
And of that other ridge whose barren back
Stretches, with all its mist and cloudy rack,
South-westward to Cleone. There she stood,
About a young bird's flutter from a wood,   180
Fair, on a sloping green of mossy tread,
By a clear pool, wherein she passioned
To see herself escaped from so sore ills,
While her robes flaunted with the daffodils.

Ah, happy Lycius! – for she was a maid
More beautiful than ever twisted braid,
Or sigh'd, or blush'd, or on spring-flower'd lea
Spread a green kirtle to the minstrelsy:
A virgin purest lipp'd, yet in the lore
Of love deep learned to the red heart's core: 190
Not one hour old, yet of sciential brain
To unperplex bliss from its neighbour pain;
Define their pettish limits, and estrange
Their points of contact, and swift counterchange;
Intrigue with the specious chaos, and dispart
Its most ambiguous atoms with sure art;
As though in Cupid's college she had spent
Sweet days a lovely graduate, still unshent,
And kept his rosy terms in idle languishment.

Why this fair creature chose so fairily   200
By the wayside to linger, we shall see;
But first 'tis fit to tell how she could muse
And dream, when in the serpent prison-house,
Of all she list, strange or magnificent:

How, ever, where she will'd her spirit went;
Whether to faint Elysium, or where
Down through tress-lifting waves the Nereids fair
Wind into Thetis' bower by many a pearly stair;
Or where God Bacchus drains his cups divine,
Stretch'd out, at ease, beneath a glutinous pine;   210
Or where in Pluto's gardens palatine
Mulciber's columns gleam in far piazzian line.
And sometimes into cities she would send
Her dream, with feast and rioting to blend;
And once, while among mortals dreaming thus,
She saw the young Corinthian Lycius
Charioting foremost in the envious race,
Like a young Jove with calm uneager face,
And fell into a swooning love of him.
Now on the moth-time of that evening dim   220
He would return that way, as well she knew,
To Corinth from the shore; for freshly blew
The eastern soft wind, and his galley now
Grated the quay-stones with her brazen prow
In port Cenchreas, from Egina isle
Fresh anchor'd; whither he had been awhile
To sacrifice to Jove, whose temple there
Waits with high marble doors for blood and incense rare.
Jove heard his vows, and better'd his desire;
For by some freakful chance he made retire   230
From his companions, and set forth to walk,
Perhaps grown wearied of their Corinth talk:
Over the solitary hills he fared,
Thoughtless at first, but ere eve's star appear'd
His phantasy was lost, where reason fades,
In the calm'd twilight of Platonic shades.
Lamia beheld him coming, near, more near –
Close to her passing, in indifference drear,
His silent sandals swept the mossy green;
So neighbour'd to him, and yet so unseen,   240

She stood: he pass'd, shut up in mysteries,
His mind wrapp'd like his mantle, while her eyes
Follow'd his steps, and her neck regal white
Turn'd – syllabling thus: 'Ah, Lycius bright!
And will you leave me on the hills alone?
Lycius, look back! and be some pity shown.'
He did; not with cold wonder, fearingly,
But Orpheus-like at an Eurydice;
For so delicious were the words she sung,
It seem'd he had loved them a whole summer long.   250
And soon his eyes had drunk her beauty up,
Leaving no drop in the bewildering cup,
And still the cup was full, – while he, afraid
Lest she should vanish ere his lip had paid
Due adoration, thus began to adore;
Her soft look growing coy, she saw his chain so sure:
'Leave thee alone! Look back! Ah, Goddess, see
Whether my eyes can ever turn from thee!
For pity do not this sad heart belie –
Even as thou vanishest so I shall die.   260
Stay! though a Naiad of the rivers, stay!
To thy far wishes will thy streams obey:
Stay! though the greenest woods be thy domain,
Alone they can drink up the morning rain;
Though a descended Pleiad, will not one
Of thine harmonious sisters keep in tune
Thy spheres, and as thy silver proxy shine?
So sweetly to these ravish'd ears of mine
Came thy sweet greeting, that if thou shouldst fade,
Thy memory will waste me to a shade.   270
For pity do not melt!' – 'If I should stay,'
Said Lamia, 'here, upon this floor of clay,
And pain my steps upon these flowers too rough,
What canst thou say or do of charm enough
To dull the nice remembrance of my home?
Thou canst not ask me with thee here to roam

Over these hills and vales, where no joy is, –
Empty of immortality and bliss!
Thou art a scholar, Lycius, and must know
That finer spirits cannot breathe below   280
In human climes, and live. Alas! poor youth,
What taste of purer air hast thou to soothe
My essence? What serener palaces,
Where I may all my many senses please
And by mysterious sleights a hundred thirsts appease?
It cannot be – Adieu!' So said, she rose
Tiptoe, with white arms spread. He, sick to lose
The amorous promise of her lone complain,
Swoon'd, murmuring of love, and pale with pain.
The cruel lady, without any show   290
Of sorrow for her tender favourite's woe,
But rather, if her eyes could brighter be,
With brighter eyes and slow amenity,
Put her new lips to his, and gave afresh
The life she had so tangled in her mesh:
And as he from one trance was wakening
Into another, she began to sing,
Happy in beauty, life, and love, and everything,
A song of love, too sweet for earthly lyres,
While, like held breath, the stars drew in their
        panting fires.   300
And then she whisper'd in such trembling tone
As those who, safe together met alone
For the first time through many anguish'd days,
Use other speech than looks; bidding him raise
His drooping head, and clear his soul of doubt,
For that she was a woman, and without
Any more subtle fluid in her veins
Than throbbing blood, and that the self-same pains
Inhabited her frail-strung heart as his.
And next she wonder'd how his eyes could miss   310
Her face so long in Corinth, where, she said,

She dwelt but half retired, and there had led
Days happy as the gold coin could invent
Without the aid of love; yet in content,
Till she saw him, as once she pass'd him by
Where 'gainst a column he leant thoughtfully
At Venus' temple porch, 'mid baskets heap'd
Of amorous herbs and flowers, newly reap'd
Late on that eve, as 'twas the night before
The Adonian feast; whereof she saw no more,   320
But wept alone those days, for why should she adore?
Lycius from death awoke into amaze
To see her still, and singing so sweet lays;
Then from amaze into delight he fell
To hear her whisper woman's lore so well;
And every word she spake enticed him on
To unperplex'd delight and pleasure known.
Let the mad poets say whate'er they please
Of the sweets of Fairies, Peris, Goddesses,
There is not such a treat among them all,   330
Haunters of cavern, lake, and waterfall,
As a real woman, lineal indeed
From Pyrrha's pebbles or old Adam's seed.
Thus gentle Lamia judged, and judged aright,
That Lycius could not love in half a fright,
So threw the goddess off, and won his heart
More pleasantly by playing woman's part,
With no more awe than what her beauty gave,
That, while it smote, still guaranteed to save.
Lycius to all made eloquent reply,   340
Marrying to every word a twin-born sigh;
And last, pointing to Corinth, ask'd her sweet,
If 'twas too far that night for her soft feet.
The way was short, for Lamia's eagerness
Made, by a spell, the triple league decrease
To a few paces; not at all surmised
By blinded Lycius. So, in her comprised,

They pass'd the city gates, he knew not how,
So noiseless, and he never thought to know.

As men talk in a dream, so Corinth all,   350
Throughout her palaces imperial,
And all her populous streets and temples lewd,
Mutter'd, like tempest in the distance brew'd,
To the wide-spreaded night above her towers.
Men, women, rich and poor, in the cool hours,
Shuffled their sandals o'er the pavement white,
Companion'd or alone; while many a light
Flared, here and there, from wealthy festivals,
And threw their moving shadows on the walls,
Or found them cluster'd in the corniced shade   360
Of some arch'd temple door or dusky colonnade.

Muffling his face, of greeting friends in fear,
Her finger he press'd hard, as one came near
With curl'd grey beard, sharp eyes, and smooth bald crown,
Slow-stepp'd, and robed in philosophic gown:
Lycius shrank closer, as they met and past,
Into his mantle, adding wings to haste,
While hurried Lamia trembled. 'Ah!' said he,
'Why do you shudder, love, so ruefully?
Why does your tender palm dissolve in dew?' –   370
'I'm wearied,' said fair Lamia: 'tell me who
Is that old man? I cannot bring to mind
His features: – Lycius! wherefore did you blind
Yourself from his quick eyes?' Lycius replied,
' 'Tis Apollonius sage, my trusty guide
And good instructor; but to-night he seems
The ghost of folly haunting my sweet dreams.'

While yet he spake they had arrived before
A pillar'd porch, with lofty portal door,
Where hung a silver lamp, whose phosphor glow   380

Reflected in the slabbèd steps below,
Mild as a star in water; for so new
And so unsullied was the marble hue,
So through the crystal polish, liquid fine,
Ran the dark veins, that none but feet divine
Could e'er have touch'd there. Sounds Æolian
Breathed from the hinges, as the ample span
Of the wide doors disclosed a place unknown
Some time to any, but those two alone,
And a few Persian mutes, who that same year   390
Were seen about the markets: none knew where
They could inhabit; the most curious
Were foil'd, who watch'd to trace them to their house:
And but the flitter-wingèd verse must tell,
For truth's sake, what woe afterwards befell,
'Twould humour many a heart to leave them thus
Shut from the busy world of more incredulous.

PART II

LOVE in a hut, with water and a crust,
Is – Love, forgive us! – cinders, ashes, dust;
Love in a palace is perhaps at last
More grievous torment than a hermit's fast: –
That is a doubtful tale from faery land,
Hard for the non-elect to understand.
Had Lycius lived to hand his story down,
He might have given the moral a fresh frown,
Or clench'd it quite: but too short was their bliss
To breed distrust and hate, that make the soft voice hiss.   10
Beside, there, nightly, with terrific glare,
Love, jealous grown of so complete a pair,
Hover'd and buzz'd his wings, with fearful roar,
Above the lintel of their chamber door,
And down the passage cast a glow upon the floor.

   For all this came a ruin: side by side
They were enthronèd, in the even tide,
Upon a couch, near to a curtaining
Whose airy texture, from a golden string,
Floated into the room, and let appear   20
Unveil'd the summer heaven, blue and clear,
Betwixt two marble shafts: – there they reposed,
Where use had made it sweet, with eyelids closed,
Saving a tithe which love still open kept,
That they might see each other while they almost slept;
When from the slope side of a suburb hill,
Deafening the swallow's twitter, came a thrill
Of trumpets. Lycius started – the sounds fled,
But left a thought, a buzzing in his head.
For the first time, since first he harbour'd in   30
That purple-linèd palace of sweet sin,
His spirit pass'd beyond its golden bourn
Into the noisy world almost forsworn.
The lady, ever watchful, penetrant,
Saw this with pain, so arguing a want
Of something more, more than her empery
Of joys; and she began to moan and sigh
Because he mused beyond her, knowing well,
That but a moment's thought is passion's passing bell.
'Why do you sigh, fair creature?' whisper'd he: 40
'Why do you think?' return'd she tenderly:
'You have deserted me; where am I now?
Not in your heart while care weighs on your brow:
No, no, you have dismiss'd me, and I go,
From your breast houseless: ay, it must be so.'
He answer'd, bending to her open eyes,
Where he was mirror'd small in paradise, –
'My silver planet, both of eve and morn!
Why will you plead yourself so sad forlorn,
While I am striving how to fill my heart   50

With deeper crimson and a double smart?
How to entangle, trammel up, and snare
Your soul in mine, and labyrinth you there,
Like the hid scent in an unbudded rose?
Ay, a sweet kiss – you see your mighty woes.
My thoughts! shall I unveil them? Listen then.
What mortal hath a prize, that other men
May be confounded and abash'd withal,
But lets it sometimes pace abroad majestical,
And triumph, as in thee I should rejoice   60
Amid the hoarse alarm of Corinth's voice.
Let my foes choke, and my friends shout afar,
While through the throngèd streets your bridal car
Wheels round its dazzling spokes.' – The lady's cheek
Trembled; she nothing said, but, pale and meek,
Arose and knelt before him, wept a rain
Of sorrows at his words; at last with pain
Beseeching him, the while his hand she wrung,
To change his purpose. He thereat was stung,
Perverse, with stronger fancy to reclaim   70
Her wild and timid nature to his aim;
Besides, for all his love, in self despite,
Against his better self, he took delight
Luxurious in her sorrows, soft and new.
His passion, cruel grown, took on a hue
Fierce and sanguineous as 'twas possible
In one whose brow had no dark veins to swell.
Fine was the mitigated fury, like
Apollo's presence when in act to strike
The serpent – Ha, the serpent! certes, she   80
Was none. She burnt, she loved the tyranny,
And, all subdued, consented to the hour
When to the bridal he shall lead his paramour.
Whispering in midnight silence, said the youth,
'Sure some sweet name thou hast, though, by my truth,
I have not ask'd it, ever thinking thee

Not mortal, but of heavenly progeny,
As still I do. Hast any mortal name,
Fit appellation for this dazzling frame?
Or friends or kinsfolk on the citied earth,   90
To share our marriage feast and nuptial mirth?'
'I have no friends,' said Lamia, 'no, not one;
My presence in wide Corinth hardly known.
My parents' bones are in their dusty urns
Sepulchred, where no kindled incense burns,
Seeing all their luckless race are dead save me,
And I neglect the holy rite for thee.
Even as you list invite your many guests;
But if, as now it seems, your vision rests
With any pleasure on me, do not bid   100
Old Apollonius – from him keep me hid.'
Lycius, perplex'd at words so blind and blank,
Made close inquiry; from whose touch she shrank,
Feigning a sleep; and he to the dull shade
Of deep sleep in a moment was betray'd.

   It was the custom then to bring away
The bride from home at blushing shut of day,
Veil'd, in a chariot, heralded along
By strewn flowers, torches, and a marriage song,
With other pageants: but this fair unknown   110
Had not a friend. So being left alone
(Lycius was gone to summon all his kin),
And knowing surely she could never win
His foolish heart from its mad pompousness,
She set herself, high-thoughted, how to dress
The misery in fit magnificence.
She did so, but 'tis doubtful how and whence
Came and who were her subtle servitors.
About the halls, and to and from the doors,
There was a noise of wings, till in short space   120
The glowing banquet-room shone with wide-archèd grace;

A haunting music, sole perhaps and lone
Supportress of the faery-roof, made moan
Throughout, as fearful the whole charm might fade,
Fresh carvèd cedar, mimicking a glade
Of palm and plantain, met from either side,
High in the midst, in honour of the bride:
Two palms and then two plantains, and so on,
From either side their stems branch'd one to one
All down the aislèd place; and beneath all   130
There ran a stream of lamps straight on from wall to wall.
So canopied, lay an untasted feast
Teeming with odours. Lamia, regal drest,
Silently paced about, and as she went,
In pale contented sort of discontent,
Mission'd her viewless servants to enrich
The fretted splendour of each nook and niche,
Between the tree-stems, marbled plain at first,
Came jasper panels; then anon there burst
Forth creeping imagery of slighter trees,   140
And with the larger wove in small intricacies.
Approving all, she faded at self-will,
And shut the chamber up, close, hush'd and still,
Complete and ready for the revels rude,
When dreadful guests would come to spoil her solitude.

    The day appear'd, and all the gossip rout.
O senseless Lycius! Madman! wherefore flout
The silent-blessing fate, warm cloister'd hours,
And show to common eyes these secret bowers?
The herd approach'd; each guest, with busy brain,   150
Arriving at the portal, gazed amain,
And enter'd marvelling: for they knew the street,
Remember'd it from childhood all complete
Without a gap, yet ne'er before had seen
That royal porch, that high-built fair demesne;
So in they hurried all, mazed, curious and keen;

Save one, who look'd thereon with eye severe,
And with calm-planted steps walk'd in austere;
'Twas Apollonius: something too he laugh'd,
As though some knotty problem, that had daft   160
His patient thought, had now begun to thaw
And solve and melt: 'twas just as he foresaw.

    He met within the murmurous vestibule
His young disciple. ' 'Tis no common rule,
Lycius,' said he, 'for uninvited guest
To force himself upon you, and infest
With an unbidden presence the bright throng
Of younger friends; yet must I do this wrong,
And you forgive me.' Lycius blush'd, and led
The old man through the inner doors broad-spread;   170
With reconciling words and courteous mien
Turning into sweet milk the sophist's spleen.

    Of wealthy lustre was the banquet-room,
Fill'd with pervading brilliance and perfume:
Before each lucid panel fuming stood
A censer fed with myrrh and spicèd wood,
Each by a sacred tripod held aloft,
Whose slender feet wide-swerved upon the soft
Wool-woofèd carpets: fifty wreaths of smoke
From fifty censers their light voyage took   180
To the high roof, still mimick'd as they rose
Along the mirror'd walls by twin-clouds odorous.
Twelve spherèd tables, by silk seats insphered,
High as the level of a man's breast rear'd
On libbard's paws, upheld the heavy gold
Of cups and goblets, and the store thrice told
Of Ceres' horn, and, in huge vessels, wine
Came from the gloomy tun with merry shine.
Thus loaded with a feast the tables stood,
Each shrining in the midst the image of a God.   190

When in an antechamber every guest
Had felt the cold full sponge to pleasure press'd
By minist'ring slaves upon his hands and feet,
And fragrant oils with ceremony meet
Pour'd on his hair, they all moved to the feast
In white robes, and themselves in order placed
Around the silken couches, wondering
Whence all this mighty cost and blaze of wealth could spring.

Soft went the music the soft air along,
While fluent Greek a vowel'd under-song   200
Kept up among the guests, discoursing low
At first, for scarcely was the wine at flow;
But when the happy vintage touch'd their brains,
Louder they talk, and louder come the strains
Of powerful instruments: – the gorgeous dyes,
The space, the splendour of the draperies,
The roof of awful richness, nectarous cheer,
Beautiful slaves, and Lamia's self, appear.
Now, when the wine has done its rosy deed
And every soul from human trammels freed,   210
No more so strange; for merry wine, sweet wine,
Will make Elysian shades not too fair, too divine.
Soon was God Bacchus at meridian height;
Flush'd were their cheeks, and bright eyes double bright;
Garlands of every green and every scent
From vales deflower'd or forest-trees branch-rent,
In baskets of bright osier'd gold were brought,
High as the handles heap'd, to suit the thought
Of every guest; that each, as he did please,
Might fancy-fit his brows, silk-pillow'd at his ease.   220

What wreath for Lamia? What for Lycius?
What for the sage, old Apollonius?
Upon her aching forehead be there hung
The leaves of willow and of adder's tongue;

And for the youth, quick, let us strip for him
The thyrsus, that his watching eyes may swim
Into forgetfulness; and, for the sage,
Let spear-grass and the spiteful thistle wage
War on his temples. Do not all charms fly
At the mere touch of cold philosophy?   230
There was an awful rainbow once in heaven:
We know her woof, her texture; she is given
In the dull catalogue of common things.
Philosophy will clip an Angel's wings,
Conquer all mysteries by rule and line,
Empty the haunted air and gnomed mine –
Unweave a rainbow, as it erewhile made
The tender-person'd Lamia melt into a shade.

    By her glad Lycius sitting, in chief place,
Scarce saw in all the room another face,   240
Till, checking his love trance, a cup he took
Full brimm'd, and opposite sent forth a look
'Cross the broad table, to beseech a glance
From his old teacher's wrinkled countenance,
And pledge him. The bald-head philosopher
Had fix'd his eye, without a twinkle or a stir,
Full on the alarmèd beauty of the bride,
Brow-beating her fair form and troubling her sweet pride.
Lycius then press'd her hand, with devout touch,
As pale it lay upon the rosy couch: 250
'Twas icy, and the cold ran through his veins;
Then sudden it grew hot, and all the pains
Of an unnatural heat shot to his heart.
'Lamia, what means this? Wherefore dost thou start?
Know'st thou that man?' Poor Lamia answer'd not.
He gazed into her eyes, and not a jot
Own'd they the lovelorn piteous appeal:
More, more he gazed: his human senses reel:
Some hungry spell that loveliness absorbs;

There was no recognition in those orbs.   260
'Lamia!' he cried – and no soft-toned reply.
The many heard, and the loud revelry
Grew hush; the stately music no more breathes;
The myrtle sicken'd in a thousand wreaths.
By faint degrees, voice, lute, and pleasure ceased;
A deadly silence step by step increased
Until it seem'd a horrid presence there,
And not a man but felt the terror in his hair.
'Lamia!' he shriek'd; and nothing but the shriek
With its sad echo did the silence break.   270
'Begone, foul dream!' he cried, gazing again
In the bride's face, where now no azure vein
Wander'd on fair-spaced temples, no soft bloom
Misted the cheek, no passion to illume
The deep-recessèd vision: – all was blight:
Lamia, no longer fair, there sat, a deadly white.
'Shut, shut those juggling eyes, thou ruthless man!
Turn them aside, wretch! or the righteous ban
Of all the Gods, whose dreadful images
Here represent their shadowy presences,   280
May pierce them on the sudden with the thorn
Of painful blindness; leaving thee forlorn,
In trembling dotage to the feeblest fright
Of conscience, for their long-offended might,
For all thine impious proud-heart sophistries,
Unlawful magic, and enticing lies.
Corinthians! look upon that grey-beard wretch!
Mark how, possess'd, his lashless eyelids stretch
Around his demon eyes! Corinthians, see!
My sweet bride withers at their potency.'   290
'Fool!' said the sophist, in an under-tone
Gruff with contempt; which a death-nighing moan
From Lycius answer'd, as, heart-struck and lost,
He sank supine beside the aching ghost.
'Fool! Fool!' repeated he, while his eyes still

Relented not, nor moved: 'from every ill
Of life have I preserved thee to this day,
And shall I see thee made a serpent's prey?'
Then Lamia breathed death-breath; the sophist's eye,
Like a sharp spear, went through her utterly,   300
Keen, cruel, perceant, stinging: she, as well
As her weak hand could any meaning tell,
Motion'd him to be silent; vainly so;
He look'd and look'd again a level – No!
'A serpent!' echoed he. No sooner said,
Than with a frightful scream she vanishèd;
And Lycius' arms were empty of delight,
As were his limbs of life, from that same night.
On the high couch he lay – his friends came round –
Supported him; no pulse or breath they found,   310
And in its marriage robe the heavy body wound.

Isabella; or, The Pot of Basil

A Story from Boccaccio

FAIR Isabel, poor simple Isabel!
    Lorenzo, a young palmer in Love's eye!
They could not in the self-same mansion dwell
    Without some stir of heart, some malady;
They could not sit at meals but feel how well
    It soothèd each to be the other by;
They could not, sure, beneath the same roof sleep,
But to each other dream, and nightly weep.

With every morn their love grew tenderer,
    With every eve deeper and tenderer still;   10
He might not in house, field, or garden stir,
    But her full shape would all his seeing fill;
And his continual voice was pleasanter
    To her, than noise of trees or hidden rill;
Her lute-string gave an echo of his name,
She spoilt her half-done broidery with the same.

He knew whose gentle hand was at the latch,
    Before the door had given her to his eyes;
And from her chamber-window he would catch
    Her beauty farther than the falcon spies;   20
And constant as her vespers would he watch,
    Because her face was turn'd to the same skies;
And with sick longing all the night outwear,
To hear her morning step upon the stair.

A whole long month of May in this sad plight
    Made their cheeks paler by the break of June:

'To-morrow will I bow to my delight,
　　To-morrow will I ask my lady's boon.' –
'O may I never see another night,
　　Lorenzo, if thy lips breathe not love's tune.' –　　　　30
So spake they to their pillows; but, alas,
Honeyless days and days did he let pass;

Until sweet Isabella's untouch'd cheek
　　Fell sick within the rose's just domain,
Fell thin as a young mother's, who doth seek
　　By every lull to cool her infant's pain:
'How ill she is!' said he, 'I may not speak
　　And yet I will, and tell my love all plain:
If looks speak love-laws, I will drink her tears,
And at the least 'twill startle off her cares.'　　　　40

So said he one fair morning, and all day
　　His heart beat awfully against his side;
And to his heart he inwardly did pray
　　For power to speak; but still the ruddy tide
Stifled his voice, and pulsed resolve away –
　　Fever'd his high conceit of such a bride,
Yet brought him to the meekness of a child:
Alas! when passion is both meek and wild!

So once more he had waked and anguishèd
　　A dreary night of love and misery,　　　　50
If Isabel's quick eye had not been wed
　　To every symbol on his forehead high;
She saw it waxing very pale and dead,
　　And straight all flush'd; so, lispèd tenderly,
'Lorenzo!' – here she ceased her timid quest,
But in her tone and look he read the rest.

'O Isabella! I can half perceive
　　That I may speak my grief into thine ear;

If thou didst ever anything believe,
    Believe how I love thee, believe how near   60
My soul is to its doom: I would not grieve
    Thy hand by unwelcome pressing, would not fear
Thine eyes by gazing; but I cannot live
Another night, and not my passion shrive.

'Love: thou art leading me from wintry cold,
    Lady! thou leadest me to summer clime,
And I must taste the blossoms that unfold
    In its ripe warmth this gracious morning time.'
So said, his erewhile timid lips grew bold,
    And poesied with hers in dewy rhyme: 70
Great bliss was with them, and great happiness
Grew, like a lusty flower in June's caress.

Parting they seem'd to tread upon the air,
    Twin roses by the zephyr blown apart
Only to meet again more close, and share
    The inward fragrance of each other's heart.
She, to her chamber gone, a ditty fair
    Sang, of delicious love and honey'd dart;
He with light steps went up a western hill,
And bade the sun farewell, and joy'd his fill.   80

All close they met again, before the dusk
    Had taken from the stars its pleasant veil,
All close they met, all eves, before the dusk
    Had taken from the stars its pleasant veil,
Close in a bower of hyacinth and musk,
    Unknown of any, free from whispering tale.
Ah! better had it been for ever so,
Than idle ears should pleasure in their woe.

Were they unhappy then? – It cannot be –
    Too many tears for lovers have been shed,   90

Too many sighs give we to them in fee,
   Too much of pity after they are dead,
Too many doleful stories do we see,
   Whose matter in bright gold were best be read;
Except in such a page where Theseus' spouse
Over the pathless waves towards him bows.

But for the general award of love,
   The little sweet doth kill much bitterness;
Though Dido silent is in under-grove,
   And Isabella's was a great distress,   100
Though young Lorenzo in warm Indian clove
   Was not embalm'd, this truth is not the less –
Even bees, the little almsmen of spring-bowers,
Know there is richest juice in poison-flowers.

With her two brothers this fair lady dwelt,
   Enrichèd from ancestral merchandise,
And for them many a weary hand did swelt
   In torchèd mines and noisy factories,
And many once proud-quiver'd loins did melt
   In blood from stinging whip; with hollow eyes   110
Many all day in dazzling river stood,
To take the rich-ored driftings of the flood.

For them the Ceylon diver held his breath,
   And went all naked to the hungry shark;
For them his ears gush'd blood; for them in death
   The seal on the cold ice with piteous bark
Lay full of darts; for them alone did seethe
   A thousand men in troubles wide and dark:
Half-ignorant, they turn'd an easy wheel,
That set sharp racks at work, to pinch and peel.   120

Why were they proud? Because their marble founts
   Gush'd with more pride than do a wretch's tears?

Why were they proud? Because fair orange-mounts
    Were of more soft ascent than lazar stairs!
Why were they proud? Because red-lined accounts
    Were richer than the songs of Grecian years?
Why were they proud? again we ask aloud,
Why in the name of Glory were they proud?

Yet were these Florentines as self-retired
    In hungry pride and gainful cowardice,   130
As two close Hebrews in that land inspired,
    Paled in and vineyarded from beggar-spies;
The hawks of ship-mast forests – the untired
    And pannier'd mules for ducats and old lies –
Quick cat's-paws on the generous stray-away, –
Great wits in Spanish, Tuscan, and Malay.

How was it these same ledger-men could spy
    Fair Isabella in her downy nest?
How could they find out in Lorenzo's eye
    A straying from his toil? Hot Egypt's pest   140
Into their vision covetous and sly!
    How could these money-bags see east and west?
Yet so they did – and every dealer fair
Must see behind, as doth the hunted hare.

O eloquent and famed Boccaccio!
    Of thee we now should ask forgiving boon,
And of thy spicy myrtles as they blow,
    And of thy roses amorous of the moon,
And of thy lilies, that do paler grow
    Now they can no more hear thy ghittern's tune,   150
For venturing syllables that ill beseem
The quiet glooms of such a piteous theme.

Grant thou a pardon here, and then the tale
    Shall move on soberly, as it is meet;

There is no other crime, no mad assail
    To make old prose in modern rhyme more sweet;
But it is done – succeed the verse or fail –
    To honour thee, and thy gone spirit greet;
To stead thee as a verse in English tongue,
An echo of thee in the north-wind sung.   160

These brethren having found by many signs
    What love Lorenzo for their sister had,
And how she loved him too, each unconfines
    His bitter thoughts to other, well-nigh mad
That he, the servant of their trade designs,
    Should in their sister's love be blithe and glad,
When 'twas their plan to coax her by degrees
To some high noble and his olive-trees.

And many a jealous conference had they,
    And many times they bit their lips alone,   170
Before they fix'd upon a surest way
    To make the youngster for his crime atone;
And at the last, these men of cruel clay
    Cut Mercy with a sharp knife to the bone;
For they resolvèd in some forest dim
To kill Lorenzo, and there bury him.

So, on a pleasant morning, as he leant
    Into the sun-rise, o'er the balustrade
Of the garden-terrace, towards him they bent
    Their footing through the dews; and to him said,   180
'You seem there in the quiet of content,
    Lorenzo, and we are most loth to invade
Calm speculation; but if you are wise,
Bestride your steed while cold is in the skies.

'To-day we purpose, ay, this hour we mount
    To spur three leagues towards the Apennine;

Come down, we pray thee, ere the hot sun count
   His dewy rosary on the eglantine.'
Lorenzo, courteously as he was wont,
   Bow'd a fair greeting to these serpents' whine,   190
And went in haste, to get in readiness,
With belt, and spur, and bracing huntsman's dress.

And as he to the court-yard pass'd along,
   Each third step did he pause, and listen'd oft
If he could hear his lady's matin-song,
   Or the light whisper of her footstep soft;
And as he thus over his passion hung,
   He heard a laugh full musical aloft;
When, looking up, he saw her features bright
Smile through an in-door lattice, all delight.   200

'Love, Isabel!' said he, 'I was in pain
   Lest I should miss to bid thee a good morrow:
Ah! what if I should lose thee, when so fain
   I am to stifle all the heavy sorrow
Of a poor three hours' absence? but we'll gain
   Out of the amorous dark what day doth borrow.
Good bye! I'll soon be back.' – 'Good bye!' said she:
And as he went she chanted merrily.

So the two brothers and their murder'd man
   Rode past fair Florence, to where Arno's stream   210
Gurgles through straiten'd banks, and still doth fan
   Itself with dancing bulrush, and the bream
Keeps head against the freshets. Sick and wan
   The brothers' faces in the ford did seem,
Lorenzo's flush with love. – They pass'd the water
Into a forest quiet for the slaughter.

There was Lorenzo slain and buried in,
   There in that forest did his great love cease;

Ah! when a soul doth thus its freedom win,
 It aches in loneliness – is ill at peace   220
As the break-covert blood-hounds of such sin:
 They dipp'd their swords in the water, and did tease
Their horses homeward, with convulsèd spur,
Each richer by his being a murderer.

They told their sister how, with sudden speed,
 Lorenzo had ta'en ship for foreign lands,
Because of some great urgency and need
 In their affairs, requiring trusty hands.
Poor girl! put on thy stifling widow's weed,
 And 'scape at once from Hope's accursèd bands;   230
To-day thou wilt not see him, nor to-morrow,
And the next day will be a day of sorrow.

She weeps alone for pleasures not to be;
 Sorely she wept until the night came on,
And then, instead of love, O misery!
 She brooded o'er the luxury alone:
His image in the dusk she seem'd to see,
 And to the silence made a gentle moan,
Spreading her perfect arms upon the air,
And on her couch low murmuring, 'Where?
    O where?'   240

But Selfishness, Love's cousin, held not long
 Its fiery vigil in her single breast;
She fretted for the golden hour, and hung
 Upon the time with feverish unrest –
Not long; for soon into her heart a throng
 Of higher occupants, a richer zest,
Came tragic; passion not to be subdued,
And sorrow for her love in travels rude.

In the mid days of autumn, on their eves
 The breath of Winter comes from far away,   250

And the sick west continually bereaves
 Of some gold tinge, and plays a roundelay
Of death among the bushes and the leaves,
 To make all bare before he dares to stray
From his north cavern. So sweet Isabel
By gradual decay from beauty fell,

Because Lorenzo came not. Oftentimes
 She ask'd her brothers, with an eye all pale
Striving to be itself, what dungeon climes
 Could keep him off so long? They spake a tale 260
Time after time, to quiet her. Their crimes
 Came on them, like a smoke from Hinnom's vale;
And every night in dreams they groan'd aloud,
To see their sister in her snowy shroud.

And she had died in drowsy ignorance,
 But for a thing more deadly dark than all;
It came like a fierce potion, drunk by chance,
 Which saves a sick man from the feather'd pall
For some few gasping moments; like a lance,
 Waking an Indian from his cloudy hall 270
With cruel pierce, and bringing him again
Sense of the gnawing fire at heart and brain.

It was a vision. In the drowsy gloom,
 The dull of midnight, at her couch's foot
Lorenzo stood, and wept: the forest tomb
 Had marr'd his glossy hair which once could shoot
Lustre into the sun, and put cold doom
 Upon his lips, and taken the soft lute
From his lorn voice, and past his loamèd ears
Had made a miry channel for his tears. 280

Strange sound it was, when the pale shadow spake,
 For there was striving, in its piteous tongue,

To speak as when on earth it was awake,
   And Isabella on its music hung:
Languor there was in it, and tremulous shake,
   As in a palsied Druid's harp unstrung;
And through it moan'd a ghostly under-song,
Like hoarse night-gusts sepulchral brièrs among.

Its eyes, though wild, were still all dewy bright
   With love, and kept all phantom fear aloof   290
From the poor girl by magic of their light,
   The while it did unthread the horrid woof
Of the late darken'd time – the murderous spite
   Of pride and avarice – the dark pine roof
In the forest – and the sodden turfèd dell,
Where, without any word, from stabs he fell.

Saying moreover, 'Isabel, my sweet!
   Red whortle-berries droop above my head,
And a large flint-stone weighs upon my feet;
   Around me beeches and high chestnuts shed   300
Their leaves and prickly nuts; a sheep-fold bleat
   Comes from beyond the river to my bed:
Go, shed one tear upon my heather-bloom,
And it shall comfort me within the tomb.

'I am a shadow now, alas! alas!
   Upon the skirts of human nature dwelling
Alone: I chant alone the holy mass,
   While little sounds of life are round my knelling,
And glossy bees at noon do fieldward pass,
   And many a chapel bell the hour is telling,   310
Paining me through: those sounds grow strange to me,
And thou art distant in Humanity.

'I know what was, I feel full well what is,
   And I should rage, if spirits could go mad;

Though I forget the taste of earthly bliss,
    That paleness warms my grave, as though I had
A seraph chosen from the bright abyss
    To be my spouse; thy paleness makes me glad;
Thy beauty grows upon me, and I feel
A greater love through all my essence steal.'   320

The Spirit mourn'd 'Adieu!' – dissolved, and left
    The atom darkness in a slow turmoil;
As when of healthful midnight sleep bereft,
    Thinking on rugged hours and fruitless toil,
We put our eyes into a pillowy cleft,
    And see the spangly gloom froth up and boil:
It made sad Isabella's eyelids ache,
And in the dawn she started up awake;

'Ha! ha!' said she, 'I knew not this hard life,
    I thought the worst was simple misery;   330
I thought some Fate with pleasure or with strife
    Portion'd us – happy days, or else to die;
But there is crime – a brother's bloody knife!
    Sweet Spirit, thou hast school'd my infancy:
I'll visit thee for this, and kiss thine eyes,
And greet thee morn and even in the skies.'

When the full morning came, she had devised
    How she might secret to the forest hie;
How she might find the clay, so dearly prized,
    And sing to it one latest lullaby;   340
How her short absence might be unsurmised,
    While she the inmost of the dream would try.
Resolved, she took with her an aged nurse,
And went into that dismal forest-hearse.

See, as they creep along the river side,
    How she doth whisper to that aged dame,

And, after looking round the champaign wide,
    Shows her a knife. – 'What feverous hectic flame
Burns in thee, child? – what good can thee betide
    That thou shouldst smile again?' – The evening
        came,   350
And they had found Lorenzo's earthy bed;
The flint was there, the berries at his head.

Who hath not loiter'd in a green church-yard,
    And let his spirit, like a demon mole,
Work through the clayey soil and gravel hard,
    To see skull, coffin'd bones, and funeral stole;
Pitying each form that hungry Death had marr'd,
    And filling it once more with human soul?
Ah! this is holiday to what was felt
When Isabella by Lorenzo knelt.   360

She gazed into the fresh-thrown mould, as though
    One glance did fully all its secrets tell;
Clearly she saw, as other eyes would know
    Pale limbs at bottom of a crystal well;
Upon the murderous spot she seem'd to grow,
    Like to a native lily of the dell:
Then with her knife, all sudden, she began
To dig more fervently than misers can.

Soon she turn'd up a soilèd glove, whereon
    Her silk had play'd in purple phantasies;   370
She kiss'd it with a lip more chill than stone,
    And put it in her bosom, where it dries
And freezes utterly unto the bone
    Those dainties made to still an infant's cries:
Then 'gan she work again; nor stay'd her care,
But to throw back at times her veiling hair.

That old nurse stood beside her wondering,
    Until her heart felt pity to the core

At sight of such a dismal labouring,
    And so she kneelèd, with her locks all hoar,   **380**
And put her lean hands to the horrid thing:
    Three hours they labour'd at this travail sore;
At last they felt the kernel of the grave,
And Isabella did not stamp and rave.

Ah! wherefore all this wormy circumstance?
    Why linger at the yawning tomb so long?
O for the gentleness of old Romance,
    The simple plaining of a minstrel's song!
Fair reader, at the old tale take a glance,
    For here, in truth, it doth not well belong   **390**
To speak: – O turn thee to the very tale,
And taste the music of that vision pale.

With duller steel than the Persèan sword
    They cut away no formless monster's head,
But one, whose gentleness did well accord
    With death, as life. The ancient harps have said,
Love never dies, but lives, immortal Lord:
    If Love impersonate was ever dead,
Pale Isabella kiss'd it, and low moan'd.
'Twas love; cold, – dead indeed, but not dethroned.   **400**

In anxious secrecy they took it home,
    And then the prize was all for Isabel:
She calm'd its wild hair with a golden comb
    And all around each eye's sepulchral cell
Pointed each fringèd lash; the smearèd loam
    With tears, as chilly as a dripping well,
She drench'd away: and still she comb'd, and kept
Sighing all day – and still she kiss'd, and wept.

Then in a silken scarf – sweet with the dews
    Of precious flowers pluck'd in Araby,   **410**

And divine liquids come with odorous ooze
    Through the cold serpent-pipe refreshfully, –
She wrapp'd it up; and for its tomb did choose
    A garden-pot, wherein she laid it by,
And cover'd it with mould, and o'er it set
Sweet Basil, which her tears kept ever wet.

And she forgot the stars, the moon, and sun,
    And she forgot the blue above the trees,
And she forgot the dells where waters run,
    And she forgot the chilly autumn breeze;   **420**
She had no knowledge when the day was done,
    And the new morn she saw not: but in peace
Hung over her sweet Basil evermore,
And moisten'd it with tears unto the core.

And so she ever fed it with thin tears,
    Whence thick, and green, and beautiful it grew,
So that it smelt more balmy than its peers
    Of Basil-tufts in Florence; for it drew
Nurture besides, and life, from human fears,
    From the fast mouldering head there shut from
        view;   **430**
So that the jewel, safely casketed,
Came forth, and in perfumèd leafits spread.

O Melancholy, linger here awhile!
    O Music, Music, breathe despondingly!
O Echo, Echo, from some sombre isle,
    Unknown, Lethean, sigh to us – O sigh!
Spirits in grief, lift up your heads, and smile;
    Lift up your heads, sweet Spirits, heavily,
And make a pale light in your cypress glooms,
Tinting with silver wan your marble tombs.   **440**

Moan hither, all ye syllables of woe,
    From the deep throat of sad Melpomene!

Through bronzèd lyre in tragic order go,
    And touch the strings into a mystery;
Sound mournfully upon the winds and low;
    For simple Isabel is soon to be
Among the dead: She withers, like a palm
Cut by an Indian for its juicy balm.

O leave the palm to wither by itself,
    Let not quick Winter chill its dying hour! –   450
It may not be – those Baälites of pelf,
    Her brethren, noted the continual shower
From her dead eyes; and many a curious elf,
    Among her kindred, wonder'd that such dower
Of youth and beauty should be thrown aside
By one mark'd out to be a Noble's bride.

And, furthermore, her brethren wonder'd much
    Why she sat drooping by the Basil green,
And why it flourish'd, as by magic touch;
    Greatly they wonder'd what the thing might mean: 460
They could not surely give belief, that such
    A very nothing would have power to wean
Her from her own fair youth, and pleasures gay,
And even remembrance of her love's delay.

Therefore they watch'd a time when they might sift
    This hidden whim; and long they watch'd in vain;
For seldom did she go to chapel-shrift,
    And seldom felt she any hunger-pain:
And when she left, she hurried back, as swift
    As bird on wing to breast its eggs again: 470
And, patient as a hen-bird, sat her there
Beside her Basil, weeping through her hair.

Yet they contrived to steal the Basil-pot,
    And to examine it in secret place:

The thing was vile with green and livid spot,
    And yet they knew it was Lorenzo's face:
The guerdon of their murder they had got,
    And so left Florence in a moment's space,
Never to turn again. – Away they went,
With blood upon their heads, to banishment.   **480**

O Melancholy, turn thine eyes away!
    O Music, Music, breathe despondingly
O Echo, Echo, on some other day,
    From isles Lethean, sigh to us – O sigh!
Spirits of grief, sing not your 'Well-a-way!'
    For Isabel, sweet Isabel, will die;
Will die a death too lone and incomplete,
Now they have ta'en away her Basil sweet.

Piteous she look'd on dead and senseless things,
    Asking for her lost Basil amorously: **490**
And with melodious chuckle in the strings
    Of her lorn voice, she oftentimes would cry
After the Pilgrim in his wanderings,
    To ask him where her Basil was; and why
'Twas hid from her: 'For cruel 'tis,' said she,
'To steal my Basil-pot away from me.'

And so she pined, and so she died forlorn,
    Imploring for her Basil to the last.
No heart was there in Florence but did mourn
    In pity of her love, so overcast.   **500**
And a sad ditty of this story borne
    From mouth to mouth through all the country pass'd:
Still is the burthen sung – 'O cruelty,
To steal my Basil-pot away from me!'

The Eve of St. Agnes

St. Agnes' Eve – Ah, bitter chill it was!
The owl, for all his feathers, was a-cold;
The hare limp'd trembling through the frozen grass,
And silent was the flock in woolly fold:
Numb were the Beadsman's fingers while he told
His rosary, and while his frosted breath,
Like pious incense from a censer old,
Seem'd taking flight for heaven, without a death,
Past the sweet Virgin's picture, while his prayer he saith.

His prayer he saith, this patient, holy man:　　10
Then takes his lamp, and riseth from his knees,
And back returneth, meagre, barefoot, wan,
Along the chapel aisle by slow degrees:
The sculptured dead, on each side, seem to freeze,
Emprison'd in black, purgatorial rails:
Knights, ladies, praying in dumb orat'ries,
He passeth by, and his weak spirit fails
To think how they may ache in icy hoods and mails.

Northward he turneth through a little door,
And scarce three steps, ere Music's golden tongue　　20
Flatter'd to tears this aged man and poor.
But no – already had his death-bell rung;
The joys of all his life were said and sung;
His was harsh penance on St. Agnes' Eve:
Another way he went, and soon among
Rough ashes sat he for his soul's reprieve,
And all night kept awake, for sinners' sake to grieve.

That ancient Beadsman heard the prelude soft;
And so it chanced, for many a door was wide,
From hurry to and fro. Soon, up aloft,   30
The silver, snarling trumpets 'gan to chide:
The level chambers, ready with their pride,
Were glowing to receive a thousand guests:
The carvèd angels, ever eager-eyed,
Stared, where upon their heads the cornice rests,
With hair blown back, and wings put crosswise on their
       breasts.

At length burst in the argent revelry,
With plume, tiara, and all rich array,
Numerous as shadows haunting fairily
The brain new-stuff'd, in youth, with triumphs gay   40
Of old romance. These let us wish away,
And turn, sole-thoughted, to one Lady there,
Whose heart had brooded, all that wintry day,
On love, and wing'd St. Agnes' saintly care,
As she had heard old dames full many times declare.

They told her how, upon St. Agnes' Eve,
Young virgins might have visions of delight,
And soft adorings from their loves receive
Upon the honey'd middle of the night,
If ceremonies due they did aright;   50
As, supperless to bed they must retire,
And couch supine their beauties, lily white;
Nor look behind, nor sideways, but require
Of Heaven with upward eyes for all that they desire.

Full of this whim was thoughtful Madeline:
The music, yearning like a God in pain,
She scarcely heard: her maiden eyes divine,
Fix'd on the floor, saw many a sweeping train

Pass by – she heeded not at all: in vain
Came many a tiptoe, amorous cavalier, 60
And back retired; not cool'd by high disdain,
But she saw not: her heart was otherwhere;
She sigh'd for Agnes' dreams, the sweetest of the year.

She danced along with vague, regardless eyes,
Anxious her lips, her breathing quick and short:
The hallow'd hour was near at hand: she sighs
Amid the timbrels, and the throng'd resort
Of whisperers in anger, or in sport;
'Mid looks of love, defiance, hate, and scorn,
Hoodwink'd with faery fancy; all amort, 70
Save to St. Agnes and her lambs unshorn,
And all the bliss to be before to-morrow morn.

So, purposing each moment to retire,
She linger'd still. Meantime, across the moors
Had come young Porphyro, with heart on fire
For Madeline. Beside the portal doors,
Buttress'd from moonlight, stands he, and implores
All saints to give him sight of Madeline,
But for one moment in the tedious hours,
That he might gaze and worship all unseen; 80
Perchance speak, kneel, touch, kiss – in sooth such things
        have been.

He ventures in: let no buzz'd whisper tell,
All eyes be muffled, or a hundred swords
Will storm his heart, Love's feverous citadel:
For him, those chambers held barbarian hordes,
Hyena foemen, and hot-blooded lords,
Whose very dogs would execrations howl
Against his lineage; not one breast affords
Him any mercy in that mansion foul,
Save one old beldame, weak in body and in soul. 90

Ah, happy chance! the aged creature came,
Shuffling along with ivory-headed wand,
To where he stood, hid from the torch's flame,
Behind a broad hall pillar, far beyond
The sound of merriment and chorus bland.
He startled her: but soon she knew his face,
And grasp'd his fingers in her palsied hand,
    Saying, 'Mercy, Porphyro! hie thee from this place;
They are all here to-night, the whole blood-thirsty race!

'Get hence! get hence! there's dwarfish Hildebrand: 100
He had a fever late, and in the fit
He curs'd thee and thine, both house and land:
Then there's that old Lord Maurice, not a whit
More tame for his grey hairs – Alas me! flit!
Flit like a ghost away.' – 'Ah, Gossip dear,
We're safe enough; here in this arm-chair sit,
    And tell me how' – 'Good Saints! not here, not here;
Follow me, child, or else these stones will be thy bier.'

He follow'd through a lowly archèd way,
Brushing the cobwebs with his lofty plume;   110
And as she mutter'd 'Well-a – well-a-day!'
He found him in a little moonlight room,
Pale, latticed, chill, and silent as a tomb.
'Now tell me where is Madeline,' said he,
'O tell me, Angela, by the holy loom
    Which none but secret sisterhood may see,
When they St. Agnes' wool are weaving piously.'

'St. Agnes! Ah! it is St. Agnes' Eve –
Yet men will murder upon holy days.
Thou must hold water in a witch's sieve,   120
And be liege-lord of all the Elves and Fays
To venture so: it fills me with amaze
To see thee, Porphyro! – St. Agnes' Eve!

God's help! my lady fair the conjurer plays
   This very night: good angels her deceive!
But let me laugh awhile, I've mickle time to grieve.'

   Feebly she laugheth in the languid moon,
   While Porphyro upon her face doth look,
   Like puzzled urchin on an aged crone
   Who keepeth closed a wondrous riddle-book,   130
   As spectacled she sits in chimney nook.
   But soon his eyes grew brilliant, when she told
   His lady's purpose; and he scarce could brook
   Tears, at the thought of those enchantments cold,
And Madeline asleep in lap of legends old.

   Sudden a thought came like a full-blown rose,
   Flushing his brow, and in his painèd heart
   Made purple riot: then doth he propose
   A stratagem, that makes the beldame start:
   'A cruel man and impious thou art!   140
   Sweet lady! let her pray, and sleep, and dream
   Alone with her good angels, far apart
   From wicked men like thee. Go, go! – I deem
Thou canst not surely be the same that thou didst seem.'

   'I will not harm her, by all saints I swear!'
   Quoth Porphyro: 'O may I ne'er find grace
   When my weak voice shall whisper its last prayer,
   If one of her soft ringlets I displace,
   Or look with ruffian passion in her face.
   Good Angela, believe me, by these tears;   150
   Or I will, even in a moment's space,
   Awake, with horrid shout, my foemen's ears,
And beard them, though they be more fang'd than wolves
          and bears.'

'Ah! why wilt thou affright a feeble soul?
A poor, weak, palsy-stricken, churchyard thing,
Whose passing-bell may ere the midnight toll;
Whose prayers for thee, each morn and evening,
Were never miss'd.' Thus plaining, doth she bring
A gentler speech from burning Porphyro;
So woeful, and of such deep sorrowing,   160
   That Angela gives promise she will do
Whatever he shall wish, betide her weal or woe.

Which was, to lead him, in close secrecy,
Even to Madeline's chamber, and there hide
Him in a closet, of such privacy
That he might see her beauty unespied,
And win perhaps that night a peerless bride,
While legion'd fairies paced the coverlet,
And pale enchantment held her sleepy-eyed.
   Never on such a night have lovers met,   170
Since Merlin paid his Demon all the monstrous debt.

'It shall be as thou wishest,' said the Dame:
'All cates and dainties shall be storèd there
Quickly on this feast-night: by the tambour frame
Her own lute thou wilt see: no time to spare,
For I am slow and feeble, and scarce dare
On such a catering trust my dizzy head.
Wait here, my child, with patience; kneel in prayer
   The while. Ah! thou must needs the lady wed,
Or may I never leave my grave among the dead.'   180

So saying, she hobbled off with busy fear.
The lover's endless minutes slowly pass'd;
The dame return'd, and whisper'd in his ear
To follow her; with aged eyes aghast
From fright of dim espial. Safe at last

Through many a dusky gallery, they gain
The maiden's chamber, silken, hush'd, and chaste;
Where Porphyro took covert, pleased amain.
His poor guide hurried back with agues in her brain.

Her faltering hand upon the balustrade,   190
Old Angela was feeling for the stair,
When Madeline, St. Agnes' charmèd maid,
Rose, like a mission'd spirit, unaware:
With silver taper's light, and pious care,
She turn'd, and down the aged gossip led
To a safe level matting. Now prepare,
Young Porphyro, for gazing on that bed;
She comes, she comes again, like ring-dove fray'd and fled.

Out went the taper as she hurried in;
Its little smoke, in pallid moonshine, died: 200
She closed the door, she panted, all akin
To spirits of the air, and visions wide:
No utter'd syllable, or, woe betide!
But to her heart, her heart was voluble,
Paining with eloquence her balmy side;
As though a tongueless nightingale should swell
Her throat in vain, and die, heart-stifled, in her dell.

A casement high and triple-arch'd there was,
All garlanded with carven imageries,
Of fruits and flowers, and bunches of knot-grass,   210
And diamonded with panes of quaint device,
Innumerable of stains and splendid dyes,
As are the tiger-moth's deep-damask'd wings;
And in the midst, 'mong thousand heraldries,
And twilight saints, and dim emblazonings,
A shielded scutcheon blush'd with blood of queens and kings.

Full on this casement shone the wintry moon,
And threw warm gules on Madeline's fair breast,

As down she knelt for Heaven's grace and boon;
Rose-bloom fell on her hands, together prest,   220
And on her silver cross soft amethyst,
And on her hair a glory, like a saint:
She seem'd a splendid angel, newly drest,
Save wings, for heaven: – Porphyro grew faint:
She knelt, so pure a thing, so free from mortal taint.

Anon his heart revives: her vespers done,
Of all its wreathèd pearls her hair she frees;
Unclasps her warmèd jewels one by one;
Loosens her fragrant boddice; by degrees
Her rich attire creeps rustling to her knees: 230
Half-hidden, like a mermaid in sea-weed,
Pensive awhile she dreams awake, and sees,
In fancy, fair St. Agnes in her bed,
But dares not look behind, or all the charm is fled.

Soon, trembling in her soft and chilly nest,
In sort of wakeful swoon, perplex'd she lay,
Until the poppied warmth of sleep oppress'd
Her soothèd limbs, and soul fatigued away;
Flown, like a thought, until the morrow-day;
Blissfully haven'd both from joy and pain;   240
Clasp'd like a missal where swart Paynims pray;
Blinded alike from sunshine and from rain,
As though a rose should shut, and be a bud again.

Stolen to this paradise, and so entranced,
Porphyro gazed upon her empty dress,
And listen'd to her breathing, if it chanced
To wake into a slumberous tenderness;
Which when he heard, that minute did he bless,
And breath'd himself: then from the closet crept,
Noiseless as fear in a wide wilderness,   250
And over the hush'd carpet, silent, stept,
And 'tween the curtains peep'd, where, lo! – how fast she slept!

Then by the bed-side, where the faded moon
Made a dim, silver twilight, soft he set
A table, and, half anguish'd, threw thereon
A cloth of woven crimson, gold, and jet: –
O for some drowsy Morphean amulet!
The boisterous, midnight, festive clarion,
The kettle-drum, and far-heard clarionet,
Affray his ears, though but in dying tone: –   260
The hall-door shuts again, and all the noise is gone.

And still she slept an azure-lidded sleep,
In blanchèd linen, smooth, and lavender'd,
While he from forth the closet brought a heap
Of candied apple, quince, and plum, and gourd;
With jellies soother than the creamy curd,
And lucent syrops, tinct with cinnamon;
Manna and dates, in argosy transferr'd
From Fez; and spicèd dainties, every one,
From silken Samarcand to cedar'd Lebanon.   270

These delicates he heap'd with glowing hand
On golden dishes and in baskets bright
Of wreathèd silver: sumptuous they stand
In the retired quiet of the night,
Filling the chilly room with perfume light. –
'And now, my love, my seraph fair, awake!
Thou art my heaven, and I thine eremite:
Open thine eyes, for meek St. Agnes' sake,
Or I shall drowse beside thee, so my soul doth ache.'

Thus whispering, his warm, unnervèd arm   280
Sank in her pillow. Shaded was her dream
By the dusk curtains: – 'twas a midnight charm
Impossible to melt as icèd stream:
The lustrous salvers in the moonlight gleam;
Broad golden fringe upon the carpet lies:

It seem'd he never, never could redeem
From such a stedfast spell his lady's eyes;
So mused awhile, entoil'd in woofèd phantasies.

Awakening up, he took her hollow lute, –
Tumultuous, – and, in chords that tenderest be,   290
He play'd an ancient ditty, long since mute,
In Provence call'd 'La belle dame sans mercy':
Close to her ear touching the melody; –
Wherewith disturb'd, she utter'd a soft moan:
He ceased – she panted quick – and suddenly
Her blue affrayèd eyes wide open shone:
Upon his knees he sank, pale as smooth-sculptured stone.

Her eyes were open, but she still beheld,
Now wide awake, the vision of her sleep:
There was a painful change, that nigh expell'd   300
The blisses of her dream so pure and deep.
At which fair Madeline began to weep,
And moan forth witless words with many a sigh,
While still her gaze on Porphyro would keep;
Who knelt, with joinèd hands and piteous eye,
Fearing to move or speak, she look'd so dreamingly.

'Ah, Porphyro!' said she, 'but even now
Thy voice was at sweet tremble in mine ear,
Made tunable with every sweetest vow;
And those sad eyes were spiritual and clear: 310
How changed thou art! how pallid, chill, and drear!
Give me that voice again, my Porphyro,
Those looks immortal, those complainings dear!
O leave me not in this eternal woe,
For if thou diest, my Love, I know not where to go.'

Beyond a mortal man impassion'd far
At these voluptuous accents, he arose,

Ethereal, flush'd, and like a throbbing star
Seen 'mid the sapphire heaven's deep repose;
Into her dream he melted, as the rose   320
Blendeth its odour with the violet, –
Solution sweet: meantime the frost-wind blows
Like Love's alarum pattering the sharp sleet
Against the window-panes; St. Agnes' moon hath set.

'Tis dark: quick pattereth the flaw-blown sleet,
'This is no dream, my bride, my Madeline!'
'Tis dark: the icèd gusts still rave and beat:
'No dream, alas! alas! and woe is mine!
Porphyro will leave me here to fade and pine.
Cruel! what traitor could thee hither bring?   330
I curse not, for my heart is lost in thine,
Though thou forsakest a deceivèd thing; –
A dove forlorn and lost with sick unprunèd wing.'

'My Madeline! sweet dreamer! lovely bride!
Say, may I be for aye thy vassal blest?
Thy beauty's shield, heart-shaped and vermeil-dyed?
Ah, silver shrine, here will I take my rest
After so many hours of toil and quest,
A famish'd pilgrim, – saved by miracle.
Though I have found, I will not rob thy nest,   340
Saving of thy sweet self; if thou think'st well
To trust, fair Madeline, to no rude infidel.

'Hark! 'tis an elfin storm from faery land,
Of haggard seeming, but a boon indeed:
Arise – arise! the morning is at hand; –
The bloated wassailers will never heed: –
Let us away, my love, with happy speed;
There are no ears to hear, or eyes to see, –
Drown'd all in Rhenish and the sleepy mead.

Awake! arise! my love, and fearless be,   350
For o'er the southern moors I have a home for thee.'

She hurried at his words, beset with fears,
For there were sleeping dragons all around,
At glaring watch, perhaps, with ready spears.
Down the wide stairs a darkling way they found;
In all the house was heard no human sound.
A chain-droop'd lamp was flickering by each door;
The arras, rich with horsemen, hawk, and hound,
Flutter'd in the besieging wind's uproar;
And the long carpets rose along the gusty floor.   360

They glide, like phantoms, into the wide hall;
Like phantoms to the iron porch they glide,
Where lay the Porter, in uneasy sprawl,
With a huge empty flagon by his side:
The wakeful bloodhound rose, and shook his hide,
But his sagacious eye an inmate owns:
By one, and one, the bolts full easy slide: –
The chains lie silent on the footworn stones;
The key turns, and the door upon its hinges groans.

And they are gone: ay, ages long ago   370
These lovers fled away into the storm.
That night the Baron dreamt of many a woe,
And all his warrior-guests with shade and form
Of witch, and demon, and large coffin-worm,
Were long be-nightmared. Angela the old
Died palsy-twitch'd, with meagre face deform;
The Beadsman, after thousand aves told,
For aye unsought-for slept among his ashes cold.

Ode to a Nightingale

My heart aches, and a drowsy numbness pains
    My sense, as though of hemlock I had drunk,
Or emptied some dull opiate to the drains
    One minute past, and Lethe-wards had sunk:
'Tis not through envy of thy happy lot,
    But being too happy in thy happiness, –
        That thou, light-wingèd Dryad of the trees,
          In some melodious plot
    Of beechen green, and shadows numberless,
        Singest of summer in full-throated ease.   10

O for a draught of vintage, that hath been
    Cool'd a long age in the deep-delvèd earth,
Tasting of Flora and the country green,
    Dance, and Provençal song, and sunburnt mirth!
O for a beaker full of the warm South,
    Full of the true, the blushful Hippocrene,
        With beaded bubbles winking at the brim,
          And purple-stainèd mouth;
    That I might drink and leave the world unseen,
And with thee fade away into the forest dim: 20

Fade far away, dissolve, and quite forget
    What thou among the leaves hast never known,
The weariness, the fever, and the fret
    Here, where men sit and hear each other groan;
Where palsy shakes a few, sad, last grey hairs,
    Where youth grows pale, and spectre-thin, and dies;
        Where but to think is to be full of sorrow
          And leaden-eyed despairs;
    Where Beauty cannot keep her lustrous eyes,
Or new Love pine at them beyond to-morrow.   30

Away! away! for I will fly to thee,
    Not charioted by Bacchus and his pards,

But on the viewless wings of Poesy,
   Though the dull brain perplexes and retards:
Already with thee! tender is the night,
    And haply the Queen-Moon is on her throne,
      Cluster'd around by all her starry Fays;
        But here there is no light,
    Save what from heaven is with the breezes blown
Through verdurous glooms and winding mossy
         ways.   **40**

I cannot see what flowers are at my feet,
   Nor what soft incense hangs upon the boughs,
But, in embalmèd darkness, guess each sweet
    Wherewith the seasonable month endows
The grass, the thicket, and the fruit-tree wild;
    White hawthorn, and the pastoral eglantine;
      Fast-fading violets cover'd up in leaves;
        And mid-May's eldest child,
    The coming musk-rose, full of dewy wine,
The murmurous haunt of flies on summer eves.   **50**

Darkling I listen; and for many a time
   I have been half in love with easeful Death,
Call'd him soft names in many a musèd rhyme,
    To take into the air my quiet breath;
Now more than ever seems it rich to die,
    To cease upon the midnight with no pain,
      While thou art pouring forth thy soul abroad
        In such an ecstasy!
    Still wouldst thou sing, and I have ears in vain –
To thy high requiem become a sod.   **60**

Thou wast not born for death, immortal Bird!
   No hungry generations tread thee down;
The voice I hear this passing night was heard
    In ancient days by emperor and clown:

Perhaps the self-same song that found a path
   Through the sad heart of Ruth, when sick for home,
     She stood in tears amid the alien corn;
      The same that oft-times hath
     Charm'd magic casements, opening on the foam
Of perilous seas, in faery lands forlorn.   **70**

Forlorn! the very word is like a bell
   To toll me back from thee to my sole self.
Adieu! the fancy cannot cheat so well
   As she is famed to do, deceiving elf,
Adieu! adieu! thy plaintive anthem fades
     Past the near meadows, over the still stream,
      Up the hill-side; and now 'tis buried deep
       In the next valley-glades:
     Was it a vision, or a waking dream?
Fled is that music: – do I wake or sleep?   **80**

Ode on a Grecian Urn

THOU still unravish'd bride of quietness!
   Thou foster-child of Silence and slow Time,
Sylvan historian, who canst thus express
   A flowery tale more sweetly than our rhyme:
What leaf-fringed legend haunts about thy shape
     Of deities or mortals, or of both,
      In Tempe or the dales of Arcady?
     What men or gods are these? What maidens loth?
What mad pursuit? What struggle to escape?
     What pipes and timbrels? What wild ecstasy?   **10**

Heard melodies are sweet, but those unheard
   Are sweeter: therefore, ye soft pipes, play on;
Not to the sensual ear, but, more endear'd,
   Pipe to the spirit ditties of no tone:

Fair youth, beneath the trees, thou canst not leave
    Thy song, nor ever can those trees be bare;
        Bold Lover, never, never canst thou kiss,
Though winning near the goal – yet, do not grieve;
        She cannot fade, though thou hast not thy bliss,
    For ever wilt thou love, and she be fair!   20

Ah, happy, happy boughs! that cannot shed
    Your leaves, nor ever bid the Spring adieu;
And, happy melodist, unwearièd,
    For ever piping songs for ever new;
More happy love! more happy, happy love!
    For ever warm and still to be enjoy'd,
        For ever panting and for ever young;
All breathing human passion far above,
    That leaves a heart high sorrowful and cloy'd,
        A burning forehead, and a parching tongue.   30

Who are these coming to the sacrifice?
    To what green altar, O mysterious priest,
Lead'st thou that heifer lowing at the skies,
    And all her silken flanks with garlands drest?
What little town by river or sea-shore,
    Or mountain-built with peaceful citadel,
        Is emptied of its folk, this pious morn?
And, little town, thy streets for evermore
    Will silent be; and not a soul to tell
        Why thou art desolate, can e'er return.   40

O Attic shape! Fair attitude! with brede
    Of marble men and maidens overwrought,
With forest branches and the trodden weed;
    Thou, silent form, dost tease us out of thought
As doth eternity: Cold Pastoral!
    When old age shall this generation waste,
        Thou shalt remain, in midst of other woe

Than ours, a friend to man, to whom thou say'st,
   'Beauty is truth, truth beauty, – that is all
      Ye know on earth, and all ye need to know.'   50

Ode to Psyche

O GODDESS! hear these tuneless numbers, wrung
   By sweet enforcement and remembrance dear,
And pardon that thy secrets should be sung,
   Even into thine own soft-conchèd ear:
Surely I dreamt to-day, or did I see
   The wingèd Psyche with awaken'd eyes?
I wander'd in a forest thoughtlessly,
   And, on the sudden, fainting with surprise,
Saw two fair creatures, couchèd side by side
   In deepest grass, beneath the whisp'ring roof   10
   Of leaves and trembled blossoms, where there ran
      A brooklet, scarce espied:

'Mid hush'd, cool-rooted flowers fragrant-eyed,
   Blue, silver-white, and budded Tyrian,
They lay calm-breathing on the bedded grass;
   Their arms embracèd, and their pinions too;
   Their lips touch'd not, but had not bade adieu
As if disjoinèd by soft-handed slumber,
And ready still past kisses to outnumber
   At tender eye-dawn of aurorean love: 20
      The wingèd boy I knew;
But who wast thou, O happy, happy dove?
      His Psyche true!

O latest-born and loveliest vision far
   Of all Olympus' faded hierarchy!
Fairer than Phœbe's sapphire-region'd star,
   Or Vesper, amorous glow-worm of the sky;
Fairer than these, though temple thou hast none,

Nor altar heap'd with flowers;
Nor virgin-choir to make delicious moan   30
   Upon the midnight hours;
No voice, no lute, no pipe, no incense sweet
  From chain-swung censer teeming;
No shrine, no grove, no oracle, no heat
  Of pale-mouth'd prophet dreaming.

O brightest! though too late for antique vows,
  Too, too late for the fond believing lyre,
When holy were the haunted forest boughs,
  Holy the air, the water, and the fire;
Yet even in these days so far retired   40
  From happy pieties, thy lucent fans,
  Fluttering among the faint Olympians
I see, and sing, by my own eyes inspired.
  So let me be thy choir, and make a moan
    Upon the midnight hours!
Thy voice, thy lute, thy pipe, thy incense sweet
  From swingèd censer teeming:
Thy shrine, thy grove, thy oracle, thy heat
  Of pale-mouth'd prophet dreaming.

Yes, I will be thy priest, and build a fane   50
  In some untrodden region of my mind,
Where branchèd thoughts, new grown with pleasant
    pain,
  Instead of pines shall murmur in the wind:
Far, far around shall those dark-cluster'd trees
  Fledge the wild-ridgèd mountains steep by steep;
And there by zephyrs, streams, and birds, and bees,
  The moss-lain Dryads shall be lull'd to sleep;
And in the midst of this wide quietness
  A rosy sanctuary will I dress
With the wreath'd trellis of a working brain,   60
  With buds, and bells, and stars without a name.

With all the gardener Fancy e'er could feign,
   Who breeding flowers, will never breed the same:
And there shall be for thee all soft delight
   That shadowy thought can win,
A bright torch, and a casement ope at night,
   To let the warm Love in!

Fancy

Ever let the Fancy roam,
Pleasure never is at home:
At a touch sweet Pleasure melteth,
Like to bubbles when rain pelteth;
Then let wingèd Fancy wander
Through the thought still spread beyond her:
Open wide the mind's cage door,
She'll dart forth, and cloudward soar,
O sweet Fancy! let her loose;
Summer's joys are spoilt by use,   10
And the enjoying of the Spring
Fades as does its blossoming:
Autumn's red-lipp'd fruitage too,
Blushing through the mist and dew,
Cloys with tasting: What do then?
Sit thee by the ingle, when
The sear faggot blazes bright,
Spirit of a winter's night;
When the soundless earth is muffled,
And the cakèd snow is shuffled   20
From the ploughboy's heavy shoon;
When the Night doth meet the Noon
In a dark conspiracy
To banish Even from her sky.
Sit thee there, and send abroad,
With a mind self-overawed,
Fancy, high-commission'd: – send her!

She has vassals to attend her:
She will bring, in spite of frost,
Beauties that the earth hath lost;   30
She will bring thee, all together,
All delights of summer weather;
All the buds and bells of May,
From dewy sward or thorny spray;
All the heapèd Autumn's wealth,
With a still, mysterious stealth:
She will mix these pleasures up
Like three fit wines in a cup,
And thou shalt quaff it: – thou shalt hear
Distant harvest-carols clear;   40
Rustle of the reapèd corn;
Sweet birds antheming the morn:
And, in the same moment – hark!
'Tis the early April lark,
Or the rooks, with busy caw,
Foraging for sticks and straw.
Thou shalt, at one glance, behold
The daisy and the marigold;
White-plumed lilies, and the first
Hedge-grown primrose that hath burst;   50
Shaded hyacinth, alway
Sapphire queen of the mid-May;
And every leaf, and every flower
Pearlèd with the self-same shower.
Thou shalt see the field-mouse peep
Meagre from its cellèd sleep;
And the snake all winter-thin
Cast on sunny bank its skin!
Freckled nest eggs thou shalt see
Hatching in the hawthorn-tree,   60
When the hen-bird's wing doth rest
Quiet on her mossy nest;
Then the hurry and alarm

When the beehive casts its swarm;
Acorns ripe down-pattering
While the autumn breezes sing.

Oh, sweet Fancy! let her loose;
Every thing is spoilt by use:
Where's the cheek that doth not fade,
Too much gazed at? Where's the maid   70
Whose lip mature is ever new?
Where's the eye, however blue,
Doth not weary? Where's the face
One would meet in every place?
Where's the voice, however soft,
One would hear so very oft?
At a touch sweet Pleasure melteth
Like to bubbles when rain pelteth.
Let, then, wingèd Fancy find
Thee a mistress to thy mind: 80
Dulcet-eyed as Ceres' daughter,
Ere the God of Torment taught her
How to frown and how to chide;
With a waist and with a side
White as Hebe's, when her zone
Slipt its golden clasp, and down
Fell her kirtle to her feet,
While she held the goblet sweet,
And Jove grew languid. – Break the mesh
Of the Fancy's silken leash;   90
Quickly break her prison-string,
And such joys as these she'll bring. –
Let the wingèd Fancy roam,
Pleasure never is at home.

Ode

BARDS of Passion and of Mirth,
Ye have left your souls on earth!
Have ye souls in heaven too,
Double-lived in regions new?
Yes, and those of heaven commune
With the spheres of sun and moon:
With the noise of fountains wondrous,
And the parle of voices thund'rous;
With the whisper of heaven's trees
And one another, in soft ease   10
Seated on Elysian lawns
Browsed by none but Dian's fawns;
Underneath large blue-bells tented,
Where the daisies are rose-scented,
And the rose herself has got
Perfume which on earth is not;
Where the nightingale doth sing
Not a senseless, trancèd thing,
But divine, melodious truth,
Philosophic numbers smooth;   20
Tales and golden histories
Of heaven and its mysteries.

   Thus ye live on high, and then
On the earth ye live again;
And the souls ye left behind you
Teach us, here, the way to find you,
Where your other souls are joying,
Never slumber'd, never cloying.
Here, your earth-born souls still speak
To mortals, of their little week;   30
Of their sorrows and delights;
Of their passions and their spites;
Of their glory and their shame;

What does strengthen, and what maim.
Thus ye teach us, every day,
Wisdom, though fled far away.

Bards of Passion and of Mirth,
Ye have left your souls on earth!
Ye have souls in heaven too,
Double-lived in regions new!   40

Lines on the Mermaid Tavern

SOULS of poets dead and gone,
What Elysium have ye known,
Happy field or mossy cavern,
Choicer than the Mermaid Tavern?
Have ye tippled drink more fine
Than mine host's Canary wine?
Or are fruits of Paradise
Sweeter than those dainty pies
Of venison? O generous food!
Drest as though bold Robin Hood   10
Would, with his maid Marian,
Sup and bowse from horn and can.

I have heard that on a day
Mine host's sign-board flew away,
Nobody knew whither, till
An astrologer's old quill
To a sheepskin gave the story,
Said he saw you in your glory,
Underneath a new old sign
Sipping beverage divine,   20
And pledging with contented smack
The Mermaid in the Zodiac.

Souls of poets dead and gone,
What Elysium have ye known,

Happy field or mossy cavern,
Choicer than the Mermaid Tavern?

Robin Hood

To a Friend

No! those days are gone away,
And their hours are old and grey,
And their minutes buried all
Under the down-trodden pall
Of the leaves of many years:
Many times have winter's shears,
Frozen North, and chilling East,
Sounded tempests to the feast
Of the forest's whispering fleeces,
Since men knew nor rent nor leases.   10

   No, the bugle sounds no more,
And the twanging bow no more;
Silent is the ivory shrill
Past the heath and up the hill;
There is no mid-forest laugh,
Where lone Echo gives the half
To some wight, amazed to hear
Jesting, deep in forest drear.

   On the fairest time of June
You may go, with sun or moon,   20
Or the seven stars to light you,
Or the polar ray to right you;
But you never may behold
Little John, or Robin bold:
Never one, of all the clan,
Thrumming on an empty can
Some old hunting ditty, while

He doth his green way beguile
To fair hostess Merriment,
Down beside the pasture Trent;   30
For he left the merry tale,
Messenger for spicy ale.

   Gone, the merry morris din;
Gone, the song of Gamelyn;
Gone, the tough-belted outlaw
Idling in the 'grené shawe';
All are gone away and past!
And if Robin should be cast
Sudden from his turfèd grave,
And if Marian should have   40
Once again her forest days,
She would weep, and he would craze;
He would swear, for all his oaks,
Fall'n beneath the dockyard strokes,
Have rotted on the briny seas;
She would weep that her wild bees
Sang not to her – strange! that honey
Can't be got without hard money!

   So it is; yet let us sing
Honour to the old bow-string!   50
Honour to the bugle-horn!
Honour to the woods unshorn!
Honour to the Lincoln green!
Honour to the archer keen!
Honour to tight little John,
And the horse he rode upon!
Honour to bold Robin Hood,
Sleeping in the underwood:
Honour to Maid Marian,
And to all the Sherwood clan!   60

Though their days have hurried by
Let us two a burden try.

To Autumn

SEASON of mists and mellow fruitfulness!
  Close bosom-friend of the maturing sun;
Conspiring with him how to load and bless
  With fruit the vines that round the thatch-eaves run;
To bend with apples the moss'd cottage-trees,
  And fill all fruit with ripeness to the core;
    To swell the gourd, and plump the hazel shells
  With a sweet kernel; to set budding more,
And still more, later flowers for the bees,
Until they think warm days will never cease,   10
    For Summer has o'er-brimm'd their clammy cells.

Who hath not seen thee oft amid thy store?
  Sometimes whoever seeks abroad may find
Thee sitting careless on a granary floor,
  Thy hair soft-lifted by the winnowing wind;
Or on a half-reap'd furrow sound asleep,
  Drowsed with the fumes of poppies, while thy hook
    Spares the next swath and all its twinèd flowers;
And sometimes like a gleaner thou dost keep
  Steady thy laden head across a brook;   20
  Or by a cider-press, with patient look,
    Thou watchest the last oozings, hours by hours.

Where are the songs of Spring? Ay, where are they?
  Think not of them, thou hast thy music too,
    While barrèd clouds bloom the soft-dying day,
And touch the stubble-plains with rosy hue;
  Then in a wailful choir the small gnats mourn
  Among the river sallows, borne aloft

Or sinking as the light wind lives or dies;
And full-grown lambs loud bleat from hilly bourn;   30
    Hedge-crickets sing; and now with treble soft
    The redbreast whistles from a garden-croft,
        And gathering swallows twitter in the skies.

Ode on Melancholy

No, no! go not to Lethe, neither twist
    Wolf's-bane, tight-rooted, for its poisonous wine;
Nor suffer thy pale forehead to be kiss'd
    By nightshade, ruby grape of Proserpine;
Make not your rosary of yew-berries,
    Nor let the beetle, nor the death-moth be
        Your mournful Psyche, nor the downy owl
A partner in your sorrow's mysteries;
    For shade to shade will come too drowsily,
        And drown the wakeful anguish of the soul.   10

But when the melancholy fit shall fall
    Sudden from heaven like a weeping cloud,
That fosters the droop-headed flowers all,
    And hides the green hill in an April shroud;
Then glut thy sorrow on a morning rose,
    Or on the rainbow of the salt sand-wave,
        Or on the wealth of globèd peonies;
Or if thy mistress some rich anger shows,
    Emprison her soft hand, and let her rave,
        And feed deep, deep upon her peerless eyes.   20

She dwells with Beauty – Beauty that must die;
    And Joy, whose hand is ever at his lips
Bidding adieu; and aching Pleasure nigh,
    Turning to poison while the bee-mouth sips:
Ay, in the very temple of Delight
    Veil'd Melancholy has her sovran shrine,

Though seen of none save him whose strenuous
      tongue
  Can burst Joy's grape against his palate fine:
His soul shall taste the sadness of her might,
  And be among her cloudy trophies hung.   30

Hyperion

BOOK I

DEEP in the shady sadness of a vale
Far sunken from the healthy breath of morn,
Far from the fiery noon, and eve's one star,
Sat grey-hair'd Saturn, quiet as a stone,
Still as the silence round about his lair;
Forest on forest hung about his head
Like cloud on cloud. No stir of air was there,
Not so much life as on a summer's day
Robs not one light seed from the feather'd grass,
But where the dead leaf fell, there did it rest.   10
A stream went voiceless by, still deadened more
By reason of his fallen divinity,
Spreading a shade: the Naiad 'mid her reeds
Press'd her cold finger closer to her lips.

  Along the margin-sand large foot-marks went,
No further than to where his feet had stray'd,
And slept there since. Upon the sodden ground
His old right hand lay nerveless, listless, dead,
Unsceptred; and his realmless eyes were closed;
While his bow'd head seem'd list'ning to the Earth,   20
His ancient mother, for some comfort yet.

  It seem'd no force could wake him from his place;
But there came one, who with a kindred hand
Touch'd his wide shoulders, after bending low

With reverence, though to one who knew it not.
She was a Goddess of the infant world;
By her in stature the tall Amazon
Had stood a pigmy's height: she would have ta'en
Achilles by the hair and bent his neck;
Or with a finger stay'd Ixion's wheel.   30
Her face was large as that of Memphian sphinx,
Pedestal'd haply in a palace-court,
When sages look'd to Egypt for their lore.
But oh! how unlike marble was that face:
How beautiful, if sorrow had not made
Sorrow more beautiful than Beauty's self.
There was a listening fear in her regard,
As if calamity had but begun;
As if the vanward clouds of evil days
Had spent their malice, and the sullen rear   40
Was with its stored thunder labouring up.
One hand she press'd upon that aching spot
Where beats the human heart, as if just there,
Though an immortal, she felt cruel pain:
The other upon Saturn's bended neck
She laid, and to the level of his ear
Leaning with parted lips, some words she spake
In solemn tenour and deep organ tone:
Some mourning words, which in our feeble tongue
Would come in these like accents; O how frail   50
To that large utterance of the early Gods!
'Saturn, look up! – though wherefore, poor old King?
I have no comfort for thee, no not one:
I cannot say, "O wherefore sleepest thou?"
For heaven is parted from thee, and the earth
Knows thee not, thus afflicted, for a God;
And ocean too, with all its solemn noise,
Has from thy sceptre pass'd; and all the air
Is emptied of thine hoary majesty.
Thy thunder, conscious of the new command,   60

Rumbles reluctant o'er our fallen house;
And thy sharp lightning in unpractised hands
Scorches and burns our once serene domain.
O aching time! O moments big as years!
All as ye pass swell out the monstrous truth,
And press it so upon our weary griefs
That unbelief has not a space to breathe.
Saturn, sleep on: — O thoughtless, why did I
Thus violate thy slumbrous solitude?
Why should I ope thy melancholy eyes?   70
Saturn, sleep on! while at thy feet I weep.'

   As when, upon a trancèd summer-night,
Those green-robed senators of mighty woods,
Tall oaks, branch-charmèd by the earnest stars,
Dream, and so dream all night without a stir,
Save from one gradual solitary gust
Which comes upon the silence, and dies off,
As if the ebbing air had but one wave:
So came these words and went; the while in tears
She touch'd her fair large forehead to the ground,   80
Just where her falling hair might be outspread
A soft and silken mat for Saturn's feet.
One moon, with alteration slow, had shed
Her silver seasons four upon the night,
And still these two were postured motionless,
Like natural sculpture in cathedral cavern;
The frozen God still couchant on the earth,
And the sad Goddess weeping at his feet:
Until at length old Saturn lifted up
His faded eyes, and saw his kingdom gone,   90
And all the gloom and sorrow of the place,
And that fair kneeling Goddess; and then spake,
As with a palsied tongue, and while his beard
Shook horrid with such aspen-malady:
'O tender spouse of gold Hyperion,

Thea, I feel thee ere I see thy face;
Look up, and let me see our doom in it;
Look up, and tell me, if this feeble shape
Is Saturn's; tell me, if thou hear'st the voice
Of Saturn; tell me, if this wrinkling brow,   100
Naked and bare of its great diadem,
Peers like the front of Saturn? Who had power
To make me desolate? whence came the strength?
How was it nurtured to such bursting forth,
While Fate seem'd strangled in my nervous grasp?
But it is so; and I am smother'd up,
And buried from all godlike exercise
Of influence benign on planets pale,
Of admonitions to the winds and seas,
Of peaceful sway above man's harvesting,   110
And all those acts which Deity supreme
Doth ease its heart of love in. I am gone
Away from my own bosom: I have left
My strong identity, my real self,
Somewhere between the throne, and where I sit
Here on this spot of earth. Search, Thea, search,
Open thine eyes eterne, and sphere them round
Upon all space: space starr'd, and lorn of light,
Space region'd with life-air; and barren void;
Spaces of fire, and all the yawn of hell.   120
Search, Thea, search! and tell me if thou seest
A certain shape or shadow, making way
With wings or chariot fierce to repossess
A heaven he lost erewhile: it must – it must
Be of ripe progress – Saturn must be King!
Yes, there must be a golden victory;
There must be Gods thrown down, and trumpets blown
Of triumph calm, and hymns of festival
Upon the gold clouds metropolitan,
Voices of soft proclaim, and silver stir   130
Of strings in hollow shells; and there shall be

Beautiful things made new, for the surprise
Of the sky-children; I will give command:
Thea! Thea! Thea! where is Saturn?'

    This passion lifted him upon his feet,
And made his hands to struggle in the air,
His Druid locks to shake and ooze with sweat,
His eyes to fever out, his voice to cease.
He stood, and heard not Thea's sobbing deep;
A little time, and then again he snatch'd   140
Utterance thus: 'But cannot I create?
Cannot I form? Cannot I fashion forth
Another world, another universe,
To overbear and crumble this to nought?
Where is another chaos? Where?' That word
Found way unto Olympus, and made quake
The rebel three. Thea was startled up,
And in her bearing was a sort of hope,
As thus she quick-voiced spake, yet full of awe.

    'This cheers our fallen house: come to our friends,   150
O Saturn! come away, and give them heart;
I know the covert, for thence came I hither.'
Thus brief, then with beseeching eyes she went
With backward footing through the shade a space:
He follow'd, and she turn'd to lead the way
Through aged boughs, that yielded like the mist
Which eagles cleave, upmounting from their nest.

    Meanwhile in other realms big tears were shed,
More sorrow like to this, and such like woe,
Too huge for mortal tongue or pen of scribe: 160
The Titans fierce, self-hid or prison-bound,
Groan'd for the old allegiance once more,
And listen'd in sharp pain for Saturn's voice.
But one of the whole mammoth-brood still kept

His sovereignty, and rule, and majesty;
Blazing Hyperion on his orbèd fire
Still sat, still snuff'd the incense, teeming up
From man to the sun's God, yet unsecure:
For as among us mortals omens drear
Fright and perplex, so also shudder'd he,   170
Not at dog's howl, or gloom-bird's hated screech,
Or the familiar visiting of one
Upon the first toll of his passing-bell,
Or prophesyings of the midnight lamp;
But horrors, portion'd to a giant nerve,
Oft made Hyperion ache. His palace bright,
Bastion'd with pyramids of glowing gold,
And touched with shade of bronzèd obelisks,
Glared a blood-red through all its thousand courts,
Arches, and domes, and fiery galleries;   180
And all its curtains of Aurorian clouds
Flush'd angerly: while sometimes eagle's wings,
Unseen before by Gods or wondering men,
Darken'd the place; and neighing steeds were heard,
Not heard before by Gods or wondering men.
Also, when he would taste the spicy wreaths
Of incense, breathed aloft from sacred hills,
Instead of sweets, his ample palate took
Savour of poisonous brass and metal sick:
And so, when harbour'd in the sleepy west,   190
After the full completion of fair day,
For rest divine upon exalted couch,
And slumber in the arms of melody,
He paced away the pleasant hours of ease
With stride colossal, on from hall to hall;
While far within each aisle and deep recess,
His wingèd minions in close clusters stood,
Amazed and full of fear; like anxious men
Who on wide plains gather in panting troops,
When earthquakes jar their battlements and towers.   200

Even now, while Saturn, roused from icy trance,
Went step for step with Thea through the woods,
Hyperion, leaving twilight in the rear,
Came slope upon the threshold of the west;
Then, as was wont, his palace-door flew ope
In smoothest silence, save what solemn tubes,
Blown by the serious Zephyrs, gave of sweet
And wandering sounds, slow-breathèd melodies;
And like a rose in vermeil tint and shape,
In fragrance soft, and coolness to the eye,   210
That inlet to severe magnificence
Stood full blown, for the God to enter in.

He enter'd, but he enter'd full of wrath;
His flaming robes streamed out beyond his heels,
And gave a roar, as if of earthly fire,
That scared away the meek ethereal Hours
And made their dove-wings tremble. On he flared
From stately nave to nave, from vault to vault,
Through bowers of fragrant and enwreathèd light,
And diamond-pavèd lustrous long arcades,   220
Until he reached the great main cupola;
There standing fierce beneath, he stampt his foot,
And from the basements deep to the high towers
Jarr'd his own golden region; and before
The quavering thunder thereupon had ceased,
His voice leapt out, despite of godlike curb,
To this result: 'O dreams of day and night!
O monstrous forms! O effigies of pain!
O spectres busy in a cold, cold gloom!
O lank-ear'd Phantoms of black-weeded pools!   230
Why do I know ye? why have I seen ye? why
Is my eternal essence thus distraught
To see and to behold these horrors new?
Saturn is fallen, am I too to fall?
Am I to leave this haven of my rest,

This cradle of my glory, this soft clime,
This calm luxuriance of blissful light,
These crystalline pavilions, and pure fanes,
Of all my lucent empire? It is left
Deserted, void, nor any haunt of mine.   240
The blaze, the splendour, and the symmetry,
I cannot see – but darkness, death and darkness.
Even here, into my centre of repose,
The shady visions come to domineer,
Insult, and blind, and stifle up my pomp –
Fall! – No, by Tellus and her briny robes!
Over the fiery frontier of my realms
I will advance a terrible right arm
Shall scare that infant thunderer, rebel Jove,
And bid old Saturn take his throne again.'   250
He spake, and ceased, the while a heavier threat
Held struggle with his throat, but came not forth;
For as in theatres of crowded men
Hubbub increases more they call out 'Hush!'
So at Hyperion's words the Phantoms pale
Bestirr'd themselves, thrice horrible and cold;
And from the mirror'd level where he stood
A mist arose, as from a scummy marsh.
At this, through all his bulk an agony
Crept gradual, from the feet unto the crown,   260
Like a lithe serpent vast and muscular
Making slow way, with head and neck convulsed
From over-strainèd might. Released, he fled
To the eastern gates, and full six dewy hours
Before the dawn in season due should blush,
He breathed fierce breath against the sleepy portals,
Clear'd them of heavy vapours, burst them wide
Suddenly on the ocean's chilly streams.
The planet orb of fire, whereon he rode
Each day from east to west the heavens through,   270
Spun round in sable curtaining of clouds;

Not therefore veilèd quite, blindfold and hid,
But ever and anon the glancing spheres,
Circles, and arcs, and broad-belting colure,
Glow'd through, and wrought upon the muffling dark
Sweet-shapèd lightnings from the nadir deep
Up to the zenith – hieroglyphics old,
Which sages and keen-eyed astrologers
Then living on the earth, with labouring thought
Won from the gaze of many centuries: 280
Now lost, save what we find on remnants huge
Of stone, or marble swart; their import gone,
Their wisdom long since fled. Two wings this orb
Possess'd for glory, two fair argent wings,
Ever exalted at the God's approach:
And now, from forth the gloom their plumes immense
Rose, one by one, till all outspreaded were;
While still the dazzling globe maintain'd eclipse,
Awaiting for Hyperion's command.
Fain would he have commanded, fain took throne   290
And bid the day begin, if but for change.
He might not: – No, though a primeval God
The sacred seasons might not be disturb'd,
Therefore the operations of the dawn
Stay'd in their birth, even as here 'tis told.
Those silver wings expanded sisterly,
Eager to sail their orb; the porches wide
Open'd upon the dusk demesnes of night;
And the bright Titan, phrenzied with new woes,
Unused to bend, by hard compulsion bent   300
His spirit to the sorrow of the time;
And all along a dismal rack of clouds,
Upon the boundaries of day and night,
He stretch'd himself in grief and radiance faint.
There as he lay, the Heaven with its stars
Look'd down on him with pity, and the voice
Of Cœlus, from the universal space,

Thus whisper'd low and solemn in his ear:
'O brightest of my children dear, earth-born
And sky-engender'd, Son of Mysteries   310
All unrevealèd even to the powers
Which met at thy creating! at whose joys
And palpitations sweet, and pleasures soft,
I, Cœlus, wonder how they came and whence;
And at the fruits thereof what shapes they be,
Distinct, and visible; symbols divine,
Manifestations of that beauteous life
Diffused unseen throughout eternal space;
Of these new-form'd art thou, oh brightest child!
Of these, thy brethren and the Goddesses!   320
There is sad feud among ye, and rebellion
Of son against his sire. I saw him fall,
I saw my first-born tumbled from his throne!
To me his arms were spread, to me his voice
Found way from forth the thunders round his head!
Pale wox I, and in vapours hid my face.
Art thou, too, near such doom? vague fear there is:
For I have seen my sons most unlike Gods.
Divine ye were created, and divine
In sad demeanour, solemn, undisturb'd,   330
Unruffled, like high Gods, ye lived and ruled:
Now I behold in you fear, hope, and wrath;
Actions of rage and passions; even as
I see them, on the mortal world beneath,
In men who die. – This is the grief, O Son!
Sad sign of ruin, sudden dismay, and fall!
Yet do thou strive; as thou art capable,
As thou canst move about, an evident God,
And canst oppose to each malignant hour
Ethereal presence: – I am but a voice;   340
My life is but the life of winds and tides,
No more than winds and tides can I avail: –
But thou canst. – Be thou therefore in the van

Of circumstance; yea, seize the arrow's barb
Before the tense string murmur. – To the earth!
For there thou wilt find Saturn, and his woes.
Meantime I will keep watch on thy bright sun,
And of thy seasons be a careful nurse.' –
Ere half this region-whisper had come down
Hyperion arose, and on the stars   350
Lifted his curvèd lids, and kept them wide
Until it ceased; and still he kept them wide:
And still they were the same bright, patient stars.
Then with a slow incline of his broad breast,
Like to a diver in the pearly seas,
Forward he stoop'd over the airy shore,
And plunged all noiseless into the deep night.

BOOK II

JUST at the self-same beat of Time's wide wings
Hyperion slid into the rustled air,
And Saturn gain'd with Thea that sad place
Where Cybele and the bruised Titans mourn'd.
It was a den where no insulting light
Could glimmer on their tears; where their own groans
They felt, but heard not, for the solid roar
Of thunderous waterfalls and torrents hoarse,
Pouring a constant bulk, uncertain where.
Crag jutting forth to crag, and rocks that seem'd   10
Ever as if just rising from a sleep,
Forehead to forehead held their monstrous horns;
And thus in thousand hugest phantasies
Made a fit roofing to this nest of woe.
Instead of thrones, hard flint they sat upon,
Couches of rugged stone, and slaty ridge
Stubborn'd with iron. All were not assembled:
Some chain'd in torture, and some wandering.
Cœus, and Gyges, and Briareüs,

Typhon and Dolor, and Porphyrion,   20
With many more, the brawniest in assault,
Were pent in regions of laborious breath;
Dungeon'd in opaque element, to keep
Their clenchèd teeth still clench'd, and all their limbs
Lock'd up like veins of metal, crampt and screw'd;
Without a motion, save of their big hearts
Heaving in pain, and horribly convulsed
With sanguine feverous boiling gurge of pulse.
Mnemosyne was straying in the world;
Far from her moon had Phœbe wanderèd;   30
And many else were free to roam abroad,
But for the main, here found they covert drear.
Scarce images of life, one here, one there,
Lay vast and edgeways; like a dismal cirque
Of Druid stones, upon a forlorn moor,
When the chill rain begins at shut of eve,
In dull November, and their chancel vault,
The heaven itself, is blinded throughout night.
Each one kept shroud, nor to his neighbour gave
Or word or look, or action of despair.   40
Creüs was one; his ponderous iron mace
Lay by him, and a shatter'd rib of rock
Told of his rage, ere he thus sank and pined.
Iapetus another; in his grasp,
A serpent's plashy neck; its barbèd tongue
Squeezed from the gorge, and all its uncurl'd length
Dead: and because the creature could not spit
Its poison in the eyes of conquering Jove.
Next Cottus: prone he lay, chin uppermost,
As though in pain; for still upon the flint   50
He ground severe his skull, with open mouth
And eyes at horrid working. Nearest him
Asia, born of most enormous Caf,
Who cost her mother Tellus keener pangs,
Though feminine, than any of her sons:

More thought than woe was in her dusky face,
For she was prophesying of her glory;
And in her wide imagination stood
Palm-shaded temples, and high rival fanes
By Oxus or in Ganges' sacred isles.   60
Even as Hope upon her anchor leans,
So leant she, not so fair, upon a tusk
Shed from the broadest of her elephants.
Above her, on a crag's uneasy shelve,
Upon his elbow raised, all prostrate else,
Shadow'd Enceladus; once tame and mild
As grazing ox unworried in the meads;
Now tiger-passion'd, lion-thoughted, wroth,
He meditated, plotted, and even now
Was hurling mountains in that second war,   70
Not long delay'd, that scared the younger Gods
To hide themselves in forms of beast and bird.
Not far hence Atlas; and beside him prone
Phorcus, the sire of Gorgons. Neighbour'd close
Oceanus, and Tethys, in whose lap
Sobbed Clymene among her tangled hair.
In midst of all lay Themis, at the feet
Of Ops the queen all clouded round from sight;
No shape distinguishable, more than when
Thick night confounds the pine-tops with the clouds;   80
And many else whose names may not be told.
For when the muse's wings are air-ward spread,
Who shall delay her flight? And she must chaunt
Of Saturn, and his guide, who now had climb'd
With damp and slippery footing from a depth
More horrid still. Above a sombre cliff
Their heads appear'd, and up their stature grew
Till on the level height their steps found ease;
Then Thea spread abroad her trembling arms
Upon the precincts of this nest of pain,   90
And sidelong fix'd her eye on Saturn's face:

There saw she direst strife; the supreme God
At war with all the frailty of grief,
Of rage, of fear, anxiety, revenge,
Remorse, spleen, hope, but most of all despair.
Against these plagues he strove in vain; for Fate
Had pour'd a mortal oil upon his head,
A disanointing poison: so that Thea,
Affrighted, kept her still, and let him pass
First onwards in, among the fallen tribe.   100

    As with us mortal men, the laden heart
Is persecuted more, and fever'd more,
When it is nighing to the mournful house
Where other hearts are sick of the same bruise;
So Saturn, as he walk'd into the midst,
Felt faint, and would have sunk among the rest,
But that he met Enceladus's eye,
Whose mightiness, and awe of him, at once
Came like an inspiration; and he shouted,
'Titans, behold your God!' at which some groan'd;   110
Some started on their feet; some also shouted,
Some wept, some wail'd – all bowed with reverence;
And Ops, uplifting her black folded veil,
Show'd her pale cheeks, and all her forehead wan,
Her eyebrows thin and jet, and hollow eyes.
There is a roaring in the bleak-grown pines
When Winter lifts his voice; there is a noise
Among immortals when a God gives sign,
With hushing finger, how he means to load
His tongue with the full weight of utterless thought,   120
With thunder, and with music, and with pomp:
Such noise is like the roar of bleak-grown pines,
Which, when it ceases in this mountain'd world,
No other sound succeeds; but ceasing here,
Among these fallen, Saturn's voice therefrom
Grew up like organ, that begins anew

Its strain, when other harmonies, stopt short,
Leave the dinn'd air vibrating silverly.
Thus grew it up: 'Not in my own sad breast,
Which is its own great judge and searcher out,   130
Can I find reason why ye should be thus:
Not in the legends of the first of days,
Studied from that old spirit-leavèd book
Which starry Uranus with finger bright
Saved from the shores of darkness, when the waves
Low-ebb'd still hid it up in shallow gloom;
And the which book ye know I ever kept
For my firm-basèd footstool: – Ah, infirm!
Not there, nor in sign, symbol, or portent
Of element, earth, water, air, and fire, –   140
At war, at peace, or inter-quarrelling
One against one, or two, or three, or all,
Each several one against the other three,
As fire with air loud warring when rain-floods
Drown both, and press them both against earth's face,
Where, finding sulphur, a quadruple wrath
Unhinges the poor world; – not in that strife,
Wherefrom I take strange lore, and read it deep,
Can I find reason why ye should be thus:
No, nowhere can unriddle, though I search,   150
And pore on Nature's universal scroll
Even to swooning, why ye, Divinities,
The first-born of all shaped and palpable Gods,
Should cower beneath what, in comparison,
Is untremendous might. Yet ye are here,
O'erwhelm'd and spurn'd, and batter'd, ye are here!
O Titans, shall I say, "Arise!" – Ye groan:
Shall I say "Crouch!" – Ye groan. What can I then?
O Heaven wide! O unseen parent dear!
What can I? Tell me, all ye brethren Gods,   160
How we can war, how engine our great wrath!
O speak your counsel now, for Saturn's ear

Is all a-hunger'd. Thou, Oceanus,
Ponderest high and deep; and in thy face
I see, astonied, that severe content
Which comes of thought and musing: give us help!'

So ended Saturn; and the God of the Sea,
Sophist and sage, from no Athenian grove,
But cogitation in his watery shades,
Arose, with locks not oozy, and began,   170
In murmurs, which his first-endeavouring tongue
Caught infant-like from the far-foamèd sands.
'O ye, whom wrath consumes! who, passion-stung,
Writhe at defeat, and nurse your agonies!
Shut up your senses, stifle up your ears,
My voice is not a bellows unto ire.
Yet listen, ye who will, whilst I bring proof
How ye, perforce, must be content to stoop:
And in the proof much comfort will I give,
If ye will take that comfort in its truth.   180
We fall by course of Nature's law, not force
Of thunder, or of Jove. Great Saturn, thou
Hast sifted well the atom-universe;
But for this reason, that thou art the King,
And only blind from sheer supremacy,
One avenue was shaded from thine eyes,
Through which I wander'd to eternal truth.
And first, as thou wast not the first of powers,
So art thou not the last; it cannot be.
Thou art not the beginning nor the end.   190
From chaos and parental darkness came
Light, the first fruits of that intestine broil,
That sullen ferment, which for wondrous ends
Was ripening in itself. The ripe hour came,
And with it light, and light, engendering
Upon its own producer, forthwith touch'd
The whole enormous matter into life.

Upon that very hour, our parentage,
The Heavens and the Earth, were manifest:
Then thou first-born, and we the giant-race, 200
Found ourselves ruling new and beauteous realms.
Now comes the pain of truth, to whom 'tis pain;
O folly! for to bear all naked truths,
And to envisage circumstance, all calm,
That is the top of sovereignty. Mark well!
As Heaven and Earth are fairer, fairer far
Than Chaos and blank Darkness, though once chief;
And as we show beyond that Heaven and Earth
In form and shape compact and beautiful,
In will, in action free, companionship, 210
And thousand other signs of purer life;
So on our heels a fresh perfection treads,
A power more strong in beauty, born of us
And fated to excel us, as we pass
In glory that old Darkness: nor are we
Thereby more conquer'd than by us the rule
Of shapeless Chaos. Say, doth the dull soil
Quarrel with the proud forests it hath fed,
And feedeth still, more comely than itself?
Can it deny the chiefdom of green groves? 220
Or shall the tree be envious of the dove
Because it cooeth, and hath snowy wings
To wander wherewithal and find its joys?
We are such forest-trees, and our fair boughs
Have bred forth, not pale solitary doves,
But eagles golden-feather'd, who do tower
Above us in their beauty, and must reign
In right thereof, for 'tis the eternal law
That first in beauty should be first in might;
Yea, by that law, another race may drive 230
Our conquerors to mourn as we do now.
Have ye beheld the young God of the Seas,
My dispossessor? Have ye seen his face?

Have ye beheld his chariot, foam'd along
By noble wingèd creatures he hath made?
I saw him on the calmèd waters scud,
With such a glow of beauty in his eyes,
That it enforced me to bid sad farewell
To all my empire: farewell sad I took,
And hither came, to see how dolorous fate   240
Had wrought upon ye; and how I might best
Give consolation in this woe extreme,
Receive the truth, and let it be your balm.'

    Whether through posed conviction, or disdain,
They guarded silence, when Oceanus
Left murmuring, what deepest thought can tell?
But so it was, none answer'd for a space,
Save one whom none regarded, Clymene:
And yet she answer'd not, only complain'd,
With hectic lips, and eyes up-looking mild,   250
Thus wording timidly among the fierce:
'O Father! I am here the simplest voice,
And all my knowledge is that joy is gone,
And this thing woe crept in among our hearts,
There to remain for ever, as I fear:
I would not bode of evil, if I thought
So weak a creature could turn off the help
Which by just right should come of mighty Gods;
Yet let me tell my sorrow, let me tell
Of what I heard, and how it made me weep,   260
And know that we had parted from all hope.
I stood upon a shore, a pleasant shore,
Where a sweet clime was breathèd from a land
Of fragrance, quietness, and trees, and flowers.
Full of calm joy it was, as I of grief;
Too full of joy and soft delicious warmth;
So that I felt a movement in my heart
To chide, and to reproach that solitude

With songs of misery, music of our woes;
And sat me down, and took a mouthèd shell   270
And murmur'd into it, and made melody –
O melody no more! for while I sang,
And with poor skill let pass into the breeze
The dull shell's echo, from a bowery strand
Just opposite, an island of the sea,
There came enchantment with the shifting wind,
That did both drown and keep alive my ears.
I threw my shell away upon the sand,
And a wave fill'd it, as my sense was fill'd
With that new blissful golden melody.   280
A living death was in each gush of sounds,
Each family of rapturous hurried notes,
That fell, one after one, yet all at once,
Like pearl beads dropping sudden from their string:
And then another, then another strain,
Each like a dove leaving its olive perch,
With music wing'd instead of silent plumes,
To hover round my head, and make me sick
Of joy and grief at once. Grief overcame,
And I was stopping up my frantic ears,   290
When, past all hindrance of my trembling hands,
A voice came, sweeter, sweeter than all tune,
And still it cried, "Apollo! young Apollo!
The morning-bright Apollo! young Apollo!"
I fled, it follow'd me, and cried "Apollo!"
O Father, and O Brethren! had ye felt
Those pains of mine; O Saturn, hadst thou felt,
Ye would not call this too indulgèd tongue
Presumptuous, in thus venturing to be heard!'

So far her voice flow'd on, like timorous brook   300
That, lingering along a pebbled coast,
Doth fear to meet the sea: but sea it met,
And shudder'd; for the overwhelming voice

Of huge Enceladus swallow'd it in wrath:
The ponderous syllables, like sullen waves
In the half-glutted hollows of reef-rocks,
Came booming thus, while still upon his arm
He lean'd; not rising, from supreme contempt.
'Or shall we listen to the over-wise,
Or to the over-foolish giant, Gods?   310
Not thunderbolt on thunderbolt, till all
That rebel Jove's whole armoury were spent,
Not world on world upon these shoulders piled,
Could agonise me more than baby-words
In midst of this dethronement horrible.
Speak! roar! shout! yell! ye sleepy Titans all.
Do ye forget the blows, the buffets vile?
Are ye not smitten by a youngling arm?
Dost thou forget, sham Monarch of the Waves,
Thy scalding in the seas? What! have I roused   320
Your spleens with so few simple words as these?
O joy! for now I see ye are not lost:
O joy! for now I see a thousand eyes
Wide glaring for revenge!' – As this he said,
He lifted up his stature vast, and stood,
Still without intermission speaking thus:
'Now ye are flames, I'll tell ye how to burn,
And purge the ether of our enemies:
How to feed fierce the crooked stings of fire,
And singe away the swollen clouds of Jove,   330
Stifling that puny essence in its tent,
O let him feel the evil he hath done!
For though I scorn Oceanus's lore,
Much pain have I for more than loss of realms:
The days of peace and slumberous calm are fled;
Those days, all innocent of scathing war,
When all the fair Existences of heaven
Came open-eyed to guess what we would speak: –
That was before our brows were taught to frown,

Before our lips knew else but solemn sounds;   340
That was before we knew the wingèd thing,
Victory, might be lost, or might be won.
And be ye mindful that Hyperion,
Our brightest brother, still is undisgraced –
Hyperion, lo! his radiance is here!'

    All eyes were on Enceladus's face,
And they beheld, while still Hyperion's name
Flew from his lips up to the vaulted rocks,
A pallid gleam across his features stern:
Not savage, for he saw full many a God   350
Wroth as himself. He look'd upon them all,
And in each face he saw a gleam of light,
But splendider in Saturn's, whose hoar locks
Shone like the bubbling foam about a keel
When the prow sweeps into a midnight cove.
In pale and silver silence they remain'd,
Till suddenly a splendour, like the morn,
Pervaded all the beetling gloomy steeps,
All the sad spaces of oblivion,
And every gulf, and every chasm old,   360
And every height, and every sullen depth,
Voiceless, or hoarse with loud tormented streams:
And all the everlasting cataracts,
And all the headlong torrents far and near,
Mantled before in darkness and huge shade,
Now saw the light and made it terrible.
It was Hyperion: – a granite peak
His bright feet touch'd, and there he stay'd to view
The misery his brilliance had betray'd
To the most hateful seeing of itself.   370
Golden his hair of short Numidian curl,
Regal his shape majestic, a vast shade
In midst of his own brightness, like the bulk
Of Memnon's image at the set of sun

To one who travels from the dusking East:
Sighs, too, as mournful as that Memnon's harp
He utter'd, while his hands contemplative
He press'd together, and in silence stood.
Despondence seized again the fallen Gods
At sight of the dejected King of Day, 380
And many hid their faces from the light:
But fierce Enceladus sent forth his eyes
Among the brotherhood; and, at their glare,
Uprose Iäpetus, and Creüs too,
And Phorcus, sea-born, and together strode
To where he tower'd on his eminence.
There those four shouted forth old Saturn's name.
Hyperion from the peak loud answer'd, 'Saturn!'
Saturn sat near the Mother of the Gods,
In whose face was no joy, though all the Gods 390
Gave from their hollow throat the name of 'Saturn!'

BOOK III

THUS, in alternate uproar and sad peace,
Amazèd were those Titans utterly.
O leave them, Muse! O leave them to their woes;
For thou art weak to sing such tumults dire:
A solitary sorrow best befits
Thy lips, and antheming a lonely grief.
Leave them, O Muse! for thou anon wilt find
Many a fallen old Divinity
Wandering in vain about bewilder'd shores.
Meantime touch piously the Delphic harp, 10
And not a wind of heaven but will breathe
In aid soft warble from the Dorian flute;
For lo! 'tis for the Father of all verse.
Flush every thing that hath a vermeil hue,
Let the rose glow intense and warm the air,
And let the clouds of even and of morn

Float in voluptuous fleeces o'er the hills;
Let the red wine within the goblet boil,
Cold as a bubbling well; let faint-lipp'd shells,
On sands or in great deeps, vermilion turn   20
Through all their labyrinths; and let the maid
Blush keenly, as with some warm kiss surprised.
Chief isle of the embowered Cyclades,
Rejoice, O Delos, with thine olives green,
And poplars, and lawn-shading palms, and beech,
In which the Zephyr breathes the loudest song,
And hazels thick, dark-stemm'd beneath the shade:
Apollo is once more the golden theme!
Where was he, when the Giant of the Sun
Stood bright, amid the sorrow of his peers?   30
Together had he left his mother fair
And his twin-sister sleeping in their bower,
And in the morning twilight wander'd forth
Beside the osiers of a rivulet,
Full ankle-deep in lilies of the vale.
The nightingale had ceased, and a few stars
Were lingering in the heavens, while the thrush
Began calm-throated. Throughout all the isle
There was no covert, no retired cave,
Unhaunted by the murmurous noise of waves,   40
Though scarcely heard in many a green recess.
He listen'd, and he wept, and his bright tears
Went trickling down the golden bow he held.
Thus with half-shut suffusèd eyes he stood,
While from beneath some cumbrous boughs hard by
With solemn step an awful Goddess came,
And there was purport in her looks for him,
Which he with eager guess began to read
Perplex'd, the while melodiously he said:
'How cam'st thou over the unfooted sea?   50
Or hath that antique mien and robèd form
Moved in these vales invisible till now?

Sure I have heard those vestments sweeping o'er
The fallen leaves, when I have sat alone
In cool mid-forest. Surely I have traced
The rustle of those ample skirts about
These grassy solitudes, and seen the flowers
Lift up their heads, as still the whisper pass'd.
Goddess! I have beheld those eyes before,
And their eternal calm, and all that face,   60
Or I have dream'd.' – 'Yes,' said the supreme shape,
'Thou hast dream'd of me; and awaking up
Didst find a lyre all golden by thy side,
Whose strings touch'd by thy fingers, all the vast
Unwearied ear of the whole universe
Listen'd in pain and pleasure at the birth
Of such new tuneful wonder. Is 't not strange
That thou shouldst weep, so gifted? Tell me, youth,
What sorrow thou canst feel; for I am sad
When thou dost shed a tear: explain thy griefs   70
To one who in this lonely isle hath been
The watcher of thy sleep and hours of life,
From the young day when first thy infant hand
Pluck'd witless the weak flowers, till thine arm
Could bend that bow heroic to all times.
Show thy heart's secrets to an ancient Power
Who hath forsaken old and sacred thrones
For prophecies of thee, and for the sake
Of loveliness new-born.' – Apollo then,
With sudden scrutiny and gloomless eyes   80
Thus answer'd, while his white melodious throat
Throbb'd with the syllables: 'Mnemosyne!
Thy name is on my tongue, I know not how;
Why should I tell thee what thou so well seest?
Why should I strive to show what from my lips
Would come no mystery? For me, dark, dark,
And painful vile oblivion seals my eyes:
I strive to search wherefore I am so sad,

Until a melancholy numbs my limbs;
And then upon the grass I sit, and moan,   90
Like one who once had wings. O why should I
Feel cursed and thwarted, when the liegeless air
Yields to my step aspirant? why should I
Spurn the green turf as hateful to my feet?
Goddess benign! point forth some unknown thing.
Are there not other regions than this isle?
What are the stars? There is the sun, the sun!
And the most patient brilliance of the moon!
And stars by thousands! Point me out the way
To any one particular beauteous star,   100
And I will flit into it with my lyre,
And make its silvery splendour pant with bliss.
I have heard the cloudy thunder: where is power?
Whose hand, whose essence, what divinity
Makes this alarum in the elements,
While I here idle listen on the shores
In fearless yet in aching ignorance?
O tell me, lonely Goddess! by thy harp,
That waileth every morn and eventide,
Tell me why thus I rave about these groves.   110
Mute thou remainest – mute! yet I can read
A wondrous lesson in thy silent face:
Knowledge enormous makes a God of me.
Names, deeds, grey legends, dire events, rebellions,
Majesties, sovran voices, agonies,
Creations and destroyings, all at once
Pour into the wide hollows of my brain,
And deify me, as if some blithe wine
Or bright elixir peerless I had drunk,
And so become immortal.' – Thus the God,   120
While his enkindled eyes, with level glance
Beneath his white soft temples, stedfast kept
Trembling with light upon Mnemosyne.
Soon wild commotions shook him, and made flush

All the immortal fairness of his limbs:
Most like the struggle at the gate of death;
Or liker still to one who should take leave
Of pale immortal death, and with a pang
As hot as death's is chill, with fierce convulse
Die into life: so young Apollo anguish'd;   130
His very hair, his golden tresses famed,
Kept undulation round his eager neck.
During the pain Mnemosyne upheld
Her arms as one who prophesied. At length
Apollo shriek'd; – and lo! from all his limbs
Celestial

.   .   .

POSTHUMOUS

AND

FUGITIVE POEMS

On Peace

O PEACE! and dost thou with thy presence bless
   The dwellings of this war-surrounded isle;
Soothing with placid brow our late distress,
   Making the triple kingdom brightly smile?
Joyful I hail thy presence; and I hail
   The sweet companions that await on thee;
Complete my joy – let not my first wish fail,
   Let the sweet mountain nymph thy favourite be,
With England's happiness proclaim Europa's liberty.
O Europe! let not sceptred tyrants see
   That thou must shelter in thy former state;
Keep thy chains burst, and boldly say thou art free;
   Give thy kings law – leave not uncurbed the great;
   So with the horrors past thou'lt win thy happier fate.

Lines written on 29 May,
the Anniversary of Charles's Restoration,
on hearing the Bells ringing

INFATUATE Britons, will you still proclaim
His memory, your direst, foulest shame?
     Nor patriots revere?
Ah! when I hear each traitorous lying bell,
'Tis gallant Sydney's, Russell's, Vane's sad knell,
     That pains my wounded ear.

Ode to Apollo

IN thy western halls of gold,
    When thou sittest in thy state,
Bards, that erst sublimely told
    Heroic deeds, and sang of fate,
With fervour seize their adamantine lyres,
Whose chords are solid rays, and twinkle radiant fires.

Here Homer with his nervous arms
    Strikes the twanging harp of war,
And even the western splendour warms,
    While the trumpets sound afar: 10
But, what creates the most intense surprise,
His soul looks out through renovated eyes.

Then, through thy Temple wide, melodious swells
    The sweet majestic tone of Maro's lyre:
The soul delighted on each accent dwells, –
    Enraptured dwells, – not daring to respire,
The while he tells of grief around a funeral pyre.

'Tis awful silence then again;
    Expectant stand the spheres;
    Breathless the laurell'd peers,   20
Nor move, till ends the lofty strain,
Nor move till Milton's tuneful thunders cease,
And leave once more the ravish'd heavens in peace.

Thou biddest Shakespeare wave his hand,
    And quickly forward spring
The Passions – a terrific band –
    And each vibrates the string
That with its tyrant temper best accords,
While from their Master's lips pour forth the inspiring words.

A silver trumpet Spenser blows,   30
    And, as its martial notes to silence flee,
From a virgin chorus flows
    A hymn in praise of spotless Chastity.
'Tis still! Wild warblings from the Æolian lyre
Enchantment softly breathe, and tremblingly expire.

Next thy Tasso's ardent numbers
    Float along the pleasèd air,
Calling youth from idle slumbers,
    Rousing them from Pleasure's lair:
Then o'er the strings his fingers gently move,   40
And melt the soul to pity and to love.

But when *Thou* joinest with the Nine,
And all the powers of song combine,
    We listen here on earth:
The dying tones that fill the air,
And charm the ear of evening fair,
From thee, great God of Bards, receive their heavenly birth.

'As from the darkening gloom a silver dove'

As from the darkening gloom a silver dove
    Upsoars, and darts into the Eastern light,
    On pinions that naught moves but pure delight,
So fled thy soul into the realms above,
Regions of peace and everlasting love;
    Where happy spirits, crowned with circlets bright
    Of starry beam, and gloriously bedight,
Taste the high joy none but the blest can prove.
There thou or joinest the immortal quire
    In melodies that even Heaven fair
Fill with superior bliss, or, at desire
    Of the omnipotent Father, cleavest the air

On holy message sent – What pleasures higher?
Wherefore does any grief our joy impair?

To Lord Byron

BYRON! how sweetly sad thy melody!
   Attuning still the soul to tenderness,
   As if soft Pity, with unusual stress,
Had touched her plaintive lute, and thou, being by,
Hadst caught the tones, nor suffered them to die.
   O'ershading sorrow doth not make thee less
   Delightful: thou thy griefs dost dress
With a bright halo, shining beamily,
As when a cloud a golden moon doth veil,
   Its sides are tinged with a resplendent glow,
Through the dark robe oft amber rays prevail,
   And like fair veins in sable marble flow;
Still warble, dying swan! still tell the tale,
   The enchanting tale, the tale of pleasing woe.

'Fill for me a brimming bowl'

FILL for me a brimming bowl
And let me in it drown my soul:
But put therein some drug, designed
To banish Woman from my mind:
For I want not the stream inspiring
That heats the sense with lewd desiring,
But I want as deep a draught
As e'er from Lethe's waves was quaffed;
From my despairing breast to charm
The Image of the fairest form   10
That e'er my revelling eyes beheld,
That e'er my wandering fancy spelled.
'Tis vain! away I cannot chase
The melting softness of that face,

The beaminess of those bright eyes,
That breast – earth's only Paradise.
My sight will never more be blessed;
For all I see has lost its zest:
Nor with delight can I explore
The Classic page, the Muse's lore.   20
Had she but known how beat my heart,
And with one smile relieved its smart,
I should have felt a sweet relief,
I should have felt 'the joy of grief'.
Yet as a Tuscan 'mid the snow
Of Lapland thinks on sweet Arno,
Even so for ever shall she be
The Halo of my Memory.

To Chatterton

O CHATTERTON! how very sad thy fate!
  Dear child of sorrow – son of misery!
  How soon the film of death obscured that eye,
Whence Genius wildly flashed, and high debate.
How soon that voice, majestic and elate,
  Melted in dying murmurs! Oh! how nigh
  Was night to thy fair morning. Thou didst die
A half-blown flower which cold blasts amate.
But this is past: thou art among the stars
  Of highest Heaven: to the rolling spheres
Thou sweetly singest: naught thy hymning mars,
  Above the ingrate world and human fears.
On earth the good man base detraction bars
  From thy fair name, and waters it with tears.

To Emma

O COME, dearest Emma! the rose is full blown,
And the riches of Flora are lavishly strown,

The air is all softness, and crystal the streams,
And the West is resplendently clothèd in beams.

We will hasten, my fair, to the opening glades,
The quaintly carved seats, and the freshening shades,
Where the faeries are chanting their evening hymns,
And in the last sunbeam the sylph lightly swims.

And when thou art weary I'll find thee a bed
Of mosses and flowers to pillow thy head;   10
There, beauteous Emma, I'll sit at thy feet,
While my story of love I enraptured repeat.

So fondly I'll breathe, and so softly I'll sigh,
Thou wilt think that some amorous Zephyr is nigh –
Ah, no! – as I breathe, I will press thy fair knee,
And then thou wilt know that the sigh comes from me.

Then why, lovely girl, should we lose all these blisses?
That mortal's a fool who such happiness misses.
So smile acquiescence, and give me thy hand,
With love-looking eyes, and with voice sweetly bland.   20

'Give me Women, Wine, and Snuff'

GIVE me Women, Wine, and Snuff
Until I cry out, 'Hold, enough!'
You may do so sans objection
Till the day of resurrection;
For, bless my beard, they aye shall be
My belovèd Trinity.

On receiving a Laurel Crown from Leigh Hunt

MINUTES are flying swiftly, and as yet
   Nothing unearthly has enticed my brain
   Into a delphic labyrinth – I would fain
Catch an immortal thought to pay the debt
I owe to the kind poet who has set
   Upon my ambitious head a glorious gain.
   Two bending laurel sprigs – 'tis nearly pain
To be conscious of such a coronet.
Still time is fleeting, and no dream arises
   Gorgeous as I would have it – only I see
A trampling down of what the world most prizes,
   Turbans and crowns, and blank regality;
And then I run into most wild surmises
   Of all the many glories that may be.

'Come hither all sweet maidens soberly'

COME hither all sweet maidens soberly,
   Down-looking aye, and with a chasten'd light
   Hid in the fringes of your eyelids white,
And meekly let your fair hands joinèd be,
As if so gentle that ye could not see,
   Untouch'd, a victim of your beauty bright
   Sinking away to his young spirit's night,
Sinking bewilder'd 'mid the dreary sea:
   'Tis young Leander toiling to his death;
   Nigh swooning, he doth purse his weary lips
For Hero's cheek, and smiles against her smile.
   O horrid dream! see how his body dips,
Dead-heavy; arms and shoulders gleam awhile:
He's gone: up bubbles all his amorous breath!

Written in Disgust of Vulgar Superstition

THE church bells toll a melancholy round,
 Calling the people to some other prayers,
 Some other gloominess, more dreadful cares,
More hearkening to the sermon's horrid sound.
Surely the mind of man is closely bound
 In some blind spell: seeing that each one tears
 Himself from fireside joys and Lydian airs,
And converse high of those with glory crown'd.
Still, still they toll, and I should feel a damp,
 A chill as from a tomb, did I not know
That they are dying like an outburnt lamp, –
 That 'tis their sighing, wailing ere they go
 Into oblivion – that fresh flowers will grow,
And many glories of immortal stamp.

'O! how I love, on a fair summer's eve'

O! how I love, on a fair summer's eve,
 When streams of light pour down the golden west,
 And on the balmy zephyrs tranquil rest
The silver clouds, far – far away to leave
All meaner thoughts, and take a sweet reprieve
 From little cares; to find, with easy quest,
 A fragrant wild, with Nature's beauty dressed,
And there into delight my soul deceive.
There warm my breast with patriotic lore,
 Musing on Milton's fate – on Sidney's bier –
 Till their stern forms before my mind arise:
Perhaps on the wing of Poesy upsoar,
 Full often dropping a delicious tear,
 When some melodious sorrow spells mine eyes.

To a Young Lady who sent me a Laurel Crown

FRESH morning gusts have blown away all fear
From my glad bosom: now from gloominess
I mount for ever – not an atom less
Than the proud laurel shall content my bier.
No! by the eternal stars! or why sit here
In the Sun's eye, and 'gainst my temples press
Apollo's very leaves, woven to bless
By thy white fingers and thy spirit clear.
Lo! who dares say, 'Do this'? Who dares call down
My will from its high purpose? Who say, 'Stand',
Or 'Go'? This very moment I would frown
On abject Caesars – not the stoutest band
Of mailèd heroes should tear off my crown:
Yet would I kneel and kiss thy gentle hand!

'After dark vapours have oppressed our plains'

AFTER dark vapours have oppressed our plains
For a long dreary season, comes a day
Born of the gentle South, and clears away
From the sick heavens all unseemly stains.
The anxious month, relieving from its pains,
Takes as a long-lost right the feel of May,
The eyelids with the passing coolness play,
Like rose leaves with the drip of summer rains.
And calmest thoughts come round us – as of leaves
Budding – fruit ripening in stillness – autumn suns
Smiling at eve upon the quiet sheaves –
Sweet Sappho's cheek – a sleeping infant's breath –
The gradual sand that through an hour-glass runs –
A woodland rivulet – a Poet's death.

Lines in a Letter to J. H. Reynolds, from Oxford

THE Gothic looks solemn –
The plain Doric column
Supports an old Bishop and crosier;
The mouldering arch,
Shaded o'er by a larch
Stands next door to Wilson the Hosier.

Vicè – that is, by turns –
O'er pale faces mourns
The black-tassled trencher and common hat;
The chantry boy sings,
The steeple bell rings,
And as for the Chancellor – *dominat.*

There are plenty of trees,
And plenty of ease,
And plenty of fat deer for parsons;
And when it is venison,
Short is the benison –
Then each on a leg or thigh fastens.

On the Sea

IT keeps eternal whisperings around
Desolate shores, and with its mighty swell
Gluts twice ten thousand caverns; till the spell
Of Hecate leaves them their old shadowy sound.
Often 'tis in such gentle temper found
That scarcely will the very smallest shell
Be moved for days from whence it sometime fell,
When last the winds of heaven were unbound.
O ye who have your eyeballs vext and tir'd,
Feast them upon the wideness of the sea;

O ye whose ears are dinned with uproar rude
    Or fed too much with cloying melody –
Sit ye near some old cavern's mouth and brood
    Until ye start as if the sea nymphs quired.

To the Ladies who saw me Crowned

WHAT is there in the universal Earth
    More lovely than a wreath from the bay tree?
    Haply a halo round the moon – a glee
Circling from three sweet pair of lips in mirth;
And haply you will say the dewy birth
    Of morning roses – ripplings tenderly
    Spread by the halcyon's breath upon the sea –
But these comparisons are nothing worth.
Then is there nothing in the world so fair?
    The silvery tears of April? Youth of May?
Or June that breathes out life for butterflies?
    No – none of these can from my favourite bear
Away the palm – yet shall it ever pay
    Due reverence to your most sovereign eyes.

Nebuchadnezzar's Dream

BEFORE he went to feed with owls and bats
    Nebuchadnezzar had an ugly dream,
    Worse than an Hus'if's when she thinks her cream
Made a Naumachia for mice and rats.
So scared, he sent for that 'Good King of Cats'
    Young Daniel, who soon did pluck away the beam
    From out his eye, and said he did not deem
The sceptre worth a straw – his Cushions old door-mats.
A horrid nightmare similar somewhat
    Of late has haunted a most motley crew,
    Most loggerheads and Chapmen – we are told

That any Daniel tho' he be a sot
   Can make the lying lips turn pale of hue
      By belching out 'ye are that head of Gold'.

'Haydon! forgive me that I cannot speak'

HAYDON! forgive me that I cannot speak
   Definitively on these mighty things;
     Forgive me that I have not Eagle's wings –
That what I want I know not where to seek:
And think that I would not be over-meek
   In rolling out up-followed thunderings,
     Even to the steep of Heliconian springs,
Were I of ample strength for such a freak –
Think too, that all those numbers should be thine;
   Whose else? In this who touch thy vesture's hem?
For when men stared at what was most divine
   With browless idiotism – o'erwise phlegm –
Thou hadst beheld the Hesperian shine
   Of their star in the East, and gone to worship them.

Hymn to Apollo

   GOD of the golden bow,
     And of the golden lyre,
  And of the golden hair,
     And of the golden fire,
      Charioteer
      Of the patient year,
    Where – where slept thine ire,
When like a blank idiot I put on thy wreath,
    Thy laurel, thy glory,
    The light of thy story,
Or was I a worm – too low crawling for death?
   O Delphic Apollo!

10

The Thunderer grasp'd and grasp'd,
   The Thunderer frown'd and frown'd;
   The eagle's feathery mane
      For wrath became stiffen'd – the sound
         Of breeding thunder
         Went drowsily under,
      Muttering to be unbound.
   O why didst thou pity, and for a worm   20
      Why touch thy soft lute
      Till the thunder was mute?
Why was I not crush'd – such a pitiful germ?
      O Delphic Apollo!

The Pleiades were up,
   Watching the silent air;
The seeds and roots in the Earth
   Were swelling for summer fare;
      The Ocean, its neighbour,
      Was at his old labour,   30
   When, who – who did dare
To tie, like a madman, thy plant round his brow,
   And grin and look proudly,
   And blaspheme so loudly,
And live for that honour, to stoop to thee now?
   O Delphic Apollo!

On seeing the Elgin Marbles

My spirit is too weak – mortality
   Weighs heavily on me like unwilling sleep,
   And each imagined pinnacle and steep
Of godlike hardship tells me I must die
Like a sick eagle looking at the sky.
   Yet 'tis a gentle luxury to weep
   That I have not the cloudy winds to keep
Fresh for the opening of the morning's eye.

Such dim-conceived glories of the brain
    Bring round the heart an undescribable feud;
So do these wonders a most dizzy pain
    That mingles Grecian grandeur with the rude
Wasting of old time – with a billowy main –
    A sun – a shadow of a magnitude.

On 'The Story of Rimini'

WHO loves to peer up at the morning sun,
    With half-shut eyes and comfortable cheek,
    Let him, with this sweet tale, full often seek
For meadows where the little rivers run;
Who loves to linger with that brightest one
    Of Heaven – Hesperus – let him lowly speak
    These numbers to the night, and starlight meek,
Or moon, if that her hunting be begun.
He who knows these delights, and too is prone
    To moralise upon a smile or tear,
Will find at once a region of his own,
    A bower for his spirit, and will steer
To alleys, where the fir-tree drops its cone,
    Where robins hop, and fallen leaves are sear.

Written on a Blank Space at the End of Chaucer's 'The Floure and the Leafe'

THIS pleasant tale is like a little copse:
    The honeyed lines do freshly interlace
    To keep the reader in so sweet a place,
So that he here and there full-hearted stops;
And oftentimes he feels the dewy drops
    Come cool and suddenly against his face,
    And by the wandering melody may trace
Which way the tender-leggèd linnet hops.
Oh! what a power has white simplicity!

What mighty power has this gentle story!
  I that do ever feel athirst for glory
Could at this moment be content to lie
  Meekly upon the grass, as those whose sobbings
  Were heard of none beside the mournful robins.

'In drear nighted December'

IN drear nighted December,
    Too happy, happy tree,
Thy branches ne'er remember
    Their green felicity –
The north cannot undo them
With a sleety whistle through them,
Nor frozen thawings glue them
    From budding at the prime.

In drear nighted December,
    Too happy, happy brook,
Thy bubblings ne'er remember
    Apollo's summer look –
But with a sweet forgetting
They stay their crystal fretting,
Never, never petting
    About the frozen time.

Ah! would 'twere so with many
    A gentle girl and boy –
But were there ever any
    Writh'd not of passed joy?
The feel of not to feel it,
When there is none to heal it,
Nor numbed sense to steel it,
    Was never said in rhyme.

10

20

'Unfelt, unheard, unseen'

UNFELT, unheard, unseen,
    I've left my little queen,
Her languid arms in silver slumber lying:
    Ah! through their nestling touch,
    Who – who could tell how much
There is for madness – cruel, or complying?

    Those faery lids how sleek!
    Those lips how moist! – they speak,
In ripest quiet, shadows of sweet sounds:
    Into my fancy's ear
    Melting a burden dear,
How 'Love doth know no fullness nor no bounds.'

    True! – tender monitors!
    I bend unto your laws:
This sweetest day for dalliance was born!
    So, without more ado,
    I'll feel my heaven anew,
For all the blushing of the hasty morn.

Stanzas

I

You say you love; but with a voice
    Chaster than a nun's, who singeth
The soft Vespers to herself
    While the chime-bell ringeth –
    O love me truly!

II

You say you love; but with a smile
    Cold as sunrise in September,
As you were Saint Cupid's nun,

And kept his weeks of Ember.
  O love me truly!

III

You say you love – but then your lips
  Coral tinted teach no blisses
More than coral in the sea –
  They never pout for kisses –
    O love me truly!

IV

You say you love; but then your hand
  No soft squeeze for squeeze returneth,
It is like a statue's, dead –
  While mine for passion burneth –
    O love me truly!

V

O breathe a word or two of fire!
  Smile, as if those words should burn me,
Squeeze as lovers should – O kiss
  And in thy heart inurn me!
    O love me truly!

'Hither, hither, love – '

HITHER, hither, love –
  'Tis a shady mead –
Hither, hither, love,
  Let us feed and feed!

Hither, hither, sweet –
  'Tis a cowslip bed –
Hither, hither, sweet!
  'Tis with dew bespread!

Hither, hither, dear –
    By the breath of life –   10
Hither, hither, dear!
    Be the summer's wife!

Though one moment's pleasure
    In one moment flies,
Though the passion's treasure
    In one moment dies;

Yet it has not passed –
    Think how near, how near! –
And while it doth last,
    Think how dear, how dear!   20

Hither, hither, hither,
    Love this boon has sent –
If I die and wither
    I shall die content.

'Think not of it, sweet one, so – '

THINK not of it, sweet one, so –
    Give it not a tear;
Sigh thou mayst, and bid it go
    Any, any where.

Do not look so sad, sweet one –
    Sad and fadingly;
Shed one drop, then it is gone,
    O 'twas born to die.

Still so pale? then, dearest, weep –
    Weep, I'll count the tears,   10
And each one shall be a bliss
    For thee in after years.

Brighter has it left thine eyes
    Than a sunny rill;
And thy whispering melodies
    Are tenderer still.

Yet – as all things mourn awhile
    At fleeting blisses,
E'en let us too! but be our dirge
    A dirge of kisses.   **20**

On sitting down to read 'King Lear' once again

O GOLDEN-TONGUED Romance with serene lute!
    Fair plumed Syren! Queen of far away!
    Leave melodizing on this wintry day,
Shut up thine olden pages, and be mute.
Adieu! for once again the fierce dispute,
    Betwixt damnation and impassion'd clay
    Must I burn through; once more humbly assay
The bitter-sweet of this Shakespearian fruit.
Chief Poet! and ye clouds of Albion,
    Begetters of our deep eternal theme,
When through the old oak forest I am gone,
    Let me not wander in a barren dream,
But when I am consumèd in the fire
Give me new Phœnix wings to fly at my desire.

To a Cat

CAT! who hast pass'd thy grand climacteric,
    How many mice and rats hast in thy days
    Destroy'd? – How many tit bits stolen? Gaze
With those bright languid segments green, and prick
Those velvet ears – but pr'ythee do not stick
    Thy latent talons in me – and upraise
    Thy gentle mew – and tell me all thy frays

Of fish and mice, and rats and tender chick.
Nay, look not down, nor lick thy dainty wrists –
    For all the wheezy asthma, – and for all
Thy tail's tip is nick'd off – and though the fists
    Of many a maid have given thee many a maul,
Still is that fur as soft as when the lists
    In youth thou enter'dst on glass-bottled wall.

'Hence Burgundy, Claret, and Port'

HENCE Burgundy, Claret, and Port,
    Away with old Hock and Madeira,
Too earthly ye are for my sport;
    There's a beverage brighter and clearer.
Instead of a pitiful rummer,
My wine overbrims a whole summer;
    My bowl is the sky,
    And I drink at my eye,
    Till I feel in the brain
    A Delphian pain –   10
Then follow, my Caius! then follow:
    On the green of the hill
    We will drink our fill
    Of golden sunshine,
    Till our brains intertwine
With the glory and grace of Apollo!
    God of the Meridian
        And of the East and West,
    To thee my soul is flown,
        And my body is earthward press'd. –   20
It is an awful mission,
A terrible division;
And leaves a gulph austere
To be fill'd with worldly fear.
Aye, when the soul is fled
To high above our head,

Affrighted do we gaze
After its airy maze,
As doth a mother wild,
When her young infant child   30
Is in an eagle's claws –
And is not this the cause
Of madness? – God of Song,
Thou bearest me along
Through sights I scarce can bear:
O let me, let me share
With the hot lyre and thee,
The staid Philosophy.
Temper my lonely hours,
And let me see thy bowers   40
More unalarm'd!

Lines on seeing a Lock of Milton's Hair

CHIEF of organic numbers!
    Old Scholar of the Spheres!
Thy spirit never slumbers,
    But rolls about our ears,
For ever, and for ever!
O what a mad endeavour
        Worketh he,
Who to thy sacred and ennobled hearse
Would offer a burnt sacrifice of verse
        And melody.   10

How heavenward thou soundest,
    Live Temple of sweet noise,
And Discord unconfoundest,
    Giving Delight new joys,
And Pleasure nobler pinions!
O, where are thy dominions?
        Lend thine ear

To a young delian oath, – aye, by thy soul,
By all that from thy mortal lips did roll,
And by the kernel of thine earthly love,   20
Beauty, in things on earth, and things above
        I swear!

    When every childish fashion
        Has vanish'd from my rhyme,
    Will I, grey-gone in passion,
        Leave to an after-time,
        Hymning and harmony
Of thee, and of thy works, and of thy life;
But vain is now the burning and the strife,
Pangs are in vain, until I grow high-rife   30
        With old Philosophy,
And mad with glimpses of futurity!

For many years my offering must be hush'd;
    When I do speak, I'll think upon this hour,
Because I feel my forehead hot and flush'd,
    Even at the simplest vassal of thy power, –
    A lock of thy bright hair, –
    Sudden it came,
And I was startled, when I caught thy name
        Coupled so unaware;   40
Yet, at the moment, temperate was my blood.
I thought I had beheld it from the flood.

'When I have fears that I may cease to be'

WHEN I have fears that I may cease to be
   Before my pen has glean'd my teeming brain,
Before high-piled books, in charactery,
   Hold like rich garners the full ripen'd grain;
When I behold, upon the night's starr'd face,
   Huge cloudy symbols of a high romance,
And think that I may never live to trace
   Their shadows, with the magic hand of chance;
And when I feel, fair creature of an hour,
   That I shall never look upon thee more,
Never have relish in the faery power
   Of unreflecting love; – then on the shore
Of the wide world I stand alone, and think
Till love and fame to nothingness do sink.

To the Nile

SON of the old moon-mountains African!
   Chief of the Pyramid and Crocodile!
   We call thee fruitful, and, that very while,
A desert fills our seeing's inward span;
Nurse of swart nations since the world began,
   Art thou so fruitful? or dost thou beguile
   Such men to honour thee, who, worn with toil,
Rest for a space 'twixt Cairo and Decan?
O may dark fancies err! they surely do;
   'Tis ignorance that makes a barren waste
Of all beyond itself, thou dost bedew
   Green rushes like our rivers, and dost taste
The pleasant sun-rise, green isles hast thou too,
   And to the sea as happily dost haste.

To a Lady seen for a few Moments at Vauxhall

TIME'S sea hath been five years at its slow ebb,
  Long hours have to and fro let creep the sand,
Since I was tangled in thy beauty's web
  And snared by the ungloving of thine hand.
And yet I never look on midnight sky
  But I behold thine eyes' well-memory'd light;
I cannot look upon the rose's dye
  But to thy cheek my soul doth take its flight;
I cannot look on any budding flower
  But my fond ear, in fancy at thy lips
And hearkening for a love-sound, doth devour
  Its sweets in the wrong sense. Thou dost eclipse
Every delight with sweet remembering,
And grief unto my darling joys dost bring.

'Spenser! a jealous honourer of thine'

SPENSER! a jealous honourer of thine,
  A forester deep in thy midmost trees,
Did last eve ask my promise to refine
  Some English that might strive thine ear to please.
But, Elfin Poet, 'tis impossible
  For an inhabitant of wintry earth
To rise like Phœbus with a golden quell,
  Fire-winged, and make a morning in his mirth.
It is impossible to escape from toil
  O' the sudden and receive thy spiriting:
The flower must drink the nature of the soil
  Before it can put forth its blossoming.
Be with me in the summer days and I
Will for thine honour and his pleasure try.

Answer to a Sonnet by J. H. Reynolds, ending –

'Dark eyes are dearer far
Than those that mock the hyacinthine bell.'

BLUE! 'Tis the life of heaven, – the domain
  Of Cynthia, – the wide palace of the sun, –
The tent of Hesperus, and all his train, –
  The bosomer of clouds, gold, grey, and dun.
Blue! 'Tis the life of waters – ocean
  And all its vassal streams: pools numberless
May rage, and foam, and fret, but never can
  Subside, if not to dark-blue nativeness.
Blue! gentle cousin of the forest-green,
  Married to green in all the sweetest flowers –
Forget-me-not, – the blue-bell, – and, that queen
  Of secrecy, the violet: what strange powers
Hast thou, as a mere shadow! But how great,
When in an Eye thou art, alive with fate!

Apollo to the Graces

APOLLO

WHICH of the fairest three
To-day will ride with me?
My steeds are all pawing at the threshold of the morn:
  Which of the fairest three
  To-day will ride with me
Across the gold Autumn's whole Kingdom of corn?

THE GRACES *ALL ANSWER*

I will, I – I – I –
O young Apollo let me fly
  Along with thee,
I will – I – , I, I,
  The many wonders see
I – I – I – I –

And thy lyre shall never have a slackened string:
    I, I, I, I,
Thro' the golden day will sing.

'O blush not so!'

I

O BLUSH not so! O blush not so!
    Or I shall think you knowing;
And if you smile the blushing while,
    Then maidenheads are going.

II

There's a blush for won't, and a blush for shan't,
    And a blush for having done it:
There's a blush for thought and a blush for naught,
    And a blush for just begun it.

III

O sigh not so! O sigh not so!
    For it sounds of Eve's sweet pippin;   10
By these loosen'd lips you have tasted the pips
    And fought in an amorous nipping.

IV

Will you play once more at nice-cut-core,
    For it only will last our youth out,
And we have the prime of the kissing time,
    We have not one sweet tooth out.

V

There's a sigh for yes, and a sigh for no,
    And a sigh for I can't bear it!

O what can be done, shall we stay or run?
  O cut the sweet apple and share it!   **20**

'O thou whose face hath felt the Winter's wind'

O THOU whose face hath felt the Winter's wind,
Whose eye has seen the snow-clouds hung in mist,
And the black elm tops 'mong the freezing stars!
To thee the spring will be a harvest time.
O thou whose only book has been the light
Of supreme darkness, which thou feddest on
Night after night, when Phœbus was away!
To thee the spring shall be a triple morn.
O fret not after knowledge. I have none,
And yet my song comes native with the warmth.
O fret not after knowledge! I have none.
And yet the evening listens. He who saddens
At thought of idleness cannot be idle,
And he's awake who thinks himself asleep.

The Human Seasons

FOUR Seasons fill the measure of the year;
  There are four seasons in the mind of man:
He has his lusty Spring, when fancy clear
  Takes in all beauty with an easy span:
He has his Summer, when luxuriously
  Spring's honey'd cud of youthful thought he loves
To ruminate, and by such dreaming high
  Is nearest unto Heaven: quiet coves
His soul has in its Autumn, when his wings
  He furleth close; contented so to look
On mists in idleness – to let fair things
  Pass by unheeded as a threshold brook.
He has his Winter too of pale misfeature,
Or else he would forego his mortal nature.

'Where be ye going, you Devon maid?'

WHERE be ye going, you Devon maid?
    And what have ye there in the basket?
Ye tight little fairy, just fresh from the dairy,
    Will ye give me some cream if I ask it?

I love your meads, and I love your flowers,
    And I love your junkets mainly,
But 'hind the door I love kissing more,
    O look not so disdainly.

I love your hills and I love your dales,
    And I love your flocks a-bleating –
But O, on the heather to lie together,
    With both our hearts a-beating!

I'll put your basket all safe in a nook,
    Your shawl I'll hang on a willow,
And we will sigh in the daisy's eye,
    And kiss on a grass-green pillow.

'For there's Bishop's Teign'

I

For there's Bishop's Teign
    And King's Teign
And Coomb at the clear Teign head –
    Where close by the stream
    You may have your cream
All spread upon barley bread.

II

There's Arch Brook
    And there's Larch Brook
Both turning many a mill;
    And cooling the drouth
    Of the salmon's mouth,
And fattening his silver gill.

III

There is Wild Wood,
    A mild hood
To the sheep on the lea o' the down,
    Where the golden furze,
    With its green, thin spurs,
Doth catch at the maiden's gown.

IV

There is Newton Marsh
    With its spear grass harsh –
A pleasant summer level
    Where the maidens sweet
    Of the Market Street
Do meet in the dusk to revel.

V

There's the barton rich
    With dyke and ditch
And hedge for the thrush to live in,
    And the hollow tree
    For the buzzing bee
And a bank for the wasp to hive in.

10

20

30

VI

And O, and O,
The daisies blow
And the primroses are wakened,
And violet white
Sits in silver plight,
And the green bud's as long as the spike end.

VII

Then who would go
Into dark Soho,
And chatter with dacked-haired critics,
When he can stay   **40**
For the new-mown hay,
And startle the dappled prickets?

To Homer

STANDING aloof in giant ignorance,
    Of thee I hear and of the Cyclades,
As one who sits ashore and longs perchance
    To visit dolphin-coral in deep seas.
So thou wast blind! – but then the veil was rent;
    For Jove uncurtain'd Heaven to let thee live,
And Neptune made for thee a spumy tent,
    And Pan made sing for thee his forest-hive;
Ay, on the shores of darkness there is light,
    And precipices show untrodden green;
There is a budding morrow in midnight;
    There is a triple sight in blindness keen;
Such seeing hadst thou, as it once befell,
To Dian, Queen of Earth, and Heaven, and Hell.

To J. H. Reynolds from Teignmouth 25 March 1818

DEAR Reynolds! as last night I lay in bed,
There came before my eyes that wonted thread
Of shapes, and shadows, and remembrances,
That every other minute vex and please:
Things all disjointed come from north and south, –
Two Witch's eyes above a Cherub's mouth,
Voltaire with casque and shield and habergeon,
And Alexander with his nightcap on;
Old Socrates a-tying his cravat,
And Hazlitt playing with Miss Edgeworth's cat;   10
And Junius Brutus, pretty well so so,
Making the best of's way towards Soho.

Few are there who escape these visitings, –
Perhaps one or two whose lives have patent wings,
And thro' whose curtains peeps no hellish nose,
No wild-boar tushes, and no Mermaid's toes;
But flowers bursting out with lusty pride,
And young Æolian harps personified;
Some Titian colours touch'd into real life, –
The sacrifice goes on; the pontiff knife   20
Gleams in the Sun, the milk-white heifer lows,
The pipes go shrilly, the libation flows:
A white sail shows above the green-head cliff,
Moves round the point, and throws her anchor stiff;
The mariners join hymn with those on land.

You know the Enchanted Castle, – it doth stand
Upon a rock, on the border of a Lake,
Nested in trees, which all do seem to shake
From some old magic-like Urganda's Sword.
O Phœbus! that I had thy sacred word   30
To show this Castle, in fair dreaming wise,
Unto my friend, while sick and ill he lies!

You know it well enough, where it doth seem
A mossy place, a Merlin's Hall, a dream;
You know the clear Lake, and the little Isles,
The mountains blue, and cold near neighbour rills.
All which elsewhere are but half animate;
There do they look alive to love and hate,
To smiles and frowns; they seem a lifted mound
Above some giant, pulsing underground.   40

Part of the Building was a chosen See,
Built by a banish'd Santon of Chaldee;
The other part, two thousand years from him,
Was built by Cuthbert de Saint Aldebrim;
Then there's a little wing, far from the Sun,
Built by a Lapland Witch turn'd maudlin Nun:
And many other juts of aged stone
Founded with many a mason-devil's groan.

The doors all look as if they op'd themselves,
The windows as if latch'd by Fays and Elves,   50
And from them comes a silver flash of light,
As from the westward of a Summer's night;
Or like a beauteous woman's large blue eyes
Gone mad thro' olden songs and poesies.

See! what is coming from the distance dim!
A golden Galley all in silken trim!
Three rows of oars are lightening, moment whiles,
Into the verd'rous bosoms of those isles;
Towards the shade, under the Castle wall,
It comes in silence, – now 'tis hidden all.   60
The Clarion sounds, and from a Postern-gate
An echo of sweet music doth create
A fear in the poor Herdsman, who doth bring
His beasts to trouble the enchanted spring, –

He tells of the sweet music, and the spot,
To all his friends, and they believe him not.

   O that our dreamings all, of sleep or wake,
Would all their colours from the sunset take:
From something of material sublime,
Rather than shadow our own soul's day-time   70
In the dark void of night. For in the world
We jostle, – but my flag is not unfurl'd
On the Admiral-staff, – and so philosophize
I dare not yet! Oh, never will the prize,
High reason, and the love of good and ill,
Be my award! Things cannot to the will
Be settled, but they tease us out of thought;
Or is it that imagination brought
Beyond its proper bound, yet still confin'd,
Lost in a sort of Purgatory blind,   80
Cannot refer to any standard law
Of either earth or heaven? It is a flaw
In happiness, to see beyond our bourn, –
It forces us in summer skies to mourn,
It spoils the singing of the Nightingale.

   Dear Reynolds! I have a mysterious tale,
And cannot speak it: the first page I read
Upon a Lampit rock of green sea-weed
Among the breakers; 'twas a quiet eve,
The rocks were silent, the wide sea did weave   90
An untumultuous fringe of silver foam
Along the flat brown sand; I was at home
And should have been most happy, – but I saw
Too far into the sea, where every maw
The greater on the less feeds evermore. –
But I saw too distinct into the core
Of an eternal fierce destruction,

And so from happiness I far was gone.
Still am I sick of it, and tho', to-day,
I've gather'd young spring-leaves, and flowers gay   100
Of periwinkle and wild strawberry,
Still do I that most fierce destruction see, –
The Shark at savage prey, – the Hawk at pounce, –
The gentle Robin, like a Pard or Ounce,
Ravening a worm. – Away, ye horrid moods!
Moods of one's mind! You know I hate them well,
You know I'd sooner be a clapping bell
To some Kamchatkan missionary church,
Than with these horrid moods be left in lurch.
Do you get health – and Tom the same – I'll dance,   110
And from detested moods in new romance
Take refuge. Of bad lines a centaine dose
Is sure enough – and so 'here follows prose' . . .

'Over the hill and over the dale'

OVER the hill and over the dale,
And over the bourn to Dawlish –
Where Gingerbread Wives have a scanty sale
And gingerbread nuts are smallish.

Rantipole Betty she ran down a hill
And kicked up her petticoats fairly.
Says I I'll be Jack if you will be Jill.
So she sat on the grass debonairly.

Here's somebody coming, here's somebody coming!
Says I, 'Tis the wind at a parley.   10
So without any fuss, any hawing and humming,
She lay on the grass debonairly.

Here's somebody here, and here's somebody there!
Says I, Hold your tongue, you young gipsy.

So she held her tongue and lay plump and fair,
And dead as a Venus tipsy.

O who wouldn't hie to Dawlish fair,
O who wouldn't stop in a meadow?
O who would not rumple the daisies there,
And make the wild fern for a bed do?

20

To J. R.

O THAT a week could be an age, and we
   Felt parting and warm meeting every week,
Then one poor year a thousand years would be,
   The flush of welcome ever on the cheek:
So could we live long life in little space,
   So time itself would be annihilate,
So a day's journey in oblivious haze
   To serve our joys would lengthen and dilate.
O to arrive each Monday morn from Ind!
   To land each Tuesday from the rich Levant!
In little time a host of joys to bind,
   And keep our souls in one eternal pant!
This morn, my friend, and yester-evening taught
Me how to harbour such a happy thought.

Fragment of an Ode to Maia

MOTHER of Hermes! and still youthful Maia!
   May I sing to thee
As thou wast hymned on the shores of Baiæ?
   Or may I woo thee
In earlier Sicilian? or thy smiles
Seek as they once were sought, in Grecian isles,
By bards who died content on pleasant sward,
   Leaving great verse unto a little clan?
O, give me their old vigour, and unheard
   Save of the quiet Primrose, and the span

Of heaven and few ears,
Rounded by thee, my song should die away
Content as theirs,
Rich in the simple worship of a day.

'Sweet, sweet is the greeting of eyes'

SWEET, sweet is the greeting of eyes,
And sweet is the voice in its greeting,
When adieus have grown old and goodbyes
Fade away where old Time is retreating.

Warm the nerve of a welcoming hand,
And earnest a kiss on the brow,
When we meet over sea and o'er land
Where furrows are new to the plough.

Acrostic

Give me your patience, sister, while I frame
Exact in capitals your golden name,
Or sue the fair Apollo, and he will
Rouse from his heavy slumber and instill
Great love in me for thee and Poesy.
Imagine not that greatest mastery
And kingdom over all the realms of verse
Nears more to Heaven in aught than when we nurse,
And surety give, to love and brotherhood.

Anthropophagi in Othello's mood,   10
Ulysses stormed, and his enchanted belt
Glow with the Muse, but they are never felt
Unbosomed so and so eternal made,
Such tender incense in their laurel shade,
To all the regent sisters of the Nine,
As this poor offering to you, sister mine.

Kind sister! ay, this third name says you are.
Enchanted has it been the Lord knows where.
And may it taste to you like good old wine,
Take you to real happiness and give   **20**
Sons, daughters and a home like honeyed hive.

On visiting the Tomb of Burns

The town, the churchyard, and the setting sun,
   The clouds, the trees, the rounded hills all seem
    Though beautiful, cold – strange – as in a dream
I dreamed long ago. Now new begun,
The short-lived, paly summer is but won
   From winter's ague for one hour's gleam;
    Though sapphire warm their stars do never beam;
All is cold beauty; pain is never done
For who has mind to relish, Minos-wise,
   The real of beauty, free from that dead hue
     Fickly imagination and sick pride
Cast wan upon it! Burns! with honour due
     I have oft honoured thee. Great shadow, hide
Thy face, I sin against thy native skies.

A Song about Myself

I

There was a naughty boy,
A naughty boy was he,
He would not stop at home,
He could not quiet be –
   He took
   In his knapsack
   A book
   Full of vowels
   And a shirt

With some towels –   10
A slight cap
For night-cap –
A hair brush,
Comb ditto,
New stockings,
For old ones
Would split O!
This knapsack
Tight at's back
He rivetted close   20
And followed his nose
To the North,
To the North,
And followed his nose
To the North.

II

There was a naughty boy
And a naughty boy was he,
For nothing would he do
But scribble poetry –
He took   30
An inkstand
In his hand
And a pen
Big as ten
In the other
And away
In a pother
He ran
To the mountains
And fountains   40
And ghostès
And postès

And witches
And ditches,
And wrote
In his coat
When the weather
Was cool –
Fear of gout –
And without   50
When the weather
Was warm.
Och, the charm
When we choose
To follow one's nose
To the North,
To the North,
To follow one's nose
To the North!

III

There was a naughty boy   60
   And a naughty boy was he,
He kept little fishes
   In washing tubs three
      In spite
      Of the might
      Of the maid,
      Nor afraid
      Of his granny-good,
      He often would
      Hurly burly   70
      Get up early
      And go,
      By hook or crook,
      To the brook
      And bring home

Miller's thumb,
Tittlebat
Not over fat,
Minnows small
As the stall   80
Of a glove,
Not above
The size
Of a nice
Little baby's
Little finger –
O he made
('Twas his trade)
Of fish a pretty kettle,
A kettle –   90
A kettle,
Of fish a pretty kettle,
A kettle!

IV

There was a naughty boy,
    And a naughty boy was he,
He ran away to Scotland
    The people for to see –
        There he found
        That the ground
        Was as hard,   100
        That a yard
        Was as long,
        That a song
        Was as merry,
        That a cherry
        Was as red,
        That lead
        Was as weighty,

That fourscore
    Was as eighty,
That a door
    Was as wooden
        As in England –
So he stood in his shoes
    And he wondered,
        He wondered,
He stood in his
        Shoes and he wondered.

To Ailsa Rock

Hearken, thou craggy ocean pyramid!
    Give answer by thy voice, the sea-fowls' screams!
    When were thy shoulders mantled in huge streams?
When from the sun was thy broad forehead hid?
How long is't since the mighty power bid
    Thee heave to airy sleep from fathom dreams?
    Sleep in the lap of thunder or sunbeams,
Or when grey clouds are thy cold coverlid?
Thou answer'st not; for thou art dead asleep.
    Thy life is but two dead eternities—
The last in air, the former in the deep,
    First with the whales, last with the eagle-skies.
Drowned wast thou till an earthquake made thee steep,
    Another cannot wake thy giant size!

Meg Merrilies

Old Meg she was a gipsy;
    And lived upon the moors:
Her bed it was the brown heath turf,
    And her house was out of doors.

Her apples were swart blackberries,
    Her currants pods o' broom;

Her wine was dew of the wild white rose
    Her book a churchyard tomb.

Her brothers were the craggy hills,
    Her sisters larchen trees;   10
Alone with her great family
    She lived as she did please.

No breakfast had she many a morn,
    No dinner many a noon,
And 'stead of supper she would stare
    Full hard against the moon.

But every morn of woodbine fresh
    She made her garlanding,
And every night the dark glen yew
    She wove, and she would sing.   20

And with her fingers old and brown
    She plaited mats o' rushes,
And gave them to the cottagers
    She met among the bushes.

Old Meg was brave as Margaret Queen,
    And tall as Amazon;
An old red blanket cloak she wore,
    A chip hat had she on.
God rest her aged bones somewhere;
    She died full long agone!   30

'Ah! ken ye what I met the day'

AH! ken ye what I met the day
    Out oure the mountains,
A-coming down by craggis grey
    An mossie fountains?

Ah! goud-haired Marie yeve I pray
   Ane minute's guessing,
For that I met upon the way
   Is past expressing.
As I stood where a rocky brig
   A torrent crosses,   10
I spied upon a misty rig
   A troup o' horses –
And as they trotted down the glen
   I sped to meet them
To see if I might know the men
   To stop and greet them.
First Willie on his sleek mare came
   At canting gallop –
His long hair rustled like a flame
   On board a shallop.   20
Then came his brother Rab and then
   Young Peggy's mither
And Peggy too – adown the glen
   They went togither.
I saw her wrappit in her hood
   Fra wind and raining –
Her cheek was flush wi' timid blood
   Twixt growth and waning.
She turn'd her dazèd head full oft
   For thence her brithers   30
Came riding with her bridegroom soft
   An mony ithers.
Young Tam came up an' eyed me quick
   With reddened cheek.
Braw Tam was daffèd like a chick –
   He could na speak.
Ah! Marie they are all gane hame
   Through blustering weather,
An' every heart is full on flame
   An' light as feather.   40

Ah! Marie they are all gone hame
    Fra happy wedding,
Whilst I – Ah! is it not a shame? –
    Sad tears am shedding.

'All gentle folks who owe a grudge'

ALL gentle folks who owe a grudge
    To any living thing,
Open your ears and stay your trudge
    Whilst I in dudgeon sing.

The gad-fly he hath stung me sore –
    O may he ne'er sting you!
But we have many a horrid bore
    He may sting black and blue.

Has any here an old grey mare
    With three legs all her store?   10
O put it to her buttocks bare
    And straight she'll run on four.

Has any here a lawyer suit
    Of 1743?
Take lawyer's nose and put it to 't
    And you the end will see.

Is there a man in Parliament
    Dumbfoundered in his speech?
O let his neighbour make a rent
    And put one in his breech.   20

O Lowther, how much better thou
    Hadst figured t'other day,
When to the folks thou mad'st a bow
    And hadst no more to say,

If lucky gad-fly had but ta'en
   His seat upon thine arse,
And put thee to a little pain
   To save thee from a worse.

Better than Southey it had been,
   Better than Mr D –,   30
Better than Wordsworth too, I ween,
   Better than Mr V – .

Forgive me pray, good people all,
   For deviating so.
In spirit sure I had a call –
   And now I on will go.

Has any here a daughter fair
   Too fond of reading novels,
Too apt to fall in love with care
   And charming Mister Lovels?   40

O put a gad-fly to that thing
   She keeps so white and pert –
I mean the finger for the ring,
   And it will breed a Wert.

Has any here a pious spouse
   Who seven times a day
Scolds as King David prayed, to chouse
   And have her holy way?

O let a gad-fly's little sting
   Persuade her sacred tongue   50
That noises are a common thing,
   But that her bell has rung.

And as this is the *summum bo-*
    num of all conquering,
I leave withouten wordès mo
    The gad-fly's little sting.

'Of late two dainties were before me plac'd'

OF late two dainties were before me plac'd
    Sweet, holy, pure, sacred and innocent,
    From the ninth sphere to me benignly sent
That Gods might know my own particular taste:
First the soft Bag-pipe mourn'd with zealous haste,
    The Stranger next with head on bosom bent
    Sigh'd; rueful again the piteous Bag-pipe went,
Again the Stranger sighings fresh did waste.
O Bag-pipe thou didst steal my heart away –
    O Stranger thou my nerves from Pipe didst charm –
O Bagpipe thou didst re-assert thy sway –
    Again thou Stranger gav'st me fresh alarm –
Alas! I could not choose. Ah! my poor heart.
Mumchance art thou with both oblig'd to part.

Sonnet written in the Cottage where Burns was born

THIS mortal body of a thousand days
Now fills, O Burns, a space in thine own room,
Where thou didst dream alone on budded bays,
Happy and thoughtless of thy day of doom!
My pulse is warm with thine own Barley-bree,
My head is light with pledging a great soul,
My eyes are wandering, and I cannot see,
Fancy is dead, and drunken at its goal;
Yet can I stamp my foot upon thy floor,
Yet can I ope thy window-sash to find
The meadow thou hast trampèd o'er and o'er, –

Yet can I think of thee till thought is blind, –
Yet can I gulp a bumper to thy name, –
O smile among the shades, for this is fame!

Lines written in the Highlands after visiting the Burns Country

THERE is a charm in footing slow across a silent plain,
Where patriot battle has been fought, where glory had the
      gain;
There is a pleasure on the heath, where Druids old have been,
Where mantles grey have rustled by, and swept the nettled
      green;
There is a joy in every spot made known in times of old,
New to the feet although each tale a hundred times be told;
There is a deeper joy than all, more solemn in the heart,
More parching to the tongue than all, of more divine a smart,
When weary steps forget themselves upon a pleasant turf,
Upon hot sand, or flinty road, or sea-shore iron scurf,   10
Toward the castle or the cot, where long ago was born
One who was great through mortal days, and died of fame
      unshorn.

Light heather-bells may tremble then, but they are far away;
Wood-lark may sing from sandy fern, – the Sun may hear
      his lay;
Runnels may kiss the grass on shelves and shallows clear, –
But their low voices are not heard, tho' come on travels drear;
Blood-red the sun may set behind black mountain peaks,
Blue tides may sluice and drench their time in caves and weedy
      creeks,
Eagles may seem to sleep wing-wide upon the air,
Ring-doves may fly convulsed across to some high cedared
      lair, –   20

But the forgotten eye is still fast lidded to the ground,
As Palmer's that with weariness mid-desert shrine hath found.

At such a time the soul's a child, in childhood is the brain,
Forgotten is the worldly heart, – alone, it beats in vain.
Ay, if a madman could have leave to pass a healthful day,
To tell his forehead's swoon and faint, when first began decay,
He might make tremble many a one, whose spirit had
      gone forth
To find a Bard's low cradle-place about the silent north!
Scanty the hour, and few the steps, beyond the bourn of care,
Beyond the sweet and bitter world, – beyond it unaware!   30
Scanty the hour, and few the steps, – because a longer stay
Would bar return and make a man forget his mortal way:
O horrible! to lose the sight of well-remember'd face,
Of Brother's eyes, of Sister's brow, – constant to every place,
Filling the air as on we move with portraiture intense,
More warm than those heroic tints that pain a painter's sense,
When shapes of old come striding by, and visages of old,
Locks shining black, hair scanty grey, and passions manifold.

No, no, – that horror cannot be! for at the cable's length
Man feels the gentle anchor pull, and gladdens in its
      strength: 40
One hour, half idiot, he stands by mossy waterfall,
But in the very next he reads his soul's memorial;
He reads it on the mountain's height, where chance he
      may sit down,
Upon rough marble diadem, that hill's eternal crown.
Yet be his anchor e'er so fast, room is there for a prayer,
That man may never lose his mind in mountains black
      and bare;
That he may stray, league after league, some great birthplace
      to find,
And keep his vision clear from speck, his inward sight unblind.

Staffa

NOT Aladdin magian
Ever such a work began;
Not the wizard of the Dee
Ever such a dream could see;
Not St. John, in Patmos' Isle,
In the passion of his toil,
When he saw the churches seven,
Golden-aisled, built up in heaven,
Gazed at such a rugged wonder,
As I stood its roofing under.   10
Lo! I saw one sleeping there,
On the marble cold and bare;
While the surges wash'd his feet,
And his garments white did beat
Drench'd about the sombre rocks;
On his neck his well-grown locks,
Lifted dry above the main,
Were upon the curl again.
'What is this? and what art thou?'
Whisper'd I, and touch'd his brow;   20
'What art thou? and what is this?'
Whisper'd I, and strove to kiss
The spirit's hand, to wake his eyes;
Up he started in a trice:
'I am Lycidas,' said he,
'Fam'd in funeral minstrelsy!
This was architectured thus
By the great Oceanus! –
Here his mighty waters play
Hollow organs all the day;   30
Here, by turns, his dolphins all,
Finny palmers, great and small,
Come to pay devotion due, –
Each a mouth of pearls must strew!

Many a mortal of these days,
Dares to pass our sacred ways;
Dares to touch, audaciously,
This cathedral of the sea!
I have been the pontiff-priest,
Where the waters never rest,   40
Where a fledgy sea-bird choir
Soars for ever; holy fire
I have hid from mortal man;
Proteus is my Sacristan!
But the dullèd eye of mortal
Hath pass'd beyond the rocky portal:
So for ever will I leave
Such a taint, and soon unweave
All the magic of the place.'
So saying, with a Spirit's glance   50
He dived!

'Read me a lesson, Muse, and speak it loud'

READ me a lesson, Muse, and speak it loud
    Upon the top of Nevis, blind in mist!
I look into the chasms, and a shroud
    Vapourous doth hide them; just so much I wist
Mankind do know of Hell. I look o'erhead,
    And there is sullen mist; even so much
Mankind can tell of Heaven. Mist is spread
    Before the earth, beneath me – even such,
Even so vague is man's sight of himself.
    Here are the craggy stones beneath my feet –
Thus much I know, that, a poor witless elf,
    I tread on them, that all my eye doth meet
Is mist and crag, not only on this height,
    But in the world of thought and mental might.

Ben Nevis: a Dialogue

MRS. C.

UPON my life Sir Nevis I am piqued
That I have so far panted tugg'd and reek'd
To do an honour to your old bald pate
And now am sitting on you just to bait,
Without your paying me one compliment.
Alas 'tis so with all, when our intent
Is plain, and in the eye of all Mankind
We fair ones show a preference, too blind,
You Gentle men immediately turn tail –
O let me then my hapless fate bewail!   10
Ungrateful Baldpate have I not disdain'd
The pleasant Valleys – have I not madbrain'd
Deserted all my Pickles and preserves
My China closet too – with wretched Nerves
To boot – say wretched ingrate have I not
Le[f]t my soft cushion chair and caudle pot?
'Tis true I had no corns – no! thank the fates,
My Shoemaker was always Mr. Bates.
And if not Mr. Bates why I'm not old!
Still dumb, ungrateful Nevis – still so cold!   20

Here the Lady took some more wiskey and was putting even more
to her lips when she dashed [it] to the Ground for the Mountain
began to grumble – which continued for a few minutes before he
thus began:

BEN NEVIS

What whining bit of tongue and Mouth thus dares
Disturb my slumber of a thousand years?
Even so long my sleep has been secure –
And to be so awaked I'll not endure.

Oh pain – for since the Eagle's earliest scream
I've had a dam[n]'d confounded ugly dream,
A Nightmare sure. What Madam was it you?
It cannot be! My old eyes are not true!
Red-Crag, my Spectacles! Now let me see!
Good Heavens Lady, how the gemini   30
Did you get here? O I shall split my sides!
I shall earthquake –

MRS. C.

Sweet Nevis, do not quake, for though I love
You[r] honest Countenance all things above,
Truly I should not like to be convey'd
So far into your Bosom – gentle Maid
Loves not too rough a treatment gentle Sir –
Pray thee be calm and do not quake nor stir
No not a Stone or I shall go in fits –

BEN NEVIS

I must – I shall – I meet not such tit bits –   40
I meet not such sweet creatures every day –
By my old night cap night cap night and day,
I must have one sweet Buss – I must and shall!
Red-Crag! – What Madam can you then repent
Of all the toil and vigour you have spent
To see Ben Nevis and to touch his nose?
Red-Crag, I say! O I must have them close!
Red-Crag, there lies beneath my farthest toe
A vein of Sulphur – go dear Red-Crag, go –
And rub your flinty back against it – budge!   50
Dear Madam I must kiss you faith I must!
I must Embrace you with my dearest gust!
Block-head, d'ye hear – Block-head I'll make her feel
There lies beneath my east leg's northern heel
A cave of young earth dragons – well my boy

Go thither quick and so complete my joy;
Take you a bundle of the largest pines
And when the sun on fiercest Phosphor shines
Fire them and ram them in the Dragon's nest,
Then will the dragons fry and fizz their best   60
Until ten thousand now no bigger than
Poor Al[l]igators – poor things of one span –
Will each one swell to twice ten times the size
Of northern whale – then for the tender prize –
The moment then – for then will Red-Crag rub
His flinty back – and I shall kiss and snub
And press my dainty morsel to my breast.
Block-head make haste!
                              O Muses weep the rest –
The Lady fainted and he thought her dead
So pulled the clouds again about his head   70
And went to sleep again – soon she was rous'd
By her affrighted servants – next day hous'd
Safe on the lowly ground she bless'd her fate
That fainting fit was not delayed too late.

Song

I

SPIRIT here that reignest!
Spirit here that painest!
Spirit here that burnest!
Spirit here that mournest!
        Spirit, I bow
        My forehead low,
    Enshaded with thy pinions.
        Spirit, I look
        All passion-struck
    Into thy pale dominions.   10

II

Spirit here that laughest!
Spirit here that quaffest!
Spirit here that dancest!
Noble soul that prancest!
  Spirit, with thee
  I join in the glee
 A-nudging the elbow of Momus.
  Spirit, I flush
  With a Bacchanal blush
Just fresh from the Banquet of Comus.   20

To his Brother George in America

'TIS the witching time of night,
Orbèd is the moon and bright,
And the stars they glisten, glisten,
Seeming with bright eyes to listen –
  For what listen they?
For a song and for a charm.
See they glisten in alarm,
And the moon is waxing warm
  To hear what I shall say.
Moon! keep wide thy golden ears –   10
Hearken, stars! and hearken, spheres! –
Hearken, thou eternal sky!
I sing an Infant's lullaby,
  A pretty lullaby.
Listen, listen, listen, listen,
Glisten, glisten, glisten, glisten,
  And hear my lullaby!
Though the rushes that will make
Its cradle still are in the lake –
Though the linen that will be   20
Its swathe, is on the cotton tree –
Though the woollen that will keep

It warm, is on the silly sheep –
Listen, starlight, listen, listen,
Glisten, glisten, glisten, glisten,
      And hear my lullaby:
Child, I see thee! Child, I've found thee
Midst of the quiet all around thee!
Child, I see thee! Child, I spy thee!
And thy mother sweet is nigh thee!   30
Child, I know thee! Child no more,
But a Poet evermore!
See, see, the lyre, the lyre,
In a flame of fire,
Upon the little cradle's top
Flaring, flaring, flaring,
Past the eyesight's bearing.
Awake it from its sleep,
And see if it can keep
Its eyes upon the blaze –   40
      Amaze, amaze!
It stares, it stares, it stares,
It dares what no one dares!
It lifts its little hand into the flame
Unharm'd, and on the strings
Paddles a little tune, and sings,
With dumb endeavour sweetly –
Bard art thou completely!
      Little child
      O' th' western wild,   50
Bard art thou completely!
Sweetly with dumb endeavour
A Poet now or never,
      Little child
      O' th' western wild,
A Poet now or never!

'Where's the Poet?'

WHERE'S the Poet? show him, show him,
Muses nine, that I may know him!
'Tis the man who with a man
Is an equal, be he King,
Or poorest of the beggar-clan,
Or any other wondrous thing
A man may be 'twixt ape and Plato;
'Tis the man who with a bird,
Wren or Eagle, finds his way to
All its instincts; he hath heard
The Lion's roaring, and can tell
What his horny throat expresseth,
And to him the Tiger's yell
Comes articulate and presseth
On his ear like mother-tongue.

Modern Love

AND what is love? It is a doll dress'd up
For idleness to cosset, nurse, and dandle;
A thing of soft misnomers, so divine
That silly youth doth think to make itself
Divine by loving, and so goes on
Yawning and doting a whole summer long,
Till Miss's comb is made a pearl tiara,
And common Wellingtons turn Romeo boots;
Then Cleopatra lives at number seven,
And Antony resides in Brunswick Square.
Fools! if some passions high have warm'd the world,
If Queens and Soldiers have play'd deep for hearts,
It is no reason why such agonies
Should be more common than the growth of weeds.
Fools! make me whole again that weighty pearl

The Queen of Egypt melted, and I'll say
That ye may love in spite of beaver hats.

The Castle Builder

Fragments of a Dialogue

CASTLE BUILDER

... In short, convince you that however wise
You may have grown from Convent libraries,
I have, by many yards at least, been carding
A longer skein of wit in Convent garden.

BERNADINE

A very Eden that same place must be!
Pray what demesne? Whose Lordship's legacy?
What, have you convents in that Gothic Isle?
Pray pardon me, I cannot help but smile.

CASTLE BUILDER

Sir, Convent Garden is a monstrous beast.
From morning, four o'clock, to twelve at noon,   10
It swallows cabbages without a spoon,
And then, from twelve till two, this Eden made is
A promenade for cooks and ancient ladies;
And then for supper, 'stead of soup and poaches,
It swallows chairmen, damns, and Hackney coaches.
In short, Sir, 'tis a very place for monks,
For it containeth twenty thousand punks,
Which any man may number for his sport,
By following fat elbows up a court.

In suchlike nonsense would I pass an hour   20
With random Friar, or Rake upon his tour,

Or one or few of that imperial host
Who came unmaimèd from the Russian frost.

To-night I'll have my friar – let me think
About my room, – I'll have it in the pink;
It should be rich and sombre, and the moon,
Just in its mid-life in the midst of June,
Should look thro' four large windows and display
Clear, but for gold-fish vases in the way,
Their glassy diamonding on Turkish floor;   30
The tapers keep aside, an hour or more,
To see what else the moon alone can show;
While the night-breeze doth softly let us know
My terrace is well-bower'd with oranges.
Upon the floor the dullest spirit sees
A guitar-ribband and a lady's glove
Beside a crumple-leavèd tale of love;
A tambour-frame, with Venus sleeping there,
All finish'd but some ringlets of her hair;
A viol-bow, strings torn, cross-wise upon   40
A glorious folio of Anacreon;
A skull upon a mat of roses lying,
Ink'd purple with a song concerning dying;
An hour-glass on the turn, amid the trails
Of passion-flower; – just in time there sails
A cloud across the moon, – the lights bring in,
And see what more my phantasy can win.
It is a gorgeous room, but somewhat sad;
The draperies are so, as tho' they had
Been made for Cleopatra's winding-sheet: 50
And opposite the stedfast eye doth meet
A spacious looking-glass, upon whose face,
In letters raven-sombre, you may trace
Old 'Mene, Mene, Tekel, Upharsin.'
Greek busts and statuary have ever been
Held, by the finest spirits, fitter far

Than vase grotesque and Siamesian jar;
Therefore 'tis sure a want of Attic taste
That I should rather love a Gothic waste
Of eyesight on cinque-coloured potter's clay, 60
Than on the marble fairness of old Greece.
My table-coverlets of Jason's fleece
And black Numidian sheep-wool should be wrought,
Gold, black, and heavy, from the Lama brought.
My ebon sofas should delicious be
With down from Leda's cygnet progeny.
My pictures all Salvator's, save a few
Of Titian's portraiture, and one, though new,
Of Haydon's in its fresh magnificence.
My wine – O good! 'tis here at my desire, 70
And I must sit to supper with my friar.

'Welcome joy, and welcome sorrow'

'Under the flag
Of each his faction, they to battle bring
Their embryo atoms.'

        –MILTON.

WELCOME joy, and welcome sorrow,
    Lethe's weed and Hermes' feather;
Come to-day and come to-morrow,
    I do love you both together!
    I love to mark sad faces in fair weather;
And hear a merry laugh amid the thunder;
    Fair and foul I love together:
Meadows sweet where flames are under,
And a giggle at a wonder;
Visage sage at pantomime; 10
Funeral, and steeple-chime;
Infant playing with a skull;
Morning fair, and shipwreck'd hull;
Nightshade with the woodbine kissing;

Serpents in red roses hissing;
Cleopatra regal-dress'd
With the aspic at her breast;
Dancing music, music sad,
Both together, sane and mad;
Muses bright and muses pale;   20
Sombre Saturn, Momus hale; –
Laugh and sigh, and laugh again;
Oh! the sweetness of the pain!
Muses bright and muses pale,
Bare your faces of the veil;
Let me see; and let me write
Of the day and of the night –
Both together: – let me slake
All my thirst for sweet heart-ache;
Let my bower be of yew,   30
Interwreath'd with myrtles new;
Pines and lime-trees full in bloom
And my couch a low grass-tomb.

'Hush, hush! Tread softly! hush, hush, my dear!'

HUSH, hush! Tread softly! hush, hush, my dear!
   All the house is asleep, but we know very well
That the jealous, the jealous old bald-pate may hear,
   Tho' you've padded his nightcap – O sweet Isabel!
      Tho' your feet are more light than a Faery's feet,
      Who dances on bubbles where brooklets meet, –
Hush, hush! soft tiptoe! hush, hush, my dear!
For less than a nothing the jealous can hear.

No leaf doth tremble, no ripple is there
   On the river, – all's still, and the night's sleepy eye   10
Closes up, and forgets all its Lethean care,
   Charm'd to death by the drone of the humming May-fly;

And the moon, whether prudish or complaisant,
   Has fled to her bower, well knowing I want
No light in the dusk, no torch in the gloom,
But my Isabel's eyes and her lips pulp'd with bloom.

Lift the latch! ah gently! ah tenderly – sweet!
   We are dead if that latchet gives one little clink.
Well done! – now those lips, and a flowery seat–
   The old man may sleep, and the planets may wink;   **20**
      The shut rose shall dream of our loves and awake
      Full-blown, and such warmth for the morning take,
The stock-dove shall hatch his soft brace and shall coo,
While I kiss to the melody, aching all through!

The Dove

I HAD a dove, and the sweet dove died;
   And I have thought it died of grieving;
O, what could it grieve for? its feet were tied
   With a silken thread of my own hand's weaving;

Sweet little red feet, why should you die?
Why should you leave me, sweet bird, why?
You lived alone in the forest tree,
Why, pretty thing! would you not live with me?
I kissed you oft and gave you white peas;
Why not live sweetly, as in the green trees?

Extracts from an Opera

I

O! WERE I one of the Olympian twelve,
Their godships should pass this into a law –
That when a man doth set himself in toil

After some beauty veilèd far away,
Each step he took should make his lady's hand
More soft, more white, and her fair cheek more fair;
And for each briar-berry he might eat,
A kiss should bud upon the tree of love,
And pulp and ripen richer every hour,
To melt away upon the traveller's lips.   10

II DAISY'S SONG

1

The sun, with his great eye,
Sees not so much as I;
And the moon, all silver-proud,
Might as well be in a cloud.

2

And O the spring – the spring!
I lead the life of a king!
Couched in the teeming grass,
I spy each pretty lass.

3

I look where no one dares,
And I stare where no one stares,   20
And when the night is nigh,
Lambs bleat my lullaby.

III FOLLY'S SONG

When wedding fiddles are a-playing,
            Huzza for folly O!
And when maidens go a-maying,
            Huzza, etc.
When a milk-pail is upset,

Huzza, etc.
And the clothes left in the wet,
    Huzza, etc.   30

When the barrel's set abroach,
    Huzza, etc.
When Kate Eyebrow keeps a coach,
    Huzza, etc.
When the pig is over-roasted,
    Huzza, etc.
And the cheese is over-toasted,
    Huzza, etc.
When Sir Snap is with his lawyer,
    Huzza, etc.   40
And Miss Chip has kissed the sawyer,
    Huzza, etc.

I V

O, I am frightened with most hateful thoughts!
Perhaps her voice is not a nightingale's,
Perhaps her teeth are not the fairest pearl;
Her eye-lashes may be, for aught I know,
Not longer than the may-fly's small fan-horns;
There may not be one dimple on her hand –
And freckles many. Ah! a careless nurse,
In haste to teach the little thing to walk,   50
May have crumped up a pair of Dian's legs
And warped the ivory of a Juno's neck.

V SONG

I

The stranger lighted from his steed,
   And ere he spake a word,
He seized my lady's lily hand,
   And kissed it all unheard.

2

The stranger walked into the hall,
    And ere he spake a word,
He kissed my lady's cherry lips,
    And kissed 'em all unheard.   60

3

The stranger walked into the bower –
    But my lady first did go:
Ay, hand in hand into the bower,
    Where my lord's roses blow.

4

My lady's maid had a silken scarf,
    And a golden ring had she,
And a kiss from the stranger, as off he went
    Again on his fair palfrey.

The Eve of Saint Mark

UPON a Sabbath-day it fell;
Twice holy was the Sabbath-bell,
That call'd the folk to evening prayer;
The city streets were clean and fair
From wholesome drench of April rains;
And, on the western window panes,
The chilly sunset faintly told
Of unmatured green valleys cold,
Of the green thorny bloomless hedge,
Of rivers new with spring-tide sedge,   10
Of primroses by shelter'd rills,
And daisies on the aguish hills.
Twice holy was the Sabbath-bell:
The silent streets were crowded well
With staid and pious companies,

Warm from their fire-side orat'ries;
And moving, with demurest air,
To even-song, and vesper prayer,
Each archèd porch, and entry low,
Was fill'd with patient folk and slow,   20
With whispers hush, and shuffling feet,
While play'd the organ loud and sweet.

The bells had ceased, the prayers begun,
And Bertha had not yet half done
A curious volume, patch'd and torn,
That all day long, from earliest morn,
Had taken captive her two eyes,
Among its golden broideries;
Perplex'd her with a thousand things, —
The stars of heaven, and angels' wings,   30
Martyrs in a fiery blaze,
Azure saints in silver rays,
Moses' breastplate, and the seven
Candlesticks John saw in heaven,
The wingèd Lion of Saint Mark,
And the Covenantal Ark,
With its many mysteries
Cherubim and golden mice.

Bertha was a maiden fair,
Dwelling in th' old Minster-square;   40
From her fire-side she could see,
Sidelong, its rich antiquity,
Far as the Bishop's garden-wall;
Where sycamores and elm-trees tall,
Full-leaved, the forest had outstript,
By no sharp north-wind ever nipt,
So shelter'd by the mighty pile.
Bertha arose, and read awhile,
With forehead 'gainst the window-pane.

Again she tried, and then again,   50
Until the dusk eve left her dark
Upon the legend of St. Mark.
From plaited lawn-frill, fine and thin,
She lifted up her soft warm chin,
With aching neck and swimming eyes,
And dazed with saintly imageries.

All was gloom, and silent all,
Save now and then the still foot-fall
Of one returning homewards late,
Past the echoing minster-gate.   60
The clamorous daws, that all the day
Above tree-tops and towers play,
Pair by pair had gone to rest,
Each in its ancient belfry-nest,
Where asleep they fall betimes,
To music and the drowsy chimes.

All was silent, all was gloom,
Abroad and in the homely room:
Down she sat, poor cheated soul!
And struck a lamp from the dismal coal;   70
Lean'd forward, with bright drooping hair
And slant book, full against the glare.
Her shadow, in uneasy guise,
Hover'd about, a giant size,
On ceiling-beam and old oak chair,
The parrot's cage, and panel square;
And the warm angled winter screen,
On which were many monsters seen,
Call'd doves of Siam, Lima mice,
And legless birds of Paradise,   80
Macaw, and tender Avadavat,
And silken-furr'd Angora cat.

Untired she read, her shadow still
Glower'd about, as it would fill
The room with wildest forms and shades,
As though some ghostly queen of spades
Had come to mock behind her back,
And dance, and ruffle her garments black.
Untired she read the legend page,
Of holy Mark, from youth to age,   90
On land, on sea, in pagan chains,
Rejoicing for his many pains.
Sometimes the learned eremite,
With golden star, or dagger bright,
Referr'd to pious poesies
Written in smallest crow-quill size
Beneath the text; and thus the rhyme
Was parcell'd out from time to time:
–'Als writith he of swevenis,
Men han beforne they wake in bliss,   100
Whanne that hir friendes thinke hem bound
In crimpèd shroude farre under grounde;
And how a litling child mote be
A saint er its nativitie,
Gif that the modre (God her blesse!)
Kepen in solitarinesse,
And kissen devoute the holy croce.
Of Goddes love, and Sathan's force, –
He writith; and thinges many mo:
Of swiche thinges I may not shew.   110
Bot I must tellen verilie
Somdel of Sainte Cicilie,
And chieflie what he auctorethe
Of Sainte Markis life and dethe':

At length her constant eyelids come
Upon the fervent martyrdom;

Then lastly to his holy shrine,
Exalt amid the tapers' shine
At Venice,–

To Sleep

O SOFT embalmer of the still midnight!
　　Shutting, with careful fingers and benign,
Our gloom-pleased eyes, embower'd from the light,
　　Enshaded in forgetfulness divine;
O soothest Sleep! if so it please thee, close,
　　In midst of this thine hymn, my willing eyes,
Or wait the amen, ere thy poppy throws
　　Around my bed its lulling charities;
　　Then save me, or the passèd day will shine
Upon my pillow, breeding many woes;
　　Save me from curious conscience, that still lords
Its strength in darkness, burrowing like a mole;
　　Turn the key deftly in the oilèd wards,
And seal the hushèd casket of my soul.

'Why did I laugh to-night?'

WHY did I laugh to-night? No voice will tell:
　　No God, no Demon of severe response,
Deigns to reply from Heaven or from Hell.
　　Then to my human heart I turn at once.
Heart! Thou and I are here, sad and alone;
　　Say, wherefore did I laugh? O mortal pain!
O Darkness! Darkness! ever must I moan,
　　To question Heaven and Hell and Heart in vain.
Why did I laugh? I know this Being's lease,
　　My fancy to its utmost blisses spreads;
Yet would I on this very midnight cease,
　　And the world's gaudy ensigns see in shreds;
Verse, Fame, and Beauty are intense indeed,
But Death intenser – Death is Life's high meed.

On a Dream after reading of Paolo and Francesca in Dante's 'Inferno'

As Hermes once took to his feathers light,
    When lullèd Argus, baffled, swoon'd and slept,
So on a Delphic reed, my idle spright,
    So play'd, so charm'd, so conquer'd, so bereft
The dragon-world of all its hundred eyes,
    And seeing it asleep, so fled away,
Not to pure Ida with its snow-cold skies,
    Nor unto Tempe, where Jove grieved a day;
But to that second circle of sad Hell,
    Where in the gust, the whirlwind, and the flaw
Of rain and hail-stones, lovers need not tell
    Their sorrows, – pale were the sweet lips I saw,
Pale were the lips I kiss'd, and fair the form
I floated with, about that melancholy storm.

'The House of Mourning written by Mr. Scott'

The House of Mourning written by Mr. Scott,
    A sermon at the Magdalen, a tear
Dropped on a greasy novel, want of cheer
    After a walk uphill to a friend's cot,
Tea with a maiden lady, a cursed lot
    Of worthy poems with the author near,
    A patron lord, a drunkenness from beer,
Haydon's great picture, a cold coffee pot
At midnight when the Muse is ripe for labour,
    The voice of Mr. Coleridge, a French bonnet
Before you in the pit, a pipe and tabour,
A damned inseparable flute and neighbour –
    All these are vile, but viler Wordsworth's sonnet
On Dover. Dover! – who *could* write upon it?

'Fame, like a wayward girl'

FAME, like a wayward girl, will still be coy
    To those who woo her with too slavish knees,
But makes surrender to some thoughtless boy,
    And dotes the more upon a heart at ease;
She is a Gipsy will not speak to those
    Who have not learnt to be content without her;
A Jilt, whose ear was never whisper'd close,
    Who thinks they scandal her who talk about her;
A very Gipsy is she, Nilus-born,
    Sister-in-law to jealous Potiphar;
Ye love-sick Bards! repay her scorn for scorn;
    Ye Artists lovelorn! madmen that ye are!
Make your best bow to her and bid adieu,
Then, if she likes it, she will follow you.

Song of Four Fairies

Fire, Air, Earth, and Water,
Salamander, Zephyr, Dusketha, and Breama.

    Sal. Happy, happy, glowing fire!
    Zeph. Fragrant air! delicious light!
    Dus. Let me to my glooms retire!
    Bre. I to green-weed rivers bright!
    Sal. Happy, happy glowing fire!
Dazzling bowers of soft retire,
Ever let my nourish'd wing,
Like a bat's, still wandering,
Faintless fan your fiery spaces,
Spirit sole in deadly places.
In unhaunted roar and blaze,
Open eyes that never daze,
Let me see the myriad shapes

10

Of men, and beasts, and fish, and apes,
Portray'd in many a fiery den,
And wrought by spumy bitumen
On the deep intenser roof,
Archèd every way aloof.
Let me breathe upon their skies,
And anger their live tapestries;   20
Free from cold, and every care
Of chilly rain and shivering air.
 Zeph. Spirit of Fire! away! away!
Or your very roundelay
Will sear my plumage newly budded
From its quillèd sheath, all studded
With the self-same dews that fell
On the May-grown Asphodel.
Spirit of Fire – away! away!
 Bre. Spirit of Fire – away! away!   30
Zephyr, blue-eyed fairy, turn,
And see my cool sedge-buried urn,
Where it rests its mossy brim
'Mid water-mint and cresses dim;
And the flowers, in sweet troubles,
Lift their eyes above the bubbles,
Like our Queen, when she would please
To sleep and Oberon *will* tease –
Love me, blue-eyed Fairy! true.
Soothly I am sick for you.   40
 Zeph. Gentle Breama! by the first
Violet young nature nurst,
I will bathe myself with thee,
So you sometimes follow me
To my home, far, far in west,
Beyond the nimble-wheelèd quest
Of the golden-browèd sun.
Come with me, o'er tops of trees,
To my fragrant palaces,

Where they ever floating are   50
Beneath the cherish of a star
Call'd Vesper, who with silver veil
Ever hides his brilliance pale,
Ever gently-drowsed doth keep
Twilight for the Fayes to sleep.
Fear not that your watery hair
Will thirst in drouthy ringlets there;
Clouds of storèd summer rains
Thou shalt taste, before the stains
Of the mountain soil they take,   60
And too unlucent for thee make.
I love thee, crystal Fairy, true!
Sooth I am as sick for you!

    Sal. Out, ye aguish Fairies, out!
Chilly lovers, what a rout
Keep ye with your frozen breath,
Colder than the mortal death!
Adder-eyed Dusketha, speak!
Shall we leave these, and go seek
In the earth's wide entrails old   70
Couches warm as theirs are cold?
O for a fiery gloom and thee,
Dusketha, so enchantingly
Freckle-wing'd and lizard-sided!

    Dus. By thee, Sprite, will I be guided!
I care not for cold or heat:
Frost and flame, or sparks, or sleet,
To my essence are the same; –
But I honour more the flame.
Sprite of Fire, I follow thee   80
Wheresoever it may be, –
To the torrid spouts and fountains,
Underneath earth-quakèd mountains;
Or, at thy supreme desire,
Touch the very pulse of fire

With my bare unlidded eyes.
    Sal. Sweet Dusketha! paradise!
Off, ye icy Spirits, fly!
Frosty creatures of the sky.
    Dus. Breathe upon them, fiery sprite!   90
    Zeph.   } Away! away to our delight!
    Bre.   }
    Sal. Go, feed on icicles, while we
Bedded in tongue-flames will be.
    Dus. Lead me to those feverous glooms,
Sprite of Fire!
    Bre.   Me to the blooms,
Blue-eyed Zephyr, of those flowers
Far in the west where the May-cloud lowers;
And the beams of still Vesper, when winds
        are all wist,
Are shed through the rain and the milder mist,   100
And twilight your floating bowers.

La Belle Dame sans Mercy

[*Indicator* version]

AH, what can ail thee, wretched wight,
  Alone and palely loitering;
The sedge is wither'd from the lake,
    And no birds sing.

Ah, what can ail thee, wretched wight,
  So haggard and so woe-begone?
The squirrel's granary is full,
    And the harvest's done.

I see a lily on thy brow,
  With anguish moist and fever dew;   10
And on thy cheek a fading rose
    Fast withereth too.

I met a Lady in the meads
    Full beautiful, a fairy's child;
Her hair was long, her foot was light,
    And her eyes were wild.

I set her on my pacing steed,
    And nothing else saw all day long;
For sideways would she lean, and sing
    A fairy's song.   20

I made a garland for her head,
    And bracelets too, and fragrant zone:
She look'd at me as she did love,
    And made sweet moan.

She found me roots of relish sweet,
    And honey wild, and manna dew;
And sure in language strange she said,
    I love thee true.

She took me to her elfin grot,
    And there she gaz'd and sighed deep,   30
And there I shut her wild sad eyes –
    So kiss'd to sleep.

And there we slumber'd on the moss,
    And there I dream'd, ah woe betide,
The latest dream I ever dream'd
    On the cold hill side.

I saw pale kings, and princes too,
    Pale warriors, death-pale were they all;
Who cried, 'La belle Dame sans mercy
    Hath thee in thrall!'   40

I saw their starv'd lips in the gloom
    With horrid warning gaped wide,

And I awoke, and found me here
　　On the cold hill side.

And this is why I sojourn here
　　Alone and palely loitering,
Though the sedge is wither'd from the lake,
　　And no birds sing.

　　　　　　　　　　　CAVIARE

La belle dame sans merci

O WHAT can ail thee knight at arms,
　　Alone and palely loitering?
The sedge has withered from the lake
　　And no birds sing!

O what can ail thee knight at arms,
　　So haggard and so woe begone?
The squirrel's granary is full
　　And the harvest's done.

I see a lilly on thy brow
　　With anguish moist and fever dew,　　　10
And on thy cheeks a fading rose
　　Fast Withereth too –

I met a Lady in the Meads
　　Full beautiful, a faery's child;
Her hair was long, her foot was light
　　And her eyes were wild –

I made a Garland for her head,
　　And bracelets too, and fragrant Zone
She look'd at me as she did love
　　And made sweet moan –　　　　　　20

I set her on my pacing steed
    And nothing else saw all day long,
For sidelong would she bend, and sing
    A faery's song –

She found me roots of relish sweet
    And honey wild and manna dew,
And sure in language strange she said
    I love thee true –

She took me to her elfin grot
    And there she wept and sigh'd full sore,   30
And there I shut her wild wild eyes
    With kisses four.

And there she lulled me asleep
    And there I dream'd – Ah! Woe betide!
The latest dream I ever dreamt
    On the cold hill side.

I saw pale kings and Princes too,
    Pale warriors, death pale were they all;
They cried 'La belle dame sans merci
    Thee hath in thrall.'   40

I saw their starv'd lips in the gloam
    With horrid warning gaped wide,
And I awoke and found me here
    On the cold hill's side.

And this is why I sojourn here
    Alone and palely loitering;
Though the sedge is wither'd from the Lake
    And no birds sing.

'How fever'd is the man, who cannot look'

'You cannot eat your cake and have it too.' – *Proverb*

How fever'd is the man, who cannot look
    Upon his mortal days with temperate blood,
Who vexes all the leaves of his life's book,
    And robs his fair name of its maidenhood;
It is as if the rose should pluck herself,
    Or the ripe plum finger its misty bloom,
As if a Naiad, like a meddling elf,
    Should darken her pure grot with muddy gloom,
But the rose leaves herself upon the briar,
    For winds to kiss and grateful bees to feed,
And the ripe plum still wears its dim attire,
    The undisturbed lake has crystal space,
    Why then should man, teasing the world for grace,
Spoil his salvation for a fierce miscreed?

'If by dull rhymes our English must be chain'd'

If by dull rhymes our English must be chain'd,
    And, like Andromeda, the Sonnet sweet
Fetter'd, in spite of pained loveliness,
    Let us find out, if we must be constrain'd,
Sandals more interwoven and complete
To fit the naked foot of Poesy:
    Let us inspect the Lyre, and weigh the stress
Of every chord, and see what may be gain'd
By ear industrious, and attention meet;
Misers of sound and syllable, no less
Than Midas of his coinage, let us be
Jealous of dead leaves in the bay wreath crown;
So, if we may not let the Muse be free,
She will be bound with garlands of her own.

Faery Songs

I

SHED no tear! oh shed no tear!
The flower will bloom another year.
Weep no more! oh weep no more!
Young buds sleep in the root's white core.
Dry your eyes! oh dry your eyes!
For I was taught in Paradise
To ease my breast of melodies –
            Shed no tear.

Overhead! look overhead!
'Mong the blossoms white and red –
Look up, look up. I flutter now
On this flush pomegranate bough.
See me! 'tis this silvery bill
Ever cures the good man's ill.
Shed no tear! Oh shed no tear!
The flower will bloom another year.
Adieu, adieu! – I fly, adieu!
I vanish in the heaven's blue –
            Adieu! Adieu!

2

AH! woe is me! poor Silver-wing!
  That I must chant thy lady's dirge,
And death to this fair haunt of spring,
Of melody, and streams of flowery verge, –
    Poor Silver-wing! ah! woe is me!
      That I must see
These blossoms snow upon thy lady's pall!
    Go, pretty page, and in her ear
    Whisper that the hour is near.
    Softly tell her not to fear

Such calm favonian burial!
  Go, pretty page! and soothly tell, –
  The blossoms hang by a melting spell,
And fall they must ere a star wink thrice
    Upon her closèd eyes,
That now in vain are weeping their last tears
  At sweet life leaving, and these arbours green, –
Rich dowry from the Spirit of the Spheres, –
    Alas! poor Queen!

Spenserian Stanzas on Charles Armitage Brown

I

HE is to weet a melancholy carle:
Thin in the waist, with bushy head of hair,
As hath the seeded thistle when in parle
It holds the Zephyr, ere it sendeth fair
Its light balloons into the summer air;
Therto his beard had not begun to bloom,
No brush had touch'd his chin or razor sheer;
No care had touch'd his cheek with mortal doom,
But new he was and bright as scarf from Persian loom.

II

Ne cared he for wine, or half-and-half   10
Ne cared he for fish or flesh or fowl,
And sauces held he worthless as the chaff;
He 'sdeigned the swine-head at the wassail-bowl;
Ne with lewd ribbalds sat he cheek by jowl;
Ne with sly Lemans in the scorner's chair;
But after water-brooks this Pilgrim's soul
Panted, and all his food was woodland air
Though he would oft-times feast on gilliflowers rare.

III

The slang of cities in no wise he knew,
   Tipping the wink to him was heathen Greek;   20
He sipp'd no olden Tom or ruin blue,
   Or nantz or cherry-brandy drank full meek
By many a damsel hoarse and rouge of cheek;
Nor did he know each aged watchman's beat,
   Nor in obscured purlieus would he seek
   For curled Jewesses, with ankles neat,
Who as they walk abroad make tinkling with their feet.

Ode on Indolence

'They toil not, neither do they spin.'

ONE morn before me were three figures seen,
   With bowèd necks, and joinèd hands, side-faced;
And one behind the other stepp'd serene,
   In placid sandals, and in white robes graced;
      They pass'd, like figures on a marble urn,
   When shifted round to see the other side;
They came again; as when the urn once more
      Is shifted round, the first seen shades return;
   And they were strange to me, as may betide
With vases, to one deep in Phidian lore.   10

How is it, Shadows! that I knew ye not?
   How came ye muffled in so hush a mask?
Was it a silent deep-disguisèd plot
   To steal away, and leave without a task
      My idle days? Ripe was the drowsy hour;
   The blissful cloud of summer-indolence
Benumb'd my eyes; my pulse grew less and less;
      Pain had no sting, and pleasure's wreath no flower:
   O, why did ye not melt, and leave my sense
Unhaunted quite of all but – nothingness?   20

A third time pass'd they by, and, passing, turn'd
    Each one the face a moment whiles to me;
Then faded, and to follow them I burn'd
    And ached for wings, because I knew the three;
        The first was a fair Maid, and Love her name;
    The second was Ambition, pale of cheek,
And ever watchful with fatiguèd eye;
        The last, whom I love more, the more of blame
    Is heap'd upon her, maiden most unmeek, –
I knew to be my demon Poesy.   30

They faded, and, forsooth! I wanted wings:
    O folly! What is Love? and where is it?
And for that poor Ambition! it springs
    From a man's little heart's short fever-fit;
        For Poesy! – no, – she has not a joy, –
    At least for me, – so sweet as drowsy noons,
And evenings steep'd in honey'd indolence;
        O, for an age so shelter'd from annoy,
    That I may never know how change the moons,
Or hear the voice of busy common-sense!   40

And once more came they by; – alas! wherefore?
    My sleep had been embroider'd with dim dreams;
My soul had been a lawn besprinkled o'er
    With flowers, and stirring shades; and baffled beams:
        The morn was clouded, but no shower fell,
    Tho' in her lids hung the sweet tears of May;
The open casement press'd a new-leaved vine,
    Let in the budding warmth and throstle's lay;
        O Shadows! 'twas a time to bid farewell!
Upon your skirts had fallen no tears of mine.   50

So, ye three Ghosts, adieu! Ye cannot raise
    My head cool-bedded in the flowery grass;
For I would not be dieted with praise,

A pet-lamb in a sentimental farce!
   Fade softly from my eyes, and be once more
In masque-like figures on the dreamy urn;
Farewell! I yet have visions for the night,
   And for the day faint visions there is store;
Vanish, ye Phantoms! from my idle spright,
   Into the clouds, and never more return!   60

A Party of Lovers

PENSIVE they sit, and roll their languid eyes,
Nibble their toast and cool their tea with sighs;
Or else forget the purpose of the night,
Forget their tea, forget their appetite.
See, with cross'd arms they sit – Ah! happy crew,
The fire is going out and no one rings
For coals, and therefore no coals Betty brings.
A fly is in the milk-pot. Must he die
Circled by a humane society?
No, no; there, Mr. Werter takes his spoon,   10
Inserts it, dips the handle, and lo! soon
The little straggler, sav'd from perils dark,
Across the teaboard draws a long wet mark.

   Romeo! Arise, take snuffers by the handle,
There's a large cauliflower in each candle.
A winding sheet – ah, me! I must away
To No. 7, just beyond the circus gay.
Alas, my friend, your coat sits very well;
Where may your Tailor live? I may not tell.
O pardon me. I'm absent now and then.   20
Where *might* my Tailor live? I say again
I cannot tell, let me no more be teased;
He lives in Wapping, might live where he pleased.

'The day is gone'

THE day is gone, and all its sweets are gone!
    Sweet voice, sweet lips, soft hand, and softer breast,
Warm breath, light whisper, tender semi-tone,
    Bright eyes, accomplish'd shape, and lang'rous waist!
Faded the flower and all its budded charms,
    Faded the sight of beauty from my eyes,
Faded the shape of beauty from my arms,
    Faded the voice, warmth, whiteness, paradise –
Vanish'd unseasonably at shut of eve,
    When the dusk holiday – or holinight
Of fragrant-curtain'd love begins to weave
    The woof of darkness thick, for hid delight;
But, as I've read love's missal through to-day,
He'll let me sleep, seeing I fast and pray.

Lines to Fanny

WHAT can I do to drive away
Remembrance from my eyes? for they have seen,
Ay, an hour ago, my brilliant Queen!
Touch has a memory. O say, love, say,
What can I do to kill it and be free
In my old liberty?
When every fair one that I saw was fair
Enough to catch me in but half a snare,
Not keep me there:
When, howe'er poor or particolour'd things,   **10**
My muse had wings,
And ever ready was to take her course
Whither I bent her force,
Unintellectual, yet divine to me; –
Divine, I say! – What sea-bird o'er the sea
Is a philosopher the while he goes

Winging along where the great water throes?
How shall I do
To get anew
Those moulted feathers, and so mount once more   20
Above, above
The reach of fluttering Love,
And make him cower lowly while I soar?
Shall I gulp wine? No, that is vulgarism,
A heresy and schism,
Foisted into the canon-law of love; –
No, – wine is only sweet to happy men;
More dismal cares
Seize on me unawares, –
Where shall I learn to get my peace again?   30
To banish thoughts of that most hateful land,
Dungeoner of my friends, that wicked strand
Where they were wreck'd and live a wreckèd life;
That monstrous region, whose dull rivers pour,
Ever from their sordid urns unto the shore,
Unown'd of any weedy-hairèd gods;
Whose winds, all zephyrless, hold scourging rods,
Iced in the great lakes, to afflict mankind;
Whose rank-grown forests, frosted, black, and blind,
Would fright a Dryad; whose harsh herbaged meads   40
Make lean and lank the starv'd ox while he feeds;
There bad flowers have no scent, birds no sweet song,
And great unerring Nature once seems wrong.

O, for some sunny spell
To dissipate the shadows of this hell!
Say they are gone, – with the new dawning light
Steps forth my lady bright!
O, let me once more rest
My soul upon that dazzling breast!
Let once again these aching arms be placed,   50
The tender gaolers of thy waist!

And let me feel that warm breath here and there
To spread a rapture in my very hair, –
O, the sweetness of the pain!
Give me those lips again!
Enough! Enough! it is enough for me
To dream of thee!

To Fanny

PHYSICIAN Nature! let my spirit blood!
O ease my heart of verse and let me rest:
Throw me upon thy Tripod, till the flood
Of stifling numbers ebbs from my full breast.
A theme! a theme! great nature! give a theme;
  Let me begin my dream.
I come – I see thee, as thou standest there,
Beckon me not into the wintry air.

Ah! dearest love, sweet home of all my fears,
And hopes, and joys, and panting miseries, –   10
To-night, if I may guess, thy beauty wears
  A smile of such delight,
  As brilliant and as bright,
As when with ravish'd, aching, vassal eyes,
  Lost in soft amaze,
   I gaze, I gaze!

Who now, with greedy looks, eats up my feast?
What stare outfaces now my silver moon?
Ah! keep that hand unravish'd at the least;
  Let, let, the amorous burn –   20
  But, pr'ythee, do not turn
The current of your heart from me so soon.
  O! save, in charity,
  The quickest pulse for me.

Save it for me, sweet love! though music breathe
Voluptuous visions into the warm air,
Though swimming through the dance's dangerous wreath:
    Be like an April day,
    Smiling and cold and gay,
A temperate lily, temperate as fair;   30
    Then, Heaven! there will be
    A warmer June for me.

Why, this – you'll say, my Fanny! is not true:
Put your soft hand upon your snowy side,
Where the heart beats: confess – 'tis nothing new –
    Must not a woman be
    A feather on the sea,
Sway'd to and fro by every wind and tide?
    Of as uncertain speed
    As blow-ball from the mead?   40

I know it – and to know it is despair
To one who loves you as I love, sweet Fanny!
Whose heart goes flutt'ring for you everywhere,
    Nor, when away you roam,
    Dare keep its wretched home,
Love, love alone, his pains severe and many:
    Then, loveliest! keep me free,
    From torturing jealousy.

Ah! if you prize my subdued soul above
The poor, the fading, brief pride of an hour;   50
Let none profane my Holy See of love,
    Or with a rude hand break
    The sacramental cake:
Let none else touch the just new-budded flower.
    If not – may my eyes close,
    Love! on their last repose.

To Fanny

I CRY your mercy – pity – love! – ay, love!
   Merciful love that tantalises not
One-thoughted, never-wandering, guileless love,
   Unmask'd, and being seen – without a blot!
O! let me have thee whole, – all – all – be mine!
   That shape, that fairness, that sweet minor zest
Of love, your kiss, – those hands, those eyes divine,
   That warm, white, lucent, million-pleasured breast, –
Yourself – your soul – in pity give me all,
   Withhold no atom's atom or I die,
Or living on, perhaps, your wretched thrall,
   Forget, in the mist of idle misery,
Life's purposes, – the palate of my mind
Losing its gust, and my ambition blind!

'This living hand, now warm and capable'

THIS living hand, now warm and capable
Of earnest grasping, would, if it were cold
And in the icy silence of the tomb,
So haunt thy days and chill thy dreaming nights
That thou would[st] wish thine own heart dry of blood
So in my veins red life might stream again,
And thou be conscience-calm'd – see here it is –
I hold it towards you.

'Bright Star, would I were stedfast as thou art'

BRIGHT Star, would I were stedfast as thou art –
   Not in lone splendor hung aloft the night
And watching, with eternal lids apart,
   Like nature's patient, sleepless Eremite,
The moving waters at their priestlike task

Of pure ablution round earth's human shores,
Or gazing on the new soft-fallen masque
    Of snow upon the mountains and the moors.
No – yet still stedfast, still unchangeable,
    Pillow'd upon my fair love's ripening breast,
To feel for ever its soft swell and fall,
    Awake for ever in a sweet unrest,
Still, still to hear her tender-taken breath,
And so live ever – or else swoon to death.

Two or three Posies

from a letter to his sister

Two or three Posies
With two or three simples –
Two or three Noses
With two or three pimples –
Two or three wise men
And two or three ninny's –
Two or three purses
And two or three guineas –
Two or three raps
At two or three doors –   10
Two or three naps
Of two or three hours –
Two or three Cats
And two or three mice –
Two or three sprats
At a very great price –
Two or three sandies
And two or three tabbies –
Two or three dandies
And two Mrs. ——— mum!   20
Two or three Smiles
And two or three frowns –

Two or three Miles
To two or three towns –
Two or three pegs
For two or three bonnets –
Two or three dove eggs
To hatch into sonnets.

'When they were come unto the Faery's Court'

WHEN they were come unto the Faery's Court
They rang – no one at home; all gone to sport
And dance and kiss and love as faeries do,
For faeries be, as humans, lovers true.
Amid the woods they were, so lone and wild,
Where even the robin feels himself exiled,
And where the very brooks as if afraid
Hurry along to some less magic shade.
'No one at home!' the fretful princess cried,
'And all for nothing such a dre[a]ry ride,   10
And all for nothing my new diamond cross,
No one to see my Persian feathers toss,
No one to see my Ape, my Dwarf, my Fool,
Or how I pace my Otaheitan mule.
Ape, Dwarf and Fool, why stand you gaping there?
Burst the door open, quick – or I declare
I'll switch you soundly and in pieces tear.'
The Dwarf began to tremble and the Ape
Star'd at the Fool, the Fool was all agape,
The Princess grasp'd her switch, but just in time   20
The dwarf with piteous face began to rhyme.
'O mighty Princess did you ne'er hear tell
What your poor servants know but too too well?
Know you the three great crimes in faery land?
The first, alas! poor Dwarf, I understand –
I made a whipstock of a faery's wand –
The next is snoring in their company –

The next, the last, the direst of the three
Is making free when they are not at home.
I was a Prince – a baby prince – my doom   30
You see, I made a whipstock of a wand –
My top has henceforth slept in faery land.
He was a Prince, the Fool, a grown up Prince,
But he has never been a King's son since
He fell a-snoring at a faery Ball –
Your poor Ape was a prince and he, poor thing,
Picklock'd a faery's boudoir – now no king,
But ape – so pray your highness stay awhile;
'Tis sooth indeed, we know it to our sorrow –
Persist and *you* may be an ape tomorrow –'   40
While the Dwarf spake the Princess all for spite
Peel'd the brown hazel twig to lily white,
Clench'd her small teeth, and held her lips apart,
Try'd to look unconcern'd with beating heart.
They saw her highness had made up her mind
And quaver'd like the reeds before the wind,
And they had had it, but, O happy chance!
The Ape for very fear began to dance
And grinn'd as all his ugliness did ache –
She staid her vixen fingers for his sake,   50
He was so very ugly: then she took
Her pocket glass mirror and began to look
First at herself and [then] at him and then
She smil'd at her own beauteous face again.
Yet for all this – for all her pretty face
She took it in her head to see the place.
Women gain little from experience
Either in Lovers, husbands or expense.
The more the beauty, the more fortune too,
Beauty before the wide world never knew.   60
So each fair reasons – tho' it oft miscarries.
She thought *her* pretty face would please the fa[e]ries.

'My darling Ape I won't whip you today –
Give me the Picklock, sirrah, and go play.'
They all three wept – but counsel was as vain
As crying cup biddy to drops of rain.
Yet lingeringly did the sad Ape forth draw
The Picklock from the Pocket in his Jaw.
The Princess took it and dismounting straight
Trip'd in blue silver'd slippers to the gate   70
And touch'd the wards, the Door full cou[r]teou[s]ly
Opened – she enter'd with her servants three.
Again it clos'd and there was nothing seen
But the Mule grazing on the herbage green.

End of Canto xii

Canto the xiii

The Mule no sooner saw himself alone
Than he prick'd up his Ears – and said 'well done!
At least, unhappy Prince, I may be free –
No more a Princess shall side-saddle me.
O King of Othaietè – tho' a Mule
"Aye every inch a King" – tho' "Fortune's fool" –   80
Well done – for by what Mr. Dwarfy said
I would not give a sixpence for her head.'
Even as he spake he trotted in high glee
To the knotty side of an old Pollard tree
Aud rub['d] his sides against the mossed bark
Till his Girths burst and left him naked stark
Except his Bridle – how get rid of that,
Buckled and tied with many a twist and plait?
At last it struck him to pretend to sleep
And then the thievish Monkeys down would creep   90
And filch the unpleasant trammels quite away.
No sooner thought of than adown he lay,
Sham'd a good snore – the Monkey-men descended
And whom they thought to injure they befriended.

They hung his Bridle on a topmost bough
And of[f] he went, run, trot, or anyhow –
   Brown is gone to bed – and I am tired of rhyming . . .

'In after-time a sage of mickle lore'

IN after-time a sage of mickle lore
Yclep'd Typographus, the Giant took
And did refit his limbs as heretofore,
And made him read in many a learned book,
And into many a lively legend look;
Thereby in goodly themes so training him,
That all his brutishness he quite forsook,
When, meeting Artegall and Talus grim,
The one he struck stone-blind, the other's eyes wox dim.

LONGER
POSTHUMOUS
POEMS

NARRATIVE AND DRAMATIC

The Fall of Hyperion: a Vision

Canto I

FANATICS have their dreams, wherewith they weave
A paradise for a sect; the savage, too,
From forth the loftiest fashion of his sleep
Guesses at heaven; pity these have not
Traced upon vellum or wild Indian leaf
The shadows of melodious utterance,
But bare of laurel they live, dream, and die;
For Poesy alone can tell her dreams, –
With the fine spell of words alone can save
Imagination from the sable chain   10
And dumb enchantment. Who alive can say,
'Thou art no Poet – mayst not tell thy dreams'?
Since every man whose soul is not a clod
Hath visions and would speak, if he had loved,
And been well nurtured in his mother tongue.
Whether the dream now purposed to rehearse
Be poet's or fanatic's will be known
When this warm scribe, my hand, is in the grave.
   Methought I stood where trees of every clime,
Palm, myrtle, oak, and sycamore, and beech,   20
With plantane and spice-blossoms, made a screen,
In neighbourhood of fountains (by the noise
Soft-showering in mine ears), and (by the touch
Of scent) not far from roses. Turning round
I saw an arbour with a drooping roof
Of trellis vines, and bells, and larger blooms,
Like floral censers, swinging light in air;
Before its wreathèd doorway, on a mound
Of moss, was spread a feast of summer fruits,

Which, nearer seen, seem'd refuse of a meal   30
By angel tasted or our Mother Eve;
For empty shells were scatter'd on the grass,
And grapestalks but half bare, and remnants more
Sweet-smelling, whose pure kinds I could not know.
Still was more plenty than the fabled horn
Thrice emptied could pour forth at banqueting,
For Proserpine return'd to her own fields,
Where the white heifers low. And appetite,
More yearning than on earth I ever felt,
Growing within, I ate deliciously, –   40
And, after not long, thirsted; for thereby
Stood a cool vessel of transparent juice
Sipp'd by the wander'd bee, the which I took,
And pledging all the mortals of the world,
And all the dead whose names are in our lips,
Drank. That full draught is parent of my theme.
No Asian poppy or elixir fine
Of the soon-fading, jealous Caliphat,
No poison gender'd in close monkish cell,
To thin the scarlet conclave of old men,   50
Could so have rapt unwilling life away.
Among the fragrant husks and berries crush'd
Upon the grass, I struggled hard against
The domineering potion, but in vain.
The cloudy swoon came on, and down I sank,
Like a Silenus on an antique vase.
How long I slumber'd 'tis a chance to guess.
When sense of life return'd, I started up
As if with wings, but the fair trees were gone,
The mossy mound and arbour were no more: 60
I look'd around upon the carvèd sides
Of an old sanctuary, with roof august,
Builded so high, it seem'd that filmèd clouds
Might spread beneath as o'er the stars of heaven.
So old the place was, I remember'd none

The like upon the earth: what I had seen
Of grey cathedrals, buttress'd walls, rent towers,
The superannuations of sunk realms,
Or Nature's rocks toil'd hard in waves and winds,
Seem'd but the faulture of decrepit things 70
To that eternal domèd monument.
Upon the marble at my feet there lay
Store of strange vessels and large draperies,
Which needs had been of dyed asbestos wove,
Or in that place the moth could not corrupt,
So white the linen, so, in zone distinct,
Ran imageries from a sombre loom.
All in a mingled heap confused there lay
Robes, golden tongs, censer and chafing-dish,
Girdles, and chains, and holy jewelries. 80
    Turning from these with awe, once more I raised
My eyes to fathom the space every way:
The embossèd roof, the silent massy range
Of columns north and south, ending in mist
Of nothing; then to eastward, where black gates
Were shut against the sunrise evermore;
Then to the west I look'd, and saw far off
An image, huge of feature as a cloud,
At level of whose feet an altar slept,
To be approach'd on either side by steps 90
And marble balustrade, and patient travail
To count with toil the innumerable degrees.
Towards the altar sober-paced I went,
Repressing haste as too unholy there;
And, coming nearer, saw beside the shrine
One ministering; and there arose a flame.
As in mid-way the sickening east wind
Shifts sudden to the south, the small warm rain
Melts out the frozen incense from all flowers,
And fills the air with so much pleasant health 100
That even the dying man forgets his shroud; —

Even so that lofty sacrificial fire,
Sending forth Maian incense, spread around
Forgetfulness of everything but bliss,
And clouded all the altar with soft smoke;
From whose white fragrant curtains thus I heard
Language pronounced: 'If thou canst not ascend
These steps, die on that marble where thou art.
Thy flesh, near cousin to the common dust,
Will parch for lack of nutriment; thy bones   110
Will wither in few years, and vanish so
That not the quickest eye could find a grain
Of what thou now art on that pavement cold.
The sands of thy short life are spent this hour,
And no hand in the universe can turn
Thy hour-glass, if these gummèd leaves be burnt
Ere thou canst mount up these immortal steps.'
I heard, I look'd: two senses both at once,
So fine, so subtle, felt the tyranny
Of that fierce threat and the hard task proposed,   120
Prodigious seem'd the toil; the leaves were yet
Burning, when suddenly a palsied chill
Struck from the pavèd level up my limbs,
And was ascending quick to put cold grasp
Upon those streams that pulse beside the throat.
I shriek'd, and the sharp anguish of my shriek
Stung my own ears; I strove hard to escape
The numbness, strove to gain the lowest step.
Slow, heavy, deadly was my pace: the cold
Grew stifling, suffocating, at the heart;   130
And when I clasp'd my hands I felt them not.
One minute before death my iced foot touch'd
The lowest stair; and, as it touch'd, life seem'd
To pour in at the toes; I mounted up
As once fair angels on a ladder flew
From the green turf to heaven. 'Holy Power,'
Cried I, approaching near the hornèd shrine,

'What am I that should so be saved from death?
What am I that another death come not
To choke my utterance sacrilegious, here?'   140
Then said the veilèd shadow: 'Thou hast felt
What 'tis to die and live again before
Thy fated hour; that thou hadst power to do so
Is thine own safety; thou hast dated on
Thy doom.' 'High Prophetess,' said I, 'purge off,
Benign, if so it please thee, my mind's film.'
'None can usurp this height,' returned that shade,
'But those to whom the miseries of the world
Are misery, and will not let them rest.
All else who find a haven in the world,   150
Where they may thoughtless sleep away their days,
If by a chance into this fane they come,
Rot on the pavement where thou rottedst half.'
'Are there not thousands in the world,' said I,
Encouraged by the sooth voice of the shade,
'Who love their fellows even to the death,
Who feel the giant agony of the world,
And more, like slaves to poor humanity,
Labour for mortal good? I sure should see
Other men here, but I am here alone.'   160
'Those whom thou spakest of are no visionaries,'
Rejoin'd that voice; 'they are no dreamers weak;
They seek no wonder but the human face,
No music but a happy-noted voice:
They come not here, they have no thought to come;
And thou art here, for thou art less than they.
What benefit canst thou, or all thy tribe,
To the great world? Thou art a dreaming thing,
A fever of thyself: think of the earth;
What bliss, even in hope, is there for thee?   170
What haven? every creature hath its home,
Every sole man hath days of joy and pain,
Whether his labours be sublime or low –

The pain alone, the joy alone, distinct:
Only the dreamer venoms all his days,
Bearing more woe than all his sins deserve.
Therefore, that happiness be somewhat shared,
Such things as thou art are admitted oft
Into like gardens thou didst pass erewhile,
And suffer'd in these temples: for that cause   180
Thou standest safe beneath this statue's knees.'
'That I am favour'd for unworthiness,
By such propitious parley medicined
In sickness not ignoble, I rejoice,
Ay, and could weep for love of such award.'
So answer'd I, continuing, 'If it please,
Majestic shadow, tell me: sure not all
Those melodies sung into the world's ear
Are useless: sure a poet is a sage;
A humanist, physician to all men.   190
That I am none I feel, as vultures feel
They are no birds when eagles are abroad.
What am I then: Thou spakest of my tribe:
What tribe?' The tall shade veil'd in drooping white
Then spake, so much more earnest, that the breath
Moved the thin linen folds that drooping hung
About a golden censer from the hand
Pendent – 'Art thou not of the dreamer tribe?
The poet and the dreamer are distinct,
Diverse, sheer opposite, antipodes.   200
The one pours out a balm upon the world,
The other vexes it.' Then shouted I
Spite of myself, and with a Pythia's spleen,
'Apollo! faded! O far flown Apollo!
Where is thy misty pestilence to creep
Into the dwellings, through the door crannies
Of all mock lyrists, large self worshippers
And careless hectorers in proud bad verse.
Though I breathe death with them it will be life

To see them sprawl before me into graves.   210
Majestic shadow, tell me where I am,
Whose altar this, for whom this incense curls;
What image this whose face I cannot see
For the broad marble knees; and who thou art,
Of accent feminine, so courteous?'
    Then the tall shade, in drooping linen veil'd,
Spoke out, so much more earnest, that her breath
Stirr'd the thin folds of gauze that drooping hung
About a golden censer from her hand
Pendent; and by her voice I knew she shed   220
Long-treasured tears. 'This temple, sad and lone,
Is all spared from the thunder of a war
Foughten long since by giant hierarchy
Against rebellion: this old image here,
Whose carvèd features wrinkled as he fell,
Is Saturn's; I, Moneta, left supreme,
Sole priestess of this desolation.'
I had no words to answer, for my tongue,
Useless, could find about its roofèd home
No syllable of a fit majesty   230
To make rejoinder to Moneta's mourn:
There was a silence, while the altar's blaze
Was fainting for sweet food. I look'd thereon,
And on the pavèd floor, where nigh were piled
Faggots of cinnamon, and many heaps
Of other crispèd spicewood: then again
I look'd upon the altar, and its horns
Whiten'd with ashes, and its languorous flame,
And then upon the offerings again;
And so, by turns, till sad Moneta cried: 240
'The sacrifice is done, but not the less
Will I be kind to thee for thy good will.
My power, which to me is still a curse,
Shall be to thee a wonder, for the scenes
Still swooning vivid through my globèd brain,

With an electral changing misery,
Thou shalt with these dull mortal eyes behold
Free from all pain, if wonder pain thee not.'
As near as an immortal's spherèd words
Could to a mother's soften were these last: 250
And yet I had a terror of her robes,
And chiefly of the veils from her brow
Hung pale, and curtain'd her in mysteries,
That made my heart too small to hold its blood.
This saw that Goddess, and with sacred hand
Parted the veils. Then saw I a wan face,
Not pined by human sorrows, but bright-blanch'd
By an immortal sickness which kills not;
It works a constant change, which happy death
Can put no end to; deathwards progressing   260
To no death was that visage; it had past
The lily and the snow; and beyond these
I must not think now, though I saw that face.
But for her eyes I should have fled away;
They held me back with a benignant light,
Soft mitigated by divinest lids
Half-closed, and visionless entire they seem'd
Of all external things; they saw me not,
But in blank splendour, beam'd like the mild moon,
Who comforts those she sees not, who knows not   270
What eyes are upward cast. As I had found
A grain of gold upon a mountain's side,
And, twinged with avarice, strain'd out my eyes
To search its sullen entrails rich with ore,
So, at the view of sad Moneta's brow,
I ask'd to see what things the hollow brain
Behind environ'd: what high tragedy
In the dark secret chambers of her skull
Was acting, that could give so dread a stress
To her cold lips, and fill with such a light   280
Her planetary eyes, and touch her voice

With such a sorrow. 'Shade of Memory!'
Cried I, with act adorant at her feet,
'By all the gloom hung round thy fallen house,
By this last temple, by the golden age,
By great Apollo, thy dear foster-child,
And by thyself, forlorn divinity,
The pale Omega of a wither'd race,
Let me behold, according as thou saidst,
What in thy brain so ferments to and fro!'   290
No sooner had this conjuration past
My devout lips, than side by side we stood
(Like a stunt bramble by a solemn pine)
Deep in the shady sadness of a vale
Far sunken from the healthy breath of morn,
Far from the fiery noon and eve's one star.
Onward I look'd beneath the gloomy boughs,
And saw what first I thought an image huge,
Like to the image pedestal'd so high
In Saturn's temple; then Moneta's voice   300
Came brief upon mine ear. 'So Saturn sat
When he had lost his realms'; whereon there grew
A power within me of enormous ken
To see as a god sees, and take the depth
Of things as nimbly as the outward eye
Can size and shape pervade. The lofty theme
At those few words hung vast before my mind
With half-unravell'd web. I sat myself
Upon an eagle's watch, that I might see,
And seeing ne'er forget. No stir of life   310
Was in this shrouded vale, – not so much air
As in the zoning of a summer's day
Robs not one light seed from the feather'd grass;
But where the dead leaf fell there did it rest.
A stream went voiceless by, still deaden'd more
By reason of the fallen divinity
Spreading more shade; the Naiad 'mid her reeds

Prest her cold finger closer to her lips.
    Along the margin-sand large foot-marks went
No farther than to where old Saturn's feet   320
Had rested, and there slept how long a sleep!
Degraded, cold, upon the sodden ground
His old right hand lay nerveless, listless, dead,
Unsceptred, and his realmless eyes were closed;
While his bow'd head seem'd listening to the Earth,
His ancient mother, for some comfort yet.
    It seem'd no force could wake him from his place;
But there came one who, with a kindred hand,
Touch'd his wide shoulders, after bending low
With reverence, though to one who knew it not.   330
Then came the grieved voice of Mnemosyne,
And grieved I hearken'd. 'That divinity
Whom thou saw'st step from yon forlornest wood,
And with slow pace approach our fallen king,
Is Thea, softest-natured of our brood.'
I mark'd the Goddess, in fair statuary
Surpassing wan Moneta by the head,
And in her sorrow nearer woman's tears.
There was a list'ning fear in her regard,
As if calamity had but begun;   340
As if the vanward clouds of evil days
Had spent their malice, and the sullen rear
Was with its storèd thunder labouring up.
One hand she press'd upon that aching spot
Where beats the human heart, as if just there,
Though an immortal, she felt cruel pain;
The other upon Saturn's bended neck
She laid, and to the level of his ear
Leaning, with parted lips some words she spoke
In solemn tenour and deep organ-tone;   350
Some mourning words, which in our feeble tongue
Would come in this-like accenting; how frail
To that large utterance of the early gods!

'Saturn, look up! and for what, poor lost king?
I have no comfort for thee; no, not one;
I cannot say, wherefore thus sleepest thou?
For Heaven is parted from thee, and the Earth
Knows thee not, so afflicted, for a god.
And Ocean, too, with all its solemn noise,
Has from thy sceptre pass'd; and all the air   360
Is emptied of thine hoary majesty.
Thy thunder, captious at the new command,
Rumbles reluctant o'er our fallen house;
And thy sharp lightning, in unpractised hands,
Scotches and burns our once serene domain.
With such remorseless speed still come new woes,
That unbelief has not a space to breathe.
Saturn! sleep on: me thoughtless, why should I
Thus violate thy slumbrous solitude?
Why should I ope thy melancholy eyes?   370
Saturn! sleep on, while at thy feet I weep.'
      As when upon a trancèd summer-night
Forests, branch-charmèd by the earnest stars,
Dream, and so dream all night without a noise,
Save from one gradual solitary gust
Swelling upon the silence, dying off,
As if the ebbing air had but one wave,
So came these words and went; the while in tears
She prest her fair large forehead to the earth,
Just where her fallen hair might spread in curls   380
A soft and silken mat for Saturn's feet.
Long, long these two were postured motionless,
Like sculpture builded-up upon the grave
Of their own power. A long awful time
I look'd upon them: still they were the same;
The frozen God still bending to the earth,
And the sad Goddess weeping at his feet;
Moneta silent. Without stay or prop
But my own weak mortality, I bore

The load of this eternal quietude,   390
The unchanging gloom and the three fixèd shapes
Ponderous upon my senses, a whole moon;
For by my burning brain I measured sure
Her silver seasons shedded on the night,
And every day by day methought I grew
More gaunt and ghostly. Oftentimes I pray'd
Intense, that death would take me from the vale
And all its burthens; gasping with despair
Of change, hour after hour I cursed myself,
Until old Saturn raised his faded eyes,   400
And look'd around and saw his kingdom gone,
And all the gloom and sorrow of the place,
And that fair kneeling Goddess at his feet.
As the moist scent of flowers, and grass, and leaves,
Fills forest-dells with a pervading air,
Known to the woodland nostril, so the words
Of Saturn fill'd the mossy glooms around,
Even to the hollows of time-eaten oaks,
And to the windings in the foxes' hole,
With sad, low tones, while thus he spake, and sent   410
Strange musings to the solitary Pan.
'Moan, brethren, moan, for we are swallow'd up
And buried from all godlike exercise
Of influence benign on planets pale,
And peaceful sway above man's harvesting.
And all those acts which Deity supreme
Doth ease its heart of love in. Moan and wail;
Moan, brethren, moan; for lo, the rebel spheres
Spin round; the stars their ancient courses keep;
Clouds still with shadowy moisture haunt the earth,   420
Still suck their fill of light from sun and moon;
Still buds the tree, and still the seashores murmur;
There is no death in all the universe,
No smell of death, – There shall be death. Moan, moan;
Moan, Cybele, moan; for thy pernicious babes

Have changed a god into a shaking palsy.
Moan, brethren, moan, for I have no strength left;
Weak as the reed, weak, feeble as my voice.
Oh! oh! the pain, the pain of feebleness;
Moan, moan, for still I thaw; or give me help;   430
Throw down those imps, and give me victory.
Let me hear other groans, and trumpets blown
Of triumph calm, and hymns of festival,
From the gold peaks of heaven's high-piled clouds;
Voices of soft proclaim, and silver stir
Of strings in hollow shells; and let there be
Beautiful things made new, for the surprise
Of the sky-children.' So he feebly ceased,
With such a poor and sickly-sounding pause,
Methought I heard some old man of the earth   440
Bewailing earthly loss; nor could my eyes
And ears act with that unison of sense
Which marries sweet sound with the grace of form,
And dolorous accent from a tragic harp
With large-limb'd visions. More I scrutinized.
Still fixt he sat beneath the sable trees,
Whose arms spread straggling in wild serpent forms,
With leaves all hush'd; his awful presence there
(Now all was silent) gave a deadly lie
To what I erewhile heard: only his lips   450
Trembled amid the white curls of his beard;
They told the truth, though round the snowy locks
Hung nobly, as upon the face of heaven
A mid-day fleece of clouds. Thea arose,
And stretcht her white arm through the hollow dark,
Pointing some whither: whereat he too rose,
Like a vast giant, seen by men at sea
To grow pale from the waves at dull midnight.
They melted from my sight into the woods;
Ere I could turn, Moneta cried, 'These twain   460
Are speeding to the families of grief,

Where, rooft in by black rocks, they waste in pain
And darkness, for no hope.' And she spake on,
As ye may read who can unwearied pass
Onward from the antechamber of this dream,
Where, even at the open doors, awhile
I must delay, and glean my memory
Of her high phrase – perhaps no further dare.

Canto II

'MORTAL, that thou mayst understand aright,
I humanize my sayings to thine ear,
Making comparisons of earthly things;
Or thou mightst better listen to the wind,
Whose language is to thee a barren noise,
Though it blows legend-laden thro' the trees.
In melancholy realms big tears are shed,
More sorrow like to this, and such like woe,
Too huge for mortal tongue or pen of scribe,
The Titans fierce, self-hid or prison-bound,   10
Groan for the old allegiance once more,
Listening in their doom for Saturn's voice.
But one of the whole eagle-brood still keeps
His sovereignty, and rule, and majesty:
Blazing Hyperion on his orbèd fire
Still sits, still snuffs the incense teeming up
From Man to the Sun's God – yet unsecure,
For as upon the earth dire prodigies
Fright and perplex, so also shudders he;
Not at dog's howl or gloom-bird's hated screech,   20
Or the familiar visiting of one
Upon the first toll of his passing bell,
But horrors, portioned to a giant nerve,
Make great Hyperion ache. His palace bright,
Bastion'd with pyramids of glowing gold,
And touch'd with shade of bronzèd obelisks,

Glares a blood-red thro' all the thousand courts,
Arches, and domes, and fiery galleries;
And all its curtains of Aurorian clouds
Flush angerly; when he would taste the wreaths   30
Of incense breathed aloft from sacred hills,
Instead of sweets, his ample palate takes
Savour of poisonous brass and metals sick;
Wherefore when harbour'd in the sleepy West,
After the full completion of fair day,
For rest divine upon exalted couch,
And slumber in the arms of melody,
He paces through the pleasant hours of ease,
With strides colossal, on from hall to hall,
While far within each aisle and deep recess   40
His wingèd minions in close clusters stand
Amazed, and full of fear; like anxious men
Who on a wide plain gather in sad troops,
When earthquakes jar their battlements and towers.
Even now where Saturn, roused from icy trance,
Goes step for step with Thea from yon woods,
Hyperion, leaving twilight in the rear,
Is sloping to the threshold of the West.
Thither we tend.' Now in clear light I stood,
Relieved from the dusk vale. Mnemosyne   50
Was sitting on a square-edged polish'd stone,
That in its lucid depth reflected pure
Her priestess' garments. My quick eyes ran on
From stately nave to nave, from vault to vault,
Through bow'rs of fragrant and enwreathèd light,
And diamond-pavèd lustrous long arcades.
Anon rush'd by the bright Hyperion;
His flaming robes stream'd out beyond his heels,
And gave a roar as if of earthly fire,
That scared away the meek ethereal hours,   60
And made their dove-wings tremble. On he flared

• • •

The Cap and Bells; or, The Jealousies
A Faery Tale – Unfinished

IN midmost Ind, beside Hydaspes cool,
There stood, or hovered, tremulous in the air,
A faery city, 'neath the potent rule
Of Emperor Elfinan; famed ev'rywhere
For love of mortal women, maidens fair,
Whose lips were solid, whose soft hands were made
Of a fit mould and beauty, ripe and rare,
To pamper his slight wooing, warm yet staid:
He loved girls smooth as shades, but hated a mere shade.

This was a crime forbidden by the law;   10
And all the priesthood of his city wept,
For ruin and dismay they well foresaw
If impious prince no bound or limit kept,
And faery Zendervester overstept;
They wept, he sinned, and still he would sin on,
They dreamt of sin, and he sinned while they slept;
In vain the pulpit thundered at the throne,
Caricature was vain, and vain the tart lampoon.

Which seeing, his high court of parliament
Laid a remonstrance at his Highness' feet,   20
Praying his royal senses to content
Themselves with what in faery land was sweet,
Befitting best that shade with shade should meet:
Whereat, to calm their fears, he promised soon
From mortal tempters all to make retreat, –
Ay, even on the first of the new moon
An immaterial wife to espouse as heaven's boon.

Meantime he sent a fluttering embassy
To Pigmio, of Imaus sovereign,
To half beg, half demand, respectfully,   30
The hand of his fair daughter Bellanaine;
An audience had, and speeching done, they gain
Their point, and bring the weeping bride away;
Whom, with but one attendant, safely lain
Upon their wings, they bore in bright array,
While little harps were touched by many a lyric fay.

As in old pictures tender cherubim
A child's soul thro' the sapphired canvas bear,
So, thro' a real heaven, on they swim
With the sweet princess on her plumaged lair,   40
Speed giving to the winds her lustrous hair;
And so she journeyed, sleeping or awake,
Save when, for healthful exercise and air,
She chose to *promener à l'aile* or take
A pigeon's somerset, for sport or change's sake.

'Dear Princess, do not whisper me so loud,'
Quoth Corallina, nurse and confidant.
'Do not you see there, lurking in a cloud,
Close at your back, that sly old Crafticant?
He hears a whisper plainer than a rant: 50
Dry up your tears, and do not look so blue;
He's Elfinan's great state-spy militant,
His running, lying, flying footman too, –
Dear mistress, let him have no handle against you!

'Show him a mouse's tail, and he will guess,
With metaphysic swiftness, at the mouse;
Show him a garden, and with speed no less
He'll surmise sagely of a dwelling-house,
And plot, in the same minute, how to chouse
The owner out of it; show him a – ' 'Peace!   60

Peace! nor contrive thy mistress' ire to rouse!'
Returned the Princess, 'my tongue shall not cease
Till from this hated match I get a free release.

'Ah, beauteous mortal!' 'Hush!' quoth Coralline,
'Really you must not talk of him, indeed.'
'You hush!' replied the mistress with a shine
Of anger in her eyes, enough to breed
In stouter hearts than nurse's fear and dread:
'Twas not the glance itself made Nursey flinch,
But of its threat she took the utmost heed;   70
Not liking in her heart an hour-long pinch,
Or a sharp needle run into her back an inch.

So she was silenced, and fair Bellanaine,
Writhing her little body with ennui,
Continued to lament and to complain,
That Fate, cross-purposing, should let her be
Ravished away far from her dear countree;
That all her feelings should be set at nought,
In trumping up this match so hastily,
With lowland blood; and lowland blood she thought   80
Poison, as every staunch true-born Imaian ought.

Sorely she grieved, and wetted three or four
White Provence rose-leaves with her faery tears,
But not for this cause; – alas! she had more
Bad reasons for her sorrow, as appears
In the famed memoirs of a thousand years,
Written by Crafticant, and publishèd
By Parpaglion and Co., (those sly compeers
Who raked up ev'ry fact against the dead,)
In Scarab Street, Panthea, at the Jubal's Head.   90

Where, after a long hypercritic howl
Against the vicious manners of the age,

He goes on to expose, with heart and soul,
What vice in this or that year was the rage,
Backbiting all the world in ev'ry page;
With special strictures on the horrid crime,
(Sectioned and subsectioned with learning sage,)
Of faeries stooping on their wings sublime
To kiss a mortal's lips, when such were in their prime.

Turn to the copious index, you will find   100
Somewhere in the column, headed letter B,
The name of Bellanaine, if you're not blind;
Then pray refer to the text, and you will see
An article made up of calumny
Against this highland princess, rating her
For giving way, so over fashionably,
To this new-fangled vice, which seems a burr
Stuck in his moral throat, no coughing e'er could stir.

There he says plainly that she loved a man!
That she around him fluttered, flirted, toyed,   110
Before her marriage with great Elfinan;
That after marriage, too, she never joyed
In husband's company, but still employed
Her wits to 'scape away to Angle-land;
Where lived the youth, who worried and annoyed
Her tender heart, and its warm ardours fanned
To such a dreadful blaze her side would scorch her hand.

But let us leave this idle tittle-tattle
To waiting-maids and bedroom coteries,
Nor till fit time against her fame wage battle.   120
Poor Elfinan is very ill at ease;
Let us resume his subject if you please;
For it may comfort and console him much
To rhyme and syllable his miseries;

Poor Elfinan! whose cruel fate was such,
He sat and cursed a bride he knew he could not touch.

Soon as (according to his promises)
The bridal embassy had taken wing,
And vanished, bird-like, o'er the suburb trees,
The Emperor, empierced with the sharp sting   130
Of love, retired, vex'd and murmuring
Like any drone shut from the fair bee-queen,
Into his cabinet, and there did fling
His limbs upon a sofa, full of spleen,
And damned his House of Commons, in complete chagrin.

'I'll trounce some of the members,' cried the Prince,
'I'll put a mark against some rebel names,
I'll make the Opposition-benches wince,
I'll show them very soon, to all their shames,
What 'tis to smother up a Prince's flames.   140
That ministers should join in it, I own,
Surprises me! – they too at these high games!
Am I an Emperor? Do I wear a crown?
Imperial Elfinan, go hang thyself or drown!

'I'll trounce 'em! – there's the square-cut chancellor,
His son shall never touch that bishopric;
And for the nephew of old Palfior,
I'll show him that his speeches made me sick,
And give the colonelcy to Phalaric;
The tiptoe marquis, moral and gallant,   150
Shall lodge in shabby taverns upon tick;
And for the Speaker's second cousin's aunt,
She sha'n't be maid of honour, – by heaven that she sha'n't.

'I'll shirk the Duke of A.; I'll cut his brother;
I'll give no garter to his eldest son;
I won't speak to his sister or his mother.

The Viscount B. shall live at cut-and-run;
But how in the world can I contrive to stun
That fellow's voice, which plagues me worse than any,
That stubborn fool, that impudent state-dun,   160
Who sets down ev'ry sovereign as a zany, –
That vulgar commoner, Esquire Biancopany?

'Monstrous affair! Pshaw! pah! what ugly minx
Will they fetch from Imaus for my bride?
Alas! my wearied heart within me sinks,
To think that I must be so near allied
To a cold dullard fay, – ah, woe betide!
Ah, fairest of all human loveliness!
Sweet Bertha! what crime can it be to glide
About the fragrant plaitings of thy dress,   170
Or kiss thine eyes, or count thy locks, tress after tress?'

So said, one minute's while his eyes remained
Half lidded, piteous, languid, innocent;
But, in a wink, their splendour they regained,
Sparkling revenge with amorous fury blent.
Love thwarted in bad temper oft has vent:
He rose, he stampt his foot, he rang the bell,
And ordered some death-warrants to be sent
For signature: – somewhere the tempest fell,   180
As many a poor fellow does not live to tell.

'At the same time, Eban,' – (this was his page,
A fay of colour, slave from top to toe,
Sent as a present, while yet under age,
From the Viceroy of Zanguebar, – wise, slow
His speech, his only words were 'Yes,' and 'No,'
But swift of look and foot and wing was he,) –
'At the same time, Eban, this instant go
To Hum the soothsayer, whose name I see
Among the fresh arrivals in our empery.

'Bring Hum to me. But stay — here, take my ring,   190
The pledge of favour, that he not suspect
Any foul play, or awkward murdering,
Tho' I have bowstrung many of his sect;
Throw in a hint, that if he should neglect
One hour the next shall see him in my grasp,
And the next after that shall see him necked
Or swallowed by my hunger-starvèd asp, —
And mention ('tis as well) the torture of the wasp.'

These orders given, the Prince, in half a pet,
Let o'er the silk his propping elbow slide,   200
Caught up his little legs, and, in a fret,
Fell on the sofa on his royal side.
The slave retreated backwards, humble-eyed,
And with a slave-like silence closed the door,
And to old Hum thro' street and alley hied;
He 'knew the city,' as we say, of yore,
And for short cuts and turns, was nobody knew more.

It was the time when wholesale houses close
Their shutters with a moody sense of wealth,
But retail dealers, diligent, let loose   210
The gas (objected to on score of health),
Conveyed in little soldered pipes by stealth,
And make it flare in many a brilliant form,
That all the powers of darkness it repell'th,
Which to the oil-trade doth great scaith and harm,
And supersedeth quite the use of the glow-worm.

Eban, untempted by the pastrycooks,
(Of pastry he got store within the palace,)
With hasty steps, wrapped cloak, and solemn looks,
Incognito upon his errand sallies,   220
His smelling-bottle ready for the alleys;
He passed the hurdygurdies with disdain,

Vowing he'd have them sent on board the galleys;
  Just as he made his vow it 'gan to rain,
Therefore he called a coach, and bade it drive amain.

  'I'll pull the string,' said he, and further said,
  'Polluted jarvey! Ah, thou filthy hack!
  Whose springs of life are all dried up and dead,
  Whose linsey-woolsey lining hangs all slack,
  Whose rug is straw, whose wholeness is a crack;   230
  And evermore thy steps go clatter-clitter;
  Whose glass once up can never be got back,
  Who prov'st, with jolting arguments and bitter,
That 'tis of modern use to travel in a litter.

  'Thou inconvenience! thou hungry crop
  For all corn! thou snail-creeper to and fro,
  Who, while thou goest, ever seem'st to stop,
  And fiddle-faddle standest while you go;
  I' the morning, freighted with a weight of woe,
  Unto some lazar-house thou journeyest,   240
  And in the evening tak'st a double row
  Of dowdies, for some dance or party drest,
Besides the goods meanwhile thou movest east and west.

  'By thy ungallant bearing and sad mien,
  An inch appears the utmost thou couldst budge;
  Yet at the slightest nod, or hint, or sign,
  Round to the curb-stone patient dost thou trudge,
  Schooled in a beckon, learnèd in a nudge,
  A dull-eyed Argus watching for a fare;
  Quiet and plodding, thou dost bear no grudge   250
  To whisking tilburies or phaetons rare,
Curricles, or mail-coaches, swift beyond compare.'

  Philosophizing thus, he pulled the check
  And bade the coachman wheel to such a street,

Who, turning much his body, more his neck,
Louted full low, and hoarsely did him greet:
'Certes, monsieur were best take to his feet,
Seeing his servant can no further drive
For press of coaches, that to-night here meet,
Many as bees about a straw-capped hive,   260
When first for April honey into faint flowers they dive.'

Eban then paid his fare, and tiptoe went
To Hum's hotel; and, as he on did pass
With head inclined, each dusky lineament
Showed in the pearl-paved street, as in a glass;
His purple vest, that ever peeping was
Rich from the fluttering crimson of his cloak,
His silvery trousers, and his silken sash,
Tied in a burnished knot, their semblance took
Upon the mirrored walls, wherever he might look.   270

He smiled at self, and, smiling, showed his teeth
And seeing his white teeth, he smiled the more;
Lifted his eye-brows, spurned the path beneath,
Showed teeth again, and smiled as heretofore,
Until he knocked at the magician's door;
Where, till the porter answered, might be seen,
In the clear panel more he could adore, –
His turban wreathed of gold, and white, and green,
Mustachios, ear-ring, nose-ring, and his sabre keen.

'Does not your master give a rout to-night?'   280
Quoth the dark page. 'Oh, no!' returned the Swiss,
'Next door but one to us, upon the right,
The *Magazin des Modes* now open is
Against the Emperor's wedding; – and, sir, this
My master finds a monstrous horrid bore;
As he retired, an hour ago I wis,

With his best beard and brimstone, to explore
And cast a quiet figure in his second floor.

'Gad! he's obliged to stick to business!
For chalk, I hear, stands at a pretty price;   290
And as for aqua vitæ – there's a mess!
The *dentes sapientiæ* of mice,
Our barber tells me too, are on the rise, –
Tinder's a lighter article, – nitre pure
Goes off like lightning, – grains of Paradise
At an enormous figure! – stars not sure! –
Zodiac will not move without a slight douceur!

'Venus won't stir a peg without a fee,
And master is too partial, *entre nous,*
To – ' 'Hush – hush!' cried Eban, 'sure that is he   300
Coming downstairs, – by St. Bartholomew!
As backwards as he can, – is 't something new?
Or is 't his custom, in the name of fun?'
'He always comes down backward, with one shoe' –
Returned the porter – 'off, and one shoe on,
Like, saving shoe for sock or stocking, my man John!'

It was indeed the great Magician,
Feeling, with careful toe, for every stair,
And retrograding careful as he can,
Backwards and downwards from his own two pair: 310
'Salpietro!' exclaimed Hum, 'is the dog there?
He's always in my way upon the mat!'
'He's in the kitchen, or the Lord knows where,' –
Replied the Swiss, – 'the nasty, whelping brat!'
'Don't beat him!' returned Hum, and on the floor came pat.

Then facing right about, he saw the page,
And said: 'Don't tell me what you want, Eban;

The Emperor is now in a huge rage, –
'Tis nine to one he'll give you the rattan!
Let us away!' Away together ran   320
    The plain-dressed sage and spangled blackamoor,
Nor rested till they stood to cool, and fan,
    And breathe themselves at th' Emperor's chamber door,
When Eban thought he heard a soft imperial snore.

'I thought you guessed, foretold, or prophesied,
    That's Majesty was in a raving fit?'
'He dreams,' said Hum, 'or I have ever lied,
    That he is tearing you, sir, bit by bit.'
'He's not asleep, and you have little wit,'
    Replied the page; 'that little buzzing noise,   330
Whate'er your palmistry may make of it,
    Comes from a plaything of the Emperor's choice,
From a Man-Tiger-Organ, prettiest of his toys.'

Eban then ushered in the learnèd seer:
    Elfinan's back was turned, but, ne'ertheless,
Both, prostrate on the carpet, ear by ear,
    Crept silently, and waited in distress,
Knowing the Emperor's moody bitterness;
    Eban especially, who on the floor 'gan
Tremble and quake to death, – he fearèd less   340
    A dose of senna-tea or nightmare Gorgon
Than the Emperor when he played on his Man-Tiger-Organ.

They kissed nine times the carpet's velvet face
    Of glossy silk, soft, smooth, and meadow-green,
Where the close eye in deep rich fur might trace
    A silver tissue, scantly to be seen,
As daisies lurked in June grass, buds in green;
    Sudden the music ceased, sudden the hand
Of majesty, by dint of passion keen,

Doubled into a common first, went grand,   350
And knocked down three cut glasses and his best inkstand.

Then turning round, he saw those trembling two:
'Eban,' said he, 'as slaves should taste the fruits
Of diligence, I shall remember you
To-morrow, or next day, as time suits,
In a finger conversation with my mutes, –
Begone! – for you, Chaldean! here remain;
Fear not, quake not, and as good wine recruits
A conjurer's spirits, what cup will you drain?
Sherry in silver, hock in gold, or glassed champagne?'   360

'Commander of the Faithful!' answered Hum,
'In preference to these, I'll merely taste
A thimble-full of old Jamaica rum.'
'A simple boon!' said Elfinan; 'thou mayst
Have Nantz, with which my morning-coffee's laced.'
'I'll have a glass of Nantz, then,' – said the seer, –
'Made racy – (sure my boldness is misplaced!) –
With the third part – (yet that is drinking dear!) –
Of the least drop of *crème de citron*, crystal clear.'

'I pledge you, Hum! and pledge my dearest love,   370
My Bertha!' 'Bertha! Bertha!' cried the sage,
'I know a many Berthas!' 'Mine's above
All Berthas!' sighed the Emperor. 'I engage,'
Said Hum, 'in duty, and in vassalage,
To mention all the Berthas in the earth; –
There's Bertha Watson, – and Miss Bertha Page, –
This famed for languid eyes, and that for mirth, –
There's Bertha Blount of York, – and Bertha Knox of Perth.'

'You seem to know' – 'I do know,' answered Hum,
'Your Majesty's in love with some fine girl   380

Named Bertha; but her surname will not come,
Without a little conjuring.' ' 'Tis Pearl,
'Tis Bertha Pearl! What makes my brains so whirl?
And she is softer, fairer than her name!'
'Where does she live?' asked Hum. 'Her fair locks curl
So brightly, they put all our fays to shame!–
Live? – O! at Canterbury, with her old grand-dame.'

'Good! good!' cried Hum, 'I've known her from a child!
She is a changeling of my management;
She was born at midnight in an Indian wild;   390
Her mother's screams with the striped tiger's blent,
While the torch-bearing slaves a halloo sent
Into the jungles; and her palanquin,
Rested amid the desert's dreariment,
Shook with her agony, till fair were seen
The little Bertha's eyes open on the stars serene.'

'I can't say,' said the monarch; 'that may be,
Just as it happened, true or else a bam!
Drink up your brandy, and sit down by me,
Feel, feel my pulse – how much in love I am!   400
And if your science is not all a sham
Tell me some means to get the lady here.'
'Upon my honour!' said the son of Cham,
'She is my dainty changeling, near and dear,
Although her story sounds at first a little queer.'

'Convey her to me, Hum, or by my crown,
My sceptre, and my cross-surmounted globe,
I'll knock you' – 'Does your majesty mean – *down*?
No, no, you never could my feelings probe
To such a depth!' The Emperor took his robe,   410
And wept upon its purple palatine,
While Hum continued, shamming half a sob,–
'In Canterbury doth your lady shine?
But let me cool your brandy with a little wine.'

Whereat a narrow Flemish glass he took,
That since belonged to Admiral De Witt,
Admired it with a connoisseuring look,
And with the ripest claret crownèd it;
And, ere the lively bead could burst and flit,
He turned it quickly, nimbly upside down,   420
His mouth being held conveniently fit
    To catch the treasure: 'Best in all the town!'
He said, smacked his moist lips, and gave a pleasant frown.

'Ah! good my Prince, weep not!' And then again
He filled a bumper. 'Great Sire, do not weep!
Your pulse is shocking, but I'll ease your pain.'
'Fetch me that ottoman, and prithee keep
Your voice low,' said the Emperor; 'and steep
Some lady's-fingers nice in Candy wine;
And prithee, Hum, behind the screen do peep   430
    For the rose-water vase, magician mine!
And sponge my forehead, – so my love doth make me pine.

'Ah, cursèd Bellanaine!' 'Don't think of her,'
Rejoined the Mago, 'but on Bertha muse;
For, by my choicest best barometer,
You shall not throttled be in marriage noose;
I've said it, Sire; you only have to choose –
Bertha or Bellanaine.' So saying, he drew
From the left pocket of his threadbare hose
    A sampler, hoarded slyly, good as new,   440
Holding it by his thumb and finger full in view.

'Sire, this is Bertha Pearl's neat handy-work;
Her *name*, see here, *Midsummer, ninety-one*.'
Elfinan snatched it with a sudden jerk,
And wept as if he never would have done,
Honouring with royal tears the poor homespun;
Whereon were broidered tigers with black eyes,

And long-tailed pheasants, and a rising sun,
   Plenty of posies, great stags, butterflies
Bigger than stags, – a moon, – with other mysteries.   450

The monarch handled o'er and o'er again
   These day-school hieroglyphics with a sigh;
Somewhat in sadness, but pleased in the main
   Till this oracular couplet met his eye
Astounded: *Cupid I, do thee defy!*
   It was too much. He shrunk back in his chair,
Grew pale as death, and fainted – very nigh.
   'Pho! nonsense!' exclaimed Hum, 'now don't despair:
She does not mean it, really. Cheer up, hearty – there!

'And listen to my words. You say you won't,   460
   On any terms, marry Miss Bellanaine;
It goes against your conscience – good! Well, don't.
   You say you love a mortal. I would fain
Persuade your honour's highness to refrain
   From peccadilloes. But, Sire, as I say,
What good would that do? And, to be more plain,
   You would do me a mischief some odd day,
Cut off my ears and hands, or head, too, by my fay!

'Besides, manners forbid that I should pass any
   Vile strictures on the conduct of a prince   470
Who should indulge his genius, if he has any,
   Not, like a subject, foolish matters mince.
Now I think on 't, perhaps I could convince
   Your Majesty there is no crime at all
In loving pretty little Bertha, since
   She's very delicate, – not over tall, –
A fairy's hand, and in the waist why – very small.'

'Ring the repeater, gentle Hum!' ' 'Tis five,'
   Said gentle Hum; 'the nights draw in apace;

The little birds, I hear, are all alive;   480
I see the dawning touched upon your face;
Shall I put out the candles, please your Grace?'
'Do put them out, and, without more ado,
Tell me how I may that sweet girl embrace, –
How you can bring her to me.' 'That's for you,
Great Emperor! to adventure, like a lover true.'

'I fetch her?' – 'Yes, an 't like your Majesty;
And as she would be frightened wide awake
To travel such a distance through the sky,
Use of some soft manœuvre you must make,   490
For your convenience and her dear nerves' sake;
Nice way would be to bring her in a swoon,
Anon, I'll tell what course were best to take;
You must away this morning.' 'Hum! so soon?'
'Sire, you must be in Kent by twelve o'clock at noon.'

At this great Cæsar started on his feet,
Lifted his wings, and stood attentive-wise.
'Those wings to Canterbury you must beat,
If you hold Bertha as a worthy prize.
Look in the Almanack – *Moore* never lies –   500
April the twenty-fourth, – this coming day,
Now breathing its new bloom upon the skies,
Will end in St. Mark's Eve; – you must away,
For on that eve alone can you the maid convey.'

Then the magician solemnly 'gan frown,
So that his frost-white eyebrows, beetling low,
Shaded his deep green eyes and wrinkles brown
Plaited upon his furnace-scorchèd brow:
Forth from his hood that hung his neck below,
He lifted a bright casket of pure gold,   510
Touched a spring-lock, and there in wool or snow,
Charmed into ever freezing, lay an old
And legend-leavèd book, mysterious to behold.

'Take this same book, – it will not bite you, Sire;
There, put it underneath your royal arm;
Though it's a pretty weight it will not tire,
But rather on your journey keep you warm:
This is the magic, this the potent charm,
That shall drive Bertha to a fainting fit!
When the time comes don't feel the least alarm,   520
But lift her from the ground, and swiftly flit
Back to your palace, where I wait for guerdon fit.'

'What shall I do with that same book?' 'Why, merely
Lay it on Bertha's table, close beside
Her work-box, and 'twill help your purpose dearly;
I say no more.' 'Or good or ill betide,
Through the wide air to Kent this morn I glide!'
Exclaimed the Emperor. 'When I return,
Ask what you will, – I'll give you my new bride!
And take some more wine, Hum; – O heavens! I burn   530
To be upon the wing! Now, now that minx I spurn!'

'Leave her to me,' rejoined the magian:
'But how shall I account, illustrious fay!
For thine imperial absence? Pho! I can
Say you are very sick, and bar the way
To your so loving courtiers for one day;
If either of their two archbishops' graces
Should talk of extreme unction, I shall say
You do not like cold pig with Latin phrases,
Which never should be used but in alarming cases.'   540

'Open the window, Hum! I'm ready now!'
'Zooks!' exclaimed Hum, as up the sash he drew,
'Behold, your Majesty, upon the brow,
Of yonder hill, what crowds of people!' 'Whew?
The monster's always after something new,'
Returned his Highness, 'they are piping hot

To see my pigsney Bellanaine. Hum! do
  Tighten my belt a little, – so, so, – not
Too tight, – the book! – my wand! – so, nothing is forgot.'

  'Wounds! how they shout!' said Hum, 'and there,
      – see, see!   550
  The ambassadors returned from Pigmio!
  The morning's very fine, – uncommonly!
  See, past the skirts of yon white cloud they go,
  Tingeing it with soft crimsons! Now below
  Those sable-pointed heads of firs and pines
  They dip, move on, and with them moves a glow
  Along the forest side! Now amber lines
Reach the hill top, and now throughout the valley shines.'

  'Why, Hum, you're getting quite poetical!
  Those *nows* you managed in a special style.'   560
  'If ever you have leisure, Sire, you shall
  See scraps of mine will make it worth your while,
  Tit-bits for Phœbus! – yes, you well may smile.
  Hark! hark! the bells!' 'A little further yet,
  Good Hum, and let me view this mighty coil.'
  Then the great Emperor full graceful set
His elbow for a prop, and snuffed his mignonette.

  The morn is full of holiday; loud bells
  With rival clamours ring from every spire;
  Cunningly-stationed music dies and swells   570
  In echoing places; when the winds respire,
  Light flags stream out like gauzy tongues of fire;
  A metropolitan murmur, lifeful, warm,
  Comes from the northern suburbs; rich attire
  Freckles with red and gold the moving swarm;
While here and there clear trumpets blow a keen alarm.

  And now the fairy escort was seen clear,
  Like the old pageant of Aurora's train,

Above a pearl-built minster, hovering near;
First wily Crafticant, the chamberlain,   580
Balanced upon his grey-grown pinions twain,
His slender wand officially revealed;
Then black gnomes scattering sixpences like rain;
Then pages three and three; and next, slave-held,
The Imaian 'scutcheon bright, – one mouse in argent field.

Gentlemen pensioners next; and after them,
A troop of wingèd Janizaries flew;
Then slaves, as presents bearing many a gem;
Then twelve physicians fluttering two and two;
And next a chaplain in a cassock new;   590
Then Lords in waiting; then (what head not reels
For pleasure?) – the fair Princess in full view,
Borne upon wings, – and very pleased she feels
To have such splendour dance attendance at her heels.

For there was more magnificence behind:
She waved her handkerchief. 'Ah, very grand!'
Cried Elfinan, and closed the window-blind;
'And, Hum, we must not shilly-shally stand, –
Adieu! adieu! I'm off for Angle-land!
I say, old Hocus, have you such a thing   600
About you, – feel your pockets, I command, –
I want, this instant, an invisible ring, –
Thank you, old mummy! – now securely I take wing.'

Then Elfinan swift vaulted from the floor,
And lighted graceful on the window-sill;
Under one arm the magic book he bore,
The other he could wave about at will;
Pale was his face, he still looked very ill:
He bowed at Bellanaine, and said – 'Poor Bell!
Farewell! farewell! and if for ever! still   610

For ever fare thee well!' – and then he fell
A laughing! – snapped his fingers! – shame it is to tell!

'By 'r Lady! he is gone!' cries Hum, 'and I –
(I own it) – have made too free with his wine;
Old Crafticant will smoke me. By the bye!
This room is full of jewels as a mine.
Dear valuable creatures, how ye shine!
Sometime to-day I must contrive a minute,
If Mercury propitiously incline,
To examine his scrutoire, and see what's in it,   620
For of superfluous diamonds I as well may thin it.

'The Emperor's horrid bad; yes, that's my cue!'
Some histories say that this was Hum's last speech;
That, being fuddled, he went reeling through
The corridor, and scarce upright could reach
The stair-head; that being glutted as a leech,
And used, as we ourselves have just now said,
To manage stairs reversely, like a peach
Too ripe, he fell, being puzzled in his head
With liquor and the staircase: verdict – *found stone dead.*   630

This as a falsehood Crafticanto treats;
And as his style is of strange elegance,
Gentle and tender, full of soft conceits,
(Much like our Boswell's,) we will take a glance
At his sweet prose, and, if we can, make dance
His woven periods into careless rhyme;
O, little faery Pegasus! rear – prance –
Trot round the quarto – ordinary time!
March, little Pegasus, with pawing hoof sublime!

Well, let us see, – *tenth book and chapter nine,* –   640
Thus Crafticant pursues his diary: –

' 'Twas twelve o'clock at night, the weather fine,
Latitude thirty-six; our scouts descry
A flight of starlings making rapidly
Towards Thibet. Mem.: – birds fly in the night;
From twelve to half-past – wings not fit to fly
For a thick fog – The Princess sulky quite;
Called for an extra shawl, and gave her nurse a bite.

'Five minutes before one – brought down a moth
With my new double-barrel – stewed the thighs   650
And made a very tolerable broth –
Princess turned dainty; to our great surprise,
Altered her mind, and thought it very nice:
Seeing her pleasant, tried her with a pun,
She frowned; a monstrous owl across us flies
About this time, – a sad old figure of fun;
Bad omen – this new match can't be a happy one.

'From two to half-past, dusky way we made,
Above the plains of Gobi, – desert, bleak;
Beheld afar off, in the hooded shade   660
Of darkness, a great mountain (strange to speak),
Spitting, from forth its sulphur-baken peak,
A fan-shaped burst of blood-red, arrowy fire,
Turbaned with smoke, which still away did reek,
Solid and black from that eternal pyre,
Upon the laden winds that scantly could respire.

'Just upon three o'clock a falling star
Created an alarm among our troop,
Killed a man-cook, a page, and broke a jar,
A tureen, and three dishes, at one swoop,   670
Then passing by the Princess, singed her hoop:
Could not conceive what Coralline was at,
She clapped her hands three times and cried out "Whoop!"

Some strange Imaian custom. A large bat
Came sudden 'fore my face, and brushed against my hat.

'Five minutes thirteen seconds after three,
Far in the west a mighty fire broke out,
Conjectured, on the instant, it might be,
The city of Balk – 'twas Balk beyond all doubt:
A griffin, wheeling here and there about,   680
Kept reconnoitring us – doubled our guard –
Lighted our torches, and kept up a shout,
Till he sheered off – the Princess very scared –
And many on their marrowbones for death prepared.

'At half-past three arose the cheerful moon –
Bivouacked for four minutes on a cloud –
Where from the earth we heard a lively tune
Of tambourines and pipes, serene and loud,
While on a flowery lawn a brilliant crowd
Cinque-parted danced, some half-asleep reposed   690
Beneath the green-faned cedars, some did shroud
In silken tents, and 'mid light fragrance dozed,
Or on the open turf their soothèd eyelids closed.

'Dropped my gold watch, and killed a kettledrum –
It went for apoplexy – foolish folks! –
Left it to pay the piper – a good sum –
(I've got a conscience, maugre people's jokes;)
To scrape a little favour 'gan to coax
Her Highness' pug-dog – got a sharp rebuff –
She wished a game at whist – make three revokes –   700
Turned from myself, her partner, in a huff;
His Majesty will know her temper time enough.

'She cried for chess – I played a game with her –
Castled her King with such a vixen look,

It bodes ill to his Majesty – (refer
To the second chapter of my fortieth book,
And see what hoity-toity airs she took).
At half-past four the morn essayed to beam –
Saluted, as we passed, an early rook –
The Princess fell asleep, and, in her dream,   710
Talked of one Master Hubert, deep in her esteem.

'About this time, – making delightful way, –
Shed a quill-feather from my larboard wing –
Wished, trusted, hoped 'twas no sign of decay –
Thank heaven, I'm hearty yet! – 'twas no such thing: –
At five the golden light began to spring,
With fiery shudder through the bloomèd east;
At six we heard Panthea's churches ring –
The city all his unhived swarms had cast,
To watch our grand approach, and hail us as we passed.   720

'As flowers turn their faces to the sun,
So on our flight with hungry eyes they gaze,
And, as we shaped our course, this, that way run,
With mad-cap pleasure, or hand-clasped amaze;
Sweet in the air a mild-toned music plays,
And progresses through its own labyrinth;
Buds gathered from the green spring's middle-days,
They scattered, – daisy, primrose, hyacinth, –
Or round white columns wreathed from capital to plinth.

'Onward we floated o'er the panting streets,   730
That seemed throughout with upheld faces paved;
Look where we will, our bird's-eye vision meets
Legions of holiday; bright standards waved,
And fluttering ensigns emulously craved
Our minute's glance; a busy thunderous roar,
From square to square, among the buildings raved,

As when the sea, at flow, gluts up once more
The craggy hollowness of a wild reefed shore.

'And "Bellanaine for ever!" shouted they;
  While that fair Princess, from her wingèd chair,   740
  Bowed low with high demeanour, and, to pay
  Their new-blown loyalty with guerdon fair,
  Still emptied, at meet distance, here and there,
  A plenty horn of jewels. And here I
  (Who wish to give the devil her due) declare
  Against that ugly piece of calumny,
Which calls them Highland pebble-stones, not worth a fly.

'Still "Bellanaine!" they shouted, while we glide
  'Slant to a light Ionic portico,
  The city's delicacy, and the pride   750
  Of our Imperial Basilic; a row
  Of lords and ladies, on each hand, make show
  Submissive of knee-bent obeisance,
  All down the steps; and as we entered, lo!
  The strangest sight, the most unlooked-for chance –
All things turned topsy-turvy in a devil's dance.

' 'Stead of his anxious Majesty and court
  At the open doors, with wide saluting eyes,
  Congées and scape-graces of every sort,
  And all the smooth routine of gallantries,   760
  Was seen, to our immoderate surprise,
  A motley crowd thick gathered in the hall,
  Lords, scullions, deputy-scullions, with wild cries
  Stunning the vestibule from wall to wall,
Where the Chief Justice on his knees and hands doth crawl.

'Counts of the palace, and the state purveyor
  Of moth's down, to make soft the royal beds,

The Common Council and my fool Lord Mayor
Marching a-row, each other slipshod treads;
Powdered bag-wigs and ruffy-tuffy heads   770
Of cinder wenches meet and soil each other;
Toe crushed with heel ill-natured fighting breeds,
Frill-rumpling elbows brew up many a bother,
And fists in the short ribs keep up the yell and pother.

'A Poet, mounted on the Court-Clown's back,
Rode to the Princess swift with spurring heels,
And close into her face, with rhyming clack,
Began a Prothalamion; – she reels,
She falls, she faints! while laughter peals
Over her woman's weakness. "Where," cried I,   780
"Where is his Majesty?" No person feels
Inclined to answer; wherefore instantly
I plunged into the crowd to find him or to die.

'Jostling my way I gained the stairs, and ran
To the first landing, where, incredible!
I met, far gone in liquor, that old man,
That vile impostor Hum, –'
                              So far so well, –
For we have proved the Mago never fell
Down stairs on Crafticanto's evidence;
And therefore duly shall proceed to tell,   790
Plain in our own original mood and tense,
The sequel of this day, though labour 'tis immense!

Now Hum, new-fledged with high authority,
Came forth to quell the hubbub in the hall . . .

Otho the Great

A TRAGEDY IN FIVE ACTS

*This play was first produced at the
St. Martin's Theatre, London on
November 26th, 1950*

DRAMATIS PERSONÆ

OTHO THE GREAT, *Emperor of Germany.*

LUDOLPH, *his Son.*

CONRAD, *Duke of Franconia.*

ALBERT, *a Knight, favoured by Otho.*

SIGIFRED, *an Officer, friend of Ludolph.*

THEODORE, *Officer.*

GONFRID, *Officer.*

ETHELBERT, *an Abbot.*

GERSA, *Prince of Hungary.*

An Hungarian Captain.

Physician.

Page.

Nobles, Knights, Attendants, and Soldiers.

ERMINIA, *Niece of Otho.*

AURANTHE, *Conrad's Sister.*

Ladies and Attendants.

SCENE: *The Castle of Friedburg, its vicinity,
and the Hungarian Camp.*

TIME: *One Day.*

ACT I

SCENE I.—*An Apartment in the Castle*

Enter Conrad.

So, I am safe emergèd from these broils!
Amid the wreck of thousands I am whole;
For every crime I have a laurel-wreath,
For every lie a lordship. Nor yet has
My ship of fortune furled her silken sails, —
Let her glide on! This dangered neck is saved,
By dexterous policy, from the rebel's axe;
And of my ducal palace not one stone
Is bruised by the Hungarian petards.
Toil hard, ye slaves, and from the miser-earth   10
Bring forth once more my bullion, treasured deep,
With all my jewelled salvers, silver and gold,
And precious goblets that make rich the wine.
But why do I stand babbling to myself?
Where is Auranthe? I have news for her
Shall —

Enter Auranthe.

Auranthe. Conrad! what tidings? Good, if I may guess
From your alert eyes and high-lifted brows.
What tidings of the battle? Albert? Ludolph?
Otho?

Conrad. You guess aright. And, sister, slurring o'er
Our by-gone quarrels, I confess my heart   20
Is beating with a child's anxiety,
To make our golden fortune known to you.

Auranthe. So serious?

Conrad.   Yes, so serious, that before
I utter even the shadow of a hint
Concerning what will make that sin-worn cheek
Blush joyous blood through every lineament,
You must make here a solemn vow to me.

Auranthe. I pr'ythee, Conrad, do not overact
The hypocrite. What vow would you impose?

Conrad. Trust me for once. That you may be assured   30
'Tis not confiding in a broken reed,
A poor court-bankrupt, outwitted and lost,
Revolve these facts in your acutest mood,
In such a mood as now you listen to me:
A few days since, I was an open rebel, –
Against the Emperor had suborned his son, –
Drawn off his nobles to revolt, – and shown
Contented fools causes for discontent,
Fresh hatched in my ambition's eagle-nest;
So thrived I as a rebel, – and, behold!   40
Now I am Otho's favourite, his dear friend,
His right hand, his brave Conrad!

Auranthe.   I confess
You have intrigued with these unsteady times
To admiration. But to be a favourite!

Conrad. I saw my moment. The Hungarians,
Collected silently in holes and corners,
Appeared, a sudden host, in the open day.
I should have perished in our empire's wreck,
But, calling interest loyalty, swore faith
To most believing Otho; and so helped   50
His blood-stained ensigns to the victory
In yesterday's hard fight, that it has turned
The edge of his sharp wrath to eager kindness.

Auranthe. So far yourself. But what is this to me
More than that I am glad? I gratulate you.

Conrad. Yes, sister, but it does regard you greatly,
Nearly, momentously, – ay, painfully!
Make me this vow—

Auranthe.   Concerning whom or what?

Conrad. Albert!

Auranthe. I would inquire somewhat of him.
You had a letter from me touching him?   60

No treason 'gainst his head in deed or word!
Surely you spared him at my earnest prayer?
Give me the letter – it should not exist.
    Conrad. At one pernicious charge of the enemy
I for a moment-whiles, was prisoner ta'en
And rifled, – stuff! the horses' hoofs have minced it!
    Auranthe. He is alive?
    Conrad.   He is! but here make oath
To alienate him from your scheming brain,
Divorce him from your solitary thoughts,
And cloud him in such utter banishment,   70
That when his person meets again your eye
Your vision shall quite lose its memory,
And wander past him as through vacancy.
    Auranthe. I'll not be perjured.
    Conrad.   No, nor great, nor mighty;
You would not wear a crown, or rule a kingdom.
To you it is indifferent.
    Auranthe.   What means this?
    Conrad. You'll not be perjured! Go to Albert then,
That camp-mushroom – dishonour of our house.
Go, page his dusty heels upon a march,
Furbish his jingling baldric while he sleeps,   80
And share his mouldy ration in a siege.
Yet stay, – perhaps a charm may call you back,
And make the widening circlets of your eyes
Sparkle with healthy fevers. – The Emperor
Hath given consent that you should marry Ludolph.
    Auranthe. Can it be, brother? For a golden crown
With a queen's awful lips I doubly thank you!
This is to wake in Paradise! Farewell,
Thou clod of yesterday! – 'twas not myself!
Not till this moment did I ever feel   90
My spirit's faculties! I'll flatter you
For this, and be you ever proud of it;
Thou, Jove-like, struck'dst thy forehead,

And from the teeming marrow of thy brain
I spring complete Minerva! But the prince –
His highness Ludolph – where is he?
    Conrad.   I know not
When, lackeying my counsel at a beck,
The rebel lords, on bended knees, received
The Emperor's pardon, Ludolph kept aloof,
Sole, in a stiff, fool-hardy, sulky pride;   100
Yet, for all this, I never saw a father
In such a sickly longing for his son.
We shall soon see him; for the Emperor
He will be here this morning.
    Auranthe.   That I heard
Among the midnight rumours from the camp.
    Conrad. You give up Albert to me?
    Auranthe.   Harm him not!
E'en for his highness Ludolph's sceptry hand,
I would not Albert suffer any wrong.
    Conrad. Have I not laboured, plotted – ?
    Auranthe.   See you spare him:
Nor be pathetic, my kind benefactor!   110
On all the many bounties of your hand,
'Twas for yourself you laboured – not for me!
Do you not count, when I am queen, to take
Advantage of your chance discoveries
Of my poor secrets, and so hold a rod
Over my life?
    Conrad. Let not this slave – this villain –
Be cause of feud between us. See! he comes!
Look, woman, look, your Albert is quite safe!
In haste it seems. Now shall I be in the way,
And wished with silent curses in my grave,   120
Or side by side with 'whelmèd mariners.

Enter Albert.

    Albert. Fair on your graces fall this early morrow!

So it is like to do, without my prayers,
For your right noble names, like favourite tunes,
Have fallen full frequent from our Emperor's lips,
High commented with smiles.
    Auranthe.   Noble Albert!
    Conrad. [Aside.] Noble!
    Auranthe.   Such salutation argues a glad heart
In our prosperity. We thank you, sir.
    Albert. Lady! O, would to Heaven your poor servant
Could do you better service than mere words!   130
But I have other greeting than mine own, –
From no less man than Otho, who has sent
This ring as pledge of dearest amity;
'Tis chosen, I hear, from Hymen's jewel'ry,
And you will prize it, lady, I doubt not,
Beyond all pleasures past, and all to come.
To you, great duke –
    Conrad.   To me! What of me, ha?
    Albert. What pleased your grace to say?
    Conrad.   Your message, sir!
    Albert. You mean not this to me?
    Conrad.   Sister, this way;
For there shall be no 'gentle Alberts' now,   *[Aside.]*   140
No 'sweet Auranthes!'
                      [Exeunt Conrad and Auranthe.]
    Albert. [Solus.] The duke is out of temper; if he knows
More than a brother of a sister ought
I should not quarrel with his peevishness.
Auranthe – Heaven preserve her always fair! –
Is in the heady, proud, ambitious vein;
I bicker not with her, – bid her farewell;
She has taken flight from me, then let her soar, –
He is a fool who stands at pining gaze!
But for poor Ludolph, he is food for sorrow: 150
No levelling bluster of my licensed thoughts,
No military swagger of my mind,

Can smother from myself the wrong I've done him, –
Without design, indeed, – yet it is so, –
And opiate for the conscience have I none! *[Exit.]*

SCENE II. – *The Court-yard of the Castle*

Martial Music. Enter, from the outer gate, Otho, Nobles,
Knights, and Attendants. The Soldiers halt at the gate with
Banners in sight.

Otho. Where is my noble herald?

Enter Conrad, from the Castle, attended by two Knights and servants.
Albert following.

                              Well, hast told
Auranthe our intent imperial?
Lest our rent banners, too o' the sudden shown,
Should fright her silken casements and dismay
Her household to our lack of entertainment.
A victory!
    Conrad. God save illustrious Otho!
    Otho. Ay, Conrad, it will pluck out all grey hairs;
It is the best physician for the spleen;
The courtliest inviter to a feast;
The subtlest excuser of small faults;
And a nice judge in the age and smack of wine.   10

Enter, from the Castle, Auranthe, followed by Pages holding up her robes,
and a train of Women. She kneels.

Hail, my sweet hostess! I do thank the stars,
Or my good soldiers, or their ladies' eyes,
That, after such a merry battle fought,
I can, all safe in body and in soul,
Kiss your fair hand and lady fortune's too.
My ring! now, on my life, it doth rejoice
These lips to feel 't on this soft ivory!
Keep it, my brightest daughter; it may prove

The little prologue to a line of kings.   20
I strove against thee and my hot-blood son,
Dull blockhead that I was to be so blind;
But now my sight is clear; forgive me, lady.
   Auranthe. My lord, I was a vassal to your frown,
And now your favour makes me but more humble;
In wintry winds the simple snow is safe,
But fadeth at the greeting of the sun:
Unto thine anger I might well have spoken,
Taking on me a woman's privilege,
But this so sudden kindness makes me dumb.   30
   Otho. What need of this? Enough, if you will be
A potent tutoress to my wayward boy,
And teach him, what it seems his nurse could not,
To say, for once, I thank you. Sigifred!
   Albert. He has not yet returned, my gracious liege.
   Otho. What then! No tidings of my friendly Arab?
   Conrad. None, mighty Otho.

[To one of his Knights, who goes out.]

Send forth instantly
An hundred horsemen from my honoured gates,
To scour the plains and search the cottages.
Cry a reward to him who shall first bring   40
News of that vanishèd Arabian,—
A full-heaped helmet of the purest gold.
   Otho. More thanks, good Conrad; for, except my son's,
There is no face I rather would behold
Than that same quick-eyed pagan's. By the saints,
This coming night of banquets must not light
Her dazzling torches; nor the music breathe
Smooth, without clashing cymbal, tones of peace
And indoor melodies; nor the ruddy wine
Ebb spouting to the lees; if I pledge not,   50
In my first cup, that Arab!
   Albert.   Mighty monarch,

I wonder not this stranger's victor-deeds
So hang upon your spirit. Twice in the fight
It was my chance to meet his olive brow,
Triumphant in the enemy's shattered rhomb;
And, to say truth, in any Christian arm
I never saw such prowess.

    Otho.   Did you ever?
O, 'tis a noble boy! – tut! – what do I say?
I mean a triple Saladin, whose eyes,
When in the glorious scuffle they met mine,   60
Seemed to say, 'Sleep, old man, in safety sleep;
I am the victory!'

    Conrad.   Pity he's not here.

    Otho. And my son too, pity he is not here.
Lady Auranthe, I would not make you blush,
But can you give a guess where Ludolph is?
Know you not of him?

    Auranthe.   Indeed, my liege, no secret –

    Otho. Nay, nay, without more words, dost know of him?

    Auranthe. I would I were so over-fortunate,
Both for his sake and mine, and to make glad
A father's ears with tidings of his son.   70

    Otho. I see 'tis like to be a tedious day.
Were Theodore and Gonfrid and the rest
Sent forth with my commands?

    Albert.   Ay, my lord.

    Otho. And no news! No news! 'Faith! 'tis very strange
He thus avoids us. Lady, is 't not strange?
Will he be truant to you too? It is a shame.

    Conrad. Wilt please your highness enter, and accept
The unworthy welcome of your servant's house?
Leaving your cares to one whose diligence
May in few hours make pleasures of them all.   80

    Otho. Not so tedious, Conrad. No, no, no, –
I must see Ludolph or the – what's that shout?

    Voices without. Huzza! huzza! Long live the Emperor!

Other Voices. Fall back! Away there!

Otho.   Say, what noise is that!

[Albert advancing from the back of the stage,
whither he had hastened on hearing the cheers of the soldiery.]

Albert. It is young Gersa, the Hungarian prince,
Picked like a red stag from the fallow herd
Of prisoners. Poor prince, forlorn he steps,
Slow, and demure, and proud in his despair.
If I may judge by his so tragic bearing,
His eye not downcast, and his folded arm,   90
He doth this moment wish himself asleep
Among his fallen captains on yon plains.

Enter Gersa, in chains, and guarded.

Otho. Well said, Sir Albert.

Gersa.   Not a word of greeting?
No welcome to a princely visitor,
Most mighty Otho? Will not my great host
Vouchsafe a syllable, before he bids
His gentlemen conduct me with all care
To some securest lodging – cold perhaps!

Otho. What mood is this? Hath fortune touched thy brain?

Gersa. O kings and princes of this fev'rous world,   100
What abject things, what mockeries must ye be,
What nerveless minions of safe palaces,
When here, a monarch, whose proud foot is used
To fallen princes' necks as to his stirrup,
Must needs exclaim that I am mad forsooth,
Because I cannot flatter with bent knees
My conqueror!

Otho.   Gersa, I think you wrong me:
I think I have a better fame abroad.

Gersa. I pr'ythee mock me not with gentle speech,
But, as a favour, bid me from thy presence;   110
Let me no longer be the wondering food

Of all these eyes; pr'ythee, command me hence!

    Otho. Do not mistake me, Gersa. That you may not,
Come, fair Auranthe, try if your soft hands
Can manage those hard rivets, to set free
So brave a prince and soldier.

    Auranthe. [Sets him free.]   Welcome task!

    Gersa. I am wound up in deep astonishment!
Thank you, fair lady. Otho! emperor!
You rob me of myself; my dignity
Is now your infant; I am a weak child.   120

    Otho. Give me your hand, and let this kindly grasp
Live in our memories.

    Gersa.   In mine it will.
I blush to think of my unchastened tongue;
But I was haunted by the monstrous ghost
Of all our slain battalions. Sire, reflect,
And pardon you will grant, that, at this hour,
The bruisèd remnants of our stricken camp
Are huddling undistinguished my dear friends,
With common thousands, into shallow graves.

    Otho. Enough, most noble Gersa. You are free   130
To cheer the brave remainder of your host
By your own healing presence, and that too,
Not as their leader merely, but their king;
For, as I hear, the wily enemy
Who eased the crownet from your infant brows,
Bloody Taraxa, is among the dead.

    Gersa. Then I retire, so generous Otho please,
Bearing with me a weight of benefits
Too heavy to be borne.

    Otho.   It is not so;
Still understand me, King of Hungary,   140
Nor judge my open purposes awry.
Though I did hold you high in my esteem
For your self's sake, I do not personate
The stage-play emperor to entrap applause,

To set the silly sort o' the world agape,
And make the politic smile; no, I have heard
How in the Council you condemned this war,
Urging the perfidy of broken faith, –
For that I am your friend.

Gersa.   If ever, sire,
You are my enemy, I dare here swear   150
'Twill not be Gersa's fault. Otho, farewell!

  Otho. Will you return, prince, to our banqueting?

  Gersa. As to my father's board I will return.

  Otho. Conrad, with all due ceremony, give
The prince a regal escort to his camp;
Albert, go thou and bear him company.
Gersa, farewell!

  Gersa.   All happiness attend you!

  Otho. Return with what good speed you may, for soon
We must consult upon our terms of peace.

[Exeunt Gersa and Albert with others.]

And thus a marble column do I build   160
To prop my empire's dome. Conrad, in thee
I have another steadfast one, to uphold
The portals of my state; and, for my own
Pre-eminence and safety, I will strive
To keep thy strength upon its pedestal.
For, without thee, this day I might have been
A show-monster about the streets of Prague,
In chains, as just now stood that noble prince:
And then to me no mercy had been shown,
For when the conquered lion is once dungeoned   170
Who lets him forth again, or dares to give
An old lion sugar-cates of mild reprieve?
Not to thine ear alone I make confession,
But to all here, as, by experience,
I know how the great basement of all power
Is frankness, and a true tongue to the world;

And how intriguing secrecy is proof
Of fear and weakness, and a hollow state.
Conrad, I owe thee much.
 Conrad.   To kiss that hand,
My Emperor, is ample recompense   180
For a mere act of duty.
 Otho.   Thou are wrong
For what can any man on earth do more?
We will make trial of your house's welcome,
My bright Auranthe!
 Conrad.   How is Friedburg honoured!

    Enter Ethelbert and six Monks.

 Ethelbert. The benison of Heaven on your head,
Imperial Otho!
 Otho. Who stays me? Speak! Quick!
 Ethelbert. Pause but one moment, mighty conqueror,
Upon the threshold of this house of joy.
 Otho. Pray, do not prose, good Ethelbert, but speak
What is your purpose.   190
 Ethelbert. The restoration of some captive maids,
Devoted to Heaven's pious ministries,
Who, driven forth from their religious cells
And kept in thraldom by our enemy,
When late this province was a lawless spoil,
Still weep amid the wild Hungarian camp,
Though hemmed around by thy victorious arms.
 Otho. Demand the holy sisterhood in our name
From Gersa's tents. Farewell, old Ethelbert.
 Ethelbert. The saints will bless you for this pious
care.   200
 Otho. Daughter, your hand; Ludolph's would fit it best.
 Conrad. Ho! let the music sound!

  [Music. Ethelbert raises his hands, as in benediction of Otho.
    Exeunt severally. The scene closes on them.]

SCENE III. — *The Country, with the Castle in the distance*

Enter Ludolph and Sigifred.

Ludolph. You have my secret; let it not be breathed.

Sigifred. Still give me leave to wonder that the Prince
Ludolph and the swift Arab are the same;
Still to rejoice that 'twas a German arm
Death doing in a turbaned masquerade.

Ludolph. The Emperor must not know it, Sigifred.

Sigifred. I pr'ythee, why? What happier hour of time
Could thy pleased star point down upon from heaven
With silver index, bidding thee make peace?

Ludolph. Still it must not be known, good Sigifred;   10
The star may point oblique.

Sigifred.   If Otho knew
His son to be that unknown Mussulman
After whose spurring heels he sent me forth,
With one of his well-pleased Olympian oaths,
The charters of man's greatness, at this hour
He would be watching round the castle walls,
And, like an anxious warder, strain his sight
For the first glimpse of such a son returned –
Ludolph! – that blast of the Hungarians,
That Saracenic meteor of the fight,   20
That silent fury, whose fell scymitar
Kept danger all aloof from Otho's head,
And left him space for wonder.

Ludolph.   Say no more.
Not as a swordsman would I pardon claim,
But as a son. The bronzed centurion,
Long toiled in foreign wars, and whose high deeds
Are shaded in a forest of tall spears,
Known only to his troop, hath greater plea
Of favour with my sire than I can have.

Sigifred. My lord, forgive me that I cannot see   30

How this proud temper with clear reason squares.
What made you then, with such an anxious love,
Hover around that life, whose bitter days
You vext with bad revolt? Was 't opium,
Or the mad-fumèd wine? Nay, do not frown,
I rather would grieve with you than upbraid.
    Ludolph. I do believe you. No, 'twas not to make
A father his son's debtor, or to heal
His deep heart-sickness for a rebel child.
'Twas done in memory of my boyish days,   40
Poor cancel for his kindness to my youth,
For all his calming of my childish griefs,
And all his smiles upon my merriment.
No, not a thousand foughten fields could sponge
Those days paternal from my memory,
Though now upon my head he heaps disgrace.
    Sigifred. My Prince, you think too harshly –
    Ludolph.   Can I so?
Hath he not galled my spirit to the quick?
And with a sullen rigour obstinate
Poured out a phial of wrath upon my faults;   50
Hunted me as the Tartar does the boar,
Driven me to the very edge o' the world,
And almost put a price upon my head?
    Sigifred. Remember how he spared the rebel lords.
    Ludolph. Yes, yes, I know he hath a noble nature
That cannot trample on the fallen. But his
Is not the only proud heart in his realm.
He hath wronged me, and I have done him wrong;
He hath loved me, and I have shown him kindness;
We should be almost equal.
    Sigifred.   Yet for all this,   60
I would you had appeared among those lords,
And ta'en his favour.
    Ludolph.   Ha! Till now I thought
My friend had held poor Ludolph's honour dear.

What! Would you have me sue before his throne
And kiss, the courtier's missal, its silk steps?
Or hug the golden housings of his steed,
Amid a camp whose steelèd swarms I dared
But yesterday? and, at the trumpet sound,
Bow, like some unknown mercenary's flag,
And lick the soilèd grass? No, no, my friend, 70
I would not, I, be pardoned in the heap,
And bless indemnity with all that scum, –
Those men I mean, who on my shoulders propped
Their weak rebellion, winning me with lies,
And pitying forsooth my many wrongs;
Poor self-deceivèd wretches, who must think
Each one himself a king in embryo,
Because some dozen vassals cried, My lord!
Cowards, who never knew their little hearts
Till flurried danger held the mirror up, 80
And then they owned themselves without a blush,
Curling, like spaniels, round my father's feet.
Such things deserted me and are forgiven,
While I, least guilty, am an outcast still, –
And will be, for I love such fair disgrace.
  Sigifred. I know the clear truth; so would Otho see,
For he is just and noble. Fain would I
Be pleader for you –
  Ludolph.   He'll hear none of it;
You know his temper, hot, proud, obstinate;
Endanger not yourself so uselessly. 90
I will encounter this thwart spleen myself,
To-day at the Duke Conrad's, where he keeps
His crowded state after the victory.
There will I be, a most unwelcome guest,
And parley with him, as a son should do
Who doubly loathes a father's tyranny;
Tell him how feeble is that tyranny;
How the relationship of father and son

Is no more valued than a silken leash
Where lions tug averse, if love grow not   100
From interchangèd love through many years.
Ay, and those turreted Franconian walls,
Like to a jealous casket, hold my pearl –
My fair Auranthe! Yes, I will be there.

 Sigifred. Be not so rash! wait till his wrath shall pass,
Until his royal spirit softly ebbs,
Self-influenced; then, in his morning dreams
He will forgive thee, and awake in grief
To have not thy good-morrow.

 Ludolph.   Yes, to-day
I must be there, while her young pulses beat   110
Among the new-plumed minions of war.
Have you seen her of late? No? Auranthe,
Franconia's fair sister, 'tis I mean.
She should be paler for my troublous days –
And there it is – my father's iron lips
Have sworn divorcement 'twixt me and my right.

 Sigifred. [Aside.] Auranthe! I had hoped this whim had passed.

 Ludolph. And, Sigifred, with all his love of justice,
When will he take that grandchild in his arms,
That, by my love I swear, shall soon be his?   120
This reconcilement is impossible,
For see – but who are these?

 Sigifred.   They are messengers
From our great emperor; to you, I doubt not,
For couriers are abroad to seek you out.

     Enter Theodore and Gonfrid.

 Theodore. Seeing so many vigilant eyes explore
The province to invite your highness back
To your high dignities, we are too happy.

 Gonfrid. We have no eloquence to colour justly
The emperor's anxious wishes.

 Ludolph. Go. I follow you.

[Exeunt Theodore and Gonfrid.]

I play the prude: it is not venturing – 130
Why should he be so earnest? Come, my friend,
Let us to Friedburg castle.

ACT II

SCENE I. – *An Ante-chamber in the Castle*

Enter Ludolph and Sigifred.

Ludolph. No more advices, no more cautioning;
I leave it all to fate – to anything!
I cannot square my conduct to time, place,
Or circumstance; to me 'tis all a mist!
Sigifred. I say no more.
Ludolph.   It seems I am to wait
Here in the ante-room; – that may be a trifle.
You see now how I dance attendance here,
Without that tyrant temper, you so blame,
Snapping the rein. You have medicined me
With good advices; and I here remain,   10
In this most honourable ante-room,
Your patient scholar.
Sigifred.   Do not wrong me, Prince.
By heavens, I'd rather kiss Duke Conrad's slipper,
When in the morning he doth yawn with pride,
Than see you humbled but a half-degree!
Truth is, the Emperor would fain dismiss
The nobles ere he sees you.

Enter Gonfrid, from the Council-room.

Ludolph.   Well, sir! what?
Gonfrid. Great honour to the Prince! The Emperor,
Hearing that his brave son had re-appeared,
Instant dismissed the Council from his sight,   20
As Jove fans off the clouds. Even now they pass.

[*Exit.*]

Enter the Nobles from the Council-room.
They cross the stage, bowing with respect to Ludolph,
he frowning on them. Conrad follows.
Exeunt.

Ludolph. Not the discoloured poisons of a fen,
Which he who breathes feels warning of his death,
Could taste so nauseous to the bodily sense,
As these prodigious sycophants disgust
The soul's fine palate.
   Conrad.   Princely Ludolph, hail!
Welcome, thou younger sceptre to the realm!
Strength to thy virgin crownet's golden buds,
That they, against the winter of thy sire,
May burst, and swell, and flourish round thy brows,   30
Maturing to a weighty diadem!
Yet be that hour far off! and may he live,
Who waits for thee, as the chapped earth for rain.
Set my life's star! I have lived long enough,
Since under my glad roof, propitiously,
Father and son each other repossess.
   Ludolph. Fine wording, Duke! but words could never yet
Forestall the fates; have you not learnt that yet?
Let me look well: your features are the same;
Your gait the same: your hair of the same shade;   40
As one I knew some passèd weeks ago,
Who sung far different notes into mine ears.
I have mine own particular comments on 't;
You have your own, perhaps.
   Conrad.   My gracious Prince,
All men may err. In truth I was deceived
In your great father's nature, as you were.
Had I known that of him I have since known,
And what you soon will learn, I would have turned
My sword to my own throat, rather than held

Its threatening edge against a good King's quiet: 50
Or with one word fevered you, gentle Prince,
Who seemed to me, as rugged times then went,
Indeed too much oppressed. May I be bold
To tell the Emperor you will haste to him?
   Ludolph. Your Dukedom's privilege will grant so much.

[Exit Conrad.]

He's very close to Otho, – a tight leech!
Your hand – I go. Ha! here the thunder comes
Sullen against the wind! If in two angry brows
My safety lies, then, Sigifred, I'm safe.

Enter Otho and Conrad.

   Otho. Will you make Titan play the lackey-page   60
To chattering pigmies? I would have you know
That such neglect of our high Majesty
Annuls all feel of kindred. What is son, –
Or friend, – or brother, – or all ties of blood, –
When the whole kingdom, centred in ourself,
Is rudely slighted? Who am I to wait?
By Peter's chair! I have upon my tongue
A word to fright the proudest spirit here! –
Death! – and slow tortures to the hardy fool
Who dares take such large charter from our smiles!   70
Conrad, we would be private. Sigifred,
Off! And none pass this way on pain of death!

[Exeunt Conrad and Sigifred.]

   Ludolph. This was but half expected, my good sire,
Yet I am grieved at it, to the full height,
As though my hopes of favour had been whole.
   Otho. How you indulge yourself! What can you hope for?
   Ludolph. Nothing, my liege; I have to hope for nothing.
I come to greet you as a loving son,
And then depart, if I may be so free,

Seeing that blood of yours in my warm veins   80
Has not yet mitigated into milk.

 Otho. What would you, sir?

 Ludolph.   A lenient banishment.
So please you, let me unmolested pass
This Conrad's gates to the wide air again.
I want no more. A rebel wants no more.

 Otho. And shall I let a rebel loose again
To muster kites and eagles 'gainst my head?
No, obstinate boy, you shall be kept caged up,
Served with harsh food, with scum for Sunday drink.

 Ludolph. Indeed!

 Otho.   And chains too heavy for your life: 90
I'll choose a gaoler whose swart monstrous face
Shall be a hell to look upon, and she –

 Ludolph. Ha!

 Otho. Shall be your fair Auranthe.

 Ludolph.   Amaze! Amaze!

 Otho. To-day you marry her.

 Ludolph. This is a sharp jest!

 Otho. No. None at all. When have I said a lie?

 Ludolph. If I sleep not, I am a waking wretch.

 Otho. Not a word more. Let me embrace my child.

 Ludolph. I dare not. 'Twould pollute so good a father!
O heavy crime! – that your son's blinded eyes
Could not see all his parent's love aright,   100
As now I see it! Be not kind to me –
Punish me not with favour.

 Otho.   Are you sure,
Ludolph, you have no saving plea in store?

 Ludolph. My father, none!

 Otho.   Then you astonish me.

 Ludolph. No, I have no plea. Disobedience,
Rebellion, obstinacy, blasphemy,
Are all my counsellors. If they can make
My crooked deeds show good and plausible,

Then grant me loving pardon, but not else,
Good gods! not else, in any way, my liege!   110
   Otho. You are a most perplexing noble boy.
   Ludolph. You not less a perplexing noble father.
   Otho. Well, you shall have free passport through the gates.
Farewell!
   Ludolph. Farewell! and by these tears believe,
And still remember, I repent in pain
All my misdeeds!
   Otho.   Ludolph, I will! I will!
But, Ludolph, ere you go, I would inquire
If you, in all your wandering, ever met
A certain Arab haunting in these parts.
   Ludolph. No, my good lord, I cannot say I did.   120
Otho. Make not your father blind before his time;
Nor let these arms paternal hunger more
For an embrace, to dull the appetite
Of my great love for thee, my supreme child!
Come close, and let me breathe into thine ear.
I knew you through disguise. You are the Arab!
You can't deny it.   *[Embracing him.]*
   Ludolph.   Happiest of days!
   Otho. We'll make it so.
   Ludolph.   'Stead of one fatted calf
Ten hecatombs shall bellow out their last,
Smote 'twixt the horns by the death-stunning mace   130
Of Mars, and all the soldiery shall feast
Nobly as Nimrod's masons, when the towers
Of Nineveh new kissed the parted clouds!
   Otho. Large as a God speak out, where all is thine.
   Ludolph. Ay, father, but the fire in my sad breast
Is quenched with inward tears! I must rejoice
For you, whose wings so shadow over me
In tender victory, but for myself
I still must mourn. The fair Auranthe mine!
Too great a boon! I pr'ythee let me ask   140

What more than I know of could so have changed
Your purpose touching her?
  Otho.   At a word, this:
In no deed did you give me more offence
Than your rejection of Erminia.
To my appalling, I saw too good proof
Of your keen-eyed suspicion, – she is naught.
  Ludolph. You are convinced?
  Otho.   Ay, spite of her sweet looks.
O that my brother's daughter should so fall!
Her fame has passed into the grosser lips
Of soldiers in their cups.
  Ludolph.   'Tis very sad.   150
  Otho. No more of her. Auranthe – Ludolph, come!
This marriage be the bond of endless peace! *[Exeunt.]*

SCENE II. – *The entrance of Gersa's Tent in the Hungarian Camp*

Enter Erminia.

Erminia. Where – where – where shall I find a messenger?
A trusty soul – a good man, in the camp?
Shall I go myself? Monstrous wickedness!
O cursèd Conrad! devilish Auranthe!
Here is proof palpable as the bright sun!
O for a voice to reach the Emperor's ears!

[Shouts in the Camp.]

Enter an Hungarian Captain.

Captain. Fair prisoner, you hear these joyous shouts?
The King – ay, now our King – but still your slave,
Young Gersa, from a short captivity
Has just returned. He bids me say, bright dame,   10
That even the homage of his rangèd chiefs
Cures not his keen impatience to behold
Such beauty once again. What ails you, lady?

Erminia. Say, is not that a German, yonder? There!

Captain. Methinks by his stout bearing he should be;
Yes – it is Albert; a Brave German knight,
And much in the Emperor's favour.

Erminia.   I would fain
Inquire of friends and kinsfolk, – how they fared
In these rough times. Brave soldier, as you pass
To royal Gersa with my humble thanks,   20
Will you send yonder knight to me?

Captain.   I will.   *[Exit.]*

Erminia. Yes, he was ever known to be a man
Frank, open, generous: Albert I may trust.
O proof! proof! proof! Albert's an honest man;
Not Ethelbert the monk, if he were here,
Would I hold more trustworthy. Now!

Enter Albert.

Albert.   Good gods!
Lady Erminia! are you prisoner
In this beleaguered camp? or are you here
Of your own will? You pleased to send for me.
By Venus, 'tis a pity I knew not   30
Your plight before, and, by her son, I swear
To do you every service you can ask.
What would the fairest – ?

Erminia.   Albert, will you swear?

Albert. I have. Well?

Erminia.   Albert, you have fame to lose.
If men, in court and camp, lie not outright,
You should be, from a thousand, chosen forth
To do an honest deed. Shall I confide—?

Albert. Ay, anything to me, fair creature. Do;
Dictate my task. Sweet woman—

Erminia.   Truce with that.
You understand me not; and, in your speech,   40

I see how far the slander is abroad.
Without proof could you think me innocent?
   Albert. Lady, I should rejoice to know you so.
   Erminia. If you have any pity for a maid
Suffering a daily death from evil tongues;
Any compassion for that Emperor's niece
Who, for your bright sword and clear honesty,
Lifted you from the crowd of common men
Into the lap of honour, – save me, knight!
   Albert. How? Make it clear, if it be possible,   50
I, by the banner of Saint Maurice, swear
To right you.
   Erminia. Possible! – Easy. O my heart!
This letter's not so soiled but you may read it; –
Possible! There – that letter! Read – read it.

                          [Gives him a letter.]

                Albert [reading].

'TO THE DUKE CONRAD, – Forget the threat you made at parting and I will forget to send the Emperor letters and papers of yours I have become possessed of. His life is no trifle to me; his death you shall find none to yourself.'

   [Speaks to himself] 'Tis me – my life that's pleaded for!   60

                [Reads.]

'He, for his own sake, will be dumb as the grave. Erminia has my shame fixed upon her, sure as a wen. We are safe.

                                AURANTHE.'

A she-devil! A dragon! I her imp!
Fire of hell! Auranthe – lewd demon!
Where got you this? Where? when?
   Erminia. I found it in the tent, among some spoils
Which, being noble, fell to Gersa's lot.

Come in, and see.   *[They go in and return.]*

   Albert.   Villainy! Villainy!
Conrad's sword, his corslet and his helm,
And his letter. Caitiff, he shall feel—   70

   Erminia. I see you are thunderstruck. Haste, haste,
away!

   Albert. O I am tortured by this villainy.

   Erminia. You needs must be. Carry it swift to Otho;
Tell him, moreover, I am prisoner
Here in this camp, where all the sisterhood,
Forced from their quiet cells, are parcelled out
For slaves among these Huns. Away! Away!

   Albert. I am gone.

   Erminia.   Swift be your steed! Within this hour
The Emperor will see it.

   Albert.   Ere I sleep:
That I can swear.   *[Hurries out.]*

   Gersa. [Without.] Brave captains! thanks. Enough   80
Of loyal homage now!

   Erminia. Hail, royal Hun!

   Gersa. What means this, fair one? Why in such alarm?
Who was it hurried by me so distract?
It seemed you were in deep discourse together;
Your doctrine has not been so harsh to him
As to my poor deserts. Come, come, be plain.
I am no jealous fool to kill you both,
Or, for such trifles, rob th' adornèd world
Of such a beauteous vestal.

   Erminia.   I grieve, my lord,
To hear you condescend to ribald-phrase.   90

   Gersa. This is too much! Hearken, my lady pure!

   Erminia. Silence! and hear the magic of a name –
Erminia! I am she, – the Emperor's niece!
Praised be the heavens, I now dare own myself!

   Gersa. Erminia! Indeed! I've heard of her.
Pr'ythee, fair lady, what chance brought you here?

Erminia. Ask your own soldiers.

Gersa.   And you dare own your name.
For loveliness you may – and for the rest
My vein is not censorious.

Erminia.   Alas! poor me!
'Tis false indeed.

Gersa.   Indeed you are too fair: 100
The swan, soft leaning on her fledgy breast,
When to the stream she launches, looks not back
With such a tender grace; nor are her wings
So white as your soul is, if that but be
Twin picture to your face. Erminia!
To-day, for the first day, I am a king,
Yet would I give my unworn crown away
To know you spotless.

Erminia.   Trust me one day more,
Generously, without more certain guarantee
Than this poor face you deign to praise so much;   110
After that, say and do whate'er you please.
If I have any knowledge of you, sir,
I think, nay I am sure, you will grieve much
To hear my story. O, be gentle to me,
For I am sick and faint with many wrongs,
Tired out, and weary-worn with contumelies.

Gersa. Poor lady!

Enter Ethelbert.

Erminia.   Gentle Prince, 'tis false indeed.
Good morrow, holy father! I have had
Your prayers, though I looked for you in vain.

Ethelbert. Blessings upon you, daughter! Sure you look   120
Too cheerful for these foul pernicious days.
Young man, you heard this virgin say 'twas false. –
'Tis false, I say. What! can you not employ
Your temper elsewhere, 'mong these burly tents,

But you must taunt this dove, for she hath lost
The Eagle Otho to beat off assault?
Fie! fie! But I will be her guard myself,
I' the Emperor's name. I here demand of you
Herself, and all her sisterhood. She false!

  Gersa. Peace! peace, old man! I cannot think she is.   130

  Ethelbert. Whom I have known from her first infancy.
Baptized her in the bosom of the Church,
Watched her, as anxious husbandmen the grain,
From the first shoot till the unripe mid-May,
Then to the tender ear of her June days,
Which, lifting sweet abroad its timid green,
Is blighted by the touch of calumny!
You cannot credit such a monstrous tale?

  Gersa. I cannot. Take her. Fair Erminia,
I follow you to Friedburg, – is 't not so?   140

  Erminia. Ay, so we purpose.

  Ethelbert.   Daughter, do you so?
How's this? I marvel! Yet you look not mad.

  Erminia. I have good news to tell you, Ethelbert.

  Gersa. Ho! ho, there! Guards!
Your blessing, father! Sweet Erminia,
Believe me, I am well nigh sure –

  Erminia.   Farewell!
Short time will show.   *[Enter Chiefs.]*

      Yes, father Ethelbert,
I have news precious as we pass along.

  Ethelbert. Dear daughter, you shall guide me.

  Erminia.   To no ill.

  Gersa. Command an escort to the Friedburg lines.   150

       [Exeunt Chiefs.]

Pray let me lead. Fair lady, forget not
Gersa, how he believed you innocent.
I follow you to Friedburg with all speed.   *[Exeunt.]*

ACT III

SCENE I. — *The Country*

Enter Albert.

Albert. O that the earth were empty, as when Cain
Had no perplexity to hide his head!
Or that the sword of some brave enemy
Had put a sudden stop to my hot breath,
And hurled me down the illimitable gulf
Of times past, unremembered! Better so
Than thus fast-limèd in a cursèd snare, –
The limbo of a wanton. This the end
Of an aspiring life! My boyhood past
In feud with wolves and bears, when no eye saw   10
The solitary warfare, fought for love
Of honour 'mid the growling wilderness;
My sturdier youth, maturing to the sword,
Won by the syren-trumpets, and the ring
Of shields upon the pavement, when bright-mailed
Henry the Fowler passed the streets of Prague.
Was 't to this end I louted and became
The menial of Mars, and held a spear,
Swayed by command, as corn is by the wind?
Is it for this, I now am lifted up   20
By Europe's thronèd Emperor, to see
My honour be my executioner, –
My love of fame, my prided honesty,
Put to the torture for confessional?
Then the damned crime of blurting to the world
A woman's secret! – though a fiend she be,
Too tender of my ignominious life;
But then to wrong the generous Emperor
In such a searching point, were to give up
My soul for foot-ball at hell's holiday!   30

I must confess, – and cut my throat, – to-day?
To-morrow? Ho! some wine!

Enter Sigifred.

   Sigifred.   A fine humour –
   Albert. Who goes there? Count Sigifred? Ha! ha!
   Sigifred. What, man, do you mistake the hollow sky
For a thronged tavern, and these stubbèd trees
For old serge hangings, – me, your humble friend,
For a poor waiter? Why, man, how you stare!
What gipsies have you been carousing with?
No, no more wine: methinks you've had enough.
   Albert. You well may laugh and banter. What a fool   **40**
An injury may make of a staid man!
You shall know all anon.
   Sigifred.   Some tavern brawl?
   Albert. 'Twas with some people out of common reach;
Revenge is difficult.
   Sigifred.   I am your friend;
We meet again to-day, and can confer
Upon it. For the present I'm in haste.
   Albert. Whither?
   Sigifred.   To fetch King Gersa to the feast.
The Emperor on this marriage is so hot,
Pray heaven it end not in apoplexy!
The very porters, as I passed the doors,   **50**
Heard his loud laugh, and answered in full choir.
I marvel, Albert, you delay so long
From these bright revelries; go, show yourself,
You may be made a duke.
   Albert.   Ay, very like.
Pray, what day has his Highness fixed upon?
   Sigifred. For what?
   Albert. The marriage. What else can I mean?
   Sigifred. To-day. O, I forgot, you could not know;
The news is scarce a minute old with me.

Albert. Married to-day! To-day! You did not say so?

Sigifred. Now, while I speak to you, their comely heads 60
Are bowed before the mitre.

Albert. O! monstrous!

Sigifred. What is this?

Albert. Nothing, Sigifred. Farewell!
We'll meet upon our subject. Farewell, Count! *[Exit.]*

Sigifred. To this clear-headed Albert? He brain-turned!
'Tis as portentous as a meteor. *[Exit.]*

SCENE II. – *An Apartment in the Castle*

Enter, as from the Marriage, Otho, Ludolph, Auranthe, Conrad,
Nobles, Knights, Ladies, etc. Music.

Otho. Now, Ludolph! Now, Auranthe! Daughter fair!
What can I find to grace your nuptial day
More than my love, and these wide realms in fee!

Ludolph. I have too much.

Auranthe. And I, my liege, by far.

Ludolph. Auranthe I have! O, my bride, my love!
Not all the gaze upon us can restrain
My eyes, too long poor exiles from thy face,
From adoration, and my foolish tongue
From uttering soft responses to the love
I see in thy mute beauty beaming forth! 10
Fair creature, bless me with a single word!
All mine!

Auranthe. Spare, spare me, my lord; I swoon else.

Ludolph. Soft beauty! by to-morrow I should die,
Wert thou not mine. *[They talk apart.]*

1st Lady. How deep she has bewitched him!

1st Knight. Ask you for her recipe for love philtres.

2nd Lady. They hold the Emperor in admiration.

Otho. If ever king was happy that am I!
What are the cities 'yond the Alps to me,
The provinces about the Danube's mouth,

The promise of fair soil beyond the Rhone;   20
Or routing out of Hyperborean hordes,
To these fair children, stars of a new age?
Unless perchance I might rejoice to win
This little ball of earth, and chuck it them
To play with!

    Auranthe. Nay, my lord, I do not know—
    Ludolph. Let me not famish.
    Otho. [To Conrad.]   Good Franconia,
You heard what oath I sware, as the sun rose,
That unless Heaven would send me back my son,
My Arab, – no soft music should enrich
The cool wine, kissed off with a soldier's smack;   30
Now all my empire, bartered for one feast,
Seems poverty.

    Conrad.   Upon the neighbour plain
The heralds have prepared a royal lists;
Your knights, found war-proof in the bloody field,
Speed to the game.

    Otho.   Well, Ludolph, what say you?
    Ludolph. My lord!
    Otho.   A tourney?
    Conrad.   Or, if't please you best—
    Ludolph. I want no more!
    1st Lady.   He soars!
    2nd Lady.   Past all reason.
    Ludolph. Though heaven's choir
Should in a vast circumference descend
And sing for my delight, I'd stop my ears!   40
Though bright Apollo's car stood burning here,
And he put out an arm to bid me mount,
His touch an immortality, not I!
This earth, this palace, this room, Auranthe!

    Otho. This is a little painful: just too much.
Conrad, if he flames longer in this wise

I shall believe in wizard-woven loves
And old romances; but I'll break the spell.
Ludolph!

    Conrad. He'll be calm, anon.

    Ludolph.   You called?
Yes, yes, yes, I offend. You must forgive me;   **50**
Not being quite recovered from the stun
Of your large bounties. A tourney, is it not?

                         [A senet heard faintly.]

    Conrad. The trumpets reach us.

    Ethelbert. [Without.]   On your peril, sirs,
Detain us!

    1st Voice. [Without.] Let not the abbot pass.

    2nd Voice. [Without.]   No!
On your lives!

    1st Voice. [Without.] Holy father, you must not.

    Ethelbert. [Without.] Otho!

    Otho.   Who calls on Otho?

    Ethelbert. [Without.]   Ethelbert.

    Otho. Let him come in.

         Enter Ethelbert, leading in Erminia.

               Thou cursèd abbot, why
Hast brought pollution to our holy rites?
Hast thou no fear of hangman, or the faggot?

    Ludolph. What portent – what strange prodigy is this?   **60**

    Conrad. Away!

    Ethelbert.   You, Duke?

    Erminia.   Albert has surely failed me!
Look at the Emperor's brow upon me bent!

    Ethelbert. A sad delay!

    Conrad.   Away, thou guilty thing!

    Ethelbert. You again, Duke? Justice, most noble Otho!
You – go to your sister there, and plot again,
A quick plot, swift as thought to save your heads;

For lo! the toils are spread around your den,
The world is all agape to see dragged forth
Two ugly monsters.

    Ludolph. What means he, my lord?

    Conrad. I cannot guess.

    Ethelbert. Best ask your lady sister   70
Whether the riddle puzzles her beyond
The power of utterance.

    Conrad. Foul barbarian, cease;
The Princess faints!

    Ludolph. Stab him! O, sweetest wife!

[Attendants bear off Auranthe.]

    Erminia. Alas!

    Ethelbert. Your wife?

    Ludolph. Ay, Satan! does that yerk ye?

    Ethelbert. Wife! so soon!

    Ludolph. Ay, wife! Oh, impudence!
Thou bitter mischief! Venomous mad priest!
How dar'st thou lift those beetle brows at me –
Me – the prince Ludolph, in this presence here,
Upon my marriage-day, and scandalize
My joys with such opprobrious surprise?   80
Wife! Why dost linger on that syllable,
As if it were some demon's name pronounced
To summon harmful lightning, and make yawn
The sleepy thunder? Hast no sense of fear?
No ounce of man in thy mortality?
Tremble! for, at my nod, the sharpened axe
Will make thy bold tongue quiver to the roots,
Those grey lids wink, and thou not know it more!

    Ethelbert. O, poor deceivèd Prince! I pity thee!
Great Otho! I claim justice—

    Ludolph. Thou shalt have 't!   90
Thine arms from forth a pulpit of hot fire
Shall sprawl distracted? O that that dull cowl

Were some most sensitive portion of thy life,
That I might give it to my hounds to tear!
Thy girdle some fine zealous-painèd nerve
To girth my saddle! And those devil's beads
Each one a life, that I might every day
Crush one with Vulcan's hammer!
    Otho.   Peace, my son;
You far outstrip my spleen in this affair.
Let us be calm, and hear the abbot's plea   100
For this intrusion.
    Ludolph.   I am silent, sire.
    Otho. Conrad, see all depart not wanted here.

[Exeunt Knights, Ladies, etc.]

Ludolph, be calm. Ethelbert, peace awhile.
This mystery demands an audience
Of a just judge, and that will Otho be.
    Ludolph. Why has he time to breathe another word?
    Otho. Ludolph, old Ethelbert, be sure, comes not
To beard us for no cause; he's not the man
To cry himself up an ambassador
Without credentials.
    Ludolph.   I'll chain up myself.   110
    Otho. Old abbot, stand here forth. Lady Erminia,
Sit. And now, abbot! what have you to say?
Our ear is open. First we here denounce
Hard penalties against thee, if't be found
The cause for which you have disturbed us here,
Making our bright hours muddy, be a thing
Of little moment.
    Ethelbert.   See this innocent!
Otho! thou father of the people called,
Is her life nothing? Her fair honour nothing?
Her tears from matins until even-song   120
Nothing? Her burst heart nothing? Emperor!
Is this your gentle niece – the simplest flower

Of the world's herbal – this fair lily blanched
Still with the dews of piety, this meek lady
Here sitting like an angel newly-shent,
Who veils its snowy wings and grows all pale, –
Is she nothing?

 Otho.   What more to the purpose, abbot?

 Ludolph. Whither is he winding?

 Conrad.   No clue yet!

 Ethelbert. You have heard, my liege, and so, no doubt, all here,
Foul, poisonous, malignant whisperings;   130
Nay open speech, rude mockery grown common,
Against the spotless nature and clear fame
Of the princess Erminia, your niece.
I have intruded here thus suddenly,
Because I hold those base weeds, with tight hand,
Which now disfigure her fair growing stem,
Waiting but for your sign to pull them up
By the dark roots, and leave her palpable,
To all men's sight, a lady innocent.
The ignominy of that whispered tale   140
About a midnight gallant, seen to climb
A window to her chamber neighboured near,
I will from her turn off, and put the load
On the right shoulders; on that wretch's head,
Who, by close stratagems, did save herself,
Chiefly by shifting to this lady's room
A rope-ladder for false witness.

 Ludolph.   Most atrocious!

 Otho. Ethelbert, proceed.

 Ethelbert.   With sad lips I shall;
For, in the healing of one wound, I fear
To make a greater. His young highness here   150
To-day was married.

 Ludolph. Good.

 Ethelbert.   Would it were good!
Yet why do I delay to spread abroad

The names of those two vipers, from whose jaw
A deadly breath went forth to taint and blast
This guileless lady?

 Otho.   Abbot, speak their names.

 Ethelbert. A minute first. It cannot be – but may
I ask, great judge, if you to-day have put
A letter by unread?

 Otho.   Does 't end in this?

 Conrad. Out with their names!

 Ethelbert.   Bold sinner, say you so?

 Ludolph. Out, tedious monk!

 Otho.   Confess, or by the wheel— 160

 Ethelbert. My evidence cannot be far away;
And, though it never come, be on my head
The crime of passing an attaint upon
The slanderers of this virgin—

 Ludolph.   Speak aloud!

 Ethelbert. Auranthe, and her brother there!

 Conrad. Amaze!

 Ludolph. Throw them from the windows!

 Otho. Do what you will!

 Ludolph.   What shall I do with them?
Something of quick dispatch, for should she hear,
My soft Auranthe, her sweet mercy would
Prevail against my fury. Damnèd priest! 170
What swift death wilt thou die? As to the lady,
I touch her not.

 Ethelbert. Illustrious Otho, stay!
An ample store of misery thou hast;
Choke not the granary of thy noble mind
With more bad bitter grain, too difficult
A cud for the repentance of a man
Grey-growing. To thee only I appeal,
Not to thy noble son, whose yeasting youth
Will clear itself, and crystal turn again.
A young man's heart, by Heaven's blessing, is 180

A wide world, where a thousand new-born hopes
Empurple fresh the melancholy blood:
But an old man's is narrow, tenantless
Of hopes, and stuffed with many memories,
Which being pleasant, ease the heavy pulse –
Painful, clog up and stagnate. Weigh this matter
Even as a miser balances his coin;
And, in the name of mercy, give command
That your knight Albert be brought here before you.
He will expound this riddle; he will show   190
A noon-day proof of bad Auranthe's guilt.
    Otho. Let Albert straight be summoned.

                              [Exit one of the Nobles.]

    Ludolph.   Impossible!
I cannot doubt – I will not – no – to doubt
Is to be ashes! – withered up to death!
    Otho. My gentle Ludolph, harbour not a fear;
You do yourself much wrong.
    Ludolph.   O, wretched dolt!
Now, when my foot is almost on thy neck,
Wilt thou infuriate me? Proof! Thou fool!
Why wilt thou tease impossibility
With such a thick-skulled persevering suit?   200
Fanatic obstinacy! Prodigy!
Monster of folly! Ghost of a turned brain!
You puzzle me, – you haunt me, when I dream
Of you my brain will split! Bold sorcerer!
Juggler! May I come near you? On my soul
I know not whether to pity, curse, or laugh.

          Enter Albert and the Nobleman.

Here, Albert, this old phantom wants a proof!
Give him his proof! A camel's load of proofs!
    Otho. Albert, I speak to you as to a man
Whose words once uttered pass like current gold;   210

And therefore fit to calmly put a close
To this brief tempest. Do you stand possessed
Of any proof against the honourableness
Of Lady Auranthe, our new-spousèd daughter?
   Albert. You chill me with astonishment. How's this?
My liege, what proof should I have 'gainst a fame
Impossible of slur?

                   [Otho rises.]

Erminia.   O, wickedness!
Ethelbert. Deluded monarch, 'tis a cruel lie.
Otho. Peace, rebel-priest!
Conrad.   Insult beyond credence!
Erminia. Almost a dream!
Ludolph.   We have awakened from   220
A foolish dream that from my brow hath wrung
A wrathful dew. O folly! why did I
So act the lion with this silly gnat?
Let them depart. Lady Erminia!
I ever grieved for you, as who did not?
But now you have, with such a brazen front,
So most maliciously, so madly striven
To dazzle the soft moon, when tenderest clouds
Should be unlooped around to curtain her,
I leave you to the desert of the world   230
Almost with pleasure. Let them be set free
For me! I take no personal revenge
More than against a nightmare, which a man
Forgets in the new dawn.   *[Exit Ludolph.]*
   Otho. Still in extremes! No, they must not be loose.
   Ethelbert. Albert, I must suspect thee of a crime
So fiendish—
   Otho.   Fear'st thou not my fury, monk?
Conrad, be they in your safe custody
Till we determine some fit punishment.
It is so mad a deed, I must reflect   240

And question them in private; for perhaps,
By patient scrutiny, we may discover
Whether they merit death, or should be placed
In care of the physicians.

> *[Exeunt Otho and Nobles, Albert following.]*

    Conrad. My guards, ho!
    Erminia.   Albert, wilt thou follow there?
Wilt thou creep dastardly behind his back,
And shrink away from a weak woman's eye?
Turn, thou court-Janus! thou forget'st thyself;
Here is the duke, waiting with open arms

> *Enter Guards.*

To thank thee; here congratulate each other;   250
Wring hands; embrace; and swear how lucky 'twas
That I, by happy chance, hit the right man
Of all the world to trust in.
    Albert.   Trust! to me!
    Conrad. [Aside.] He is the sole one in this mystery.
    Erminia. Well, I give up, and save my prayers for Heaven!
You, who could do this deed, would ne'er relent,
Though, at my words, the hollow prison-vaults
Would groan for pity.
    Conrad.   Manacle them both!
    Ethelbert. I know it – it must be – I see it all!
Albert, thou art the minion!
    Erminia.   Ah! too plain—   260
Conrad. Silence! Gag up their mouth! I cannot bear
More of this brawling. That the Emperor
Had placed you in some other custody!
Bring them away.   *[Exeunt all but Albert.]*
    Albert. Though my name perish from the book of honour,
Almost before the recent ink is dry,
And be no more remembered after death

Than any drummer's in the muster-roll;
Yet shall I season high my sudden fall
With triumph o'er that evil-witted duke!   270
He shall feel what it is to have the hand
Of a man drowning, on his hateful throat.

Enter Gersa and Sigifred.

Gersa. What discord is at ferment in this house?
Sigifred. We are without conjecture; not a soul
We met could answer any certainty.
Gersa. Young Ludolph, like a fiery arrow, shot
By us.
Sigifred. The Emperor, with crossed arms, in thought.
Gersa. In one room music, in another sadness,
Perplexity everywhere!
Albert.   A trifle more!
Follow; your presence will much avail   280
To tune our jarrèd spirits. I'll explain.   *[Exeunt.]*

ACT IV

SCENE I. – *Auranthe's Apartment*

Auranthe and Conrad discovered.

Conrad. Well, well, I know what ugly jeopardy
We are caged in; you need not pester that
Into my ears. Pr'ythee, let me be spared
A foolish tongue, that I may bethink me
Of remedies with some deliberation.
You cannot doubt but 'tis in Albert's power
To crush or save us?
Auranthe.   No, I cannot doubt.
He has, assure yourself, by some strange means,
My secret; which I ever hid from him,
Knowing his mawkish honesty.

Conrad.   Cursed slave!   10

Auranthe. Ay, I could almost curse him now myself.
Wretched impediment! Evil genius!
A glue upon my wings, that cannot spread,
When they should span the provinces! A snake,
A scorpion, sprawling on the first gold step,
Conducting to the throne high canopied.

Conrad. You would not hear my counsel, when his life
Might have been trodden out, all sure and hushed;
Now the dull animal forsooth must be
Entreated, managed! When can you contrive   20
The interview he demands?

Auranthe.   As speedily
It must be done as my bribed woman can
Unseen conduct him to me; but I fear
'Twill be impossible, while the broad day
Comes through the panes with persecuting glare.
Methinks, if 't now were night I could intrigue
With darkness, bring the stars to second me,
And settle all this trouble.

Conrad.   Nonsense! Child!
See him immediately; why not now?

Auranthe. Do you forget that even the senseless doorposts   30
Are on the watch and gape through all the house?
How many whisperers there are about,
Hungry for evidence to ruin me, –
Men I have spurned, and women I have taunted?
Besides, the foolish prince sends, minute whiles,
His pages – so they tell me – to inquire
After my health, entreating, if I please,
To see me.

Conrad. Well, suppose this Albert here;
What is your power with him?

Auranthe.   He should be
My echo, my taught parrot! but I fear   40
He will be cur enough to bark at me;

Have his own say; read me some silly creed
'Bout shame and pity.

  Conrad.   What will you do then?

  Auranthe. What I shall do, I know not: what I would
Cannot be done; for see, this chamber-floor
Will not yield to the pick-axe and the spade, –
Here is no quiet depth of hollow ground.

  Conrad. Sister, you have grown sensible and wise,
Seconding, ere I speak it, what is now,
I hope, resolved between us.

  Auranthe.   Say, what is 't?

  Conrad. You need not be his sexton, too: a man
May carry that with him shall make him die
Elsewhere, – give that to him; pretend the while
You will to-morrow succumb to his wishes,
Be what they may, and send him from the Castle
On some fool's errand; let his latest groan
Frighten the wolves!

  Auranthe.   Alas! he must not die!

  Conrad. Would you were both hearsed up in stifling lead!
Detested—

  Auranthe. Conrad, hold! I would not bear
The little thunder of your fretful tongue,
Tho' I alone were taken in these toils,   60
And you could free me; but remember, sir,
You live alone in my security:
So keep your wits at work, for your own sake,
Not mine, and be more mannerly.

  Conrad.   Thou wasp!
If my domains were emptied of these folk,
And I had thee to starve—

  Auranthe.   O, marvellous!
But, Conrad, now be gone; the host is looked for;
Cringe to the Emperor, entertain the lords.
And, do ye mind, above all things, proclaim   70
My sickness, with a brother's saddened eye,

Condoling with Prince Ludolph. In fit time
Return to me.
    Conrad.   I leave you to your thoughts.

                [Exit.]

  Auranthe. [Sola.] Down, down, proud temper! down,
    Auranthe's pride!
Why do I anger him when I should kneel?
Conrad! Albert! help! help! What can I do?
O, wretched woman! lost, wrecked, swallowed up,
Accursèd, blasted! O, thou golden Crown,
Orbing along the serene firmament
Of a wide empire, like a glowing moon;   80
And thou, bright sceptre! lustrous in my eyes
There – as the fabled fair Hesperian tree,
Bearing a fruit more precious! graceful thing,
Delicate, godlike, magic! must I leave
Thee to melt in the visionary air,
Ere, by one grasp, this common hand is made
Imperial? I do not know the time
When I have wept for sorrow; but methinks
I could now sit upon the ground, and shed
Tears, tears of misery. O, the heavy day!   90
How shall I bear my life till Albert comes?
Ludolph! Erminia! Proofs! O heavy day!
Bring me some mourning weeds, that I may 'tire
Myself as fits one wailing her own death:
Cut off these curls, and brand this lily hand,
And throw these jewels from my loathing sight, –
Fetch me a missal, and a string of beads, –
A cup of bittered water, and a crust, –
I will confess, O holy Abbot! – How?
What is this? Auranthe! thou fool, dolt,   100
Whimpering idiot! up! up! and quell!
I am safe! Coward! why am I in fear?

Albert! he cannot stickle, chew the cud
In such a fine extreme, – impossible!
Who knocks?   *[Goes to the door, listens, and opens it.]*

Enter Albert.

Albert, I have been waiting for you here
With such an aching heart, such swooning throbs
On my poor brain, such cruel, cruel sorrow,
That I should claim your pity! Art not well?
   Albert. Yes, lady, well.
   Auranthe.   You look not so, alas!   110
But pale, as if you brought some heavy news.
   Albert. You know full well what makes me look so pale.
   Auranthe. No! Do I? Surely I am still to learn
Some horror; all I know, this present, is
I am near hustled to a dangerous gulf,
Which you can save me from, – and therefore safe,
So trusting in thy love; that should not make
Thee pale, my Albert.
   Albert.   It doth make me freeze.
   Auranthe. Why should it, love?
   Albert.   You should not ask me that,
But make your own heart monitor, and save   120
Me the great pain of telling. You must know.
   Auranthe. Something has vext you, Albert. There are times
When simplest things put on a sombre cast;
A melancholy mood will haunt a man,
Until most easy matters take the shape
Of unachievable tasks; small rivulets
Then seem impassable.
   Albert.   Do not cheat yourself
With hope that gloss of words, or suppliant action,
Or tears, or ravings, or self-threatened death,
Can alter my resolve.
   Auranthe.   You make me tremble,   130

Not so much at your threats, as at your voice,
Untuned, and harsh, and barren of all love.
    Albert. You suffocate me! Stop this devil's parley,
And listen to me; know me once for all.
    Auranthe. I thought I did. Alas! I am deceived.
    Albert. No, you are not deceived. You took me for
A man detesting all inhuman crime;
And therefore kept from me your demon's plot
Against Erminia. Silent? Be so still;
For ever! Speak no more; but hear my words,   140
Thy fate. Your safety I have bought to-day
By blazoning a lie, which in the dawn
I'll expiate with truth.
    Auranthe.   O cruel traitor!
Albert. For I would not set eyes upon thy shame;
I would not see thee dragged to death by the hair,
Penanced, and taunted on a scaffolding!
To-night, upon the skirts of the blind wood
That blackens northward of these horrid towers,
I wait for you with horses. Choose your fate.
Farewell!
    Auranthe. Albert, you jest; I'm sure you must.   150
You, an ambitious Soldier! I, a Queen,
One who could say, – Here, rule these Provinces!
Take tribute from these cities for thyself!
Empty these armouries, these treasuries,
Muster thy warlike thousands at a nod!
Go! conquer Italy!
    Albert.   Auranthe, you have made
The whole world chaff to me. Your doom is fixed.
    Auranthe. Out, villain! dastard!
    Albert.   Look there to the door!
Who is it?
    Auranthe. Conrad, traitor!
    Albert.   Let him in.

Enter Conrad.

Do not affect amazement, hypocrite,   160
At seeing me in this chamber.
   Conrad.   Auranthe?
   Albert. Talk not with eyes, but speak your curses out
Against me, who would sooner crush and grind
A brace of toads, than league with them t' oppress
An innocent lady, gull an Emperor,
More generous to me than autumn sun
To ripening harvests.
   Auranthe.   No more insult, sir!
   Albert. Ay, clutch your scabbard: but, for prudence sake,
Draw not the sword; 'twould make an uproar, Duke,
You would not hear the end of. At nightfall   170
Your lady sister, if I guess aright,
Will leave this busy castle. You had best
Take farewell too of worldly vanities.
   Conrad. Vassal!
   Albert. To-morrow, when the Emperor sends
For loving Conrad, see you fawn on him.
Good even!
   Auranthe. You'll be seen!
   Albert.   See the coast clear then.
   Auranthe. [As he goes.] Remorseless Albert! Cruel, cruel
      wretch!   *[She lets him out.]*
   Conrad. So we must lick the dust?
   Auranthe.   I follow him.
   Conrad. How? Where? The plan of your escape?
   Auranthe.   He waits
For me with horses by the forest-side,   180
Northward.
   Conrad. Good, good! he dies. You go, say you?
   Auranthe. Perforce.
   Conrad.   Be speedy, darkness! Till that comes,

Fiends keep you company!   *[Exit.]*
   Auranthe.   And you! and you!
And all men! Vanish!   *[Retires to an inner apartment.]*

SCENE II. — *An Apartment in the Castle*

Enter Ludolph and Page.

  Page. Still very sick, my lord; but now I went,
And there her women, in a mournful throng,
Stood in the passage whispering; if any
Moved 'twas with careful steps, and hushed as death.
They bade me stop.
  Ludolph.   Good fellow, once again
Make soft inquiry; pr'ythee, be not stayed
By any hindrance, but with gentlest force
Break through her weeping servants, till thou com'st
E'en to her chamber-door, and there, fair boy, –   10
If with thy mother's milk thou hast sucked in
Any divine eloquence, – woo her ears
With plaints for me, more tender than the voice
Of dying Echo, echoed.
  Page.   Kindest master!
To know thee sad thus, will unloose my tongue
In mournful syllables. Let but my words reach
Her ears, and she shall take them coupled with
Moans from my heart, and sighs not counterfeit.
May I speed better!   *[Exit Page.]*
  Ludolph. [Solus.] Auranthe! My life!
Long have I loved thee, yet till now not loved: 20
Remembering, as I do, hard-hearted times
When I had heard e'en of thy death perhaps,
And – thoughtless! – suffered thee to pass alone
Into Elysium! – now I follow thee,
A substance or a shadow, wheresoe'er
Thou leadest me – whether thy white feet press,
With pleasant weight, the amorous-aching earth,

Or thro' the air thou pioneerest me,
A shade! Yet sadly I predestinate!
O, unbenignest Love, why wilt thou let   30
Darkness steal out upon the sleepy world
So wearily, as if Night's chariot wheels
Were clogged in some thick cloud? O, changeful Love,
Let not her steeds with drowsy-footed pace
Pass the high stars, before sweet embassage
Comes from the pillowed beauty of that fair
Completion of all-delicate Nature's wit!
Pout her faint lips anew with rubious health;
And, with thine infant fingers, lift the fringe
Of her sick eyelids; that those eyes may glow   40
With wooing light upon me ere the morn
Peers with disrelish, grey, barren, and cold!

Enter Gersa and Courtiers.

Otho calls me his Lion, – should I blush
To be so tamed? so—
 Gersa.   Do me the courtesy,
Gentlemen, to pass on.
 1st Knight.   We are your servants.
         [Exeunt Courtiers.]
 Ludolph. It seems then, sir, you have found out the man
You would confer with; – me?
 Gersa.   If I break not
Too much upon your thoughtful mood, I will
Claim a brief while your patience.
 Ludolph.   For what cause
Soe'er, I shall be honoured.
 Gersa.   I not less.   50
 Ludolph. What may it be? No trifle can take place
Of such deliberate prologue, serious 'haviour.
But, be it what it may, I cannot fail
To listen with no common interest;
For though so new your presence is to me,

I have a soldier's friendship for your fame.
Please you explain.

    Gersa.   As thus: – for, pardon me,
I cannot, in plain terms, grossly assault
A noble nature; and would faintly sketch
What your quick apprehension will fill up;   60
So finely I esteem you.

    Ludolph.   I attend.

    Gersa. Your generous father, most illustrious Otho,
Sits in the banquet-room among his chiefs;
His wine is bitter, for you are not there;
His eyes are fixed still on the open doors,
And ev'ry passer in he frowns upon,
Seeing no Ludolph comes.

    Ludolph.   I do neglect.

    Gersa. And for your absence may I guess the cause?

    Ludolph. Stay there! No – guess? More princely you must be
Than to make guesses at me. 'Tis enough.   70
I'm sorry I can hear no more.

    Gersa.   And I
As grieved to force it on you so abrupt;
Yet, one day, you must know a grief, whose sting
Will sharpen more the longer 'tis concealed.

    Ludolph. Say it at once, sir! Dead – dead? – is she dead?

    Gersa. Mine is a cruel task: she is not dead,
And would, for your sake, she were innocent.

    Ludolph. Hungarian! thou amazest me beyond
All scope of thought, convulsest my heart's blood
To deadly churning! Gersa, you are young,   80
As I am; let me observe you, face to face;
Not grey-browed like the poisonous Ethelbert,
No rheumèd eyes, no furrowing of age,
No wrinkles, where all vices nestle in
Like crannied vermin, – no! but fresh, and young,
And hopeful-featured. Ha! by heaven, you weep!
Tears, human tears! Do you repent you then

Of a cursed torturer's office? Why shouldst join –
Tell me, – the league of devils? Confess – confess –
The lie!

  Gersa. Lie! – but begone all ceremonious points   90
Of honour battailous! I could not turn
My wrath against thee for the orbèd world.

  Ludolph. Your wrath, weak boy? Tremble at mine, unless
Retraction follow close upon the heels
Of that late 'stounding insult! Why has my sword
Not done already a sheer judgment on thee?
Despair, or eat thy words! Why, thou wast nigh
Whimpering away my reason! Hark ye, sir,
It is no secret, that Erminia,
Erminia, sir, was hidden in your tent, –   100
O, blessed asylum! comfortable home!
Begone! I pity thee; thou art a gull,
Erminia's last new puppet!

Gersa.   Furious fire!
Thou mak'st me boil as hot as thou canst flame!
And in thy teeth I give thee back the lie!
Thou liest! Thou, Auranthe's fool! A wittol!

  Ludolph. Look! look at this bright sword;
There is no part of it, to the very hilt,
But shall indulge itself about thine heart!
Draw! but remember thou must cower thy plumes,   110
As yesterday the Arab made thee stoop.

  Gersa. Patience! Not here; I would not spill thy blood
Here, underneath this roof where Otho breathes, –
Thy father, – almost mine,

  Ludolph.   O, faltering coward!

        Enter Page.

Stay, stay; here is one I have half a word with.
Well? What ails thee, child?

  Page.   My lord!

  Ludolph.   What wouldst say?

Page. They are fled!

Ludolph.   They! Who?

Page.   When anxiously
I hastened back, your grieving messenger,
I found the stairs all dark, the lamps extinct,
And not a foot or whisper to be heard.   120
I thought her dead, and on the lowest step
Sat listening; when presently came by
Two muffled up, – one sighing heavily,
The other cursing low, whose voice I knew
For the Duke Conrad's. Close I followed them
Thro' the dark ways they chose to the open air,
And, as I followed, heard my lady speak.

    Ludolph. Thy life answers the truth!

    Page.   The chamber's empty!

    Ludolph. As I will be of mercy! So, at last,
This nail is in my temples!

    Gersa. Be calm in this.   130

    Ludolph. I am.

    Gersa. And Albert, too, has disappeared;
Ere I met you, I sought him everywhere;
You would not hearken.

    Ludolph. Which way went they, boy?

    Gersa. I'll hunt with you.

    Ludolph.   No, no, no. My senses are
Still whole. I have survived. My arm is strong –
My appetite sharp – for revenge! I'll no sharer
In my feast; my injury is all my own,
And so is my revenge, my lawful chattels!
Terrier, ferret them out! Burn – burn the witch!
Trace me their footsteps! Away!   *[Exeunt.]*   140

ACT V

SCENE I. – *A part of the Forest*

Enter Conrad and Auranthe.

Auranthe. Go no further; not a step more. Thou art
A master-plague in the midst of miseries.
Go, – I fear thee! I tremble, every limb,
Who never shook before. There's moody death
In thy resolvèd looks! Yes, I could kneel
To pray thee far away! Conrad, go! go! –
There! yonder, underneath the boughs I see
Our horses!
    Conrad. Ay, and the man.
    Auranthe.   Yes, he is there!
Go, go, – no blood! no blood! – go, gentle Conrad!
    Conrad. Farewell!
    Auranthe.   Farewell! For this Heaven pardon you!   10

                          [Exit Auranthe.]

    Conrad. If he survive one hour, then may I die
In unimagined tortures, or breathe through
A long life in the foulest sink o' the world!
He dies! 'Tis well she do not advertise
The caitiff of the cold steel at his back.   *[Exit Conrad.]*

           Enter Ludolph and Page.

    Ludolph. Missed the way, boy? Say not that on your peril!
    Page. Indeed, indeed, I cannot trace them further.
    Ludolph. Must I stop here? Here solitary die
Stifled beneath the thick oppressive shade
Of these dull boughs – this even of dark thickets –   20
Silent, – without revenge? – pshaw! bitter end, –
A bitter death – a suffocating death, –
A gnawing – silent – deadly, quiet death!
Escaped? – fled? – vanished? melted into air?
She's gone! I cannot clutch her! no revenge!
A muffled death, ensnared in horrid silence!
Sucked to my grave amid a dreamy calm!
O, where is that illustrious noise of war,
To smother up this sound of labouring breath,
This rustle of the trees!

[Auranthe shrieks at a distance.]

Page. My lord, a noise! 30
This way — hark!
Ludolph. Yes, yes! A hope! A music!
A glorious clamour! How I live again! *[Exeunt.]*

SCENE II. — *Another part of the Forest*

Enter Albert, wounded.

Albert. Oh! for enough life to support me on
To Otho's feet!

Enter Ludolph.

Ludolph. Thrice villainous, stay there!
Tell me where that detested woman is,
Or this is through thee!
Albert. My good Prince, with me
The sword has done its worst; not without worst
Done to another, — Conrad has it home!
I see you know it all!
Ludolph. Where is his sister?

Enter Auranthe.

Auranthe. Albert!
Ludolph. Ha! There! there! He is the paramour! —
There — hug him — dying! O, thou innocence,
Shrine him and comfort him at his last gasp; 10
Kiss down his eyelids! Was he not thy love?
Wilt thou forsake him at his latest hour?
Keep fearful and aloof from his last gaze,
His most uneasy moments, when cold death
Stands with the door ajar to let him in?
Albert. O that that door with hollow slam would close
Upon me sudden! for I cannot meet,
In all the unknown chambers of the dead,
Such horrors!

Ludolph.   Auranthe! what can he mean?
What horrors? Is it not a joyous time?   20
Am I not married to a paragon
'Of personal beauty and untainted soul'?
A blushing fair-eyed purity? A sylph,
Whose snowy timid hand has never sinned
Beyond a flower plucked, white as itself?
Albert, you do insult my bride – your mistress –
To talk of horrors on our wedding-night!
     Albert. Alas! poor Prince, I would you knew my heart!
'Tis not so guilty –
     Ludolph.   Hear! he pleads not guilty!
You are not? or, if so, what matters it?   30
You have escaped me, free as the dusk air,
Hid in the forest, safe from my revenge;
I cannot catch you! You should laugh at me,
Poor cheated Ludolph! Make the forest hiss
With jeers at me! You tremble – faint at once,
You will come to again. O cockatrice,
I have you! Whither wander those fair eyes
To entice the devil to your help, that he
May change you to a spider, so to crawl
Into some cranny to escape my wrath?   40
     Albert. Sometimes the counsel of a dying man
Doth operate quietly when his breath is gone:
Disjoin those hands – part – part – do not destroy
Each other – forget her! – Our miseries
Are equal shared, and mercy is—
     Ludolph.   A boon
When one can compass it. Auranthe, try
Your oratory; your breath is not so hitched.
Ay, stare for help!   *[Albert dies.]*
               There goes a spotted soul
Howling in vain along the hollow night!
Hear him! He calls you – sweet Auranthe, come!   50
     Auranthe. Kill me!

Ludolph. No! What? Upon our marriage night?
The earth would shudder at so foul a deed!
A fair bride! A sweet bride! An innocent bride!
No! we must revel it, as 'tis in use
In times of delicate brilliant ceremony:
Come, let me lead you to our halls again!
Nay, linger not; make no resistance, sweet; –
Will you? Ah, wretch, thou canst not, for I have
The strength of twenty lions 'gainst a lamb!
Now – one adieu for Albert! Come away! *[Exeunt.]* 60

SCENE III. – *An inner Court of the Castle*

Enter Sigifred, Gonfrid, and Theodore, meeting.

1st Knight. Was ever such a night?
Sigifred. What horrors more?
Things unbelieved one hour, so strange they are,
The next hour stamps with credit.
1st Knight. Your last news?
Gonfrid. After the page's story of the death
Of Albert and Duke Conrad?
Sigifred. And the return
Of Ludolph with the Princess.
Gonfrid. No more, save
Prince Gersa's freeing Abbot Ethelbert,
And the sweet lady, fair Erminia,
From prison.
1st Knight. Where are they now? Hast yet heard?
Gonfrid. With the sad Emperor they are closeted; 10
I saw the three pass slowly up the stairs,
The lady weeping, the old abbot cowled.
Sigifred. What next?
1st Knight. I ache to think on 't.
Gonfrid. 'Tis with fate.
1st Knight. One while these proud towers are hushed as death.

Gonfrid. The next our poor Prince fills the archèd rooms
With ghastly ravings.
    Sigifred.   I do fear his brain.
    Gonfrid. I will see more. Bear you so stout a heart?

[Exeunt into the Castle.]

SCENE IV. — *A Cabinet, opening towards a Terrace*

Otho, Erminia, Ethelbert and a Physician, discovered.

    Otho. O, my poor boy! My son! My son! My Ludolph!
Have ye no comfort for me, ye physicians
Of the weak body and soul?
    Ethelbert.   'Tis not in medicine,
Either of heaven or earth, to cure, unless
Fit time be chosen to administer.
    Otho. A kind forbearance, holy abbot. Come,
Erminia; here, sit by me, gentle girl;
Give me thy hand; hast thou forgiven me?
    Erminia. Would I were with the saints to pray for you!
    Otho. Why will ye keep me from my darling child?   10
    Physician. Forgive me, but he must not see thy face.
    Otho. Is then a father's countenance a Gorgon?
Hath it not comfort in it? Would it not
Console my poor boy, cheer him, heal his spirits?
Let me embrace him; let me speak to him;
I will! Who hinders me? Who's Emperor?
    Physician. You may not, Sire; 'twould overwhelm him quite,
He is so full of grief and passionate wrath;
Too heavy a sigh would kill him, or do worse.
He must be saved by fine contrivances;   20
And, most especially, we must keep clear
Out of his sight a father whom he loves;
His heart is full, it can contain no more.
And do its ruddy office.

Ethelbert.   Sage advice;
We must endeavour how to ease and slacken
The tight-wound energies of his despair,
Not make them tenser.
    Otho.   Enough! I hear, I hear.
Yet you were about to advise more, – I listen.
    Ethelbert. This learned doctor will agree with me,
That not in the smallest point should he be thwarted,   30
Or gainsaid by one word; his very motions,
Nods, becks, and hints, should be obeyed with care,
Even on the moment; so his troubled mind
May cure itself.
    Physician.   There are no other means.
    Otho. Open the door; let's hear if all is quiet.
    Physician. Beseech you, Sire, forbear.
    Erminia.   Do, do.
    Otho.   I command!
Open it straight: – hush! – quiet! – my lost boy!
My miserable child!
    Ludolph. [Indistinctly without.] Fill, fill my goblet, – here's a health!
    Erminia.   O, close the door!
    Otho. Let, let me hear his voice; this cannot last;   40
And fain would I catch up his dying words,
Though my own knell they be! This cannot last!
O let me catch his voice – for lo! I hear
A whisper in this silence that he's dead!
It is so! Gersa?

Enter Gersa.

    Physician.   Say, how fares the Prince?
    Gersa. More calm; his features are less wild and flushed;
Once he complained of weariness.
    Physician.   Indeed!
'Tis good, – 'tis good; let him but fall asleep,
That saves him.

Otho.   Gersa, watch him like a child;
Ward him from harm, – and bring me better news!   50
     Physician. Humour him to the height. I fear to go;
For should he catch a glimpse of my dull garb,
It might affright him, fill him with suspicion
That we believe him sick, which must not be.
     Gersa. I will invent what soothing means I can.

[Exit Gersa.]

     Physician. This should cheer up your Highness; weariness
Is a good symptom, and most favourable;
It gives me pleasant hopes. Please you, walk forth
Upon the terrace; the refreshing air
Will blow one half of your sad doubts away.   *[Exeunt.]*   60

SCENE V. – *A Banqueting Hall, brilliantly illuminated,*
and set forth with all costly magnificence with supper-tables laden with
services of gold and silver. A door in the back scene, guarded by two Soldiers,
Lords, Ladies, Knights, Gentlemen, etc., whispering sadly, and ranging
themselves; part entering and part discovered

     1st Knight. Grievously are we tantalized, one and all;
Swayed here and there, commanded to and fro,
As though we were the shadows of a sleep,
And linked to a dreaming fancy. What do we here?
     Gonfrid. I am no seer; you know we must obey
The Prince from A to Z, though it should be
To set the place in flames. I pray, hast heard
Where the most wicked Princess is?
     1st Knight.   There, sir,
In the next room; have you remarked those two
Stout Soldiers posted at the door?
     Gonfrid. For what?

[They whisper.]

     1st Lady. How ghast a train!

2nd Lady. Sure this should be some splendid burial.
1st Lady. What fearful whispering! See, see, – Gersa there!

Enter Gersa.

Gersa. Put on your brightest looks; smile if you can;
Behave as all were happy; keep your eyes
From the least watch upon him; if he speaks
To any one, answer, collectedly,
Without surprise, his questions, howe'er strange.
Do this to the utmost, – though, alas! with me
The remedy grows hopeless! Here he comes, –   20
Observe what I have said, – show no surprise.

Enter Ludolph, followed by Sigifred and Page.

Ludolph. A splendid company! rare beauties here!
I should have Orphean lips, and Plato's fancy,
Amphion's utterance, tonèd with his lyre,
Or the deep key of Jove's sonorous mouth,
To give fit salutation. Methought I heard,
As I came in, some whispers, – what of that?
'Tis natural men should whisper; at the kiss
Of Psyche given by Love, there was a buzz
Among the gods! – and silence is as natural.   30
These draperies are fine, and being a mortal,
I should desire no better; yet, in truth,
There must be some superior costliness
Some wider-domèd high magnificence!
I would have, as a mortal I may not,
Hangings of heaven's clouds, purple and gold,
Slung from the spheres; gauzes of silver mist,
Looped up with cords of twisted wreathèd light,
And tasselled round with weeping meteors!
These pendent lamps and chandeliers are bright   40
As earthly fires from dull dross can be cleansed;
Yet could my eyes drink up intenser beams
Undazzled; – this is darkness, – when I close

These lids, I see far fiercer brilliances,—
Skies full of splendid moons, and shooting stars,
And spouting exhalations, diamond fires,
And panting fountains quivering with deep glows.
Yes — this is dark — is it not dark?

 Sigifred.   My lord,
'Tis late; the lights of festival are ever
Quenched in the morn.

 Ludolph.   'Tis not to-morrow then?   50
 Sigifred. 'Tis early dawn.

 Gersa.   Indeed full time we slept;
Say you so, Prince?

 Ludolph.   I say I quarrelled with you;
We did not tilt each other, — that's a blessing, —
Good gods! no innocent blood upon my head!

 Sigifred. Retire, Gersa!

 Ludolph.   There should be three more here:
For two of them, they stay away perhaps,
Being gloomy-minded, haters of fair revels, —
They know their own thoughts best.

         As for the third,
Deep blue eyes, semi-shaded in white lids,
Finished with lashes fine for more soft shade;   60
Completed by her twin-arched ebon-brows;
White temples, of exactest elegance,
Of even mould, felicitous and smooth;
Cheeks fashioned tenderly on either side,
So perfect, so divine, that our poor eyes
Are dazzled with the sweet proportioning,
And wonder that 'tis so, — the magic chance!
Her nostrils, small, fragrant, fairy-delicate;
Her lips — I swear no human bones e'er wore
So taking a disguise; — you shall behold her!   70
We'll have her presently; ay, you shall see her,
And wonder at her, friends, she is so fair;
She is the world's chief jewel, and, by heaven!

She's mine by right of marriage! – she is mine!
Patience, good people, in fit time I send
A summoner, – she will obey my call,
Being a wife most mild and dutiful.
First I would hear what music is prepared
To herald and receive her; let me hear!
   Sigifred. Bid the musicians soothe him tenderly. 80

[A soft strain of music.]

   Ludolph. Ye have none better? No, I am content;
'Tis a rich sobbing melody, with reliefs
Full and majestic; it is well enough,
And will be sweeter, when ye see her pace
Sweeping into this presence, glistened o'er
With emptied caskets, and her train upheld
By ladies habited in robes of lawn,
Sprinkled with golden crescents, others bright
In silks, with spangles showered, and bowed to
By Duchesses and pearlèd Margravines! 90
Sad! that the fairest creature of the earth –
I pray you mind me not – 'tis sad, I say,
That the extremest beauty of the world
Should so entrench herself away from me,
Behind a barrier of engendered guilt!
   2nd Lady. Ah! what a moan!
   1st Knight.   Most piteous indeed!
   Ludolph. She shall be brought before this company,
And then – then –
   1st Lady.   He muses.
   Gersa.   O, Fortune! where will this end?
   Sigifred. I guess his purpose! Indeed he must not have
That pestilence brought in, – that cannot be, 100
There we must stop him.
   Gersa.   I am lost! Hush, hush!
He is about to rave again.

Ludolph. A barrier of guilt! I was the fool,
She was the cheater! Who's the cheater now,
And who the fool? The entrapped, the cagèd fool,
The bird-limed raven? She shall croak to death
Secure! Methinks I have her in my fist,
To crush her with my heel! Wait, wait! I marvel
My father keeps away. Good friend — ah! Sigifred?
Do bring him to me, — and Erminia,   110
I fain would see before I sleep — and Ethelbert,
That he may bless me, as I know he will,
Though I have cursed him.
    Sigifred.   Rather suffer me
To lead you to them.
    Ludolph.   No, excuse me, – no!
The day is not quite done. Go, bring them hither.

                          [Exit Sigifred.]

Certes, a father's smile should, like sunlight,
Slant on my sheavèd harvest of ripe bliss.
Besides, I thirst to pledge my lovely bride
In a deep goblet; let me see — what wine?
The strong Iberian juice or mellow Greek?   120
Or pale Calabrian? Or the Tuscan grape?
Or of old Ætna's pulpy wine-presses,
Black stained with the fat vintage, as it were
The purple slaughter-house, where Bacchus' self
Pricked his own swollen veins! Where is my page?
    Page. Here, here!
    Ludolph. Be ready to obey me; anon thou shalt
Bear a soft message for me; for the hour
Draws near when I must make a winding up
Of bridal mysteries — a fine-spun vengeance!
Carve it on my tomb, that, when I rest beneath,   130
Men shall confess, this Prince was gulled and cheated,
But from the ashes of disgrace he rose

More than a fiery dragon, and did burn
His ignominy up in purging fires!
Did I not send, sir, but a moment past,
For my father?

    Gersa.   You did.

    Ludolph.   Perhaps 'twould be
Much better he came not.

    Gersa.   He enters now!

    Enter Otho, Erminia, Ethelbert, Sigifred, and Physician.

    Ludolph. O! thou good man, against whose sacred head
I was a mad conspirator, chiefly too
For the sake of my fair newly wedded wife,   140
Now to be punished! – do not look so sad!
Those charitable eyes will thaw my heart,
Those tears will wash away a just resolve,
A verdict ten times sworn! Awake – awake –
Put on a judge's brow, and use a tongue
Made iron-stern by habit! Thou shalt see
A deed to be applauded, 'scribed in gold!
Join a loud voice to mine, and so denounce
What I alone will execute!

    Otho.   Dear son,
What is it? By your father's love, I sue   150
That it be nothing merciless!

    Ludolph.   To that demon?
Not so! No! She is in temple-stall,
Being garnished for the sacrifice, and I,
The Priest of Justice, will immolate her
Upon the altar of wrath! She stings me through! –
Even as the worm doth feed upon the nut,
So she, a scorpion, preys upon my brain!
I feel her gnawing here! Let her but vanish
Then, father, I will lead your legions forth,
Compact in steelèd squares and spearèd files,   160

And bid our trumpets speak a fell rebuke
To nations drowsed in peace!
    Otho.   To-morrow, son,
Be your word law; forget to-day –
    Ludolph.   I will,
When I have finished it! Now, – now, I'm pight,
Tight-footed for the deed!
    Erminia.   Alas! Alas!
    Ludolph. What angel's voice is that? Erminia.
Ah! gentlest creature, whose sweet innocence
Was almost murdered; I am penitent.
Wilt thou forgive me? And thou, holy man,
Good Ethelbert, shall I die in peace with you?   **170**
    Erminia. Die, my lord?
    Ludolph.   I feel it possible.
    Otho.   Physician?
    Physician. I fear he is past my skill.
    Otho.   Not so!
    Ludolph. I see it – I see it – I have been wandering!
Half mad – not right here – I forget my purpose.
Bestir – bestir – Auranthe! Ha! ha! ha!
Youngster! page! go bid them drag her to me!
Obey! This shall finish it!   *[Draws a dagger.]*
    Otho.   Oh, my son! my son
    Sigifred. This must not be – stop there!
    Ludolph.   Am I obeyed?
A little talk with her – no harm – haste! haste!   *[Exit Page.]*
Set her before me – never fear I can strike.   **180**
    Several Voices. My lord! My lord!
    Gersa.   Good Prince!
    Ludolph. Why do ye trouble me? out – out – away!
There she is! take that! and that! no, no,
That's not well done – where is she?

    The doors open. Enter Page. Several Women are seen grouped
        about Auranthe in the inner room.

Page. Alas! My lord, my lord! they cannot move her!
Her arms are stiff – her fingers clenched and cold.
   Ludolph. She's dead!   *[Staggers and falls into their arms.]*
   Ethelbert.   Take away the dagger.
   Gersa.   Softly; so!
   Otho. Thank God for that!
   Sigifred.   It could not harm him now.
   Gersa. No! – brief be his anguish!
   Ludolph. She's gone! I am content. Nobles, good night!   190
We are all weary – faint – set ope the doors –
I will to bed! To-morrow—   *[Dies.]*

THE CURTAIN FALLS

King Stephen

Fragment of a Tragedy

ACT I

SCENE I. — *Field of Battle*

Alarum. Enter King Stephen, Knights, and Soldiers.

Stephen. If shame can on a soldier's vein-swoll'n front
Spread deeper crimson than the battle's toil,
Blush in your casing helmets! for see, see!
Yonder my chivalry, my pride of war,
Wrenched with an iron hand from firm array,
Are routed loose about the plashy meads,
Of honour forfeit. O that my known voice
Could reach your dastard ears, and fright you more!
Fly, cowards, fly! Gloucester is at your backs!
Throw your slack bridles o'er the flurried manes,
Ply well the rowel with faint trembling heels,
Scampering to death at last!
    1st Knight.   The enemy
Bears his flaunt standard close upon their rear.
    2nd Knight. Sure of a bloody prey, seeing the fens
Will swamp them girth-deep.
    Stephen.   Over head and ears.
No matter! 'Tis a gallant enemy;
How like a comet he goes streaming on.
But we must plague him in the flank, — hey, friends?
We are well breathed — follow!

Enter Earl Baldwin and Soldiers, as defeated.

    Stephen.   De Redvers!

10

What is the monstrous bugbear that can fright
Baldwin?   20
   Baldwin. No scarecrow, but the fortunate star
Of boisterous Chester, whose fell truncheon now
Points level to the goal of victory.
This way he comes, and if you would maintain
Your person unaffronted by vile odds,
Take horse, my Lord.
   Stephen.   And which way spur for life?
Now I thank heaven I am in the toils,
That soldiers may bear witness how my arm
Can burst the meshes. Not the eagle more
Loves to beat up against a tyrannous blast,   30
Than I to meet the torrent of my foes.
This is a brag – be 't so, – but if I fall,
Carve it upon my 'scutcheoned sepulchre.
On, fellow soldiers! Earl of Redvers, back!
Not twenty Earls of Chester shall brow-beat
The diadem.   *[Exeunt. Alarum.]*

SCENE II. – *Another part of the Field*

Trumpets sounding a Victory.
Enter Gloucester, Knights, and Forces.

   Gloucester. Now may we lift our bruisèd visors up
And take the flattering freshness of the air,
While the wild din of battle dies away
Into times past, yet to be echoed sure
In the silent pages of our chroniclers.
   1st Knight. Will Stephen's death be marked there, my good Lord,
Or that we give him lodging in yon towers?
   Gloucester. Fain would I know the great usurper's fate.

Enter two Captains severally.

   1st Captain. My Lord!
   2nd Captain. Most noble Earl!

1st Captain. The King –

2nd Captain.   The Empress greets – 10

Gloucester. What of the King?

1st Captain.   He sole and lone maintains
A hopeless bustle 'mid our swarming arms,
And with a nimble savageness attacks,
Escapes, makes fiercer onset, then anew
Eludes death, giving death to most that dare
Trespass within the circuit of his sword!
He must by this have fallen. Baldwin is taken;
And for the Duke of Bretagne, like a stag
He flies, for the Welsh beagles to hunt down.
God save the Empress!

Gloucester.   Now our dreaded Queen: 20
What message from her Highness?

2nd Captain.   Royal Maud
From the thronged towers of Lincoln hath looked down,
Like Pallas from the walls of Ilion,
And seen her enemies havocked at her feet.
She greets most noble Gloucester from her heart,
Entreating him, his captains, and brave knights,
To grace a banquet. The high city gates
Are envious which shall see your triumph pass;
The streets are full of music.

Enter 2nd Knight.

Gloucester. Whence come you?

2nd Knight. From Stephen, my good Prince – Stephen!
    Stephen! 30

Gloucester. Why do you make such echoing of his name?

2nd Knight. Because I think, my Lord, he is no man,
But a fierce demon, 'nointed safe from wounds,
And misbaptizèd with a Christian name.

Gloucester. A mighty soldier! – Does he still hold out?

2nd Knight. He shames our victory. His valour still
Keeps elbow-room amid our eager swords,

And holds our bladed falchions all aloof.
His gleaming battle-axe, being slaughter-sick,
Smote on the morion of a Flemish knight,   40
Broke short in his hand; upon the which he flung
The heft away with such a vengeful force
It paunched the Earl of Chester's horse, who then
Spleen-hearted came in full career at him.

    Gloucester. Did no one take him at a vantage then?
    2nd Knight. Three then with tiger leap upon him flew,
Whom with his sword swift drawn and nimbly held,
He stung away again, and stood to breathe,
Smiling. Anon upon him rushed once more
A throng of foes, and in this renewed strife,   50
My sword met his and snapped off at the hilt.

    Gloucester. Come, lead me to this Mars and let us move
In silence, not insulting his sad doom
With clamorous trumpets. To the Empress bear
My salutation as befits the time.

[Exeunt Gloucester and Forces.]

SCENE III. — *The Field of Battle*

Enter Stephen, unarmed.

    Stephen. Another sword! And what if I could seize
One from Bellona's gleaming armoury,
Or choose the fairest of her sheavèd spears!
Where are my enemies? Here, close at hand,
Here come the testy brood. O, for a sword!
I'm faint — a biting sword! A noble sword!
A hedge-stake — or a ponderous stone to hurl
With brawny vengeance, like the labourer Cain.
Come on! Farewell my kingdom, and all hail
Thou superb, plumed, and helmeted renown!   10
All hail! I would not truck this brilliant day

To rule in Pylos with a Nestor's beard –
Come on!

Enter De Kaims and Knights, etc.

    De Kaims. Is 't madness, or a hunger after death,
That makes thee thus unarmed throw taunts at us?
Yield, Stephen, or my sword's point dips in
The gloomy current of a traitor's heart.
    Stephen. Do it, De Kaims, I will not budge an inch.
    De Kaims. Yes, of thy madness thou shalt take the meed.
    Stephen. Darest thou?
    De Kaims. How dare, against a man disarmed?
    Stephen. What weapons has the lion but himself?   20
Come not near me, De Kaims, for by the price
Of all the glory I have won this day,
Being a king, I will not yield alive
To any but the second man of the realm,
Robert of Gloucester.
    De Kaims.   Thou shalt vail to me.
    Stephen. Shall I, when I have sworn against it, sir?
Thou think'st it brave to take a breathing king,
That, on a court-day bowed to haughty Maud,
The awèd presence-chamber may be bold
To whisper, There's the man who took alive   30
Stephen – me – prisoner. Certes, De Kaims,
The ambition is a noble one.
    De Kaims.   'Tis true.
And, Stephen, I must compass it.
    Stephen.   No, no,
Do not tempt me to throttle you on the gorge,
Or with my gauntlet crush your hollow breast,
Just when your knighthood is grown ripe and full
For lordship.
    A Soldier. Is an honest yeoman's spear
Of no use at a need? Take that.

Stephen.   Ah, dastard!

De Kaims. What, you are vulnerable! my prisoner!

Stephen. No, not yet. I disclaim it, and demand   **40**
Death as a sovereign right unto a king
Who 'sdains to yield to any but his peer,
If not in title, yet in noble deeds,
The Earl of Gloucester. Stab to the hilt, De Kaims,
For I will never by mean hands be led
From this so famous field. Do ye hear! Be quick!

[Trumpets. Enter the Earl of Chester and Knights.]

SCENE IV. — *A Presence Chamber. Queen Maud in a Chair of State,
the Earls of Gloucester and Chester, Lords, Attendants*

Maud. Gloucester, no more. I will behold that Boulogne:
Set him before me. Not for the poor sake
Of regal pomp and a vain-glorious hour,
As thou with wary speech, yet near enough,
Hast hinted

Gloucester. Faithful counsel have I given;
If wary, for your Highness' benefit.

Maud. The Heavens forbid that I should not think so,
For by thy valour have I won this realm
Which by thy wisdom I will ever keep.
To sage advisers let me ever bend   **10**
A meek attentive ear, so that they treat
Of the wide kingdom's rule and government,
Not trenching on our actions personal.
Advised, not schooled, I would be; and henceforth
Spoken to in clear, plain, and open terms,
Not side-ways sermoned at.

Gloucester.   Then, in plain terms,
Once more for the fallen king —

Maud.   Your pardon, brother,
I would no more of that; for, as I said,
'Tis not for worldly pomp I wish to see

The rebel, but as dooming judge to give   20
A sentence something worthy of his guilt.
 Gloucester. If 't must be so, I'll bring him to your presence.

       [Exit Gloucester.]

 Maud. A meaner summoner might do as well.
My Lord of Chester, is 't true what I hear
Of Stephen of Boulogne, our prisoner,
That he, as a fit penance for his crimes,
Eats wholesome, sweet, and palatable food
Off Gloucester's golden dishes – drinks pure wine,
Lodges soft?
 Chester. More than that, my gracious Queen,
Has angered me. The noble Earl, methinks,   30
Full soldier as he is, and without peer
In counsel, dreams too much among his books.
It may read well, but sure 'tis out of date
To play the Alexander with Darius.
 Maud. Truth! I think so. By Heavens, it shall not last!
 Chester. It would amaze your Highness now to mark
How Gloucester overstrains his courtesy
To that crime-loving rebel, that Boulogne –
 Maud. That ingrate!
 Chester.   For whose vast ingratitude
To our late sovereign lord, your noble sire,   40
The generous Earl condoles in his mishaps,
And with a sort of lackeying friendliness
Talks off the mighty frowning from his brow,
Woos him to hold a duet in a smile,
Or, if it please him, play an hour at chess –
 Maud. A perjured slave!
 Chester.   And for his perjury,
Gloucester has fit rewards – nay, I believe,
He sets his bustling household's wits at work
For flatteries to ease this Stephen's hours,
And make a heaven of his purgatory;   50

Adorning bondage with the pleasant gloss
Of feasts and music, and all idle shows
Of indoor pageantry; while syren whispers,
Predestined for his ear, 'scape as half-checked
From lips the courtliest and the rubiest
Of all the realm, admiring of his deeds.

   Maud. A frost upon his summer!

   Chester.   A queen's nod
Can make his June December. Here he comes.

SELECTED LETTERS

My dear Bailey,

   ... O I wish I was as certain of the end of all your troubles as that of your momentary start about the authenticity of the Imagination. I am certain of nothing but of the holiness of the Heart's affections and the truth of Imagination—What the imagination seizes as Beauty must be truth—whether it existed before or not—for I have the same Idea of all our Passions as of Love they are all in their sublime, creative of essential Beauty—In a Word, you may know my favorite Speculation by my first Book and the little song I sent in my last—which is a representation from the fancy of the probable mode of operating in these Matters—The Imagination may be compared to Adam's dream—he awoke and found it truth. I am the more zealous in this affair, because I have never yet been able to perceive how any thing can be known for truth by consequitive reasoning—and yet it must be—Can it be that even the greatest Philosopher ever arrived at his goal without putting aside numerous objections—However it may be, O for a Life of Sensations rather than of Thoughts! It is 'a Vision in the form of Youth' a Shadow of reality to come—and this consideration has further conv[i]nced me for it has come as auxiliary to another favorite Speculation of mine, that we shall enjoy ourselves here after by having what we called happiness on Earth repeated in a finer tone and so repeated—And yet such a fate can only befall those who delight in sensation rather than hunger as you do after Truth—Adam's dream will do here and seems to be a conviction that Imagination and its empyreal reflection is the same as human Life and its spiritual repetition. But as I was saying—the simple imaginative Mind may have its rewards in the repeti[ti]on of its own silent Working coming continually on the spirit with a fine suddenness—to compare great things with small—have you never by being surprised with an old Melody—in a delicious place—by a delicious voice, fe[l]t over again your very speculations and surmises at the time it first operated on your soul—do you not remember forming to yourself the singer's face more beautiful that [*for* than] it was possible and yet with the elevation of the Moment you did not think so—even then you were mounted on the Wings of Imagination so high—that the Prototype must be here after—that delicious face you will see—What a time! I am continually running away from the subject—sure this cannot be exactly the case with a complex Mind—one that is imaginative and at the same time careful of its fruits—who would exist partly on sensation partly on thought—to whom it is necessary that years should bring the philosophic Mind—such an one I consider your's and therefore it is necessary to your eternal Happiness that you not only drink this old Wine of Heaven which I shall call the redigestion of our most ethereal Musings on Earth; but also increase in knowledge and know all things. I am glad to hear you are in a fair Way for Easter—you will soon get through your unpleasant reading and then!—but the world is full of troubles and I have not much reason to think myself pestered with many—I think Jane or Marianne has a better opinion of me than I deserve—for really and truly I do not think my Brothers illness connected with mine—you know more of the real Cause than they do—nor have I any chance of being rack'd as you have been—you perhaps at one time thought there was such a thing as Worldly Happiness to be arrived at, at certain periods of time marked out—you have of necessity from your disposition been thus led away—I scarcely remember counting upon any Happiness—I look not for it if it be not in the present hour—nothing startles me beyond the Moment. The setting sun will always set me to rights—or if a Sparrow come before my Window I take part in its existence and pick about the Gravel. The first thing that strikes me on hea[r]ing a Misfortune having befalled another is this. 'Well it cannot be helped.—he will have the pleasure of trying the resources of his spirit, and I beg now my dear Bailey that hereafter should you observe any thing cold in me not to but [*for* put] it to the account of heartlessness but abstraction—for I assure you I sometimes feel not the influence of a Passion or Affection during a whole week—and so long this sometimes continues I begin to suspect myself and the genuiness of my feelings at other times—thinking them a few barren Tragedy-tears— . . .

Your affectionate friend
John Keats

I want to say much more to you—a few hints will set me going Direct Burford Bridge near dorking

To George and Tom Keats, 21, 27 (?) December 1817

Hampstead Sunday
22 December 1818

My dear Brothers

I must crave your pardon for not having written ere this & & I saw Kean return to the public in Richard III, & finely he did it, & at the request of Reynolds I went to criticise his Luke in Riches—the critique is in todays champion, which I send you with the Examiner in which you will find very proper lamentation on the obsoletion of christmas Gambols & pastimes: but it was mixed up with so much egotism of that drivelling nature that pleasure is entirely lost. Hone the publisher's trial, you must find very amusing; & as Englishmen very encouraging—his *Not Guilty* is a thing, which not to have been, would have dulled still more Liberty's Emblazoning—Lord Ellenborough has been paid in his own coin—Wooler & Hone have done us an essential service—I have had two very pleasant evenings with Dilke yesterday & today; & am at this moment just come from him & feel in the humour to go on with this, began in the morning, & from which he came to fetch me. I spent Friday evening with Wells & went the next morning to see *Death on the Pale horse.* It is a wonderful picture, when West's age is considered; But there is nothing to be intense upon; no women one feels mad to kiss; no face swelling into reality. the excellence of every Art is its intensity, capable of making all disagreeables evaporate, from their being in close relationship with Beauty & Truth—Examine King Lear & you will find this examplified throughout; but in this picture we have unpleasantness without any momentous depth of speculation excited, in which to bury its repulsiveness—The picture is larger than Christ rejected—I dined with Haydon the sunday after you left, & had a very pleasant day, I dined too (for I have been out too much lately) with Horace Smith & met his two brothers with Hill & Kingston & one Du Bois, they only served to convince me, how superior humour is to wit in respect to enjoyment—These men say things which make one start, without making one feel, they are all alike; their manners are alike; they all know fashionables; they have a mannerism in their very eating & drinking, in their mere handling a Decanter—They talked of Kean & his low company—Would I were with that company instead of yours said I to myself! I know such like acquaintance will never do for me & yet I am going to Reynolds, on wednesday—Brown & Dilke walked with me & back from the Christmas pantomime. I had not a dispute but a disquisition with Dilke, on various subjects; several things dovetailed in my mind, & at once it struck me, what quality went to form a Man of Achievement especially in Literature & which Shakespeare posessed so enormously—I mean *Negative Capability*, that is when man is capable of being in uncertainties, Mysteries, doubts, without any irritable reaching after fact & reason—Coleridge, for instance, would let go by a fine isolated verisimilitude caught from the Penetralium of mystery, from being incapable of remaining content with half knowledge. This pursued through Volumes would perhaps take us no further than this, that with a great poet the sense of Beauty overcomes every other consideration, or rather obliterates all consideration.

Shelley's poem is out & there are words about its being objected too, as much as Queen Mab was. Poor Shelley I think he has his Quota of good qualities, in sooth la!! Write soon to your most sincere friend & affectionate Brother

John

To J. H. Reynolds, 3 February 1818

Hampstead Tuesday.

My dear Reynolds,

... It may be said that we ought to read our Contemporaries. that Wordsworth &c should have their due from us. but for the sake of a few fine imaginative or domestic passages, are we to be bullied into a certain Philosophy engendered in the whims of an Egotist— Every man has his speculations, but every man does not brood and peacock over them till he makes a false coinage and deceives himself—Many a man can travel to the very bourne of Heaven, and yet want confidence to put down his halfseeing. Sancho will invent a Journey heavenward as well as any body. We hate poetry that has a palpable design upon us—and if we do not agree, seems to put its hand in its breeches pocket. Poetry should be great & unobtrusive, a thing which enters into one's soul, and does not startle it or amaze it with itself but with its subject.—How beautiful are the retired flowers! how would they lose their beauty were they to throng into the highway crying out, "admire me I am a violet! dote upon me I am a primrose! Modern poets differ from the Elizabethans in this. Each of the moderns like an Elector of Hanover governs his petty state, & knows how many straws are swept daily from the Causeways in all his dominions & has a continual itching that all the Housewives should have their coppers well scoured: the antients were Emperors of vast Provinces, they had only heard of the remote ones and scarcely cared to visit them.—I will cut all this—I will have no more of Wordsworth or Hunt in particular—Why should we be of the tribe of Manasseh when we can wander with Esau? why should we kick against the Pricks, when we can walk on Roses? Why should we be owls, when we can be Eagles? Why be teased with "nice Eyed wagtails," when we have in sight "the Cherub Contemplation"?—Why with Wordsworths "Matthew with a bough of wilding in his hand" when we can have Jacques "under an oak &c"—The secret of the Bough of Wilding will run through your head faster than I can write it—Old Matthew spoke to him some years ago on some nothing, & because he happens in an Evening Walk to imagine the figure of the old man—he must stamp it down in black & white, and it is henceforth sacred—I don't mean to deny Wordsworth's grandeur & Hunt's merit, but I mean to say we need not be teazed with grandeur & merit—when we can have them uncontaminated & unobtrusive. Let us have the old Poets, & robin Hood Your letter and its sonnets gave me more pleasure than will the 4th Book of Childe Harold & the whole of any body's life & opinions. . . .

> Yr sincere friend and Coscribbler
> John Keats.

To John Taylor, 27 February 1818

> Hampstead 27 Feby—

My dear Taylor,

Your alteration strikes me as being a great improvement—the page looks much better. And now I will attend to the Punctuations you speak of—the comma should be at *soberly,* and in the other passage the comma should follow *quiet,*. I am extremely indebted to you for this attention and also for your after admonitions—It is a sorry thing for me that any one should have to overcome Prejudices in reading my Verses—that affects me more than any hypercriticism on any particular Passage. In *Endymion* I have most likely but moved into the Go-cart from the leading strings. In Poetry I have a few Axioms, and you will see how far I am from their Centre. 1st I think Poetry should surprise by a fine excess and not by Singularity—it should strike the Reader as a wording of his own highest thoughts, and appear-almost a Remembrance—2nd Its touches of Beauty should never be half way therby making the reader breathless instead of content: the rise, the progress, the setting of imagery should like the Sun come natural natural too him—shine over him and set soberly although in magnificence leaving him in the Luxury of twilight—but it is easier to think what Poetry should be than to write it—and this leads me on to another axiom. That if Poetry comes not as naturally as the Leaves to a tree it had better not come at all. However it may be with me I cannot help looking into new countries with 'O for a Muse of fire to ascend!'—If Endymion serves me as a Pioneer perhaps I ought to be content. I have great reason to be content, for thank God I can read and perhaps understand Shakespeare to his depths, and I have I am sure many friends, who, if I fail, will attribute any change in my Life and Temper to Humbleness rather than to Pride—to a cowering under the Wings of great Poets rather than to a Bitterness that I am not appreciated. I am anxious to get Endymion printed that I may forget it and proceed....

Your sincere and oblig^d friend
John Keats—

P.S. You shall have a sho[r]t *Preface* in good time—

To John Taylor, 24 April 1818

Teignmouth Friday

My dear Taylor,

I think I Did very wrong to leave you to all the trouble of Endymion—but I could not help it then—another time I shall be more bent to all sort of troubles and disagreeables—Young Men for some time have an idea that such a thing as happiness is to be had and therefore are extremely impatient under any unpleasant restraining—in time however, of such stuff is the world about them, they know better and instead of striving from Uneasiness greet it as an habitual sensation, a pannier which is to weigh upon them through life.

And in proportion to my disgust at the task is my sense of your kindness & anxiety—the book pleased me much—it is very free from faults; and although there are one or two words I should wish replaced, I see in many places an improvement greatly to the purpose—

I think those speeches which are related—those parts where the speaker repeats a speech—such as Glaucus' repetition of Circe's words, should have inverted commas to every line—In this there is a little confusion. If we divide the speeches into *identical* and *related:* and to the former put merely one inverted comma at the beginning and another at the end; and to the latter inverted commas before every line, the book will be better understood at the first glance. Look at pages 126 and 127 you will find in the 3 line the beginning of a *related* speech marked thus "Ah! art awake—while at the same time in the next page the continuation of the *identical speech* is mark'd in the same manner "Young Man of Latmos—You will find on the other side all the parts which should have inverted commas to every line—I was purposing to travel over the north this Summer—there is but one thing to prevent me—I know nothing I have read nothing and I mean to follow Solomon's directions of 'get Wisdom—get understanding'—I find cavalier days are gone by. I find that I can have no enjoyment in the World but continual drinking of Knowledge—I find there is no worthy pursuit but the idea of doing some good for the world—some do it with their society—some with their wit—some with their benevolence—some with a sort of power of conferring pleasure and good humour on all they meet and in a thousand ways all equally dutiful to the command of Great Nature—there is but one way for me—the road lies th[r]ough application study and thought. I will pursue it and to that end purpose retiring for some years. I have been hovering for some time between an exquisite sense of the luxurious and a love for Philosophy—were I calculated for the former I should be glad—but as I am not I shall turn all my soul to the latter. My Brother Tom is getting better and I hope I shall see both him and Reynolds well before I retire from the World. I shall see you soon and have some talk about what Books I shall take with me—

Your very sincere friend
John Keats

Remember me to Hessey—Woodhouse and Percy Street

I cannot discover any other error—the preface is well without those thing you have left out—Adieu—

To J. H. Reynolds, 3 May 1818

Teignmouth May 3ᵈ

My dear Reynolds.

... Were I to study physic or rather Medicine again,—I feel it would not make the least difference in my Poetry; when the Mind is in its infancy a Bias is in reality a Bias, but when we have acquired more strength, a Bias becomes no Bias. Every department of knowledge we see excellent and calculated towards a great whole. I am so convinced of this, that I am glad at not having given away my medical Books, which I shall again look over to keep alive the little I know thitherwards; and moreover intend through you and Rice to become a sort of Pip-civilian. An extensive knowledge is needful to thinking people—it takes away the heat and fever; and helps, by widening speculation, to ease the Burden of the Mystery: a thing I begin to understand a little, and which weighed upon you in the most gloomy and true sentence in your Letter. The difference of high Sensations with and without knowledge appears to me this— in the latter case we are falling continually ten thousand fathoms deep and being blown up again without wings and with all [the] horror of a bare shoulderd Creature—in the former case, our shoulders are fledge, and we go thro' the same air and space without fear.

... You say "I fear there is little chance of any thing else in this life." You seem by that to have been going through with a more painful and acute zest the same labyrinth that I have—I have come to the same conclusion thus far. My Branchings out therefrom have been numerous: one of them is the consideration of Wordsworth's genius and as a help, in the manner of gold being the meridian Line of worldly wealth,—how he differs from Milton.—And here I have nothing but surmises, from an uncertainty whether Miltons apparently less anxiety for Humanity proceeds from his seeing further or no than Wordsworth: And whether Wordsworth has in truth epic passion, and martyrs himself to the human heart, the main region of his song—In regard to his genius alone—we find what he says true as far as we have experienced and we can judge no further but by larger experience—for axioms in philosophy are not axioms until they are proved upon our pulses: We read fine——things but never feel them to thee full until we have gone the same steps as the Author.—I know this is not plain; you will know exactly my meaning when I say, that now I shall relish Hamlet more than I ever have done—Or, better—You are sensible no man can set down Venery as a bestial or joyless thing until he is sick of it and therefore all philosophizing on it would be mere wording. Until we are sick, we understand not;—in fine, as Byron says, "Knowledge is Sorrow"; and I go on to say that "Sorrow is Wisdom"—and further for aught we can know for certainty! "Wisdom is folly"— . . .

I will return to Wordsworth—whether or no he has an extended vision or a circumscribed grandeur—whether he is an eagle in his nest, or on the wing—And to be more explicit and to show you how tall I stand by the giant, I will put down a simile of human life as far as I now perceive it; that is, to the point to which I say we both have arrived at—' Well—I compare human life to a large Mansion of Many Apartments, two of which I can only describe, the doors of the rest being as yet shut upon me—The first we step into we call the infant or thoughtless Chamber, in which we remain as long as we do not think—We remain there a long while, and notwithstanding the doors of the second Chamber remain wide open, showing a bright appearance, we care not to hasten to it; but are at length imperceptibly impelled by the awakening of the thinking principle—within us—we no sooner get into the second Chamber, which I shall call the Chamber of Maiden-Thought, than we become intoxicated with the light and the atmosphere, we see nothing but pleasant wonders, and think of delaying there for ever in delight: However among the effects this breathing is father of is that tremendous one of sharpening one's vision into the heart and nature of Man—of convincing ones nerves that the World is full of Misery and Heratbreak, Pain, Sickness and oppression—whereby This Chamber of Maiden Thought becomes gradually darken'd and at the same time on all sides of it many doors are set open—but all dark—all leading to dark passages—We see not the balance of good and evil. We are in a Mist—*We* are now in that state—We feel the "burden of the Mystery," To this point was Wordsworth come, as far as I can conceive when he wrote 'Tintern Abbey' and it seems to me that his Genius is explorative of those dark Passages. Now if we live, and go on thinking, we too shall explore them. he is a Genius and superior [to] us, in so far as he can, more than we, make discoveries, and shed a light in them—Here I must think Wordsworth is deeper than Milton—though I think it has depended more upon the general and gregarious advance of intellect, than individual greatness of Mind—From the Paradise Lost and the other Works of Milton, I hope it is not too presuming, even between ourselves to say, his Philosophy, human and divine, may be tolerably understood by one not much advanced in years, In his time englishmen were just emancipated from a great superstition—and Men had got hold of certain points and resting places in reasoning which were too newly born to be doubted, and too much opposed by the Mass of Europe not to be thought etherial and authentically divine—who could gainsay his ideas on virtue, vice, and Chastity in Comus, just at the time of the dismissal of Cod-pieces and a hundred other disgraces? who would not rest satisfied with his hintings at good and evil in the Paradise Lost, when just free from the inquisition and burning in Smithfield? The Reformation produced such immediate and great benefits, that Protestantism was considered under the immediate eye of heaven, and its own remaining Dogmas and superstitions, then, as it were, regenerated, constituted those resting places and seeming sure points of Reasoning—from that I have mentioned, Milton, whatever he may have thought in the sequel, appears to have been content with these by his writings—He did not think into the human heart, as Wordsworth has done—Yet Milton as a Philosopher, had sure as great powers as Wordsworth—What is then to be inferr'd? O many things—It proves there is really a grand march of intellect—, It proves that a mighty providence subdues the mightiest Minds to the service of the time being, whether it be in human Knowledge or Religion—I have often pitied a Tutor who has to hear "Nom^e: Musa"—so often dinn'd into his ears—I hope you may not have the same pain in this scribbling—I may have read these things before, but I never had even a thus dim perception of them: and moreover I like to say my lesson to one who will endure my tediousness for my own sake—After all there is certainly something real in the World—Moore's present to Hazlitt is real—I like that Moore, and am glad I saw him at the Theatre just before I left Town. Tom has spit a leetle blood this afternoon, and that is rather a damper—but I know—the truth is there is something real in the World Your third Chamber of Life shall be a lucky and a gentle one—stored with the wine of love—and the Bread of Friendship—When you see George if he should not have reced a letter from me tell him he will find one at home most likely—tell Bailey I hope soon to see him—Remember me to all The leaves have been out here, for MONY a day—I have written to George for the first stanzas of my Isabel—I shall have them soon and will copy the whole out for you.

Your affectionate friend
John Keats.

To Richard Woodhouse, 27 October 1818

My dear Woodhouse,

Your Letter gave me a great satisfaction; more on account of its friendliness, than any relish of that matter in it which is accounted so acceptable in the 'genus irritabile' The best answer I can give you is in a clerklike manner to make some observations on two principle points, which seem to point like indices into the midst of the whole pro and con, about genius, and views and atchievements and ambition and cœtera. 1st As to the poetical Character itself, (I mean that sort of which, if I am any thing, I am a Member; that sort distinguished from the wordsworthian or egotistical sublime; which is a thing per se and stands alone) it is not itself—it has no self—it is every thing and nothing—It has no character—it enjoys light and shade; it lives in gusto, be it foul or fair, high or low, rich or poor, mean or elevated—It has as much delight in conceiving an Iago as an Imogen. What shocks the virtuous philosop[h]er, delights the camelion Poet. It does no harm from its relish of the dark side of things any more than from its taste for the bright one; because they both end in speculation. A Poet is the most unpoetical of any thing in existence; because he has no Identity—he is continually in for—and filling some other Body—The Sun, the Moon, the Sea and Men and Women who are creatures of impulse are poetical and have about them an unchangeable attribute—the poet has none; no identity—he is certainly the most unpoetical of all God's Creatures. If then he has no self, and if I am a Poet, where is the Wonder that I should say I would write no more? Might I not at that very instant [have] been cogitating on the Characters of saturn and Ops? It is a wretched thing to confess; but is a very fact that not one word I ever utter can be taken for granted as an opinion growing out of my identical nature—how can it, when I have no nature? When I am in a room with People if I ever am free from speculating on creations of my own brain, then not myself goes home to myself: but the identity of every one in the room begins to [*for so*] to press upon me that, I am in a very little time an[ni]hilated—not only among Men; it would be the same in a Nursery of children: I know not whether I make myself wholly understood: I hope enough so to let you see that no dependence is to be placed on what I said that day.

In the second place I will speak of my views, and of the life I purpose to myself—I am ambitious of doing the world some good: if I should be spared that may be the work of maturer years—in the interval I will assay to reach to as high a summit in Poetry as the nerve bestowed upon me will suffer. The faint conceptions I have of Poems to come brings the blood frequently into my forehead—All I hope is that I may not lose all interest in human affairs—that the solitary indifference I feel for applause even from the finest Spirits, will not blunt any acuteness of vision I may have. I do not think it will—I feel assured I should write from the mere yearning and fondness I have for the Beautiful even if my night's labours should be burnt every morning and no eye ever shine upon them. But even now I am perhaps not speaking from myself; but from some character in whose soul I now live. I am sure however that this next sentence is from myself. I feel your anxiety, good opinion and friendliness in the highest degree, and am

Your's most sincerely
John Keats

To George and Georgiana Keats, 14 February to 3 May 1819

March 19 ——

... Very few men have ever arrived at a complete disinterestedness of Mind: very few have been influenced by a pure desire of the benefit of others—in the greater part of the Benefactors & to Humanity some meretricious motive has sullied their greatness—some melodramatic scenery has fascinated them—From the manner in which I feel Haslam's misfortune I perceive how far I am from any humble standard of disinterestedness—Yet this feeling ought to be carried to its highest pitch, as there is no fear of its ever injuring society—which it would do I fear pushed to an extremity—For in wild nature the Hawk would loose his Breakfast of Robins and the Robin his of Worms The Lion must starve as well as the swallow—The greater part of Men make their way with the same instinctiveness, the same unwandering eye from their purposes, the same animal eagerness as the Hawk—The Hawk wants a Mate, so does the Man—look at them both they set about it and procure on[e] in the same manner—They want both a nest and they both set about one in the same manner—they get their food in the same manner—The noble animal Man for his amusement smokes his pipe—the Hawk balances about the Clouds—that is the only difference of their leisures. This it is that makes the Amusements of Life—to a speculative Mind. I go among the Feilds and catch a glimpse of a stoat or a fieldmouse peeping out of the withered grass—the creature hath a purpose and its eyes are bright with it—I go amongst the buildings of a city and I see a Man hurrying along—to what? The Creature has a purpose and his eyes are bright with it. But then as Wordsworth says, "We have all one human heart"—there is an ellectric fire in human nature tending to purify—so that among these human creature[s] there is continually some birth of new heroism—The pity is that we must wonder at it: as we should at finding a pearl in rubbish—I have no doubt that thousands of people never heard of have had hearts comp[l]etely disinterested: I can remember but two—Socrates and Jesus—their Histories evince it—What I heard a little time ago, Taylor observe with respect to Socrates, may be said of Jesus— That he was so great a man that though he transmitted no writing of his own to posterity, we have his Mind and his sayings and his greatness handed to us by others. It is to be lamented that the history of the latter was written and revised by Men interested in the pious frauds of Religion. Yet through all this I see his splendour. Even here though I myself am pursueing the same instinctive course as the veriest human animal you can think of—I am however young writing at random—straining at particles of light in the midst of a great darkness—without knowing the bearing of any one assertion of any one opinion. Yet may I not in this be free from sin? May there not be superior beings amused with any graceful, though instinctive attitude my mind m[a]y fall into, as I am entertained with the alertness of a Stoat or the anxiety of a Deer? Though a quarrel in the streets is a thing to be hated, the energies displayed in it are fine; the commonest Man shows a grace in his quarrel—By a superior being our reasoning[s] may take the same tone—though erroneous they may be fine—This is the very thing in which consists poetry; and if so it is not so fine a thing as philosophy—For the same reason that an eagle is not so fine a thing as a truth—Give me this credit—Do you not think I strive—to know myself? Give me this credit—and you will not think that on my own accou[n]t I repeat Milton's lines

> "How charming is divine Philosophy
> Not harsh and crabbed as dull fools suppose
> But musical as is Apollo's lute"—

No—no for myself—feeling grateful as I do to have got into a state of mind to relish them properly—Nothing ever becomes real till it is experienced—Even a Proverb is no proverb to you till your Life has illustrated it— ...

April 21 ──

... I have been reading lately two very different books Robertson's America and Voltaire's Siecle De Louis xiv It is like walking arm and arm between Pizarro and the great-little Monarch. In How lementabl[e] a case do we see the great body of the people in both instances: in the first, where Men might seem to inherit quiet of Mind from unsophisticated senses; from uncontamination of civilisation; and especially from their being as it were estranged from the mutual helps of Society and its mutual injuries – and thereby more immediately under the Protection of Providence – even there they had mortal pains to bear as bad; or even worse than Baliffs, Debts and Poverties of civilised Life – The whole appears to resolve into this – that Man is originally 'a poor forked creature subject to the same mischances as the beasts of the forest, destined to hardships and disquietude of some kind or other. If he improves by degrees his bodily accommodations and comforts – at each stage, at each accent there are waiting for him a fresh set of annoyances – he is mortal and there is still a heaven with its Stars abov[e] his head. The most interesting question that can come before us is, How far by the persevering endeavours of a seldom appearing Socrates Mankind may be made happy – I can imagine such happiness carried to an extreme – but what must it end in? – Death – and who could in such a case bear with death – the whole troubles of life which are now frittered away in a series of years, would the[n] be accumulated for the last days of a being who instead of hailing its approach, would leave this world as Eve left Paradise—But in truth I do not at all believe in this sort of perfectibility – the nature of the world will not admit of it – the inhabitants of the world will correspond to itself—Let the fish philosophise the ice away from the Rivers in winter time and they shall be at continual play in the tepid delight of summer. Look at the Poles and at the sands of Africa, Whirlpools and volcanoes – Let men exterminate them and I will say that they may arrive at earthly Happiness – The point at which Man may arrive is as far as the paralel state in inanimate nature and no further – For instance suppose a rose to have sensation, it blooms on a beautiful morning it enjoys itself – but there comes a cold wind, a hot sun – it can not escape it, it cannot destroy its annoyances – they are as native to the world as itself: no more can man be happy in spite, the world[l]y elements will prey upon his nature – The common cognomen of this world among the misguided and superstitious is 'a vale of tears' from which we are to be redeemed by a certain arbitrary interposition of God and taken to Heaven – What a little circumscribe[d] straightened notion! Call the world if you Please " 'The vale of Soulmaking" Then you will find out the use of the world (I am speaking now in the highest terms for human nature admitting it to be immortal which I will here take for granted for the purpose of showing a thought which has struck me concerning it) I say 'Soul making' Soul as distinguished from an Intelligence – There may be intelligence or sparks of the divinity in millions – but they are not Souls till they acquire identities, till each one is personally itself. I[n]telligences are atoms of perception – they know and they see and they are pure, in short they are God – how then are Souls to be made? How then are these sparks which are God to have identity given them – so as ever to possess a bliss peculiar to each ones individual existence? How, but by the medium of a world like this? This point I sincerely wish to consider because I think it a grander system of salvation than the chrystain religion – or rather it is a system of Spiritcreation – This is effected by three grand materials acting the one upon the other for a series of years – These three Materials are the *Intelligence–* the *human heart* (as distinguished from intelligence or Mind) and the *World* or *Elemental space* suited for the proper action of *Mind and Heart* on each other for the purpose of forming the *Soul* or *Intelligence destined to possess the sense of Identity.* I can scarcely express what I but dimly perceive – and yet I think I perceive it – that you may judge the more clearly I will put it in the most homely form possible – I will call the *world* a School instituted for the purpose of teaching little children to read – I will call the *human heart* the *horn Book* used in that School – and I will call the *Child able to read, the Soul* made from that *school* and its *hornbook.* Do you not see how necessary a World of Pains and troubles is to school an Intelligence and make it a soul? A Place where the heart must feel and suffer in a thousand diverse ways! Not merely is the Heart a Hornbook, It is the Minds

Bible, it is the Minds experience, it is the teat from which the Mind or intelligence sucks its identity – As various as the Lives of Men are – so various become their souls, and thus does God make individual beings, Souls, Identical Souls of the sparks of his own essence – This appears to me a faint sketch of a system of Salvation which does not affront our reason and humanity – I am convinced that many difficulties which christians labour under would vanish before it – There is one wh[i]ch even now Strikes me – the Salvation of Children – In them the Spark or intelligence returns to God without any identity – it having had no time to learn of, and be altered by, the heart – or seat of the human Passions – It is pretty generally suspected that the chr[i]stian scheme has been coppied from the ancient persian and greek Philosophers. Why may they not have made this simple thing even more simple for common apprehension by introducing Mediators and Personages in the same manner as in the hethen mythology abstractions are personified – Seriously I think it probable that this System of Soul-making – may have been the Parent of all the more palpable and personal Schemes of Redemption, among the Zoroastrians the Christians and the Hindoos. For as one part of the human species must have their carved Jupiter; so another part must have the palpable and named Mediatior and saviour, their Christ their Oromanes and their Vishnu – If what I have said should not be plain enough, as I fear it may not be, I will but [*for* put] you in the place where I began in this series of thoughts – I mean, I began by seeing how man was formed by circumstances – and what are circumstances? – but touchstones of his heart –? and what are touch stones? – but proovings of his hearrt? – and what are proovings of his heart but fortifiers or alterers of his nature? and what is his altered nature but his soul? – and what was his soul before it came into the world and had These provings and alterations and perfectionings? – An intelligence – without Identity – and how is this Identity to be made? Through the medium of the Heart? And how is the heart to become this Medium but in a world of Circumstances? – There now I think what with Poetry and Theology you may thank your Stars that my pen is not very long winded . . .

To Fanny Brawne, 25 July 1819

Sunday Night.

My sweet Girl,

I hope you did not blame me much for not obeying your request of a Letter on Saturday: we have had four in our small room playing at cards night and morning leaving me no undisturb'd opportunity to write. Now Rice and Martin are gone, I am at liberty. Brown to my sorrow confirms the account you give of your ill health. You cannot conceive how I ache to be with you: how I would die for one hour——for what is in the world? I say you cannot conceive; it is impossible you should look with such eyes upon me as I have upon you: it cannot be. Forgive me if I wander a little this evening, for I have been all day employ'd in a very abstr[a]ct Poem and I am in deep love with you—two things which must excuse me. I have, believe me, not been an age in letting you take possession of me; the very first week I knew you I wrote myself your vassal; but burnt the Letter as the very next time I saw you I thought you manifested some dislike to me. If you should ever feel for Man at the first sight what I did for you, I am lost. Yet I should not quarrel with you, but hate myself if such a thing were to happen—only I should burst if the thing were not as fine as a Man as you are as a Woman. Perhaps I am too vehement, then fancy me on my knees, especially when I mention a part of you Letter which hurt me; you say speaking of Mr. Severn 'but you must be satisfied in knowing that I admired you much more than your friend.' My dear love, I cannot believe there ever was or ever could be any thing to admire in me especially as far as sight goes—I cannot be admired, I am not a thing to be admired. You are, I love you; all I can bring you is a swooning admiration of your Beauty. I hold that place among Men which snub-nos'd brunettes with meeting eyebrows do among women—they are trash to me—unless I should find one among them with a fire in her heart like the one that burns in mine. You absorb me in spite of myself—you alone: for I look not forward with any pleasure to what is call'd being settled in the world; I tremble at domestic cares—yet for you I would meet them, though if it would leave you the happier I would rather die than do so. I have two luxuries to brood over in my walks, your Loveliness and the hour of my death. O that I could have possession of them both in the same minute. I hate the world: it batters too much the wings of my self-will, and would I could take a sweet poison from your lips to send me out of it. From no others would I take it. I am indeed astonish'd to find myself so careless of all cha[r]ms but yours—remembring as I do the time when even a bit of ribband was a matter of interest with me. What softer words can I find for you after this—what it is I will not read. Nor will I say more here, but in a Postscript answer any thing else you may have mentioned in your Letter in so many words—for I am distracted with a thousand thoughts. I will imagine you Venus to night and pray, pray, pray to your star like a Hethen.

Your's ever, fair Star,
John Keats.

My seal is mark'd like a family table cloth with my mother's initial F for Fanny: put between my Father's initials. You will soon hear from me again. My respectful Compts to your Mother. Tell Margaret I'll send her a reef of best rocks and tell Sam I will give him my light bay hunter if he will tie the Bishop hand and foot and pack him in a hamper and send him down for me to bathe him for his health with a Necklace of good snubby stones about his Neck.

To Percy Bysshe Shelley, 16 August 1820

Hampstead August 16th

My dear Shelley,

I am very much gratified that you, in a foreign country, and with a mind almost over occupied, should write to me in the strain of the Letter beside me. If I do not take advantage of your invitation it will be prevented by a circumstance I have very much at heart to prophesy—There is no doubt that an english winter would put an end to me, and do so in a lingering hateful manner, therefore I must either voyage or journey to Italy as a soldier marches up to a battery. My nerves at present are the worst part of me, yet they feel soothed when I think that come what extreme may, I shall not be destined to remain in one spot long enough to take a hatred of any four particular bed-posts. I am glad you take any pleasure in my poor Poem;—which I would willingly take the trouble to unwrite, if possible, did I care so much as I have done about Reputation. I received a copy of the Cenci, as from yourself from Hunt. There is only one part of it I am judge of; the Poetry, and dramatic effect, which by many spirits now a days is considered the mammon. A modern work it is said must have a purpose, which may be the God—*an artist* must serve Mammon—he must have "self concentration" selfishness perhaps. You I am sure will forgive me for sincerely remarking that you might curb your magnanimity and be more of an artist, and 'load every rift' of your subject with ore The thought of such discipline must fall like cold chains upon you, who perhaps never sat with your wings furl'd for six Months together. And is not this extraordina[r]y talk for the writer of Endymion? whose mind was like a pack of scattered cards—I am pick'd up and sorted to a pip. My Imagination is a Monastry and I am its Monk— you must explain my metap^{cs} [*for* metaphysics] to yourself. I am in expectation of Prometheus every day. Could I have my own wish for its interest effected you would have it still in manuscript—or be but now putting an end to the second act. I remember you advising me not to publish my first-blights, on Hampstead heath—I am returning advice upon your hands. Most of the Poems in the volume I send you have been written above two years, and would never have been publish'd but from a hope of gain; so you see I am inclined enough to take your advice now. I must exp[r]ess once more my deep sense of your kindness, adding my sincere thanks and respects for Mrs Shelley. In the hope of soon seeing you [I] remain

most sincerely [yours,]

John Keats—

To Charles Brown, 30 September 1820

Saturday Septr 28 [*for* 30]
Maria Crowther
off Yarmouth isle
of wight—

My dear Brown,

The time has not yet come for a pleasant Letter from me. I have
delayed writing to you from time to time because I felt how impos-
sible it was to enliven you with one heartening hope of my recov-
ery; this morning in bed the matter struck me in a different
manner; I thought I would write "while I was in some liking" or I
might become too ill to write at all and then if the desire to have
written should become strong it would be a great affliction to me. I
have many more Letters to write and I bless my stars that I have
begun, for time seems to press,—this may be my best opportunity.
We are in a calm and I am easy enough this morning. If my spirits
seem too low you may in some degree impute it to our having been
at sea a fortmight [*for* fortnight] without making any way. I was very
disappointed at not meeting you at bedhampton [*for* Bedhampton],
and am very provoked at the thought of you being at Chichester to
day. I should have delighted in setting off for London for the sensa-
tion merely—for what should I do there? I could not leave my
lungs or stomach or other worse things behind me. I wish to write
on subjects that will not agitate me much—there is one I must
mention and have done with it. Even if my body would recover of
itself, this would prevent it—The very thing which I want to live
most for will be a great occasion of my death. I cannot help it. Who
can help it? Were I in health it would make me ill, and how can I
bear it in my state? I dare say you will be able to guess on what sub-
ject I am harping—you know what was my greatest pain during the
first part of my illness at your house. I wish for death every day and
night to deliver me from these pains, and then I wish death away,
for death would destroy even those pains which are better than

nothing. Land and Sea, weakness and decline are great seperators, but death is the great divorcer for ever. When the pang of this thought has passed through my mind, I may say the bitterness of death is passed. I often wish for you that you might flatter me with the best. I think without my mentioning it for my sake you would be a friend to Miss Brawne when I am dead. You think she has many faults—but, for my sake, think she has not one——if there is any thing you can do for her by word or deed I know you will do it. I am in a state at present in which woman merely as woman can have no more power over me than stocks and stones, and yet the difference of my sensations with respect to Miss Brawne and my Sister is amazing. The one seems to absorb the other to a degree incredible. I seldom think of my Brother and Sister in america. The thought of leaving Miss Brawne is beyond every thing horrible—the sense of darkness coming over me—I eternally see her figure eternally vanishing. Some of the phrases she was in the habit of using during my last nursing at Wen(t)worth place ring in my ears—Is there another Life? Shall I awake and find all this a dream? There must be we cannot be created for this sort of suffering. The receiving of this letter is to be one of yours—I will say nothing about our friendship or rather yours to me more than that as you deserve to escape you will never be so unhappy as I am. I should think of—you in my last moments. I shall endeavour to write to Miss Brawne if possible to day. A sudden stop to my life in the middle of one of these Letters would be no bad thing for it keeps one in a sort of fever awhile. Though fatigued with a Letter longer than any I have written for a long while it would be better to go on for ever than awake to a sense of contrary winds. We expect to put into Portland roads to night. The Captn the Crew and the Passengers are all illtemper'd and weary. I shall write to dilke. I feel as if I was closing my last letter to you—My dear Brown

Your affectionate friend
John Keats

To Charles Brown, 30 November 1820

Rome. 30 November 1820.

My dear Brown,

'Tis the most difficult thing in the world to me to write a letter. My stomach continues so bad, that I feel it worse on opening any book,—yet I am much better than I was in Quarantine. Then I am afraid to encounter the proing and conning of any thing interesting to me in England. I have an habitual feeling of my real life having past, and that I am leading a posthumous existence. God knows how it would have been—but it appears to me—however, I will not speak of that subject. I must have been at Bedhampton nearly at the time you were writing to me from Chichester—how unfortunate— and to pass on the river too! There was my star predominant! I cannot answer any thing in your letter, which followed me from Naples to Rome, because I am afraid to look it over again. I am so weak (in mind) that I cannot bear the sight of any hand writing of a friend I love so much as I do you. Yet I ride the little horse,—and, at my worst, even in Quarantine, summoned up more puns, in a sort of desperation, in one week than in any year of my life. There is one thought enough to kill me—I have been well, healthy, alert &c, walking with her—and now—the knowledge of contrast, feeling for light and shade, all that information (primitive sense) necessary for a poem are great enemies to the recovery of the stomach. There, you rogue, I put you to the torture,—but you must bring your philosophy to bear—as I do mine, really—or how should I be able to live? Dr Clarke is very attentive to me; he says, there is very little the matter with my lungs, but my stomach, he says, is very bad. I am well disappointed in hearing good news from George,— for it runs in my head we shall all die young. I have not written to x x x x x yet, which he must think very neglectful; being anxious to send him a good account of my health, I have delayed it from week to week. If I recover, I will do all in my power to correct the mistakes made during sickness; and if I should not, all my faults will be forgiven. I shall write to x x x to-morrow, or next day. I will write to x x x x x in the middle of next week. Servern is very well, though he leads so dull a life with me. Remember me to all friends, and tell x x x x I should not have left London without taking leave of him, but from being so low in body and mind. Write to George as soon as you receive this, and tell him how I am, as far as you can guess;— and also a note to my sister—who walks about my imagination like a ghost—she is so like Tom. I can scarcely bid you good bye even in a letter. I always made an awkward bow.

God bless you!
John Keats.

Notes

On first looking into Chapman's Homer (p. 43)

Written in October 1816. Keats's former schoolteacher Charles Cowden Clarke introduced him one evening to the Elizabethan poet George Chapman's translation of Homer's *Odyssey*. They read through the night, and Keats walked home at daybreak, composing this poem on the way; he sent it to Clarke by ten o'clock the same morning.

line 1 *realms of gold:* the phrase may refer, at least literally, to books with gold leaf embossing on their covers and spines.

line 4 *bards:* poets. *in fealty:* bound by the feudal obligation of loyalty. *Apollo:* Greek god of poetry and the sun.

line 6 *demesne:* realm, feudal possession.

line 7 *serene:* clear, bright, or calm sky.

line 11 *Cortez:* a Spanish conquistador; technically, it was Balboa, a Spanish explorer, who first saw the Pacific Ocean from the top of a mountain in Panama.

line 14 *Darien:* a town in Panama; the name used to refer to the Isthmus of Panama, the narrow strip of land separating the Atlantic and Pacific Oceans.

SLEEP AND POETRY (P. 47)

Written in the cottage of Keats's friend Leigh Hunt in Hampstead, beginning sometime after October 9, 1816, and completed in December 1816. Charles Cowden Clarke described the scene: "It was in the library at Hunt's cottage, where an extemporary bed had been made up for him on the sofa, that [Keats] composed the framework and many lines of the poem . . . the last sixty or seventy being an inventory of the art garniture of the room."

Epigraph: from *The Floure and the Leafe*, lines 17–21, a poem of unknown provenance, formerly attributed to Chaucer. *full unmete:* entirely unaccommodating. *ne might:* might not. *ne wist:* did not know. *n'as:* was no. *wight:* person. *hertis ese:* heart's ease. *n'ad:* had no.

line 5   *blowing:* blooming.

line 9   *Cordelia:* Lear's third and most loving daughter in Shakespeare's *King Lear*.

line 14   *poppy buds:* the sleep- and dream-inducing drugs opium and morphine are made from poppies.

line 33   *aerial liming:* outlines in the air; or, outlining themselves in the air.

line 48   *denizen:* a foreigner admitted to partial citizenship.

line 58   *bays:* wreath made of dark-green leaves of the bay tree, a Mediterranean laurel tree; in classical times, a garland of bay leaves signifed success as a poet.

line 64   *elysium:* the dwelling place after death of mortals who have been made immortal by the gods; paradise; by extension, a place of perfect happiness.

line 74   *Meander:* the ancient name of a river in Asia Minor (modern Turkey) known for its sinuous, winding path.

line 76   *awfuller:* more awe inspiring.

line 79   *tablets:* notebooks, writing pads.

lines 88–89   *steep / Of Montmorenci:* the waterfall of the Montmorency River in Quebec, 251 feet high.

line 102   *Flora:* Roman goddess of flowers and gardens. *Pan:* Greek god of pastoral nature, including pastures, woods, and animal life; the presiding deity in most pastoral poetry, that is, idealized poetry about shepherds and their lives.

line 126   *car:* chariot; Apollo, god of poetry and the sun, traverses the sky in a chariot.

line 170   *Jove:* Jupiter, or Zeus, chief of the gods of Olympus.

line 172   *paragon:* surpass.

line 174   *aye:* always.

line 187   *Pegasus:* the winged horse, favorite of the Muses (the goddesses who inspire artists, including poets); by extension, poetry itself.

line 198   *the certain wands of Jacob's wit:* in Genesis 30:25–43, Jacob uses poplar, hazel, and chestnut rods to selectively breed Laban's flocks of cattle, goats, and sheep, having been promised ownership of all spotted livestock. *wit:* intelligence, knowledge.

line 202   *bright Lyrist:* Apollo, god of the sun and poetry.

line 206   *Boileau:* Nicolas Boileau (1636–1711), a French poet and critic who set out neoclassical poetic principles in his influential *L'art poétique* (1674). *ye:* you English poets.

line 209   *boundly:* boundless; or, perhaps, bounden, dutiful.

line 214   *Avon:* English river that runs through the town of Stratford, Shakespeare's birthplace and childhood home.

line 216   *laurel:* see note for line 58, above.

line 218   *lone spirits:* promising poets who died young, such as Thomas Chatterton (see note for dedication of *Endymion*) and Henry Kirke White (1785–1806).

line 226   *ebon:* black.

line 228   *pipe:* piping, birdsong.

line 234   *Polyphemes:* ones who resemble Polyphemus, the strong, clumsy, one-eyed giant in the *Odyssey.*

line 248   *myrtle:* evergreen shrub with aromatic foliage, white flowers, and purple berries, sacred to Venus.

line 249   *Paphos:* town on the island of Cyprus in the northeastern Mediterranean, birthplace of Venus, goddess of love.

line 257   *Yeanèd:* brought forth, born.

line 258   *sward:* grassy turf.

line 276   *fane:* temple.

line 284   *dower:* natural gift or talent.

line 285   *spanning:* extending far.

line 303   *Dedalian wings:* the waxed wings Daedalus made for his son Icarus, who flew too close to the sun; his wings melted and he plunged into the sea, to his death.

line 322   *rout:* uproar, clamor; or, perhaps, a large evening party or other gathering.

line 335   *Bacchus:* god of wine, also called Dionysus.

line 336 *Ariadne:* daughter of King Minos of Crete, abandoned by her lover Theseus on the island of Naxos, where Bacchus found her and became her lover.

line 338 *portfolio:* portfolio of engravings of paintings, common in the early nineteenth century.

line 354 *a poet's house:* Leigh Hunt's cottage.

line 374 *lawny mantle:* loose, sleeveless cloak made of fine linen or cotton.

line 379 *unshent:* unsullied, unspoiled, undamaged.

line 381 *Sappho:* Greek lyric poet (fl. c. 610–c. 580 B.C.E.); here, a sculpture of her bust.

line 385 *Great Alfred:* King Alfred the Great (849–899), king of Wessex (871–899); he resisted the Danish invasions and was responsible for a revival of learning and literature in western England.

line 387 *Kosciusko:* Thaddeus Kosciusko (1746–1817), Polish patriot, soldier, and revolutionary admired by English liberals.

line 389 *Petrarch:* influential Italian poet (1304–1374), best known for his love poems inspired by the idealized woman he called Laura.

ENDYMION: A POETIC ROMANCE (P. 59)

Begun sometime in April 1817 at Carisbrooke, on the Isle of Wight; finished at Burford Bridge, Surrey, by November 28, 1817. Keats considered the poem "a test, a trial of my Powers of Imagination and chiefly of my invention which is a rare thing indeed—by which I must make 4000 Lines of one bare circumstance and fill them with Poetry. . . . Do not the Lovers of Poetry like to have a little Region to wander in where they may pick and choose, and in which the images are so numerous that many are forgotten and found new in a second Reading . . . ? Besides a long Poem is a test of Invention which I take to be the Polar Star of Poetry, as Fancy is the Sails, and Imagination the Rudder. Did our great Poets ever write short Pieces?" Sir Benjamin Richardson related an anecdote that Henry Stephens, a fellow student of Keats's, told him about one evening when he and Keats were sitting together, "Stephens at his medical studies, Keats at his dreaming. Keats breaks out to Stephens that he has composed a new line:—'A thing of beauty is a constant joy.' 'What think you of that, Stephens?' 'It has the true ring, but is wanting in some way,' replies the latter, as he dips once more into his medical studies. An interval of silence, and again the poet:—'A thing of beauty is a joy for ever.' 'What think of that, Stephens?' 'That it will live for ever.' "

Epigraph: the line is from Shakespeare's Sonnet 17.

Dedication:

> *Thomas Chatterton:* (1752–1770), poet, author of pseudomedieval poetry supposed to have been translated from the manuscripts of a fifteenth-century monk named Thomas Rowley; he killed himself when he was just seventeen, and a myth grew up around him of young genius killed by public neglect. Keats once called him "the purest writer in the English language."

BOOK I

line 50   *vermeil:* vermilion, bright red.

line 62   *thorough:* through.

line 63   *Latmos:* mountain in Caria (modern southwestern Turkey) where Endymion's sheep graze.

line 76   *pard:* leopard.

line 78   *aye:* always.

line 100 *eglantine:* sweetbrier, a fragrant wild rose with prickly thorns.

line 132 *unmew:* set free.

line 140 *Arcadian books:* pastoral literature, concerning idealized shepherds and their lives; pastorals were often set in Arcadia, a mountainous region in southern Greece.

line 141 *Apollo:* god of music, poetry, medicine, and the sun; exiled for nine years in Thessaly, he lived there as a shepherd and taught the other shepherds to play musical instruments, including the pipe.

line 150 *Begirt:* surrounded.

line 154 *mingled wine:* during sacrifices, different wines would be blended together.

line 158 *Leda's love:* Jupiter (or Jove), who coupled with the girl Leda in the form of a swan.

line 160 *poll:* the area of the head where hair grows.

line 170 *Ganymede:* a beautiful youth of the Trojan royal line, carried to heaven by Jupiter (Jove) to be his lover and the cupbearer of the gods.

line 174 *nervy:* muscular, strong.

line 177 *groves Elysian:* the abode, after death, of mortals who have been made immortal by the gods; paradise.

line 192 *chase:* unenclosed land for hunting.

line 199 *overtop:* make top-heavy; crown.

line 206 *Triton's horn:* the conch shell blown into by Triton, the son of Neptune, to make the roar of the ocean.

line 208 *scrip:* small bag or satchel.

line 236 *hamadryads:* nymphs residing in trees; nymphs are female spirits or minor deities of natural places.

line 241 *pipy hemlock:* a poisonous plant with hollow stems.

line 243 *Syrinx:* a nymph of Arcadia; she was pursued by the god Pan, but when she came to the river Ladon and could not cross it, she prayed to be transformed, and became marsh reeds. Pan uprooted some of the reeds, cut them to different lengths, waxed them together, and made the first panpipes.

line 246 *Pan:* see note for line 102 of "Sleep and Poetry."

line 247 *turtles:* turtledoves.

line 248 *Passion:* to impassion.

line 256 *chuckling:* clucking.

line 258 *pent-up:* still in the chrysalis.

line 261 *pine:* an emblem of Pan.

line 263 *faun and satyr:* male spirits, like young men with horns, the legs of goats, and large genitals; they inhabit woods and unplowed fields.

line 272 *Naiads:* river nymphs.

line 285 *undescribèd sounds:* Pan was considered responsible for all mysterious sounds heard in remote places.

line 290 *Dryope:* here, a nymph of Arcadia who was the mother of Pan.

line 295 *bourne:* boundary.

line 306 *Mount Lycean:* Lycaeus, a mountain in Arcadia, was sacred to Jupiter and Pan; it was the site of Pan's festivals (known as Lycaea).

line 310 *Ionian:* that part of the Mediterranean Sea between southern Italy and Greece.

line 318 *Thermopylæ:* a narrow mountain pass between northern and southern Greece (i.e., between Thessaly and Locris) that three hundred Spartans defended bravely but in vain against a massive Persian army in 480 B.C.E.

line 320 *genitors:* progenitors, ancestors.

line 326 *quoit:* quoits is a game in which players throw rings (quoits) at a peg.

line 328 *Hyacinthus:* a youth beloved by Apollo, killed by a quoit when Zephyr, the west wind, blew it so that it struck him in the head. His blood was transformed into a flower called the hyacinth, whose petals spell out the lament *ai ai!*

line 330 *Phœbus:* "the Bright One," an epithet of Apollo, god of the sun.

line 334 *raft:* torn off.

line 338 *Niobe:* a woman who, for bragging about her children, saw them killed by Apollo and Diana with bows and arrows; she was so stunned she turned to stone.

line 341 *paly:* pale.

line 347 *Argonauts:* sailors on the *Argo,* the ship Jason captained in search of the Golden Fleece as told in the *Argonautica,* by Apollonius of Rhodes.

line 348 *Neptune:* god of the sea.

line 358 *eld:* old age.

line 363 *Vesper:* Hesperus; that is, the planet Venus when it appears as the evening star.

line 367 *fire-tail'd exhalations:* comets.

line 379 *feathery sails:* wings.

line 384 *Mercury:* Hermes, messenger of the gods.

line 386 *champaign:* field.

line 406 *tale Arabian:* "The Story of the Young King of the Black Islands," one of the tales in *The Arabian Nights,* also known as *The Thousand and One Nights.* The young king is turned to stone from the waist down by his unfaithful wife.

line 423 *shallop:* small boat.

line 432 *fingering:* a kind of fine wool or yarn used for knitting; here, the vegetation; also, the knitting or weaving itself.

line 453 *comfortable:* comforting, calming. *bird:* the halcyon, a mythical bird that could charm the sea into calmness.

line 481 *poll:* cut off the top of a tree, lop its branches off.

line 495 *Dryope:* a girl who was transformed into a tree while she nursed her child.

line 499 *Delphic:* divinely inspired; Delphi was a temple of Apollo where his female oracle or priestess gave prophecies inspired by the god.

line 510 *Paphian dove:* a dove from the temple of Venus in Paphos, on the island of Cyprus; Venus is the goddess of love.

line 512 *Dian:* Diana, virgin goddess of hunting and the moon; because Actaeon glimpsed her bathing naked, he was transformed into a stag, and his own hunting dogs tore him apart.

line 517 *bland:* mild.

line 531 *Lucifer:* the planet Venus when it appears as the morning star.

line 552 *snorting four:* the four horses drawing Apollo's chariot.

line 553 *zodiac-lion:* the constellation Leo.

line 555   *ditamy:* a plant sacred to Diana, supposedly able to cause weapons to be removed from wounds. *poppies:* sacred to Diana; see also note for line 14 of "Sleep and Poetry."

line 559   *Morpheus:* god of sleep.

line 563   *his rod:* Mercury's caduceus, a magic rod wound round by two serpents; with it he can lull others to sleep, resurrect the dead, and conduct the souls of the dead to the underworld.

line 571   *gulph'd:* engulfed.

line 595   *argent:* silvery.

line 605   *Olympus:* a mountain in Greece; home of the gods.

line 614   *gordian'd up:* tied in knots.

line 628   *pavilion:* large, decorated tent.

line 666   *alp:* mountain pasture.

line 671   *Oread:* mountain nymph.

line 683   *ouzel:* a European thrush.

line 696   *vermeil:* vermilion, bright red.

line 702   *under darkness:* the underworld.

line 714   *enchased:* covered with decorated armor.

line 723   *middle earth:* the earth, between heaven and the underworld.

line 732   *yew-tree:* tree associated with death because it is often planted in cemeteries.

line 759   *high-fronted:* noble-featured.

line 762   *plaited:* knitted, furrowed.

line 764   *fans:* wings.

line 765   *careless:* carefree.

line 766   *manna-dew:* manna is the miraculous food gathered by the Israelites in the wilderness.

line 786   *Æolian:* the aeolian lyre is a musical instrument that sounds when blown upon by the wind.

line 791   *clarions:* high-pitched trumpets. *bruit:* sound.

line 792   *giant battle:* between the gods and the Titans.

line 794   *Orpheus:* the great poet of Greek myth, who charmed and animated nature with his playing of the lyre.

line 799   *self-destroying:* producing forgetfulness of the sense of selfhood or self-consciousness.

line 808   *genders:* engenders, produces.

line 814   *pith:* essence.

line 815   *pelican brood:* the offspring of the pelican, which was thought to feed its young with its own blood.

line 816   *unsating:* not cloying or overfilling.

line 817 *van:* vanguard, forefront.

line 823 *Elysium:* paradise.

line 837 *mail:* armor.

line 838 *dower:* gift, endowment.

line 850 *wildered:* bewildered.

line 851 *atomies:* tiny gnats, mites, or other minuscule beings.

line 862 *Latona:* mother of Apollo and Diana.

line 907 *gnawing sloth:* here, a species of Indian bear.

line 943 *grot:* grotto, picturesque cave.

line 944 *Proserpine:* goddess of vegetation, daughter of Ceres and Jupiter; every winter she is carried into the underworld to be the spouse of Pluto, as the queen of Hades; in the summer she lives on earth.

line 947 *Echo:* a nymph who pined away out of love for Narcissus, until only her voice was left.

line 962 *freaks:* tricks.

line 966 *Delos:* an island of the Cyclades, birthplace of Apollo and Diana.

line 989 *car:* chariot.

BOOK II

line 12 *amain:* with full force.

line 13 *close:* embrace. *Troilus and Cressid:* lovers during the Trojan war; their story is told in Shakespeare's *Troilus and Cressida,* among other works.

line 15 *Swart:* dark, black.

line 23 *the great Athenian admiral:* Themistocles, whose debate with his officers about whether to make an attack was interrupted by an owl alighting on the mast of their ship, an event they interpreted as a good omen.

line 24 *Alexander:* Alexander the Great, who crossed the Indus River with his Macedonian army in 326 B.C.E.

line 26 *Odysseus:* in Book IX of the *Odyssey,* the hero Odysseus gets the Cyclops drunk and then blinds the one-eyed giant while he sleeps, so that he and his men can escape the giant's cave.

line 31 *Hero:* the lover of Leander in Marlowe's poem *Hero and Leander. Imogen:* the heroine of Shakespeare's *Cymbeline.*

line 32 *Pastorella:* heroine in Book VI of Spenser's *Faerie Queene;* she is kidnapped by bandits.

line 60 *pight:* pitched, poised, settled.

line 62 *character'd:* written, engraved.

line 81   *holy bark:* small ship carrying religious pilgrims.

line 82   *Delphi:* see note for Book I, line 499, above.

line 91   *mealy gold:* gold-colored dust on a butterfly's wings.

line 109 *Amphitrite:* the sea; as a goddess, she is the daughter of Oceanus and Tethys and the wife of Neptune, god of the sea.

line 116 *charming:* magical, enchanting.

line 118 *Meander:* see note for line 74 of "Sleep and Poetry"

line 138 *burr:* a blurry circle of light around the moon; here, mental blurriness.

line 145 *travelling:* travailing, toiling, working hard.

line 164 *Orphean lute:* a musical instrument of Orpheus, the great poet and husband of Eurydice; his playing was famously enchanting.

line 170 *Cynthia:* another name for Diana, virgin goddess of hunting and the moon; she was born on Mount Cynthus.

line 180 *Cupids:* love gods; Diana is famous for being chaste and virginal.

line 197 *Deucalion:* man who survived the flood sent by Jupiter to destroy the world, by waiting on Mount Parnassus.

line 198 *Orion:* a giant hunter who was blinded by King Oenopion; he regained his sight by turning toward the rising sun.

line 204 *sparry:* sparkling; that is, rich in spar, a lustrous crystal.

line 206 *thy threshold:* Mount Latmos, where Endymion pastured his sheep.

line 230 *antre:* cavern. *woof:* woven fabric.

line 231 *Vulcan's rainbow:* metal rainbow made by Vulcan, the blacksmith-god.

line 240 *vast:* vastness.

line 245 *fray:* frighten.

line 247 *stun:* stunning effect.

line 251 *sphering time:* the time during which the earth will continue to circle the sun.

line 253 *mighty ones:* great poets.

line 262 *quiver'd Dian:* Diana, goddess of hunting, with her quiver of arrows. *awfully:* full of awe.

line 277 *fog-born elf:* will-o'-the-wisp, a malignant spirit that lures people into swamps.

line 282 *raught:* reached.

line 288 *cloudy rack:* clouds driven before the wind.

line 292 *surcharged:* overloaded.

line 298 *chief:* upper end.

line 301 *plain:* complain.

line 308 *disparted:* separated.

line 309   *crescent:* crescent moon, emblem of Diana.

line 318   *zephyr-boughs:* waving boughs, blown by the west wind.

line 341   *sallows:* willows.

line 360   *Arion:* famous lyric poet and musician.

line 363   *Tyrian:* the sea near the city of Tyre, on the eastern shore of the Mediterranean.

line 373   *the Carian:* Endymion, who is from Caria.

line 376   *swart abysm:* dark abyss.

line 396   *coverlids:* coverlets, bedspreads.

line 405   *damask:* damask rose, a sweet-scented, pink rose with very soft petals.

line 407   *Disparts:* opens.

line 413   *Ethiop:* black.

line 415   *streakèd vases flush:* the abundant streaked, vase-shaped flowers of vines in the morning-glory family.

line 416   *creeper:* Virginia creeper, which turns red in the fall.

line 417   *virgin's bower:* clematis, a woody climbing vine.

line 421   *pathos:* moving sound of the lyre.

line 443   *Ariadne:* see note for line 336 of "Sleep and Poetry."

line 445   *Vertumnus:* Roman god of orchards and the spring; he wooed, and was initially rejected by, Pomona, the goddess of gardens and fruit trees.

line 448   *Amalthea:* daughter of Melisseus, the king of Crete; she fed Jupiter with goat's milk.

line 452   *manna:* here, apparently, the golden apples of the Hesperides.

line 453   *Hesperides:* nymphs who guarded the golden apples that Jupiter gave Juno as a wedding present.

line 458   *sea-born goddess:* Venus, goddess of love, who was born from the sea.

line 459   *mortal youth:* Adonis.

line 475   *plainings:* complainings.

line 492   *Cytherea:* Venus, who was born near Cythera.

line 494   *clamant:* clamorous, crying out.

line 497   *Pigeons and doves:* birds sacred to Venus.

line 517   *Disparted:* separated.

line 518   *car:* chariot.

line 532   *unchariest:* least bashful or coy.

line 535   *Love's self:* Cupid or Eros, god of love; he is the son of Venus. *superb:* stately, majestic.

line 537   *quell:* the power to destroy.

line 569   *zoned:* encircled.

line 611   *float:* boat. *Thetis:* sea goddess, mother of Achilles, the Greek hero of the Trojan War.

line 625   *aloof:* at some remove; here, in the far-off future.

line 627   *Protean:* changing shape, like the sea god Proteus, who could assume any shape he wished.

line 629   *griesly gapes:* terrifying chasms.

line 636   *purblind:* partly blinded. *wolds:* hilly uplands.

line 640   *Cybele:* earth-mother goddess. She is always pictured as very pregnant, often crowned with rising turrets; she rides in a chariot drawn by tame lions.

line 641   *foldings:* enfolding robes.

line 646   *nervy:* muscular, strong.

line 658   *eagle:* bird sacred to Jupiter.

line 663   *asphodel:* in Greek myth, a flower growing in Elysium, or paradise.

line 674   *Hesperean:* westward; Hesperus is the evening star, which appears in the west.

line 688   *gates of heaven:* the sun, home of the sun nymphs, also known as the Hours, or Horae, and the goddesses of the changing seasons.

line 689   *starry seven:* the Pleiades, daughters of the Titan Atlas, were transformed into a constellation by Jupiter.

line 690   *maid of the waters:* sea nymph.

line 691   *Triton:* a sea god.

line 693   *scions:* shoots or twigs.

line 696   *Aurora:* goddess of the dawn.

line 700   *vest:* vestment, garment.

line 716   *Helicon:* a mountain in Boeotia, Greece; site of the Hippocrene, a spring; both the mountain and the spring are sacred to the Muses, goddesses who inspire poets and other artists.

line 753   *Elysium:* the dwelling place for mortals who have been made immortal by the gods after death; paradise.

line 761   *Ida:* the mountain where Venus, goddess of love, was chosen as most beautiful by Paris of Troy, rather than Minerva or Juno; by extension, love, or the site of love's triumph.

line 791   *Minerva:* goddess of wisdom.

line 793   *vail'd:* lowered as a token of respect.

line 799   *Pallas:* Minerva, goddess of wisdom; also called Athena.

line 819   *empyrean:* heavenly.

line 866   *Æolian tuned:* finely tuned, like the strings of an aeolian harp, which makes harmonious music when blown upon by the wind.

line 875 *Alecto:* one of the Furies, who pursues the guilty; her head is covered with serpents.

line 876 *Hermes' pipe:* the pipe with which Hermes, messenger of the gods, lulled Argus, the hundred-eyed monster, to sleep.

line 899 *maw:* here, entrails, bowels.

line 911 *Olympian eagle:* the sacred eagle of Jupiter.

line 912 *the parentage of chaos:* Chaos gave birth to Erebus (darkness) and Nyx (night); "parentage" apparently means "offspring" here.

line 936 *Arethusa:* a wood nymph, one of Diana's attendants. Madly pursued by Alpheus (see note for line 952, below), she was transformed into a stream by Diana.

line 945 *rillets:* rivulets.

line 952 *Cruel god:* Alpheus, a river god, in love with Arethusa.

line 955 *syren:* dangerously enchanting and tempting.

line 961 *Oread-Queen:* Diana; oreads are mountain nymphs.

line 994 *Saturn in his exile:* Saturn and the Titans were overthrown by the Olympian gods.

line 1008 *sudden fell:* a reference to the story that Diana opened a secret passage under the earth and sea where Arethusa, in the form of a stream, disappeared, only to rise again on the island of Ortygia near Sicily. Alpheus, in the form of a river, followed her, so that now anything thrown into the Alpheus in Greece will rise again in the fountain of Arethusa on Ortygia.

line 1010 *Latmian:* Endymion, from Mount Latmos.

BOOK III

line 7 *Fire-branded foxes:* a reference to Judges 15:4–5, in which Samson sets the tails of foxes on fire and sends them into the Philistines' fields to burn their crops.

line 10 *dight:* dressed, arrayed.

line 13 *blown:* inflated, conceited.

line 31 *bourne:* here: realm, domain.

line 38 *Ceres:* goddess of grain and harvests, mother of Proserpine.

line 42 *Eterne:* eternal. *thy Sister:* Diana, goddess of the moon.

line 57 *kine:* cattle.

line 70 *spooming:* foaming. *Ocean:* a Titan; moved by the moon, he thus causes the tides.

line 71 *Tellus:* a Titan, she presided over the earth.

line 72 *Cynthia:* another name for Diana.

line 78   *Vesper:* the planet Venus, the evening star.

line 82   *Neptune:* god of the sea.

line 83   *love-spangles:* reflected moonlight.

line 97   *Leander:* lover of Hero; he swam the sea for her love.

line 98   *Orpheus:* poet, husband of Eurydice; he descended to the under-
          world to bring her back to earth.

line 99   *Pluto:* god of the underworld, lover of Proserpine; he ascended to
          earth to abduct her and take her to the underworld.

line 100 *wingèd Chieftain:* Cupid, or Eros, god of love.

line 106 *warm:* warmth.

line 113 *Aurora:* goddess of the dawn.

line 120 *vast:* the sea.

line 122 *Morpheus:* god of sleep.

line 124 *brazen beaks:* bronze prows or figureheads of wrecked warships.
          targe: shield.

line 129 *Saturn's vintage:* an earlier age; Saturn was chief of the Titans, who
          preceded the Olympian gods.

line 133 *Nox:* Night.

line 134 *behemoth:* a biblical land monster, sometimes identified with the
          hippopotamus. *leviathan:* a biblical sea monster, sometimes identi-
          fied with the whale.

line 153 *dibble:* a tool for making holes in the ground to plant seeds or
          seedlings.

line 157 *mesh:* braid, interweave.

line 158 *spright:* sprite; spirit or fairy.

line 176 *Felicity's abyss:* deep pleasure, bliss.

line 182 *blind:* a reference to the tradition that the moon could make one
          insane or blind.

line 192 *old man:* Glaucus, a sea god.

line 203 *woof:* woven fabric.

line 204 *'twixt cape and cape:* between Cape Horn (the southern tip of
          South America) and the Cape of Good Hope (the southern tip of
          Africa); that is, throughout the oceans.

line 205 *gulphing:* engulfing; also, perhaps, rushing like a whirlpool.

line 211 *Neptune:* god of the sea, more powerful than any other god
          except his brother Jupiter.

line 214 *conn'd:* read.

line 215 *denizen:* inhabitant; alien who has been made a partial citizen.

line 230 *stole:* long robe.

line 240   *cast:* sloughed off. *serpent-skin:* Glaucus's lower body is the tail of a scaly fish.

line 241   *syrens:* bird-women who live out at sea; their singing tempts sailors to their deaths.

line 243   *giant:* Typhoeus, a giant with a hundred serpent or dragon heads; Jupiter slew him with a thunderbolt and buried him under Mount Etna in Sicily.

line 251   *Sisters three:* the three Fates, divine beings who determine the course of events in human life.

line 265   *magian:* magical.

line 269   *Tartarus:* a region of the underworld where the most guilty are punished.

line 274   *garner'd:* gathered up and stored.

line 285   *contumelious:* contemptuous; patronizingly arrogant.

line 286   *Rheum:* tears.

line 305   *case:* body.

line 315   *the midway from mortality:* halfway between life and death.

line 338   *trod no measures:* did not dance.

line 341   *sea-mew:* seagull.

line 342   *Plaining:* complaining. *discrepant:* apart, alone.

line 351   *gulph'd:* swallowed.

line 364   *Æthon:* one of Apollo's horses.

line 366   *brim of day-tide:* noon. *lea:* meadow.

line 373   *Latmian:* Endymion, from Mount Latmos.

line 375   *distempered:* disordered, deranged.

line 376   *ocean's sire:* Neptune.

line 386   *self-intent:* selfhood, self-consciousness.

line 399   *Scylla:* a beautiful virgin, daughter of Typhoeus; loved by Glaucus, she was changed into a grotesque sea monster by jealous Circe.

line 402   *white of truth:* absolute and complete truth.

line 406   *Hercules:* a hero who ended his story by burning himself to death on a pyre on Mount Etna in Sicily.

line 412   *Circe:* a sorceress.

line 414   *Phœbus' daughter:* Apollo's daughter; here, Circe (although she is usually considered to be the daughter of Helios, another sun god).

line 415   *Æœa's isle:* island off the coast of Italy, home of Circe.

line 428   *Elysium:* paradise.

line 454 *ambrosia:* the sweet and fragrant food of the gods, sometimes used by goddesses to perfume themselves before seducing someone.

line 459 *arbitrary:* tyrannical, despotic.

line 461 *Amphion:* the inventor of music.

line 474 *Pluto:* god of the underworld, death, and funerals.

line 488 *complain:* complaint.

line 494 *gordian:* knotted or coiled.

line 500 *wizard:* enchanted. *brute:* animal; Circe turns men into animals.

line 503 *Charon:* the boatman who conveys the souls of the dead over the rivers Styx and Acheron to the underworld, for the fee of an obolus (roughly equivalent to a penny).

line 504 *pelf:* money.

line 505 *rushes Stygian:* marsh plants on the edges of the river Styx.

line 515 *phial:* vial, small glass bottle.

line 528 *wildering:* perplexing.

line 529 *writhen:* twisted.

line 530 *Python:* a great serpent.

line 531 *Boreas:* the north wind.

line 534 *fauns . . . nymphs . . . satyrs:* minor nature deities or spirits. *stark:* harsh; or powerful.

line 536 *centaurs:* creatures half horse, half man. *rapine:* plunder.

line 544 *phalanx:* a unit of infantry in close formation.

line 567 *Dis:* Pluto, god of the underworld.

line 588 *thews:* bodily strength.

line 653 *Æolus:* god of winds. *spleen:* bad temper.

line 656 *shrouds:* sets of ropes supporting the masts of a ship; the rigging.

line 659 *gulphing:* swallowing (of the ship by the sea).

line 661 *eld:* old age.

line 675 *aguish:* shivering as if with fever.

line 685 *Atlas-line:* lines as strong as the Titan Atlas, who held up the sky on his shoulders.

line 710 *elect:* chosen.

line 728 *Mars:* god of war.

line 756 *clue:* clew, a ball of yarn or thread.

line 762 *charactery:* writing.

line 775 *wight:* person.

line 776 *diadem:* crown.

line 778 *corse:* corpse.

line 786 *Apollo's touch:* the touch of the sun's rays.

line 789   *Latmian:* Endymion.

line 808   *Neptunus:* Neptune, god of the sea.

line 819   *spar:* sparkling crystals.

line 830   *sea-marks:* landmarks seen from the sea.

line 845   *fragment up:* collect or treasure up in fragments. *mere:* pure.

line 846   *lavish:* lavishly plentiful. *vast:* vastness.

line 849   *Memphis . . . Babylon . . . Nineveh:* magnificent ancient cities.

line 851   *Iris:* goddess of rainbows.

line 853   *Paphian army:* army of lovers.

line 856   *raught:* reached.

line 880   *As:* as if it were a.

line 883   *portraiture:* reflections.

line 884   *amaze:* amazing spectacle.

line 886   *dome pomp:* splendid dome. *in extremes:* above and below.

line 888   *Triton:* a sea god.

line 889   *Nereids:* sea nymphs. *Syrens:* see note for Book III, line 241, above.

line 893   *ooze-born Goddess:* Venus, goddess of love; she was born from the sea.

line 897   *doves:* Venus's attendants.

line 899   *Nais:* Glaucus's mother; Neptune is his father.

line 918   *Cythera:* island in the Aegean sea, sacred to Venus.

line 919   *Cupid:* Eros, god of love; Venus's son. *Adonis:* Venus's lover.

line 923   *accents halcyon:* calming words.

line 927   *pleach'd:* intertwined.

line 930   *coverture:* shelter.

line 940   *Muses:* goddesses who inspire poets and other artists.

line 951   *Æolus:* god of the winds.

line 956   *Gulphs:* gulps; or rushes forward.

line 973   *Æolian twang:* the sound of an aeolian harp, which is played by the wind.

line 975   *Cytherea:* Venus.

line 994   *Oceanus:* old god of the sea; one of the Titans.

line 997   *lucid:* here, shining.

line 1000   *Doris:* a sea goddess. *Ægean seer:* Nereus, Doris's spouse and a sea god with the gift of prophecy; the Aegean sea is east of mainland Greece.

line 1002   *Amphion:* the inventor of music.

line 1004   *Amphitrite:* Neptune's wife, mother of Triton.

line 1005   *Thetis:* see note for Book II, line 611, above.

BOOK IV

line 10 *eastern voice of solemn mood:* the Bible.

line 11 *Nine:* the nine Muses of classical literature.

line 15 *Ausonia:* Italy, home of Virgil and Dante.

line 26 *shrives:* here, confesses.

line 39 *hecatomb:* a ceremonial religious sacrifice.

line 56 *Phœbe:* Diana, "the Bright One."

line 66 *Hist!:* Silence! Listen! *Hermes' wand:* see note for Book I, line 563, above.

line 68 *Hyacinthus:* see note for Book I, line 328, above.

line 101 *covert:* hiding place.

line 110 *sith:* since.

line 121 *Erebus:* Hades, the underworld; named for the god Erebus, off-spring of Chaos and Darkness.

line 129 *gorgon:* monstrous, petrifying.

line 145 *roundelay:* short, simple song with a refrain.

line 148 *vermeil:* vermilion, bright red.

line 157 *spry:* spray.

line 196 *Bacchus:* god of wine.

line 210 *ivy-dart:* Bacchus's thyrsus, a spear bound with ivy (a plant sacred to him) was an emblem of revelry and intoxication.

line 212 *imbrued:* stained.

line 215 *Silenus:* an older satyr, always drunk; he is the tutor and foster father of Bacchus.

line 218 *Damsels:* the bacchantes, female worshipers of Bacchus.

line 228 *Satyrs:* fertility spirits, often represented as young men with horns, goats' legs, and large genitals; they preside over woods and unplowed fields.

line 241 *leopards:* Bacchus's chariot is drawn by leopards.

line 247 *coil:* bustle, noisy disturbance.

line 257 *Osirian Egypt:* Egypt, where one of the chief gods is Osiris.

line 259 *Abyssinia:* modern Ethiopia.

line 262 *Tartary:* region in central Asia and eastern Europe.

line 263 *Ind:* India. *vail:* lower as a gesture of respect.

line 265 *Great Brahma:* in Hinduism, the Absolute; God.

line 331 *Mercury:* Hermes, messenger of the gods.

line 336 *his wand:* see note for Book I, line 563, above.

line 346 *in spleen:* hot-tempered.

line 349 *Exhaled:* evaporated. *Phœbus:* Apollo, that is, the sun.

line 369   *Zephyr:* the west wind.

line 375   *Cimmerian:* dark, obscure; the Cimmerians were a mythical peo-
            ple who lived in perpetual darkness.

line 380   *Jove's daughter:* Diana, or Phoebe.

line 385   *litter:* a vehicle including a curtained couch and carried by men or
            animals.

line 392   *sallows:* willows.

line 394   *old Skiddaw:* the mountain above Keswick in the north of the Lake
            District in England.

line 399   *splenetic:* angry.

line 400   *blood wide:* distended, flushed with blood.

line 409   *fain:* content.

line 410   *proud birds:* peacocks, considered Juno's birds.

line 411   *nerve:* strength. *Phœbus:* Apollo.

line 413   *Pallas:* Minerva, or Athena, goddess of wisdom, war, and the lib-
            eral arts; in one hand she wields a spear; in the other, a shield de-
            picting the head of the monster Medusa.

line 415   *Hebe:* cupbearer of the gods before she was supplanted by
            Ganymede.

line 422   *kirtled:* skirted.

line 424   *Hours:* see note for Book II, line 688, above.

line 426   *floating morris:* dance in the air.

line 427   *Dis:* Pluto, god of the underworld.

line 430   *crescented:* the crescent moon is one of Diana's emblems.

line 438   *Phœbe:* Diana.

line 441   *He who died:* Icarus, who flew too close to the sun, so that the wax
            of his artificial wings melted and he plunged into the sea.

line 459   *dædale:* cunning.

line 461   *bourne:* boundary.

line 479   *Nemesis:* goddess of vengeance; she punishes impiety and rewards
            virtue.

line 485   *Vesper:* the planet Venus as the evening star.

line 531   *death-watch tick:* according to superstition, the ticking of the
            death-watch beetle portends death, and is "stifled" at the moment
            of death.

line 536   *Semele:* mother of Bacchus, god of wine.

line 553   *parley:* meeting between enemies on the battlefield for negotiation
            or other communication.

line 557   *or:* ere, before.

line 558   *mask:* here, the procession which was often part of a mask, or masque, an elaborate aristocratic dramatic entertainment; this procession is "skyey" in part because its characters are "pinion'd," or winged.

line 570 *Zephyrus:* the west wind. *Flora:* goddess of flowers and gardens.

line 571 *bibbers:* drinkers.

line 575 *balm:* an aromatic garden plant. *golden pines:* pineapples.

line 576 *Savory:* an herb. *latter-mint:* late-season mint.

line 581 *belt of heaven:* the constellations of the zodiac.

line 582 *Aquarius:* a constellation, the water carrier; identified with Ganymede, the cupbearer of the gods.

line 589 *Star-Queen:* Diana, the moon.

line 591 *Castor:* with Pollux, one of the twins in the constellation Gemini. *Lion:* the constellation Leo.

line 592 *Bear:* the constellation Ursa Major. *Pollux:* part of Gemini.

line 595 *ramping:* rushing, raging; or reared up with front hooves in the air. *Centaur:* the constellation Sagittarius.

line 599 *shent:* disgraced.

line 602 *Andromeda:* lover of Perseus ("Danae's son"), who rescued her after her father, King Cepheus of Ethiopia, chained her to a rock to appease a sea monster. After death, they were both made into constellations.

line 611 *Daphne:* a girl who, pursued by the lustful Apollo, was turned into a laurel tree.

line 686 *syrinx:* panpipes; see note for Book I, line 243, above. *flag:* leaf.

line 697 *eglantine:* see note for Book I, line 100, above.

line 699 *trace:* write

line 701 *Vesta:* goddess of virgins and fire; a fire was kept lit by virgins who were dedicated to her service.

line 702 *Phœbus:* Apollo.

line 704 *Vesper:* the planet Venus as the evening star.

line 706 *Flora:* goddess of flowers and gardens.

line 709 *Naiads:* river nymphs.

line 713 *Delphos:* an oracle, like the oracle of Apollo in his temple at Delphi.

line 730 *feather'd tyrant:* Cupid (or Eros), god of love.

line 754 *gorgon:* petrifying, monstrous.

line 761 *trammels:* nets.

line 769 *cirque:* circle.

line 774 *lute-voiced brother:* Apollo, Diana's brother, god of music.

line 783 *amaranth:* mythical flower that never fades.

line 784   *garden-ground:* paradise.

line 786   *poppy dream:* opium dream.

line 790   *charactery:* symbols (cut into the tree bark).

line 792   *fear'd:* frightened.

line 884   *monitor:* guide.

line 929   *serene father:* Apollo, the sun.

line 936   *sward:* grass turf.

line 942   *bale:* misery.

line 943   *Titan's foe:* Jupiter.

line 950   *seemlihed:* seemliness, becoming appearance.

line 953   *Rhadamanthus:* one of the judges in the underworld; he makes the dead confess their crimes and metes out punishments.

line 959   *lorn:* forlorn.

line 967   *vesper:* evening.

LAMIA (P. 187)

Written at Shanklin on the Isle of Wight and at Winchester, probably late June to September 5, 1819; revised March 1820. As the source of his plot, Keats cited the following story from Robert Burton's *Anatomy of Melancholy* (1621; III.ii.1.1):

Philostratus, in his fourth book *de Vita Apollonii,* hath a memorable instance in this kind, which I may not omit, of one Menippus Lycius, a young man twenty-five years of age, that going betwixt Cenchreas and Corinth, met such a phantasm in the habit of a fair gentlewoman, which taking him by the hand, carried him home to her house, in the suburbs of Corinth, and told him she was a Phoenician by birth, and if he would tarry with her, he should hear her sing and play, and drink such wine as never any drank, and no man should molest him; but she, being fair and lovely, would live and die with him, that was fair and lovely to behold. The young man, a philosopher, otherwise staid and discreet, able to moderate his passions, though not this of love, tarried with her a while to his great content, and at last married her, to whose wedding, amongst other guests, came Apollonius; who, by some probable conjectures, found her out to be a serpent, a lamia; and that all her furniture was, like Tantalus' gold, described by Homer, no substance but mere illusions. When she saw herself descried, she wept, and desired Apollonius to be silent, but he would not be moved, and thereupon she, plate, house, and all that was in it, vanished in an instant: many thousands took notice of this fact, for it was done in the midst of Greece.

Lamia: in ancient demonology, a monster in woman's form who preyed on human beings.

PART I

line 1   *faery broods:* generations of supernatural spirits (fairies) belonging to the postclassical age.

line 2   *Nymph:* in classical myth, one of a class of minor female divinities or spirits residing in particular places in nature, such as streams, trees, and mountains, often represented as beautiful young women or girls. *Satyr:* see note for *Endymion*, Book IV, line 228.

line 3   *King Oberon:* king of the fairies. *diadem:* crown.

line 5   *Dryads:* tree nymphs. *Fauns:* the Roman name for satyrs.

line 6   *cowslipp'd:* filled with primroses, which have fragrant yellow flowers.

line 7   *Hermes:* winged messenger god, often sent by Jove on errands; also known as Mercury.

line 9   *Olympus:* a mountain in Greece, home of the gods and goddesses. *light:* lightly; swiftly and quietly.

line 10 *Jove:* chief of the gods and goddesses, also known as Jupiter and Zeus.

line 15 *Tritons:* minor sea gods.

line 18 *meads:* meadows.

line 19 *Muse:* a goddess who inspires poets and other artists.

line 20 *Fancy:* imagination. *casket:* box, treasure chest.

line 46 *cirque-couchant:* lying in a coil.

line 47 *gordian:* knotted or coiled.

line 49 *pard:* leopard.

line 55 *penanced lady elf:* an elf punished by having been transformed into an animal.

line 57 *wannish:* dim.

line 58 *Ariadne's tiar:* Ariadne was transformed into a constellation; she was represented as wearing a crown, or tiara, of stars.

line 60 *pearls:* teeth.

line 63 *Proserpine:* see note for *Endymion*, Book I, line 944; Proserpine was carried off to Hades by Pluto from the field of Enna, in Sicily.

line 66 *pinions:* wings.

line 67 *stoop'd:* plunging.

line 74 *Apollo:* god of poetry, music, and the sun.

line 78   *Phœbean dart:* ray of sunlight; the sun god's name is Phoebus Apollo.

line 81   *star of Lethe:* Hermes, who appeared like a star on the banks of Lethe, a river in the underworld, in order to guide the souls of the dead to the lower regions.

line 89   *serpent rod:* see note for *Endymion*, Book I, line 563.

line 103   *Silenus:* see note for *Endymion*, Book IV, line 215.

line 107   *weïrd:* magic; as accented here, the word has two syllables. *syrops:* syrups.

line 114   *psalterian:* like the sound of a psaltery, an ancient stringed instrument; or, perhaps, like a psalm, a religious poem or song.

line 115   *Circean:* like that of Circe, an enchantress in the *Odyssey* who seduces Odysseus and turns his men into animals.

line 116   *a live damask:* a living damask rose, a large and fragrant pink rose.

line 119   *Corinth:* ancient city in Greece.

line 131   *lighting:* alighting, landing. *printless verdure:* untrodden greenery.

line 133   *put to proof:* put to the test. *lithe Caducean charm:* flexible caduceus's magic; see note for *Endymion*, Book IV, line 215.

line 141   *bland:* softly.

line 148   *besprent:* sprinkled.

line 151   *sear:* dry, burning.

line 155   *volcanian:* sulfuric, as if spewed from a volcano.

line 156   *milder-moonèd:* silvery.

line 157   *mead:* meadow.

line 158   *mail:* interlinked metal rings, as in chain-mail armor. *brede:* braid; interwoven patterns.

line 163   *rubious-argent:* reddish silver.

line 167   *luting:* sounding like a lute.

line 169   *hoar:* snowy.

line 174   *Cenchreas':* Cenchreae was the harbor of the city of Corinth.

line 179   *Cleone:* a village south of Corinth.

line 182   *passioned:* grew impassioned.

line 187   *lea:* meadow.

line 188   *kirtle:* skirt. *minstrelsy:* singers and musicians.

line 191   *sciential:* wise, knowledgeable.

line 192   *unperplex:* disentangle.

line 193   *pettish:* moody, changeable. *estrange:* separate out, distinguish.

line 194   *counterchange:* changing of one into the other, and vice versa.

line 195   *Intrigue with:* turn to her own purposes. *dispart:* distinguish.

line 198 *unshent:* unspoiled.

line 199 *terms:* academic terms, semesters.

line 204 *list:* wished.

line 206 *Elysium:* see note for *Endymion,* Book II, line 753.

line 207 *Nereids:* sea nymphs.

line 208 *Thetis:* see note for *Endymion,* Book II, line 611.

line 209 *Bacchus:* god of wine.

line 210 *glutinous:* secreting gluelike sap or resin.

line 211 *Pluto:* god of the underworld. *palatine:* palatial.

line 212 *Mulciber:* blacksmith god, god of fire and metalworking, also known as Vulcan. *far piazzian line:* long lines around piazzas (open courtyards).

line 223 *galley:* ship.

line 224 *quay-stones:* stones of the harbor.

line 236 *Platonic shades:* the shadowy or obscure philosophy of Plato.

line 242 *mantle:* cloak.

line 244 *syllabling:* saying.

line 248 *Orpheus:* the supreme poet and musician of Greek myth. *Eurydice:* wife of Orpheus; when she died, Pluto allowed Orpheus to lead her out of the underworld and back to earth, but forbade him from looking back at her until they were out of Hades. He loved her so much he could not resist looking back, and so lost her again.

line 261 *Naiad:* river nymph.

line 265 *Pleiad:* one of the seven sisters immortalized as stars in the constellation Pleiades.

line 267 *spheres:* a reference to the ancient model of the universe, whereby the stars were attached to enormous, transparent concentric spheres, at the center of which was the Earth; the turning of these spheres was thought to produce a harmonious sound known as "the music of the spheres."

line 270 *shade:* ghost.

line 271 *melt:* disappear.

line 275 *nice:* finely detailed, accurate.

line 281 *climes:* climates, regions.

line 288 *complain:* amorous complaint; expression of desire.

line 293 *amenity:* quality of being pleasing or pleasureable.

line 312 *retired:* secluded.

line 317 *Venus:* goddess of love.

line 320   *Adonian feast:* fertility festival of Adonis, a mortal beloved by Venus; the time of this ceremony was supposed to be unlucky.

line 322   *amaze:* amazement.

line 323   *lays:* songs.

line 327   *unperplex'd:* unmixed with pain.

line 329   *Peris:* fairylike creatures of Persian myth.

line 332   *lineal:* descended.

line 333   *Pyrrha's pebbles:* the pebbles with which Pyrrha and Deucalion (see note for *Endymion,* Book II, line 197) repopulated the earth after the great flood, by throwing them behind their backs; the ones Pyrrha threw became women.

line 345   *league:* about three miles.

line 347   *comprised:* wrapped up in; absorbed.

line 352   *temples lewd:* Burton's *Anatomy of Melancholy* (III.ii.2.1), Keats's source for his plot, says that in one temple of Venus in Corinth "a thousand whores did prostitute themselves ... all nations resorted thither as to a school of Venus."

line 386   *sounds Æolian:* sounds like those of the aeolian harp, an instrument played by the wind, not unlike a wind chime; Aeolus is the god of winds.

PART II

line 9   *clench'd:* clinched, proven.

line 12   *Love:* Cupid or Eros, god of love.

line 17   *even tide:* evening.

line 24   *tithe:* one-tenth part, little bit.

line 32   *bourn:* limit.

line 33   *forsworn:* sworn off, abandoned.

line 34   *penetrant:* penetrating, keenly perceptive.

line 35   *so arguing:* as evidence of.

line 36   *empery:* empire.

line 39   *passing bell:* death knell, bell rung at one's death.

line 48   *silver planet:* Venus, which is both the evening and the morning star.

line 51   *smart:* pain.

line 69   *thereat:* at that.

line 70   *fancy:* desire.

line 76   *sanguineous:* red-faced, angry.

line 80   *the serpent:* Python, a serpent killed by Apollo, god of the sun. *certes:* certainly.

line 83   *bridal:* wedding. *paramour:* lover.

line 98   *list:* desire, want.

line 100   *bid:* invite.

line 123   *faery:* magic.

line 136   *Mission'd:* ordered. *viewless:* invisible.

line 137   *fretted:* adorned with interlaced patterns, fretwork.

line 139   *jasper:* opaque quartz of various colors.

line 142   *faded:* disappeared, grew invisible.

line 145   *dreadful:* terrifying.

line 146   *gossip rout:* crowd of talking friends.

line 151   *amain:* intently.

line 155   *demesne:* territory, estate.

line 156   *mazed:* amazed.

line 159   *something:* somewhat, a little.

line 160   *daft:* baffled or daunted.

line 172   *sophist:* wise man, philosopher, teacher; particularly one who teaches rhetoric and argumentative technique without regard to the truthfulness of arguments. *spleen:* ill temper.

line 175   *lucid:* bright.

line 176   *censer:* a vessel for burning incense or other aromatic substances. *myrrh:* sweet-smelling tree-gum resin used in making incense and perfume.

line 179   *woofèd:* woven.

line 183   *spherèd:* here, circular.

line 185   *libbard's paws:* leopard's paws; the carved shape of the tables' feet.

line 186   *store:* supply. *told:* counted.

line 187   *Ceres' horn:* the cornucopia, or horn of plenty, filled with the fruits, grains, and vegetables whose source is Ceres, goddess of vegetation and harvests.

line 188   *tun:* barrel, cask.

line 194   *meet:* appropriate.

line 207   *awful:* awesome. *nectarous:* wine-induced.

line 210   *trammels:* entanglements.

line 212   *Elysian shades:* spirits of paradise; see also note for *Endymion,* Book II, line 753.

line 213   *Bacchus:* Dionysus, god of wine. *meridian height:* apex, highest point.

line 217   *osier'd:* woven, plaited; an osier is a willow whose flexible branches are used in basketry.

line 220   *fancy-fit:* wreathe according to his desire and imagination.

line 224   *adder's tongue:* a fern whose fronds resemble a serpent's tongue; like the willow, it is an emblem of grief.

line 226   *thyrsus:* see note for *Endymion,* Book IV, line 210.

line 229   *charms fly:* magic spells disappear.

line 231   *awful:* awesome.

line 232   *woof:* weave.

line 236   *gnomed:* filled with gnomes, magical, fairylike creatures who live underground.

line 237   *erewhile:* before long.

line 238   *shade:* shadow, spirit, ghost.

line 245   *pledge:* drink a toast to.

line 257   *Own'd:* acknowledged.

line 264   *myrtle:* a plant sacred to Venus, goddess of love.

line 277   *juggling:* conjuring, deceiving, tricking.

line 278   *ban:* proclamation, curse.

line 283   *dotage:* feeblemindedness, senility.

line 285   *sophistries:* specious (that is, attractive but false) arguments.

line 291   *sophist:* see note for Part II, line 172, above.

line 292   *nighing:* nearing.

line 294   *supine:* on his back.

line 301   *perceant:* piercing.

line 302   *tell:* make, express.

ISABELLA; OR, THE POT OF BASIL (P. 208)

Begun before March 4, 1818, in Hampstead and finished by April 27, 1818, in Teignmouth. The poem follows the plot of the fifth novel of the fourth day of Boccaccio's *Decameron.*

line 2   *palmer:* religious pilgrim.

line 4   *malady:* sickness; here, lovesickness.

line 21   *vespers:* evening prayers.

line 26   *break:* beginning, first.

line 46   *conceit:* conception, idea; also, fanciful notion.

line 52   *symbol on his forehead high:* facial expression.

line 62   *fear:* affright, make afraid.

line 64   *shrive:* confess.

line 78   *dart:* Cupid's arrow.

line 80   *joyed:* rejoiced.

line 81   *close:* close together; also, in secret.

line 95   *Theseus' spouse:* Ariadne, daughter of Minos, king of Crete. She helped Theseus escape from her father's labyrinth after he killed the Minotaur, a monster. As promised, Theseus took her away with him, but he abandoned her on the island of Naxos. In some versions of the story, she killed herself; in others, she married Bacchus (or Dionysus), god of wine.

line 99   *Dido:* queen of Carthage; she is famous as the lover of Aeneas, the Trojan hero of Virgil's *Aeneid* who escapes the Trojan War and goes to Latium in Italy to found the Roman Empire. Between Troy and Italy, Aeneas stops in Carthage, where he becomes Dido's lover, only to abandon her to follow his destiny. Heartbroken, Dido kills herself. *under-grove:* in the *Aeneid,* the grove of myrtle trees in the underworld where the spirits of broken-hearted lovers reside.

line 101   *clove:* cloves, a pungent, aromatic spice.

line 103   *almsmen:* people who depended on the charity of others, sometimes in return for praying for the souls of their benefactors; their prayers were often murmured.

line 107   *swelt:* swelter because of intense heat; also swoon, faint.

line 123   *orange-mounts:* hills covered with orange trees.

line 124   *lazar:* lazar house, a house for lepers or the poor.

line 131   *that land inspired:* Palestine.

line 133   *hawks:* hawkers, sellers.

line 134   *pannier'd:* hung with a pair of bags or baskets.

line 135   *generous stray-aways:* free-spending departers from the straight and narrow.

line 140   *Hot Egypt's pest:* the plague of darkness that God visited upon Egypt in Exodus 10:21–23.

line 150   *ghittern:* cittern, a kind of guitar.

line 159   *stead:* render service to.

line 188   *eglantine:* see note for *Endymion,* Book I, line 100.

line 200   *in-door lattice:* window crisscrossed with mullions, set in a door.

line 221   *covert:* hiding place, cover.

line 251   *west:* west wind.

line 252   *roundelay:* short, simple song with a refrain.

line 262   *Hinnom's vale:* a valley used by the ancient Hebrews to burn refuse and corpses.

line 268   *pall:* cloth spread over a coffin.

line 292   *woof:* woven fabric.

line 317   *seraph:* angel. *bright abyss:* heaven.

line 339   *clay:* corpse.

line 356   *stole:* long robe.

line 393   *Persèan sword:* the supernaturally hard and sharp sword the Greek hero Perseus used to cut off the head of Medusa, the monstrous Gorgon.

line 409   *dews:* perfumes.

line 412   *cold serpent-pipe:* coiled pipe used in the manufacture of perfume.

line 432   *leafits:* small leaves.

line 436   *Lethean:* forgotten; the Lethe is a river in the underworld whose waters bestow complete forgetfulness of the past on those who drink from it.

line 442   *Melpomene:* Muse of tragedy; the Muses are goddesses who inspire poets and preside over the arts and sciences.

line 451   *Baälites:* worshipers of Baal, a "false god" in the Bible. *pelf:* money, wealth.

line 454   *dower:* natural endowment or gift.

line 467   *chapel-shrift:* confession in church.

line 477   *guerdon:* reward.

line 503   *burthen:* refrain.

THE EVE OF ST. AGNES (P. 224)

Written at Bedhampton and Chichester, January 18 to February 2, 1819; revised September 1819. Considering the subject of this poem, it seems relevant that Keats met a young woman named Fanny Brawne in the autumn of 1818; they fell in love, and became engaged the same year on Christmas Day.

St. Agnes: the patron saint of virgins, martyred about the year 304 at the age of thirteen. According to legend, if a virtuous young girl correctly performs a certain ritual, she will dream of her future husband on the evening before St. Agnes's Day, which is January 21.

line 5   *Beadsman:* an old pensioner or poor almsman charged with the duty of praying for someone else, usually his benefactor. *told His rosary:* counted his prayers on his string of prayer beads.

line 8   *without a death:* although the Beadsman hadn't died.

line 15   *purgatorial rails:* rails encircling the tombs, like bars imprisoning the souls of the dead in Purgatory, where, according to Catholic doctrine, saved sinners go after death to be punished for their sins.

line 16 *dumb orat'ries:* silent chapels.

line 18 *mails:* chain-mail armor.

line 21 *Flatter'd:* charmed, beguiled.

line 32 *pride:* splendid decoration.

line 37 *argent revelry:* revelers clothed in silver.

line 40 *triumphs gay:* high-spirited pageants or processions.

line 52 *couch supine:* lie down on their backs.

line 53 *require:* ask.

line 55: a revised version of the poem included the following stanza:

'Twas said her future lord would there appear
Offering, as sacrifice—all in the dream—
Delicious food, even to her lips brought near,
Viands, and wine, and fruit, and sugar'd cream,
To touch her palate with the fine extreme
Of relish: then soft music heard, and then
More pleasures follow'd in a dizzy stream
Palpable almost: then to wake again
Warm in the virgin moon, no weeping Magdalen.

virgin moon: Diana, the moon goddess, is a virgin. *Magdalen:* Mary Magdalen, the woman in the Gospels who washes Jesus's feet with her hair, has traditionally been identified with the adulterous woman whom Jesus forgives for her sin and hence is sometimes portrayed as weeping; "Madeline" is an alternative spelling of "Magdalen."

line 58 *train:* long, dragging skirt.

line 67 *timbrels:* tambourines. *throng'd resort:* crowded place of rest (from the dancing).

line 70 *Hoodwink'd with faery fancy:* blinded by her charmed imagination. *all amort:* dead to all; oblivious to all.

line 71 *her lambs unshorn:* On St. Agnes's Day, two unshorn lambs are brought to the altar of the basilica of St. Agnes Fuori le Mura in Rome to be blessed, and nuns weave their wool into cloth. This refers to the legend that, after her death, St. Agnes's parents saw a vision of her with a lamb standing beside her. The name "Agnes" itself means lamb.

line 75 *Porphyro:* from the Greek, meaning "purple"; porphyry is a hard, beautiful, and valuable purple stone.

line 77 *Buttress'd from moonlight:* sheltered from the moonlight by flying buttresses, great architectural supports jutting out from the wall.

line 81 *sooth:* truth.

line 84 *feverous:* feverish; hot and delirious.

line 90 *beldame:* in English, an old woman, although in the original French it translates to "lovely lady."

line 92 *wand:* staff.

line 95 *bland:* soft, smooth.

line 98 *hie thee:* hurry.

line 105 *Gossip:* female friend; godmother.

line 110 *plume:* tuft of feathers or similar decoration on his helmet.

line 117 *St. Agnes' wool:* see note for line 71, above.

line 120 *witch's sieve:* a sieve enchanted to be able to hold water.

line 121 *Fays:* fairies.

line 122 *amaze:* amazement.

line 126 *mickle:* plenty of.

line 133 *brook:* here, restrain.

line 146 *grace:* heavenly salvation.

line 153 *beard them:* literally, pluck hairs from their beards; insult them.

line 156 *passing-bell:* death knell; bell rung when one has died.

line 158 *plaining:* complaining.

line 171 *Merlin paid his Demon all the monstrous debt:* the sorcerer Merlin of Arthurian legend was imprisoned forever in a rock by his mistress the enchantress Nimuë, on an enchanted night when she turned one of his own spells against him.

line 173 *cates:* delicacies.

line 174 *tambour frame:* an embroidery frame shaped like a tambourine.

line 185 *dim espial:* being seen in the dim light.

line 188 *amain:* exceedingly, mightily.

line 189 *agues:* chills.

line 193 *mission'd spirit:* an angel sent on a mission.

line 198 *ring-dove:* a European wood pigeon that has a white spot on each side of its neck. *fray'd:* frightened.

line 205 *balmy:* fragrant, perfumed.

line 207 *dell:* little valley.

line 211 *of quaint device:* elaborately and ingeniously designed.

line 213   *damask'd:* woven with ornamental patterns that are picked out by the play of light.

line 214   *heraldries:* genealogical emblems on a heraldic shield.

line 215   *emblazonings:* symbols on a heraldic shield.

line 216   *shielded scutcheon:* heraldic shield bearing a coat of arms. *blush'd with blood of queens and kings:* in heraldry, red signifies that the family the shield symbolizes is of royal blood.

line 218   *gules:* red; this is the term used in heraldry.

line 222   *glory:* halo, circle of light.

line 226   *Anon:* soon, presently. *vespers:* evening prayers.

line 241   *missal:* Christian prayer book. *swart Paynims:* dark-skinned pagans.

line 257   *Morphean:* sleep-inducing; Morpheus is the classical god of sleep.

line 258   *clarion:* a high-pitched trumpet.

line 265   *quince:* tart, pear-shaped, yellow fruit. *gourd:* melon.

line 266   *soother:* softer, smoother.

line 267   *lucent:* clear, bright. *tinct:* tinctured, tinged.

line 268   *Manna:* sweet gums. *argosy:* a great merchant ship.

line 269   *Fez:* a trading city in northern Morocco.

line 270   *Samarcand:* an ancient Persian city dominating the trade route between China and the Near East.

line 276   *seraph:* angel.

line 277   *eremite:* religious hermit.

line 279   *so:* so much.

line 280   *unnervèd:* weakened, slack.

line 284   *salvers:* ornamental silver trays.

line 285   *Broad golden fringe:* of the tablecloth.

line 288   *entoil'd:* entangled. *woofed:* woven.

line 292   *Provence:* a region in southern France famous for its medieval troubadours (singing poets). *La belle dame sans mercy:* "The Beautiful Lady Without Pity," title of a work by the medieval poet Alain Chartier; Keats later wrote a poem of his own with the same title.

line 293   *touching:* plucking, playing.

line 296   *affrayèd:* disturbed; frightened.

lines 314–22   the revised version of the poem replaces these lines with the following:

See, while she speaks his arms encroaching slow,
Have zoned her, heart to heart,—loud, loud the dark winds blow!

For on the midnight came a tempest fell;
More sooth, for that his quick rejoinder flows
Into her burning ear; and still the spell
Unbroken guards her in serene repose.
With her wild dream he mingled, as a rose
Marrieth its odour to a violet.
Still, still she dreams, louder the frost wind blows.

zoned: encircled. *fell:* fierce. *sooth:* soothingly.

line 322   *solution:* mixture.

line 323   *alarum:* alarm, signal of danger.

line 325   *flaw:* gust of wind.

line 333   *unprunèd:* unpreened, its feathers untrimmed by the beak.

line 335   *for aye:* forever. *vassal:* servant

line 336   *vermeil:* vermilion, bright red.

line 339   *pilgrim:* traveler on a religious journey to a holy place.

line 342   *infidel:* unbeliever, heathen; unfaithful person.

line 343   *Hark:* listen. *elfin:* magical, enchanted.

line 344   *Of haggard:* wild, untamed.

line 349   *Rhenish:* wine produced near the Rhine River in Germany. *sleepy:* narcotic, sleep-inducing. *mead:* a heavy alcoholic drink made with honey.

line 351   *moors:* uncultivated, open grassy lands.

line 353   *dragons:* dragoons, soldiers.

line 355   *darkling:* in darkness.

line 358   *arras:* a wall-hanging or screen made of tapestry.

line 364   *flagon:* drinking vessel with a handle, spout, and lid; or a large, globe-shaped glass bottle.

line 366   *inmate:* member of the household.

line 377   *aves:* Ave Marias, prayers beginning with the Latin words *Ave Maria,* "Hail Mary."

line 378   *For aye:* forever.

ODE TO A NIGHTINGALE (P. 236)

Written in Hampstead, May 1819. Seventeen years after the event, Keats's friend Charles Brown recalled it this way: "In the spring of 1819 a nightingale had built her nest near my house. Keats felt a tranquil and continual joy in her song; and one morning he took his chair from the breakfast-table to the grass-plot under a plum-tree, where he sat for two or three hours. When he came into the house, I perceived he had some scraps of paper in his hand, and these he was quietly thrusting behind the books. On inquiry, I found those scraps, four or five in number, contained his poetic feeling on the song of our nightingale. The writing was not well legible; and it was difficult to arrange the stanzas on so many scraps. With his assistance I succeeded, and this was his *Ode to a Nightingale*, a poem which has been the delight of every one."

line 2   *hemlock:* a plant that can be made into a powerful sedative drug or deadly poison.

line 4   *Lethe-wards:* see note for "Isabella," line 436.

line 7   *Dryad:* tree nymph.

line 11   *a draught of vintage:* a deep drink of wine.

line 13   *Flora:* Roman goddess of flowering plants and fertility, worshiped at a spring festival; by extension, the flowers themselves.

line 14   *Provençal:* see note for "The Eve of St. Agnes," line 292.

line 16   *Hippocrene:* a spring near Mount Helicon, one of the mountains where, in Greek myth, the Muses reside; by extension, the waters of poetic inspiration, here treated as a kind of wine.

line 26   *youth grows pale . . . and dies:* Keats's brother Tom had died of tuberculosis the preceding winter.

line 32   *Bacchus:* Greek god of wine and intoxication, also called Dionysus; "pards" are the leopards that pull the god's chariot.

line 33   *viewless:* invisible.

line 36   *haply:* perhaps. *Queen-Moon:* an Anglicized image of Diana, Greek goddess of chastity, hunting, and the moon. Thus she is attended here not by Greek nymphs but English "Fays," or fairies.

line 43   *embalmèd:* filled and covered with balms, that is, fragrant oils derived from herbs, as when dead bodies are embalmed to preserve them from decomposition; here, by extension, brushed by soothing and fragrant (balmy) breezes.

line 51   *Darkling:* in darkness.

line 53   *musèd:* meditated; perhaps also inspired by a muse; Keats had called on "easeful Death" in such poems as the sonnets "Why did I laugh to-night?" and "Bright Star, would I were stedfast as thou art."

line 60   *requiem:* mass sung for the dead. *sod:* a clump of earth with grass growing on it.

line 64   *clown:* peasant.

lines 66–7   *Ruth:* In the biblical Book of Ruth, Ruth leaves a famine in her native land of Moab to glean surplus corn (grain) in the fields of her kinsman Boaz, near Bethlehem.

line 70   *faery lands:* worlds of magic and chivalric romance, as in Edmund Spenser's *Faerie Queene* or Keats's own "La belle dame sans merci."

line 73   *fancy:* imagination, especially in its light, superficial sense.

ODE ON A GRECIAN URN (P. 238)

Written in 1819, possibly in May.

line 1   *Thou:* addressed to the ancient Greek urn of the title, a vessel for holding the ashes of the dead, often decorated with scenes from ancient myth or everyday life; such urns usually have black figures on a rust-red background, or rust-red figures on a black background.

line 3   *Sylvan historian:* teller of an old story of woodland life.

line 7   *Tempe:* a beautiful and fertile valley in Thessaly, a region of Greece. *Arcady:* an idyllic sheep-herding region in the Peloponnesus, a region of Greece famous as a setting for much pastoral poetry (see note for line 45, below).

line 8   *maidens loth:* unwilling or reluctant girls.

line 10   *timbrels:* tambourines.

line 29   *cloy'd:* glutted, oversatiated with sweetness.

line 41   *Attic:* Greek. *attitude:* posture. *brede:* anything plaited or interwoven, a braid.

line 45   *Pastoral:* idealized literature about shepherds and their life, often involving shepherds who are poets, lovers, and players of pipes; a mode invented by the ancient Greeks. The urn is called a pastoral because it depicts scenes that might be found in a pastoral story.

ODE TO PSYCHE (P. 240)

Probably written in late April 1819. Keats sent a copy of the poem to his brother George and his wife on or shortly after April 30, with these comments: "The following Poem—the last I have written is the first and the only one with which I have taken even moderate pains—I have for the most part dash'd of[f] my lines in a hurry—This I have done leisurely—I think it reads the more richly for it and will I hope encourage me to write other thing[s] in even a more peac[e]able and healthy spirit. You must recollect that Psyche was not embodied as a goddess before the time of Apulieus [sic] the Platonist who lived after the A[u]gustan age, and consequently the Goddess was never worshipped or sacrificed to with any of the ancient fervour—and perhaps never thought of in the old religion—I am more orthodox tha[n] to let a he[a]then Goddess be so neglected." The letter shows that Keats followed the account of Psyche in his edition of Lemprière's *Bibliotheca Classica:* "a nymph whom Cupid married and carried into a place of bliss, where he long enjoyed her company. Venus put her to death because she had robbed the world of her son; but Jupiter, at the request of Cupid, granted immortality to Psyche. The word signifies *the soul,* and this personification of Psyche is posterior to the Augustan age, though still it is connected with ancient mythology. Psyche is generally represented with the wings of a butterfly, to intimate the lightness of the soul, of which the butterfly is the symbol, and on that account, among the ancients, when a man had just expired, a butterfly appeared fluttering above, as if rising from the mouth of the deceased." The Greek word *psyche* means both "soul" and "butterfly." See also the famous passage on the world as a "vale of Soul-making" in Keats's letter, written a few days before he copied out the poem.

line 1   *numbers:* verses.
line 4   *soft-conchèd:* like a soft seashell.
line 12 *scarce espied:* barely seen.
line 14 *Tyrian:* purple, like the dye made in the ancient Phoenician city of Tyre.
line 16 *pinions:* wings.
line 18 *disjoinèd:* parted from one another.
line 20 *eye-dawn:* awakening. *aurorean love:* early-morning lovemaking.
line 21 *wingèd boy:* Cupid, or Eros, god of love; he is one of the lovers.
line 25 *Olympus' faded hierarchy:* the classical Greek gods and goddesses, who live on Mount Olympus; they are "faded" because they are no longer worshiped.
line 26 *Phoebe's sapphire-region'd star:* the moon; Phoebe is the moon goddess, also called Diana.
line 27 *Vesper:* the evening star, Venus (hence "amorous," since Venus is the goddess of love).
line 30 *virgin-choir:* Diana, the virgin goddess of the moon, was worshiped by virgins.
line 41 *lucent fans:* shining wings.
line 50 *fane:* temple.
line 55 *Fledge:* feather. *steep:* mountainside.
line 57 *Dryads:* in Greek myth, female divinities or spirits residing in trees.
line 62 *Fancy:* imagination. *feign:* invent.
line 66 *casement ope:* window open.

line 67 *Love:* that is, Cupid, or Eros, god of love (see note for line 21, above).

TO AUTUMN (P. 249)

Written at Winchester on September 19, 1819. On September 21, Keats described his inspiration in a letter to J. H. Reynolds: "How beautiful the season is now—How fine the air. A temperate sharpness about it. Really, without joking, chaste weather—Dian skies—I never lik'd stubble fields so much as now—Aye better than the chilly green of the spring. Somehow a stubble plain looks warm—in the same way that some pictures look warm—this struck me so much in my sunday's walk that I composed upon it." "Dian" is Diana, the Greek goddess of chastity, hunting, and the moon.

line 12 *thee:* autumn personified as a woman or goddess. *store:* harvest.
line 15 *winnowing wind:* the wind that blows the chaff from the grain in the process of winnowing.
line 17 *hook:* scythe.
line 18 *swath:* the area of grass or grain cut by a mower's scythe in one sweep.
line 25 *barrèd clouds:* as in a mackerel sky, with rows of cirrocumulus (small, white, rounded) clouds at high altitudes, resembling the pattern on a mackerel's back.
line 28 *sallows:* willows.
line 30 *bourn:* boundary between fields; region.
line 32 *garden-croft:* an enclosed plot of land adjoining a cottage and containing a garden.

ODE ON MELANCHOLY (P. 250)

Probably written in May 1819.

In an earlier version, never published by Keats, the poem began with the following stanza:

Though you should build a bark of dead men's bones,
    And rear a phantom gibbet for a mast,
Stitch creeds together for a sail, with groans
    To fill it out, bloodstained and aghast;
Although your rudder be a Dragon's tail,
    Long sever'd, yet still hard with agony,
Your cordage large uprootings from the skull
    Of bald Medusa; certes you would fail

To find the Melancholy, whether she
  Dreameth in any isle of Lethe dull.

>*should:* were to. *cordage:* ropes. *Medusa:* in Greek myth, a female monster with serpents for hair. *certes:* certainly. *Lethe:* see note for "Isabella," line 436.
>
>*Melancholy:* melancholy (sad thoughtfulness) personified as a goddess—here, ironically, an object of desire; the reader is imagined as searching for her.

line 2   *Wolf's-bane:* a poisonous herb.

line 3   *suffer:* allow.

line 4   *nightshade:* a plant with poisonous berries; also called deadly nightshade. *Proserpine:* in Greek myth, the queen of the underworld.

line 5   *yew-berries:* poisonous red berries of the yew tree or shrub, which often grows in graveyards and is associated with death.

line 6   *beetle:* the deathwatch beetle. *death-moth:* the death's-head moth, which has markings on its wings that resemble a human skull.

line 7   *Psyche:* in Greek myth, the soul, often represented as a butterfly; in Greek, *psyche* means both "soul" and "butterfly." *owl:* a bird sometimes associated with death.

line 8   *mysteries:* secret religious rites.

line 9   *shade:* shadow; spirit, ghost.

line 14   *shroud:* heavy veil; here, suggesting a death shroud, a veil covering the face of a corpse.

line 15   *glut thy sorrow on:* fulfill or satisfy your sorrow by thinking about or gazing upon.

line 18   *thy mistress:* the goddess Melancholy, or perhaps an imagined lover of the reader, or both.

line 28   *palate fine:* the sensitive roof of the mouth; also, a discriminating sense of taste.

line 30   *cloudy trophies:* the souls of Melancholy's previous lovers, kept like trophies of victory, as in classical temples; they are cloudy because they are immaterial.

HYPERION (P. 251)

Written in the autumn of 1818 and abandoned during or before April 1819.

>*Hyperion:* one of the Titans, a race of giants overthrown by the gods of ancient Greek myth; he is the old sun god, the precursor

of Apollo. Apollo takes Hyperion's place and becomes the god of poetry, music, and medicine, as well as the sun.

BOOK I

line 4   *Saturn:* chief of the Titans, also known as Cronus; he overthrew his father, Uranus, or Coelus, and later was himself overthrown, together with his siblings the Titans, by his rebellious son Zeus, or Jupiter, and *his* siblings, the Olympian gods.

line 13   *Naiad:* river nymph.

line 20   *Earth:* Tellus, or Terra, the Earth, is the mother of the Titans: Coelus, Oceanus, Hyperion, Creus, Rhea, Japetus, Themis, Saturn, Phoebe, and Tethys, among others. Coelus, her son (and later her husband), the old god of the heavens, is the father of the Titans.

line 23   *one:* Thea, wife of Hyperion.

line 29   *Achilles:* the Greek hero of the Trojan War.

line 30   *Ixion's wheel:* Jupiter punished Ixion for his insolence by having him tied to an eternally turning wheel in Hades.

line 31   *Memphian:* of Memphis, the second largest city in ancient Egypt. *sphinx:* huge Egyptian sculpture with the head of a woman and the body of a lion.

line 61   *fallen house:* the family of Titans.

line 87   *couchant:* lying down.

line 94   *horrid:* bristling (the Latin meaning of the word).

line 102   *front:* forehead.

line 105   *nervous:* strong, vigorous.

line 138   *fever out:* grow swollen as with fever.

line 146   *Olympus:* mountain in northern Thessaly in Greece; home of the gods.

line 147   *rebel three:* Jupiter, Neptune, and Pluto, Saturn's sons; after they overthrew him they split his kingdom into thirds and became the gods of heaven, the sea, and the underworld, respectively.

line 152   *covert:* hiding place.

line 171   *gloom-bird:* the owl, often considered a bad omen.

line 172   *familiar visiting:* refers to the notion that the spirit of a dead person appears to his or her relatives at the moment of death; or, perhaps, to the well-known feelings ("visitings") of someone hearing the first stroke of his or her own death knell, which was the ringing of a bell when one was close to death, inviting hearers to pray for the soul of the dying person.

line 181   *Aurorian:* lit by Aurora, the dawn.

line 182   *angerly:* angrily. *eagle's wings:* a bad omen.

line 184   *neighing steeds:* a bad omen.

line 216   *Hours:* see note for *Endymion*, Book II, line 688.

lines 227–30   *dreams . . . forms . . . effigies . . . spectres . . . Phantoms:* various synonyms for "ghosts"; considered to be portents of disaster.

line 239   *lucent:* shining.

line 246   *Tellus:* the Earth, mother of the other Titans.

line 274   *colure:* one of two circles that intersect one another at right angles at the poles of a sphere.

line 277   *hieroglyphics old:* here, signs of the zodiac.

line 282   *swart:* black.

line 311   *the powers:* Tellus, the Earth, and Coelus, the old god of the heavens, parents of the Titans, including Hyperion.

line 323   *first-born:* Saturn.

line 326   *wox:* waxed, grew.

line 349   *region-whisper:* whisper from the sky.

Book II

line 4   *Cybele:* daughter of Coelus and Tellus and wife of Saturn; also known as Ops.

line 29   *Mnemosyne:* Memory; she is a daughter of Coelus and Tellus and the mother of the nine Muses, of whom Jupiter is the father.

line 30   *Phœbe:* the moon.

line 52   *at horrid working:* rolling in anguish.

line 53   *Caf:* a huge mountain in Moslem cosmology; Keats's source may be William Beckford's *Vathek*.

line 66   *Enceladus:* strongest of all the giants who conspired to overthrow Jupiter.

line 73   *Atlas:* a Titan who bears the heavens on his shoulders; also a mountain in northwest Africa.

line 74   *Phorcus:* a sea deity, the offspring of Pontus (the Sea) and Terra, or Tellus (the Earth); with his sister Ceto, a sea monster, he fathered various monsters, including the Gorgons. *Gorgons:* monsters with snaky hair, brass hands, wings of gold, lolling red tongues, and tusks; they were so hideous that anyone who glimpsed their faces turned to stone.

line 75   *Oceanus:* the old sea god, usually depicted as an old man with a beard. *Tethys:* sea goddess, wife of Oceanus and mother of all the river gods.

line 76   *Clymene:* daughter of Oceanus and Tethys.

line 77   *Themis:* a Titan.

line 78   *Ops:* Saturn's wife, also known as Cybele.

line 120   *utterless:* unutterable.

line 134   *Uranus:* another name for Coelus, the old god of the heavens and the father of the Titans.

line 191   *chaos:* oldest of all the deities; mother of Tellus, the Earth, and Coelus, the Heavens.

line 192   *intestine broil:* civil war.

line 199   *Heavens:* Coelus. *Earth:* Tellus.

line 232   *young God of the Seas:* Neptune, often represented wielding a trident while riding in a chariot made of a shell, which is drawn by sea horses, dolphins, or winged horses.

line 244   *posed:* assumed, or pretended.

line 248   *Clymene:* see note for Book II, line 76, above.

line 304   *Enceladus:* see note for Book II, line 66, above.

line 341   *the wingèd thing:* victory, represented as a woman or goddess with wings.

Book III

line 2   *Amazèd:* stunned, bewildered, terrified.

line 10   *Delphic:* see note for *Endymion,* Book I, line 499.

line 12   *Dorian:* an ancient Greek mode of music characterized by simplicity and solemnity, usually played on flutes and recorders.

line 13   *the Father of all verse:* Apollo, god of poetry, music, medicine, and the sun.

line 14   *vermeil:* vermilion, bright red.

line 23   *Cyclades:* a group of islands in the Aegean Sea, off Greece. *Delos:* see note for *Endymion,* Book I, line 966.

line 26   *Zephyr:* god of the west wind.

line 29   *Giant of the Sun:* Hyperion.

line 31   *his mother:* Latona.

line 32   *his twin-sister:* Diana, virgin goddess of hunting and the moon.

line 34   *osiers:* willow trees.

line 46   *awful Goddess:* Mnemosyne, or Memory, mother of the Muses.

line 77   *old and sacred thrones:* of the Titans.

line 92   *liegeless:* free, unsubjected.

line 136   Richard Woodhouse commented, "The poem, if completed, would have treated of the dethronement of Hyperion, the former God of the Sun, by Apollo—and incidentally, of those of Oceanus by Neptune, of Saturn by Jupiter, etc.—and of the war of the Giants for Saturn's re-establishment, with other events, of which we have but very dark hints in the mythological poets of Greece and Rome."

ON THE SEA (P. 288)

Written around April 17, 1817. Keats was staying at Carisbrooke, on the Isle of Wight, and was planning to begin work on *Endymion*. He sent the poem in a letter to J. H. Reynolds dated April 17–18, 1817, introducing it by saying he had been "rather *narvus*—and the passage in Lear—'Do you not hear the Sea?' has haunted me intensely" [paraphrased; *King Lear,* IV.vi.4]. After the poem he continues, saying, "I had become all in a Tremble from not having written anything of late—the Sonnet over leaf did me some good."

line 4   *Hecate:* former Titan and goddess identified with Diana and the moon, and hence the tides; also goddess of magic.

line 9   *vext:* vexed, troubled, strained.

line 12   *cloying:* oppressively sweet.

line 14   *sea nymphs:* female spirits or minor divinities inhabiting the sea. *quired:* choired, sang together.

ON SEEING THE ELGIN MARBLES (P. 291)

Written before March 3, 1817. Keats visited the British Museum with his friend B. R. Haydon and saw marble statues and friezes that had adorned the Parthenon in Athens. They had been brought to England in 1806 by Lord Elgin, and purchased for the museum by the government in 1816.

line 13   *billowy main:* rough sea.

ON SITTING DOWN TO READ 'KING LEAR' ONCE AGAIN (P. 297)

Written on January 22, 1818, while Keats was revising his poem *Endymion: A Poetic Romance*.

line 2   *Syren:* in Greek mythology, a bird-woman whose singing lures sailors to their deaths; in the Greek poetic romance known as the

Argonautica, Orpheus, the archetypal poet, drowns out the Sirens with his lyre and saves the Argonauts. Some authors tell how the Sirens once had a singing contest with the Muses (the goddesses who inspire artists); the Muses won, and crowned themselves with Siren feathers.

line 9   *Albion:* the old Celtic name for England; *King Lear* is set in Celtic England.

line 14   *Phœnix:* the mythical bird that, after living for five hundred years, burns itself to ashes on a pyre of twigs ignited by the sun, fanning the flames with its own wings—and then rises again from its ashes with renewed youth to live another five hundred years.

'WHEN I HAVE FEARS THAT I MAY CEASE TO BE' (P. 301)

Written between January 22 and 31, 1818.

line 2   *glean'd:* collected the grain scattered in the field after the harvest.

line 3   *charactery:* printed words; writing.

line 4   *garners:* storehouses or granaries.

line 11   *faery:* magical.

TO HOMER (P. 308)

Probably written in April 1818.

Homer: Greek epic poet (9th–8th? cent. B.C.E.), presumed author of the *Iliad* and the *Odyssey.* He is believed to have been blind.

line 2   *Cyclades:* see note for *Hyperion,* Book III, line 23.

line 6   *Jove:* Jupiter or Zeus, chief of the gods of Olympus; god of the sky.

line 7   *Neptune:* god of the sea. *spumy:* foamy.

line 8   *Pan:* god of pastoral, earthly nature.

line 14   *Dian:* Diana, virgin goddess of hunting and the moon; in later cults, she was worshiped as the goddess of nature, the moon, and the underworld.

TO SLEEP (P. 346)

Probably written in April 1819.

line 1   *embalmer:* one who preserves a corpse from decay by filling it with preservatives, often including balms and aromatic oils; also, a source of balm, that is, something soothing and fragrant.

line 5   *soothest:* most soothing; smoothest.

line 7   *poppy:* here, the narcotic drug opium, made from dried poppy juice.

line 11   *curious:* scrupulous.

line 13   *wards:* the ridges inside a lock that fit to the notches of the key.

line 14   *casket:* small, often ornamental box or chest for holding such things as jewels and letters, commonly, as here, secured with a lock.

'WHY DID I LAUGH TO-NIGHT?' (P. 346)

Written before March 19, 1819. Keats introduced the poem to his brother and sister-in-law in a letter as follows: "I am ever affraid that your anxiety for me will lead you to fear for the violence of my temperament continually smothered down: for that reason I did not intend to have sent you the following sonnet—but look over the last two pages and ask yourselves whether I have not that in me which will well bear the buffets of the world. It will be the best comment on my sonnet; it will show you that it was written with no Agony but that of ignorance; with no thirst of any thing but knowledge when pushed to the point though the first steps to it were throug[h] my human passions—they went away, and I wrote with my Mind—and perhaps I must confess a little bit of my heart—... I went to bed, and enjoyed an uninterrupted sleep—Sane I went to bed and sane I arose."

line 10   *fancy:* imagination.

line 12   *ensigns:* banners, flags.

LA BELLE DAME SANS MERCI (P. 353)

Written on April 21, 1819.

La belle dame sans merci: The beautiful lady without pity. The title is taken from a medieval French poem by Alain Chartier.

line 3   *sedge:* expanse of grasslike plants that grow in wet areas.

line 18   *Zone:* belt.

line 25   *relish:* flavor.

line 26   *manna:* in the Bible, the substance miraculously supplied as food to the Israelites in the wilderness; by extension, an unexpected benefit, spiritual nourishment.

line 29   *elfin:* enchanted. *grot:* grotto, small picturesque cave.
line 35   *latest:* last.
line 41   *starv'd:* dead; thin. *gloam:* twilight.
line 45   *sojourn:* travel.

'IF BY DULL RHYMES OUR ENGLISH MUST BE CHAIN'D' (P. 355)

Written in late April or early May 1819. Keats included the poem in a letter to George and Georgiana Keats in which he remarked, "I have been endeavouring to discover a better sonnet stanza than we have. The legitimate [Petrarchan] does not suit the language over-well from the pouncing rhymes—the other kind [Shakespearean] appears too elegiac—and the couplet at the end of it has seldom a pleasing effect—I do not pretend to have succeeded—It will explain itself."

line 2   *Andromeda:* see note for *Endymion*, Book IV, line 602.
line 7   *Lyre:* a small U-shaped harp, played usually with a plectrum (a pick) to accompany the voice; lyric poems, originally sung while playing the lyre, derive their name from it.
line 9   *meet:* appropriate.
line 11   *Midas:* the legendary King Midas, a notorious miser.
line 12   *bay wreath crown:* garland of leaves from the bay tree, symbolizing success in poetry.

ODE ON INDOLENCE (P. 358)

Probably written in late May or early June 1819. The poem was inspired by Keats's rereading of a passage in a letter he had written on March 19, 1819, to George and Georgiana Keats: "This morning I am in a sort of temper indolent and supremely careless. . . . Neither Poetry, nor Ambition, nor Love have any alertness of countenance as they pass by me: they seem rather like three figures on a greek vase—a Man and two women—whom no one but myself could distinguish in their disguisement. This is the only happiness; and is a rare instance of advantage in the body overpowering the Mind."

They toil not, neither do they spin.: from Matthew 6:28, in which Jesus urges his hearers not to be anxious, saying, "Consider the lilies of the field, how they grow; they toil not, neither do they spin."
line 9   *betide:* happen.

line 10 *Phidian:* Phidias was the great Athenian sculptor who designed the marble sculptures for the Parthenon in the fifth century B.C.E.

line 11 *Shadows:* images, spirits, ghosts.

line 12 *mask:* here, a pantomime, a dramatic entertainment without dialogue.

line 31 *forsooth:* indeed, in truth.

line 38 *annoy:* harm, pain; annoyance.

line 44 *baffled beams:* impeded sunbeams.

line 48 *throstle's lay:* thrush's song.

line 53 *dieted:* fed.

line 59 *spright:* spirit.

'THIS LIVING HAND, NOW WARM AND CAPABLE' (P. 365)

Probably written in November or December 1819. The poem was written on the manuscript of *The Cap and Bells,* and was most likely composed at the same time. It is not clear whether "This living hand" was intended as a complete poem or for use in a later verse play or other poem.

'BRIGHT STAR, WOULD I WERE STEDFAST AS THOU ART' (P. 365)

Probably written in 1819. While on a tour of the Lake Country of England in 1818, Keats saw Lake Windermere, and remarked in a letter to his brother Tom, dated 25–27 June 1818, "the two views we have had of it are of the most noble tenderness—they can never fade away—they make one forget the divisions of life; age, youth, poverty and riches; and refine one's sensual vision into a sort of north star which can never cease to be open lidded and stedfast over the wonders of the great Power." He copied this poem into his volume of Shakespeare's poems around the end of September or the beginning of October 1820 while in Italy, on his way to his death from tuberculosis.

line 4 *Eremite:* religious hermit.

line 6 *ablution:* washing, purification as part of a religious ceremony.

THE FALL OF HYPERION: A VISION (P. 373)

Written beginning in mid-July 1819 at Shanklin on the Isle of Wight; abandoned around September 21 the same year.

Canto I

line 1   *Fanatics:* religious zealots.

line 3   *fashion:* fashionings.

line 35   *fabled horn:* the horn of plenty; see note for *Lamia,* Part II, line 187. Ceres is the mother of Proserpine.

line 37   *Proserpine:* see note for *Endymion,* Book I, line 944.

line 47   *Asian poppy:* opium.

line 48   *Caliphat:* council of caliphs, Islamic civil and religious rulers, who sometimes poisoned one another in their struggles for power.

line 50   *scarlet conclave:* the College of Cardinals of the Catholic Church, also sometimes the scene of political murders.

line 56   *Silenus:* see note for *Endymion,* Book IV, line 228.

line 68   *superannuations:* things that are too old, obsolete; here, ruins.

line 70   *faulture:* broken ruins.

line 71   *To:* compared to.

line 74   *asbestos:* nonflammable fiber.

line 75   *that place the moth could not corrupt:* heaven; a reference to Matthew 6:20: "Lay up for yourselves treasures in heaven, where neither moth nor rust doth corrupt."

line 77   *imageries:* patterns woven into the cloth.

line 78   *in a mingled heap:* worshipers used to lay offerings to the gods on the floors of ancient Greek temples.

line 88   *An image:* a statue of Saturn, chief of the Titans; the Titans were overthrown by the gods, led by Saturn's son Jupiter.

line 91   *travail:* work, travel.

line 96   *One ministering:* Moneta, the priestess of the temple; her name is Latin for "the admonisher."

line 103 *Maian incense:* a scent like that of May flowers; Maia is the goddess of May.

line 116 *gummèd leaves:* leaves covered in aromatic gum or sap.

line 135 *As once fair angels on a ladder flew:* in Genesis 28:12, Jacob sees angels, in a dream, going up and down a ladder reaching from heaven to earth.

line 137 *hornèd shrine:* altar adorned with horns on its corners.

line 144 *dated on:* postponed.

line 152 *fane:* temple.

line 155 *sooth:* smooth; true.

line 203 *Pythia:* the priestess and oracle of Apollo at Delphi; she delivered the answers of the god to those who consulted her, often with great fury, howling and crying out. *spleen:* anger, ill humor.

line 204 *Apollo:* god of poetry, music, medicine, and the sun.

line 205 *misty pestilence:* Apollo was the god who inflicted plagues, appearing surrounded by clouds when he did so.

line 222 *Is all spared:* is all that is spared. *war:* the war between the gods and Titans.

line 245 *swooning vivid:* so vivid as to make one swoon.

line 246 *electral:* electrical.

line 267 *visionless:* unseeing.

line 283 *adorant:* adoring.

line 285 *golden age:* the Golden Age of Saturn's rule.

line 288 *Omega:* the final letter of the Greek alphabet.

line 303 *ken:* range of vision.

line 308 *half-unravell'd web:* half-revealed pattern; or half-unraveled weave (as of a tapestry).

line 312 *zoning:* course; the (apparent) circling of the sun around the earth.

line 317 *Naiad:* river nymph.

line 326 *ancient mother:* Tellus, or Terra, the Earth, mother of the Titans.

line 331 *Mnemosyne:* goddess of memory, mother of the nine Muses; here, an alternative name for Moneta. See line 282 above, where Moneta is called "Shade of Memory."

line 335 *Thea:* Hyperion's sister and wife.

line 337 *Surpassing:* taller than.

line 341 *vanward:* front-line.

line 362 *captious at:* taking exception to.

line 367 *space:* moment.

line 368 *me thoughtless:* how thoughtless of me.

line 411 *Pan:* the god of pastoral nature.

line 425 *Cybele:* Saturn's sister and wife, mother of the gods.

line 431 *those imps:* Saturn's rebellious children, the gods.

line 435 *proclaim:* proclamation.

line 458 *grow:* emerge.

CANTO 2

line 15 *orbèd fire:* the sun; Hyperion was the sun god.

line 18 *dire prodigies:* terrifying omens.

line 20 *gloom-bird:* owl.

line 21 *familiar visiting:* refers to the notion that the spirit of a dead person appears to his or her relatives at the moment of death; or, perhaps, to the well-known feelings ("visitings") of someone hearing the first stroke of his or her own death knell, which was the ringing of a bell when one was close to death, inviting hearers to pray for the soul of the dying person.

line 29 *Aurorian:* lit up by Aurora, the dawn.

line 30 *angerly:* angrily.

line 50 *Mnemosyne:* Moneta.

line 60 *hours:* see note for *Endymion,* Book II, line 688.

line 61 the manuscript breaks off at this point.

Sources

The Compact Oxford English Dictionary, 2nd ed. Oxford: Oxford University Press, 1989, 1991.

Keats, John. *Letters of John Keats: A Selection.* Edited by Robert Gittings. Oxford: Oxford University Press, 1970.

Tripp, Edward. *The Meridian Handbook of Classical Mythology.* New York: Penguin Meridian, 1970, 1974.

INDEX OF TITLES

First lines are shown in roman type; titles in *italic* type

INDEX OF FIRST LINES

COMMENTARY

LEIGH HUNT

JOHN WILSON CROKER

Z. [JOHN GIBSON LOCKHART]

MATTHEW ARNOLD

T. S. ELIOT

WALTER JACKSON BATE

LEIGH HUNT

Many of our readers ... have perhaps observed for themselves, that there has been a new school of poetry rising of late, which promises to extinguish the French one that has prevailed among us since the time of Charles the 2d. It began with something excessive, like most revolutions, but this gradually wore away; and an evident aspiration after real nature and original fancy remained, which called to mind the finer times of the English Muse. In fact it is wrong to call it a new school, and still more so to represent it as one of innovation, its only object being to restore the same love of Nature, and of *thinking* instead of mere *talking,* which formerly rendered us real poets, and not merely versifying wits, and bead-rollers of couplets. ...

The object of the present article is merely to notice three young writers, who appear to us to promise a considerable addition of strength to the new school.

The last of [the] young aspirants whom we have met with, and who promise to help the new school to revive Nature and

> To put a spirit of youth in every thing,—

is, we believe, the youngest of them all, and just of age. His name is JOHN KEATS. He has not yet published any thing except in a newspaper; but a set of his manuscripts was handed us the other day, and fairly surprised us with the truth of their ambition, and ardent grappling with Nature. In the following Sonnet there is one incorrect rhyme, which might be easily altered, but which shall serve in the mean time as a peace-offering to the rhyming critics. The rest of the composition, with the exception of a little vagueness in calling the regions of poetry "the realms of gold," we do not hesitate to pronounce excellent, especially the last six lines. The word *swims* is complete; and the whole conclusion is equally powerful and quiet:—

ON FIRST LOOKING INTO CHAPMAN'S HOMER.

> Much have I travel'd in the realms of Gold,
> And many goodly States and Kingdoms seen;
> Round many western Islands have I been,
> Which Bards in fealty to Apollo hold;

But of one wide expanse had I been told,
That deep-brow'd Homer ruled as his demesne;
Yet could I never judge what men could mean,
Till I heard Chapman speak out loud and bold.
Then felt I like some watcher of the skies,
When a new planet swims into his ken;
Or like stout Cortez, when with eagle eyes
He stared at the Pacific,—and all his men
Looked at each other with a wild surmise,—
Silent, upon a peak in Darien. . . .

We have spoken with the less scruple of these poetical promises, because we really are not in the habit of lavishing praises and announcements, and because we have no fear of any pettier vanity on the part of young men, who promise to understand human nature so well.

From *The Examiner*, December 1, 1816

JOHN WILSON CROKER

Reviewers have been sometimes accused of not reading the works which they affected to criticise. On the present occasion we shall anticipate the author's complaint, and honestly confess that we have not read [*Endymion: A Poetic Romance*]. Not that we have been wanting in our duty—far from it—indeed, we have made efforts almost as superhuman as the story itself appears to be, to get through it; but with the fullest stretch of our perseverance, we are forced to confess that we have not been able to struggle beyond the first of the four books of which this Poetic Romance consists. We should extremely lament this want of energy, or whatever it may be, on our parts, were it not for one consolation—namely, that we are no better acquainted with the meaning of the book through which we have so painfully toiled, than we are with that of the three which we have not looked into.

It is not that Mr. Keats, (if that be his real name, for we almost doubt that any man in his senses would put his real name to such a rhapsody,) it is not, we say, that the author has not powers of language, rays of fancy, and gleams of genius—he has all these; but he is unhappily a disciple of the new school of what has been somewhere called Cockney poetry; which may be defined to consist of the most incongruous ideas in the most uncouth language. . . .

[Mr. Keats] is a copyist of Mr. Hunt; but he is more unintelligible, almost as rugged, twice as diffuse, and ten times more tiresome and absurd than his prototype, who, though he impudently presumed to seat himself in the chair of criticism, and to measure his own poetry by his own standard, yet generally had a meaning. But Mr. Keats had advanced no dogmas which he was bound to support by examples: his nonsense therefore is quite gratuitous; he writes it for its own sake, and, being bitten by Mr. Leigh Hunt's insane criticism, more than rivals the insanity of his poetry. . . .

Of the story we have been able to make out but little it seems to be mythological, and probably relates to the loves of Diana and Endymion; but of this, as the scope of the work has altogether escaped us, we cannot speak with any degree of certainty; and must therefore content ourselves with giving some instances of its diction and versification:—and here again we are perplexed and puzzled.—At first it appeared to us, that Mr. Keats had been amusing himself and wearying his readers with an immeasurable game at *boutsrimés* [a game in which the player improvises a poem from rhyme words that have been supplied]; but, if we recollect rightly, it is an indispensable condition at this play, that the rhymes when filled up shall have a meaning; and our author, as we have already hinted, has no meaning. He seems to us to write a line at random, and then he follows not the thought excited by this line, but that suggested by the *rhyme* with which it concludes. There is hardly a complete couplet inclosing a complete idea in the whole book. He wanders from one subject to another, from the association, not of ideas but of sounds, and the work is composed of hemistichs which, it is quite evident, have forced themselves upon the author by the mere force of the catchwords on which they turn.

We shall select, not as the most striking instance, but as that least liable to suspicion, a passage from the opening of the poem.

> Such the sun, the moon,
> Trees old and young, sprouting a shady boon
> For simple sheep; and such are daffodils
> With the green world they live in; and clear rills
> That for themselves a cooling covert make
> 'Gainst the hot season: the mid forest brake,
> Rich with a sprinkling of fair musk-rose blooms:
> And such too is the grandeur of the dooms
> We have imagined for the mighty dead; &c. &c. . . .

Here it is clear that the word, and not the idea, *moon* produced the simple sheep and their shady *boon,* and that 'the *dooms* of the mighty dead' would never have intruded themselves but for the '*fair musk-rose blooms.*' . . .

We come now to the author's taste in versification. He cannot indeed write a sentence, but perhaps he may be able to spin a line. Let us see. The following are specimens of his prosodial notions of our English Heroic metre.

> Dear as the temple's self, so does the moon,
> The passion poesy, glories infinite. . . .
> So plenteously all weed-hidden roots. . . .
> Of some strange history, potent to send. . . .
> Before the deep intoxication. . . .
> Her scarf into a fluttering pavilion. . . .

By this time our readers must be pretty well satisfied as to the meaning of his sentences and the structure of his lines: we now present them with some of the new words with which, in imitation of Mr. Leigh Hunt, he adorns our language.

We are told that 'turtles *passion* their voices,' . . . ; that 'an arbour was *nested*,' . . . ; and a lady's locks '*gordian'd* up,' . . .; and to supply the place of the nouns thus verbalized Mr. Keats, with great fecundity, spawns new ones; such as 'men-slugs and human *serpentry*'. . . .

But enough of Mr. Leigh Hunt and his simple neophyte.—If any one should be bold enough to purchase this 'Poetic Romance,' and so much more patient, than ourselves, as to get beyond the first book, and so much more fortunate as to find a meaning, we entreat him to make us acquainted with his success; we shall then return to the task which we now abandon in despair, and endeavour to make all due amends to Mr. Keats and to our readers.

From *The Quarterly Review*, April 1818

Z. [JOHN GIBSON LOCKHART]

Of all the manias of this mad age, the most incurable, as well as the most common, seems to be no other than the *Metromanie*. The just celebrity of Robert Burns and Miss Baillie has had the melancholy effect of turning the heads of we know not how many farm-servants and unmarried ladies; our very footmen compose tragedies, and there is scarcely a superannuated governess in the island that does not leave a roll of lyrics behind her in her band-box. . . . [Mr John Keats] appears to have received from nature talents of an excellent, perhaps even of a superior order—talents which, devoted to the purposes of any useful profession, must have rendered him a respectable, if not an eminent citizen. His friends, we understand, destined him to the career of medicine, and he was bound apprentice some years ago to a worthy apothecary in town. But all has been undone by a sudden attack of the malady to which we have alluded. . . .

The readers of the *Examiner* newspaper were informed, some time ago, by a solemn paragraph, in Mr Hunt's best style, of the appearance of two new stars of glorious magnitude and splendour in the poetical horizon of the land of Cockaigne. One of these turned out, by and by, to be no other than Mr John Keats. This precocious adulation confirmed the wavering apprentice in his desire to quit the gallipots, and at the same time excited in his too susceptible mind a fatal admiration for the character and talents of the most worthless and affected of all the versifiers of our time. One of his first productions was the [opening sonnet in "Poems,"] "*written on the day when Mr. Leigh Hunt left prison.*" . . . The absurdity of the thought in this sonnet is. . . . if possible, surpassed in another, "*addressed to Haydon*" the painter, that clever, but most affected artist, who as little resembles Raphael in genius as he does in person, notwithstanding the foppery of having his hair curled over his shoulders in the old Italian fashion. In this exquisite piece it will be observed, that Mr Keats classes together WORDSWORTH, HUNT, and HAYDON, as the three greatest spirits of the age, and that he alludes to himself, and some others of the rising brood of Cockneys, as likely to attain hereafter an equally honourable elevation. Wordsworth and Hunt! what a juxta-position! The purest, the loftiest, and, we do not fear to say it, the most classical of living English poets, joined together in the same compliment with the meanest, the filthiest, and the most vulgar of Cockney poetasters. No wonder that he who could be guilty of this should class Haydon with Raphael, and himself with Spencer. . . . Above all things, it is most pitiably ridiculous to hear men, of whom their country will always have reason to be proud, reviled by uneducated and flimsy striplings, who are not capable of understanding either their merits, or those of any other *men of power*—fanciful dreaming tea-drinkers, who, without logic enough to analyse a single idea, or imagination enough to form one original image, or learning enough to distinguish between the written language of Englishmen and the spoken jargon of Cockneys, presume to talk with contempt of some of the most exquisite spirits the world ever produced, merely because they did not happen to exert their faculties in laborious affected descriptions of flowers seen in window-pots, or cascades heard at Vauxhall; in short, because they chose to be wits, philosophers, patriots, and poets, rather than to found the Cockney school of versification, morality, and politics, a century before its time. . . .

As for Mr Keats' "Endymion," it has just as much to do with Greece as it has with "old Tartary the fierce;" no man, whose mind has ever been imbued with the smallest knowledge or feeling of classical poetry or classical history, could have stooped to profane and vulgarise every association in the manner which has been adopted by this "son of promise." . . . [We] must inform our readers that this romance is meant to be written in English heroic rhyme. To those who have read any of Hunt's poems, this hint might indeed be needless. Mr. Keats has adopted the loose, nerveless versification, and Cockney rhymes of the poet of Rimini; but in fairness to that gentleman, we must add, that the defects of the system are tenfold more conspicuous in his disciple's work than in his own. Mr Hunt is a small poet, but he is a clever man. Mr Keats is a still smaller poet, and he is only a boy of pretty abilities, which he has done everything in his power to spoil.

And now, good-morrow to "the Muses' son of Promise;" as for "the feats he yet may do," as we do not pretend to say, like himself, "Muse of my native land am I inspired," we shall adhere to the safe old rule of *pauca verba* [few words].

We venture to make one small prophecy, that his bookseller will not a second time venture £50 upon any thing he can write. It is a better and a wiser thing to be a starved apothecary than a starved poet; so back to the shop Mr John, back to "plasters, pills, and ointment boxes," &c. But, for Heaven's sake, young Sangrado, be a little more sparing of extenuatives and soporifics in your practice than you have been in your poetry.

From *Blackwood's Edinburgh Magazine,* August 1818

MATTHEW ARNOLD

Poetry, according to Milton's famous saying, should be "simple, sensuous, impassioned." No one can question the eminency, in Keats's poetry, of the quality of sensuousness. Keats as a poet is abundantly and enchantingly sensuous; the question with some people will be, whether he is anything else? Many things may be brought forward which seem to show him as under the fascination and sole dominion of sense, and desiring nothing better. There is the exclamation in one of his letters: "O for a life of sensations rather than of thoughts!" There is the thesis, in another, "that with a great Poet the sense of Beauty overcomes every other consideration, or rather obliterates all consideration." There is Haydon's story of him, how "he once covered his tongue and throat as far as he could reach with Cayenne pepper, in order to appreciate the delicious coldness of claret in all its glory—his own expression." One is not much surprised when Haydon further tells us, of the hero of such a story, that once for six weeks together he was hardly ever sober. "He had no decision of character," Haydon adds; "no object upon which to direct his great powers."

Character and self-control, the *virtus verusque labor* so necessary for every kind of greatness, and for the great artist, too, indispensable, appear to be wanting, certainly, to this Keats of Haydon's portraiture. They are wanting also to the Keats of the *Letters to Fanny Brawne*. These letters make as unpleasing an impression as Haydon's anecdotes. The editor of Haydon's journals could not well omit what Haydon said of his friend, but for the publication of the *Letters to Fanny Brawne* I can see no good reason whatever. Their publication appears to me, I confess, inexcusable; they ought never to have been published. But published they are, and we have to take notice of them. Letters written when Keats was near his end, under the throttling and unmanning grasp of mortal disease, we will not judge. But here is a letter written some months before he was taken ill. It is printed just as Keats wrote it:—

"You have absorb'd me. I have a sensation at the present moment as though I was dissolving—I should be exquisitely miserable without the hope of soon seeing you. I should be afraid to separate myself far from you. My sweet Fanny, will your heart never change? My love, will it? I have no limit now to my love. . . . Your note came in just here. I cannot be happier away from you. 'Tis richer than an Argosy of Pearles. Do not threat me even in jest. I have been astonished that Men could die Martyrs for religion—I have shuddered at it. I shudder no more—I could be martyred for my Religion—Love is my religion—I could die for that. I could die for you. My Creed is Love and you are its only tenet. You have ravished me away by a Power I cannot resist; and yet I could resist till I saw you; and even since I have seen you I have endeavoured often 'to reason against the reasons of my Love.' I can do that no more—the pain would be too great. My love is selfish. I cannot breathe without you."

A man who writes love-letters in this strain is probable predestined, one may observe, to misfortune in his love-affairs; but that is nothing. The complete enervation of the writer is the real point for remark. We have the tone, or rather the entire want of tone, the abandonment of all reticence and all dignity, of the merely sensuous man, of the man who "is passion's slave." Nay, we have them in such wise that one is tempted to speak even as *Blackwood* or the *Quarterly* were in the old days wont to speak; one is tempted to say that Keats's love-letter is the love-letter of a surgeon's apprentice. It has in its relaxed self-abandonment something underbred and ignoble, as of a youth ill brought up, without the training which teaches us that we must put some constraint upon our feelings and upon the expression of them. It is the sort of love-letter of a surgeon's apprentice which one might hear read out in a breach of promise case, or in the Divorce Court. The sensuous man speaks in it, and the sensuous man of a badly bred and badly trained sort. That many who are themselves also badly bred and badly trained should enjoy it, and should even think it a beautiful and characteristic production of him whom they call their "lovely and beloved Keats," does not make it better. These are the admirers whose pawing and fondness does not good but harm to the fame of Keats; who concentrate attention upon what in him is least wholesome and most questionable; who worship him, and would have the world worship him too, as the poet of

> "Light feet, dark violet eyes, and parted hair,
> Soft dimpled hands, white neck, and creamy breast."

This sensuous strain Keats had, and a man of his poetic powers could not, whatever his strain, but show his talent in it. But he has something more, and something better. We who believe Keats to have been by his promise, at any rate, if not fully by his performance, one of the very greatest of English poets, and who believe also that a merely sensuous man cannot either by promise or by performance be a very great poet, because poetry interprets life, and so large and noble a part of life is outside of such a man's ken,—we cannot but look for signs in him of something more than sensuousness, for signs of character and virtue. And indeed the elements of high character Keats undoubtedly has, and the effort to develop them; the effort is frustrated and cut short by misfortune, and disease, and time, but for the due understanding of Keats's worth the recognition of this effort, and of the elements on which it worked, is necessary.

Lord Houghton, who praises very discriminatingly the poetry of Keats, has on his character also a remark full of discrimination. He says: "The faults of Keats's disposition were precisely the contrary of those attributed to him by common opinion." And he gives a letter written after the death of Keats by his brother George, in which the writer, speaking of the fantastic *Johnny Keats* invented for common opinion by Lord Byron and by the reviewers, declares indignantly: "John was the very soul of manliness and courage, and as much like the Holy Ghost as *Johnny Keats.*" It is important to note this testimony, and to look well for whatever illustrates and confirms it. . . .

Signs of virtue, in the true and large sense of the word, the instinct for virtue passing into the life of Keats and strengthening it, I find in the admirable wisdom and temper of what he says to his friend Bailey on the occasion of a quarrel between Reynolds and Haydon:—

"Things have happened lately of great perplexity; you must have heard of them; Reynolds and Haydon retorting and recriminating, and parting for ever. The same thing has happened between Haydon and Hunt. It is unfortunate; men should bear with each other; there lives not the man who may not be cut up, aye, lashed to pieces, on his weakest side. The best of men have but a portion of good in them. . . . The sure way, Bailey, is first to know a man's faults, and then be passive. If, after that, he insensibly draws you towards him, then you have no power to break the link. Before I felt interested in either Reynolds or Haydon, I was well read in their faults; yet, knowing them, I have been cementing gradually with both. I have an affection for them both, for reasons almost opposite; and to both must I of necessity cling, supported always by the hope that when a little time, a few years, shall have tried me more fully in their esteem, I may be able to bring them together."

Butler has well said that "endeavouring to enforce upon our own minds a practical sense of virtue, or to beget in others that practical sense of it which a man really has himself, is a virtuous *act*." And such an "endeavouring" is that of Keats in those words written to Bailey. It is more than mere words; so justly thought and so discreetly urged as it is, it rises to the height of a virtuous *act*. It is proof of character.

The same thing may be said of some words written to his friend Charles Brown, whose kindness, willingly exerted whenever Keats chose to avail himself of it, seemed to free him from any pressing necessity of earning his own living. Keats felt that he must not allow this state of things to continue. He determined to set himself to "fag on as others do" at periodical literature, rather than to endanger his independence and his self-respect; and he writes to Brown:—

"I had got into a habit of mind of looking towards you as a help in all difficulties. This very habit would be the parent of idleness and difficulties. You will see it is a duty I owe to myself to break the neck of it. I do nothing for my subsistence—make no exertion. At the end of another year you shall applaud me, not for verses, but for conduct."

He had not, alas, another year of health before him when he announced that wholesome resolve; it then wanted but six months of the day of his fatal attack. But in the brief time allowed to him he did what he could to keep his word.

What character, again, what strength and clearness of judgment, in his criticism of his own productions, of the public, and of "the literary circles"! His words after the severe reviews of *Endymion* have often been quoted; they cannot be quoted too often:—

"Praise or blame has but a momentary effect on the man whose love of beauty in the abstract makes him a severe critic on his own works. My own criticism has given me pain without comparison beyond what *Blackwood* or the *Quarterly* could possibly inflict; and also, when I feel I am right, no external praise can give me such a glow as my own solitary reperception and ratification of what is fine. J. S. is perfectly right in regard to the 'slip-shod Endymion.' That it is so is no fault of mine. No! though it may sound a little paradoxical, it is as good as I had power to make it by myself." . . .

Young poets almost inevitably overrate what they call "the might of poesy," and its power over the world which now is. Keats is not a dupe on this matter any more than he is a dupe about the merit of his own performances:—

"I have no trust whatever in poetry. I don't wonder at it; the marvel is to me how people read so much of it."

His attitude towards the public is that of a strong man, not of a weakling avid of praise, and made to "be snuff'd out by an article":—

"I shall ever consider the public as debtors to me for verses, not myself to them for admiration, which I can do without."

And again, in a passage where one may perhaps find fault with the capital letters, but surely with nothing else:—

"I have not the slightest feel of humility towards the public or to anything in existence but the Eternal Being, the Principle of Beauty, and the Memory of great Men. . . . I would be subdued before my friends, and thank them for subduing me; but among multitudes of men I have no feel of stooping; I hate the idea of humility to them. I never wrote one single line of poetry with the least shadow of thought about their opinion. Forgive me for vexing you, but it eases me to tell you: I could not live without the love of my friends; I would jump down Etna for any great public good—but I hate a mawkish popularity. I cannot be subdued before them. My glory would be to daunt and dazzle the thousand jabberers about pictures and books."

Against these artistic and literary "jabberers," amongst whom Byron fancied Keats, probably, to be always living, flattering them and flattered by them, he has yet another outburst:—

"Just so much as I am humbled by the genius above my grasp, am I exalted and look with hate and contempt upon the literary world. Who could wish to be among the commonplace crowd of the little famous, who are each individually lost in a throng made up of themselves?"

And he loves Fanny Brawne the more, he tells her, because he believes that she has liked him for his own sake and for nothing else. "I have met with women who I really think would like to be married to a Poem and to be given away by a Novel."

There is a tone of too much bitterness and defiance in all this, a tone which he with great propriety subdued and corrected when he wrote his beautiful preface to *Endymion*. But the thing to be seized is that Keats had flint and iron in him, that he had character; that he was, as his brother George says, "as much like the Holy Ghost as *Johnny Keats*,"—as that imagined sensuous weakling, the delight of the literary circles of Hampstead. . . .

And of Milton, instead of resting in Milton's incomparable phrases, Keats could say, although indeed all the while "looking upon fine phrases," as he himself tells us, "like a lover"—

"Milton had an exquisite passion for what is properly, in the sense of ease and pleasure, poetical luxury; and with that, it appears to me, he would fain have been content, if he could, so doing, preserve his self-respect and feeling of duty performed; but there was working in him, as it were, that same sort of thing which operates in the great world to the end of a prophecy's being accomplished. Therefore he devoted himself rather to the ardours than the pleasures of song, solacing himself at intervals with cups of old wine."

In his own poetry, too, Keats felt that place must be found for "the ardours rather than the pleasures of song," although he was aware that he was not yet ripe for it—

> "But my flag is not unfurl'd
>   On the Admiral-staff, and to philosophise
>   I dare not yet."

Even in his pursuit of "the pleasures of song," however, there is that stamp of high work which is akin to character, which is character passing into intellectual production. "*The best sort of poetry*—that," he truly says, "is all I care for, all I live for." It is curious to observe how this severe addiction of his to the best sort of poetry affects him with a certain coldness, as if the addiction had been to mathematics, towards those prime objects of a sensuous and passionate poet's regard, love and women. He speaks of "the opinion I have formed of the generality of women, who appear to me as children to whom I would rather give a sugar-plum than my time." He confesses "a tendency to class women in my books with roses and sweetmeats—they never see themselves dominant"; and he can understand how the unpopularity of his poems may be in part due to "the offence which the ladies," not unnaturally "take at him" from this cause. Even to Fanny Brawne he can write "a flint-worded letter" when his "mind is heaped to the full" with poetry:—

"I know the generality of women would hate me for this; that I should have so unsoftened, so hard a mind as to forget them; forget the brightest realities for the dull imaginations of my own brain. . . . My heart seems now made of iron—I could not write a proper answer to an invitation to Idalia."

The truth is that "the yearning passion for the Beautiful," which was with Keats, as he himself truly says, the master-passion, is not a passion of the sensuous or sentimental man, is not a passion of the sensuous or sentimental poet. It is an intellectual and spiritual passion. It is "connected and made one," as

Keats declares that in his case it was, "with the ambition of the intellect." It is, as he again says, "the mighty *abstract idea* of Beauty in all things." And in his last days Keats wrote: "If I should die, I have left no immortal work behind me—nothing to make my friends proud of my memory; *but I have loved the principle of beauty in all things,* and if I had had time I would have made myself remembered." He *has* made himself remembered, and remembered as no merely sensuous poet could be; and he has done it by having "loved the principle of beauty in all things."

For to see things in their beauty is to see things in their truth, and Keats knew it. "What the Imagination seizes as Beauty must be Truth," he says in prose; and in immortal verse he has said the same thing—

"Beauty is truth, truth beauty,—that is all
Ye know on earth, and all ye need to know."

No, it is not all; but it is true, deeply true, and we have deep need to know it. And with beauty goes not only truth, joy goes with her also; and this too Keats saw and said, as in the famous first line of his *Endymion* it stands written—

"A thing of beauty is a joy for ever."

It is no small thing to have so loved the principle of beauty as to perceive the necessary relation of beauty with truth, and of both with joy. Keats was a great spirit, and counts for far more than many even of his admirers suppose, because this just and high perception made itself clear to him. Therefore a dignity and a glory shed gleams over his life, and happiness, too, was not a stranger to it. "Nothing startles me beyond the moment," he says; "the setting sun will always set me to rights, or if a sparrow come before my window I take part in its existence and pick about the gravel." But he had terrible bafflers—consuming disease and early death. "I think," he writes to Reynolds, "if I had a free and healthy and lasting organisation of heart, and lungs as strong as an ox's, so as to be able to bear unhurt the shock of extreme thought and sensation without weariness, I could pass my life very nearly alone, though it should last eighty years. But I feel my body too weak to support me to the height; I am obliged continually to check myself, and be nothing." He had against him even more than this; he had against him the blind power which we call Fortune. "O that something fortunate," he cries in the closing months of his life, "had ever happened to me or my brothers!—then I might hope,—but despair is forced upon me as a habit." So baffled and so sorely tried,—while laden, at the same time, with a mighty formative thought requiring health, and many days, and favouring circumstances, for its adequate manifestation,—what wonder if the achievement of Keats be partial and incomplete?

Nevertheless, let and hindered as he was, and with a short term and imperfect experience,—"young," as he says of himself, "and writing at random, straining after particles of light in the midst of a great darkness, without knowing the bearing of any one assertion, of any one opinion,"—notwithstanding all this, by virtue of his feeling for beauty and of his perception of the vital connection of beauty with truth, Keats accomplished so much in poetry, that in one of the two great modes by which poetry interprets, in the faculty of naturalistic interpretation, in what we call natural magic, he ranks with Shakespeare. "The tongue of Kean," he says in an admirable criticism of that great actor and of his enchanting elocution, "the tongue of Kean must seem to have robbed the Hybla bees and left them honeyless. There is an indescribable *gusto* in his voice;—in *Richard,* 'Be stirring with the lark to-morrow, gentle Norfolk!' comes from him as through the morning atmosphere towards which he yearns." This magic, this "indescribable *gusto* in the voice," Keats himself, too, exhibits in his poetic expression. No one else in English poetry, save Shakespeare, has in expression quite the fascinating felicity of Keats, his perfection of loveliness. "I think," he said humbly, "I shall be among the English poets after my death." He is; he is with Shakespeare.

For the second great half of poetic interpretation, for that faculty of moral interpretation which is in Shakespeare, and is informed by him with the same power of beauty as his naturalistic interpretation, Keats was not ripe. For the architectonics of poetry, the faculty which presides at the evolution of works like the *Agamemnon* or *Lear,* he was not ripe. His *Endymion,* as he himself well saw, is a failure, and his *Hyperion,* fine things as it contains, is not a success. But in shorter things, where the matured power of moral interpretation, and the high architectonics which go with complete poetic development, are not required, he is perfect. The poems which follow prove it,—prove it far better by themselves than anything which can be said about them will prove it. Therefore I have chiefly spoken here of the man, and of the elements in him which explain the production of such work. Shakespearian work it is; not imitative, indeed, of Shakespeare, but Shakespearian, because its expression has that rounded perfection and felicity of loveliness of which Shakespeare is the great master. To show such work is to praise it.

From "John Keats," in Essays in Criticism, 1880

T. S. ELIOT

Keats [is] a singular figure in a varied and remarkable period.

Keats seems to me also a great poet. I am not happy about *Hyperion:* it contains great lines, but I do not know whether it is a great poem. The Odes—especially perhaps the *Ode to Psyche*—are enough for his reputation. But I am not so much concerned with the degree of his greatness as with its kind; and its kind is manifested more clearly in his Letters than in his poems; and in contrast with the kinds we have been reviewing, it seems to me to be much more the kind of Shakespeare. The Letters are certainly the most notable and the most important ever written by any English poet. Keats's egotism, such as it is, is that of youth which time would have redeemed. His letters are what letters ought to be: the fine things come in unexpectedly, neither introduced nor shown out, but between trifle and trifle. His observations suggested by Wordsworth's *Gypsey*, in a letter to Bailey of 1817, are of the finest quality of criticism, and the deepest penetration:

> It seems to me that if Wordsworth had thought a little deeper at that moment, he would not have written the poem at all. I should judge it to have been written in one of the most comfortable moods of his life—it is a kind of sketchy intellectual landscape, not a search for truth.

And in a letter to the same correspondent a few days later he says:

> In passing, however, I must say one thing that has pressed upon me lately, and increased my Humility and capability of submission—and that is this truth—Men of Genius are great as certain ethereal chemicals operating on the Mass of neutral intellect—but they have not any individuality, any determined character—I would call the top and head of those who have a proper self Men of Power.

This is the sort of remark, which, when made by a man so young as was Keats, can only be called the result of genius. There is hardly one statement of Keats about poetry, which, when considered carefully and with due allowance for the difficulties of communication, will not be found to be true: and what is more, true for greater and more mature poetry than anything that Keats ever wrote.

But I am being tempted into a descant upon the general brilliance and profundity of the observations scattered through Keats's letters, and should probably be tempted further into remarking upon their merit as models of correspondence (not that one should ever take a model in letter-writing) and their revelation of a charming personality. My design, in this very narrow frame, has been only to refer to them as evidence of a very different kind of poetic mind than any of those I have just been considering [William Wordsworth and Percy Bysshe Shelley]. Keats's sayings about poetry, thrown out in the course of private correspondence, keep pretty close to intuition; and they have no apparent bearing upon his own times, as he himself does not appear to have taken any absorbing interest in public affairs—though when he did turn to such matters, he brought to bear a shrewd and penetrating intellect. Wordsworth had a very delicate sensibility to social life and social changes. Wordsworth and Shelley both theorise. Keats has no theory, and to have formed one was irrelevant to his interests, and alien to his mind. If we take either Wordsworth or Shelley as representative of his age, as being a voice of the age, we cannot so take Keats. But we cannot accuse Keats of any withdrawal, or refusal; he was merely about his business. He had no theories, yet in the sense appropriate to the poet, in the same sense, though to a lesser degree than Shakespeare, he had a 'philosophic' mind. He was occupied only with the highest use of poetry; but that does not imply that poets of other types may not rightly and sometimes by obligation be concerned about the other uses.

> From "Shelley and Keats," in *The Use of Poetry and the Use of Criticism:*
> *Studies in the Relation of Criticism to Poetry in England,* 1933

WALTER JACKSON BATE

The second and longer of the crucial parts of the "Negative Capability" letter is preceded by some more remarks about what [Keats] has been doing since his brothers left, and the remarks provide a significant preface. He had dinner—"I have been out too much lately"—with "Horace Smith & met his two Brothers with [Thomas] Hill & [John] Kingston & one [Edward] Du Bois."

Partly because he himself was so direct and—as Bailey said—"transparent," he was ordinarily tolerant of the more innocent affectations by which people hope to establish superiority. Moreover, such affectations appealed to his enormous relish for the idiosyncratic. As the next year passed, the very futility of such brief postures—the pointless intricacy of these doomed stratagems—against the vast backdrop of a universe of constantly unfolding "uncertainties, Mysteries, doubts," was also to take on a pathos for him. In fact, only a month after he tells his brothers about this dinner with Horace Smith and his literary friends, he was to write Bailey, speaking of "Reynolds and Haydon retorting and recriminating—and parting for ever—the same thing has happened between Haydon and Hunt":

> Men should bear with each other—there lives not the Man who may not be cut
> up, aye lashed to pieces on his weakest side. The best of Men have but a por-
> tion of good in them—a kind of spiritual yeast in their frames which creates

the ferment of existence—by which a Man is propell'd to act and strive and buffet with Circumstance.

Even so, during these important transitional months he is entering, moments inevitably occur when the familiar comic sense and the deepening charity are suspended. Affectations particularly bother him at such moments. It is a great pity, as he tells Haydon (March 21), that "people should by associating themselves with the fine[st] things, spoil them—Hunt has damned Hampstead [and] Masks and Sonnets and [I]talian tales—Wordsworth ha[s] damned the lakes," and so on. Hazlitt is "your only good damner," because he damns in a different spirit. And Keats was enormously—almost amusingly—disturbed when Reynolds told him that his self-defensive Preface to *Endymion* savored of "affectation" in its own way. Keats kept protesting that, whatever else it showed, it certainly did not show "affectation," though he at once began anxiously to rewrite it.

So at Horace Smith's dinner, which he describes to George and Tom, where he met five other men of literary interests. Their entire way of talking about literature fatigued him for the moment. The possible uses of literature seemed frozen into posture, into mannerism. Given his attempts to approach his new ideal of "disinterestedness," and the thoughts of "Humility" and of openness to amplitude that had become more specific, even more convinced, within the last few months, the gathering typified the exact opposite of what was wanted:

> They only served to convince me, how superior humour is to wit in respect to enjoyment—These men say things which make one start, without making one feel, they are all alike; their manners are alike; they all know fashionables; they have a mannerism in their very eating & drinking, in their mere handling a Decanter—They talked of Kean & his low company—Would I were with that company instead of yours said I to myself! I know such like acquaintance will never do for me.

But his humor was to return when he found himself again in Kingston's company at Haydon's a week and a half afterwards. The "mannerism" in the "mere handling a Decanter" had caught his fancy as a symbol of the entire evening. At Haydon's, as he gleefully told George and Tom, "I astonished Kingston at supper . . . keeping my two glasses at work in a knowing way."

Shortly after Smith's literary party, he went to the Christmas pantomime at Drury Lane with Charles Brown and Charles Dilke. Walking with them back to Hampstead, he found himself having not a dispute but a disquisition with Dilke, on various subjects; several things dovetailed in my mind, & at once it struck me, what quality went to form a Man of Achievement especially in Literature & which Shakespeare possessed so enormously—I mean *Negative Capability*, that is when man is capable of being in uncertainties, Mysteries, doubts, without any irritable reaching after fact & reason—Coleridge, for instance, would let go by a fine isolated verisimilitude caught from the Penetralium of mystery, from being incapable of remaining content with half knowledge. This pursued through Volumes would perhaps take us no further than this, that with a great poet the sense of Beauty overcomes every other consideration, or rather obliterates all consideration.

Using what we know of the background, we could paraphrase these famous sentences as follows. In our life of uncertainties, where no one system or formula can explain everything—where even a word is at best, in Bacon's phrase, a "wager of thought"—what is needed is an imaginative openness of mind and heightened receptivity to reality in its full and diverse concreteness. This, however, involves negating one's own ego. Keats's friend Dilke, as he said later, "was a Man who cannot feel he has a personal identity unless he has made up his Mind about everything. The only means of strengthening one's intellect is to make up ones mind about nothing—to let the mind be a thoroughfare for all thoughts. ... Dilke will never come at a truth as long as he lives; because he is always trying at it." To be dissatisfied with such insights as one may attain through this openness, to reject them unless they can be wrenched into a part of a systematic structure of one's own making, is an egoistic assertion of one's own identity. The remark, "without any irritable reaching after fact and reason," is often cited as though the pejorative words are "fact and reason," and as though uncertainties were being preferred for their own sake. But the significant word, of course, is "irritable." We should also stress "capable"—"capable of being in uncertainties, Mysteries, doubts" without the "irritable" need to extend our identities and rationalize our "half knowledge."* For a "great poet" especially, a sympathetic absorption in the essential significance of his object (caught and relished in that active cooperation of the mind in which the emerging "Truth" is felt as "Beauty," and in which the harmony of the human imagination and its object is attained) "overcomes every other con-

---

*The mention of Coleridge's allowing "a fine isolated verisimilitude" to "go by" seems ludicrously inept, though forgivable considering how little Keats had read of him. However much Coleridge yearned for system, he could never attain it simply because he was able to let so little "go by"; and the glory of his critical writing consists in its numerous "isolated verisimilitudes."

sideration" (considerations that an "irritable reaching after fact and reason" might otherwise itch to pursue). Indeed, it goes beyond and "obliterates" the act of "consideration"—of deliberating, analyzing, and piecing experience together through "consequitive reasoning."

From *John Keats,* 1963

STUDY GUIDE

1. Compare the speakers of "Ode on a Grecian Urn" and "Ode to a Nightingale." How would you describe each speaker's state of mind? In both poems, something exterior to the speaker serves as a catalyst for a vision. What is the vision that each speaker experiences? Are these visions compatible or competing? Discuss why it might be significant that "Ode on a Grecian Urn" ends with a statement while "Ode to a Nightingale" ends with a question.

2. Consider the role of the human senses in Keats's poems. Compare two or more poems that invoke the senses (such as "Ode to a Nightingale" or "The Eve of St. Agnes"). Why are the senses important? Do the poems value certain senses more than others? What is the relationship between the senses and poetic imagination/poetic insight that each of these poems offers?

3. Discuss the role of female figures in Keats's poems. Examine poems such as "The Eve of St. Agnes," and "La Belle Dame sans Merci." How are female figures used in each?

4. Consider Keats's letters as a statement of poetics. Discuss, in particular, Keats's letter to Richard Woodhouse, in which he claims, "A Poet is the most unpoetical of any thing in existence, because he has no Identity." What does he mean by this? What does he imagine is the poet's function

in society—interpreter? creator? visionary? What, according to Keats, motivates the poet to write? Discuss his claim that, "I feel assured I should write from the mere yearning and fondness I have for the Beautiful even if my night's labours should be burnt every morning and no eye ever shine upon them."

5. Discuss Keats's definition of "Negative Capability" in his letter to George and Thomas Keats. What is Negative Capability, and who, according to Keats, possesses it? How might Negative Capability be related to his notion that the poet "has no identity"?

6. Keats's first collection of poems, published in 1817, received a barrage of negative criticism from Tory politicians. Examine John Wilson Croker's and John Gibson Lockhart's critiques of Keats's poems. What, specifically, do they find so offensive about Keats's language? What do they think is the appropriate language for poetry? In what ways does Keats's assertion that "with a great poet the sense of Beauty overcomes every other consideration, or rather obliterates all consideration" threaten Croker's and Lockhart's assumptions about poetry?

MODERN LIBRARY IS ONLINE AT WWW.MODERNLIBRARY.COM

MODERN LIBRARY ONLINE IS YOUR GUIDE
TO CLASSIC LITERATURE ON THE WEB

THE MODERN LIBRARY E-NEWSLETTER

Our free e-mail newsletter is sent to subscribers, and features sample chapters, interviews with and essays by our authors, upcoming books, special promotions, announcements, and news.

To subscribe to the Modern Library e-newsletter, send a blank e-mail to: **sub_modernlibrary@info.randomhouse.com** or visit **www.modernlibrary.com**

THE MODERN LIBRARY WEBSITE

Check out the Modern Library website at
www.modernlibrary.com for:

- The Modern Library e-newsletter
- A list of our current and upcoming titles and series
- Reading Group Guides and exclusive author spotlights
- Special features with information on the classics and other paperback series
- Excerpts from new releases and other titles
- A list of our e-books and information on where to buy them
- The Modern Library Editorial Board's 100 Best Novels and 100 Best Nonfiction Books of the Twentieth Century written in the English language
- News and announcements

Questions? E-mail us at **modernlibrary@randomhouse.com**
For questions about examination or desk copies, please visit
the Random House Academic Resources site at
www.randomhouse.com/academic